ANOTHER DIMENSION TO THE BLACK DIASPORA

DIET, DISEASE, AND RACISM

ANOTHER DIMENSION TO THE BLACK DIASPORA

DIET, DISEASE, AND RACISM

KENNETH F. KIPLE
Department of History, Bowling Green State University

VIRGINIA HIMMELSTEIB KING

CAMBRIDGE UNIVERSITY PRESS

Cambridge
London   New York   New Rochelle
Melbourne   Sydney

Published by the Press Syndicate of the University of Cambridge
The Pitt Building, Trumpington Street, Cambridge CB2 1RP
32 East 57th Street, New York, NY 10022, USA
296 Beaconsfield Parade, Middle Park, Melbourne 3206, Australia

First published 1981

Printed in the United States of America

Library of Congress Cataloging in Publication Data
Kiple, Kenneth F., 1939–
Another dimension to the Black diaspora.
Bibliography: p.
Includes index.
1. Afro-Americans – Diseases – History.
2. Slavery – United States – Condition of
slaves.   3. Afro-Americans – Nutrition –
History.   4. Health and race – United States –
History.   I. King, Virginia Himmelsteib.
II. Title.
RA448.5.N4K56,   616'.008996073   81-7696
ISBN 0 521 23664 9   AACR2

For
CARRIE
and
GRAHAM

Man in all his variations is indeed as heterogeneous in his illnesses as he is in his culture.

Richard Allen Williams, "Black-Related Disease: An Overview," *Journal of Black Health Perspectives*, 1 (1974), 36.

CONTENTS

Contents

PREFACE

I

Since World War II the black people have been studied with enormous intensity by the social scientist and the scientist alike. The reasons for the interest of the social scientist lie somewhere within the parameters of the racism of Nazi Germany (which sensitized white Americans to their own racial intolerance), the postwar groundswell of black power, a new black consciousness, and a determination of both blacks and whites to correct the pages of black history with the hope that a better understanding of the black past will bring racial accommodation.

For the scientist the African on his ancestral continent has become a subject of extraordinary interest over the past few decades as black genetic anomalies have been revealed and then linked with various forms of disease protection. Moreover, the African in America has recently come to occupy other scientists, whose attention has been riveted on black "differences" such as their inability to drink milk, problems with sickle cell anemia and hypertension, and their nutritional requirements, which may well differ substantially from those of whites.

The result is that today a huge corpus of literature covers every aspect of the Afro-American experience. The social sciences have probed exhaustively into the black's West African background, the slave trade, slavery, his postbellum adjustments to freedom and twentieth-century life. Specialized studies have concentrated on myriad problems ranging from questions of why the black was enslaved in the first place to questions of American racism to longitudinal problems of black natality and mortality levels. An equally large mass of scientific literature touches on equally diverse subjects running the gamut from African blood anomalies, black nutritional requirements, and lower black than white birth weights to heat and cold tolerance to the African's skeletal mass.

Yet although both bodies of literature deal directly with the black, with few exceptions, little has been done to unite them. Rather, for the most part, social scientists and physical scientists alike have remained oblivious of one another's findings. Illustrative is Kenneth Stampp's declaration in his fine study, *The Peculiar Institution*, that "innately

Negroes *are*, after all, only white men with black skins, nothing more, nothing less."[1] Somewhat ironically the statement was made in 1956, shortly after A. C. Allison correlated the high frequency of sickle trait in Africa with areas of endemic falciparum malaria and demonstrated that sickle trait conferred malaria protection. Allison's discovery sounded the starting gun for the rush to Africa of geneticists who made more and more such discoveries – discoveries that have turned Stampp's well-intentioned words inside out.

Blacks and whites in fact do differ innately in many important respects, and it is only with an appreciation of these differences and how these differences have been perceived historically that a holistic understanding of the Afro-American's past can be achieved. The black's ability to resist tropical diseases that whites and Indians could not, such as yellow fever and malaria, was both a reason for and a rationale of American Negro slavery, for out of this phenomenon was born the notion that only blacks were suited for labor in warm climates. On the other hand, if slaves had special immunities they also had susceptibilities to diseases that not only afflicted a much higher percentage of blacks than whites, but also tended to set the black apart, in first the antebellum and then the postbellum medical mind, as decidedly different from and inferior to the white man.

One theme that is prevalent throughout this book is that a differential black and white disease experience has had much to do with slavery and racism, two of the most wrenching aspects of the Afro-American's past. Another is that genetic circumstances wrought by virtue of West African ancestry have coupled with the climatic and cultural circumstances of North America to create much of this differential by producing a black susceptibility to a number of illnesses, which we have chosen to call "black-related diseases." A final purpose is to examine the pathologies of these diseases, as well as black immunities, within the context of a differential black and white disease experience.

II

The phrase "black-related diseases" is not ours. Rather it was coined by Dr. Richard Allen Williams to indicate "not only those illnesses to which Blacks are particularly prone, but also those conditions to which Blacks manifest an unusually severe or idiosyncratic reaction."[2] The concept of diseases with racial preferences, while scarcely a new one, is sufficiently novel that some explanation as well as a few illustrations seem in order. The most familiar of these diseases are those with a genetic basis, such as sickle cell anemia, which afflicts principally blacks, or Tay-Sachs disease, which exhibits a much higher than normal frequency in Jews. These are both good straightforward examples of genetic illnesses. Then there are diseases carried by parasites with racial preferences. Different kinds of lice, for example, prefer different races. Consequently, one racial group within a community might conceivably be plagued by a particular louseborne disease, while another group within that same community escapes the disease altogether.[3] Another example can be found in some worms – hookworm, for example (see Chapters 1 and 7) – that seem to favor different races with a resulting differential in worm-related afflictions.

In still another category are illnesses to which a genetic condition predisposes. An example here is the historically higher black than white incidence of rickets in North America. The disease is a product of vitamin D deficiency caused in part by the black's pigmentation. Additionally, there are diseases born of inexperience, whereby a people who have had no opportunity to build up resistance to particular pathogens suddenly are confronted with them. The classic example of this is the decimation of the American Indian population by European disease. In this case, of course, the susceptibility is not racial, although it frequently appears to be. Finally, a body of evidence has recently been amassed that indicates that persons with certain blood groups are more prone to certain diseases and that at least "one of the factors in these diseases is genetic."[4]

Naturally, one normally thinks of blood groups in genetic rather than in racial terms. Yet certain hemoglobin abnormalities[5] do occur with a high rate of frequency among different racial groups, with the Negroid race for the moment seeming to possess more dramatic abnormalities than the Caucasoid or Mongoloid. But here, in particular, one must be especially careful about ascribing blood characteristics to race, because these abnormalities in many cases have resulted from genetic adaptation to a peculiar disease environment, all of which leads directly to that "iron curtain" which divides the biologic and social sciences – their differing concepts of race.

Biologic scientists tend to conceive of races as biologic subspecies based on the consistency of gene frequency differences, whereas social scientists are uncomfortable with the concept in large part because of their acute awareness of the strong associative link historically between race and racism. The latter has been defined for our purposes as the conviction on the part of members of one race that they are somehow innately superior to members of another. And because notions of innate superiority imply a genetic excellence transmissible from generation to generation, many social scientists are acutely suspicious of any concept based on the occurrence of gene frequencies.

Indeed, following the Jewish Holocaust of World War II and concomitant recognition by white Americans of their own overt and covert racism, loud calls came from social scientists that we should rid ourselves totally of race as a concept. It is a concept whose agonizing history seemed proof enough of its capacity for evil.[6] The need for urgency in conducting this ablutionary process was brought home sharply to many more individuals by the recent furor over alleged intelligence differences by race.

The inherent capacity for mischief contained in this intelligence testing has worried social scientists since the first tests were carried out during World War I and, in fact, had much to do with summoning the counterattack against race mounted by the environmentalists among them, who find immediate physical surroundings far more important in accounting for behavioral and intelligence variants (as well as general differences between ethnic groups) than genetic makeup. "Genetics" for them has been a dirty word, the kind best to ignore.

The curious who may be interested in the etymology of even a dirty word, however, will immediately recognize that the term "genetics" explicitly suggests the oneness of man. Indeed analyses of blood types have reinforced the tenet that *Homo sapiens* is descended from lower primates by establishing a blood "kinship" (if you will) between them. Thus, most investigators of racial differences start with the assumption of a monophyletic origin of man in Africa some 3 million plus years ago, probably from a small prehomid group, intermediate between the lower primates and *Homo sapiens.*

It follows then that if man sprang from a single progenitor stock, the broad differences indentifiable in man today should logically be the result of adaptation to regions into which he subsequently wandered – their climates, disease environments, available food, and so forth. Yet there are immense difficulties with correlating peoples and regions, for no sooner had different groups of men settled into a homeland than successive ice ages chased them out again. Man was propelled into new climates, new ecologic surroundings, and brought into contact with new peoples, all of which meant an extraordinarily wide range of genetic recombinations.

Thus, because of migration there are no true or pure races. On the other hand, because of genetic selection and mutation called into play by the evolutionary process of adaptation, different groupings, especially the generally recognized and broadly defined Caucasians, Mongolians, and Negroes, came to share many outward characteristics that doubtless have contributed to the tenacity of race as a notion in the popular mind.

In the scientific mind, race continues to be a viable concept because of the consistency with which differences in gene frequency appear in various groups. This consistency means that across the globe major constellations of combinations of frequencies are clearly identifiable. An important method of identifying these combinations is the study of blood groupings, which serve as maps to indicate the kinds of adaptations men have made as they traveled prehistoric roads. Keys to these

maps include serum and plasma proteins and red and white cell enzymes, but science is just now learning how to use these keys, so the
maps in question promise to be the subject of scrutiny for some time to
come.

Hence despite the abhorrence of many social scientists for the term
"race" (and we too confess a distaste for the word), its tough viability
makes its usage difficult to avoid, particularly in a work such as this.
Consequently, readers will find it employed to connote both ethnic
identification and subspecies defined by gene frequencies, with the
context indicating its meaning of the moment.

Now for a word or two about environment versus heredity. Clearly,
if man's differences have been wrought by adaptation to different
physical environments, then geneticists too are environmentalists. The
problem is one of time: long-run environmental factors (to borrow the
economists' nomenclature) versus short-run circumstances of the immediate environment.

Yet the two are far from mutually exclusive. A good example might
be the Jewish ability to resist tuberculosis far better than most other
peoples. One of the selective factors operative for Jews must surely
have been urbanization. During the last millennium, when man experienced city life at its most intense, European Jews have probably been
exposed to urban conditions far longer than any other population.[7]
Tuberculosis is an urban disease; the Jewish resistance to it therefore is
very likely a genetic response, encouraged by the environment in the
relatively short run.

Narrowing the focus, the childbearing experiences of women under
conditions of famine during and immediately after World War II demonstrated how severe deprivation could adversely affect the birth weights
of infants. After the war, with the return of nutritional plenty, birth
weights again rose (see Chapter 13). But suppose that severe deprivation had continued for a number of generations, a deprivation that
would produce in women the deformed pelves generally characteristic
of malnutrition. The immediate result could have been generation after
generation necessarily born with low birth weights because only smaller
infants would survive the birth process. But might not another result
have been a selective factor for low birth weights with all of the implications this would have had for the products of this deprivation?

On the other hand, if the effects of short-run environmental circumstances can ultimately produce genetic traits, so too can the immediate
environment modify those traits. Many social scientists are troubled by
genetics and fear, perhaps, that if traits are innate, then they are also
immutable. But this is not true. A specific example is the genetically
occasioned, metabolic disease phenylketonuria (PKU), which in times
past usually cursed victims with mental retardation. But today infants
genetically prone to the disease are fed a special diet to prevent brain

damage. In other words, a genetic trait has become modifiable by the environment. On the more general level, biochemists have suggested what they term a "genetotrophic approach" to many genetic liabilities, feeling that these liabilities can frequently be overcome by good nutrition (an immediate environmental factor).[8] Hence heritability of a particular trait does not mean the trait cannot be modified by manipulating the environment.

Finally, it is not coincidence that our examples of environmental manipulation are nutritional. On the contrary, one of the most important concerns of this study is a centuries-old problem of black nutritional deprivation. This problem began in precolonial West Africa and continued through the days of slavery to remain a serious threat to the health of many twentieth-century Afro-Americans. Thus throughout this book, nutritional chemistry is employed to link in systematic fashion diet with the black genetic heritage and the whole to that body of black-related diseases which has historically plagued the black.

III

The risks in producing a work such as this are many, and not the least is that the nutritionists, biomedical scientists, geneticists, epidemiologists, geographers, demographers, and physicians, whose tools we have borrowed, all know a layman when they see one and may not be all that forgiving of laymen's errors.

Another risk has to do with the subject treated and the possibility that parts will be employed out of context for racist ends. It would be fatuous, of course, to suppose that stern warnings here could prevent this. But we do hope that this and similar studies that seek to explain biologic differences among peoples will help to remove the mystery from these differences, and thus much of the racist mischief that mystery creates.

Finally, in addition to the hazard of deliberate misuse of the materials presented, there are very real perils of being honestly misunderstood. To guard against this we have not only provided many notes of elaboration and explanation but also introductions to each of the study's five major sections. These introductions discuss the evidence and arguments to be advanced and erect signposts of caution regarding speculative portions.

Against all these risks, however, is an opportunity that far outweighs them: to draw together the findings of many diverse fields, unite them within an historical framework, and thereby provide still *Another Dimension to the Black Diaspora.*

K.F.K.

Coimbra, Portugal

ACKNOWLEDGMENTS

We wish to thank the *Journal of Social History* for permission to use materials from an article that originally appeared as "Slave Child Mortality: Some Nutritional Answers to a Perennial Puzzle," 10:3 (March 1977), 284–309. We are also grateful to the *Journal of Southern History* for permission to reprint portions of "Black Tongue and Black Men: Pellagra in the Antebellum South," 63:3 (August 1977), 411–28; to *Social Science History* for permission to employ portions of "Black Yellow Fever Immunities, Both Acquired and Innate as Revealed in the American South," 1:4 (Summer 1977), 419–36; and to *Phylon* for permission to use portions of "The African Connection: Slavery, Disease, and Racism" 41 (Fall, 1980), 211–22.

Our debt to the Bowling Green Faculty Research Committee is enormous, for without its support this book truly could not have been written. It was the committee, in the form of research fellowships and travel grants, that supported research and free time for writing during the years 1976 to 1980 and also supplied the funds for duplicating the manuscript so that it could be read and criticized by so many. Thomas Berry Cobb, Carol L. Davis, and Ronald J. Etzel of the Research Services office all have given selflessly of their time and energies in assisting us with the myriad difficulties of funding this and related projects over the years. We are grateful too for an award from the Joint Social Science Research Council and the American Council of Learned Societies which has provided the opportunity for conducting extensive Caribbean research on black health problems. Some of the results of this inquiry have been incorporated in the pages that follow.

The archivists and librarians who contributed their patience as well as their knowledge to this project are legion. Special thanks go to Harriet Heidelberg, Department of Archives and History, Jackson, Mississippi; Virginia Jones, Alabama State Archives, Montgomery, Alabama; Mary Kincannon, John Brister Library, Memphis State University, Memphis, Tennessee; Sally Daly, Rudolph Matas Medical Library, Tulane School of Medicine; the staff of the Howard-Tilton Memorial Library, Tulane University, New Orleans, Louisiana; Margaret Fisher and Marshal Miller, Department of Archives, Louisiana State University, Baton Rouge, Louisiana; Beth White, Houston Academy of Medicine, Texas Medical Center Library, Houston Texas; Nancy Parker and Ola Moore, Fondren Library, Rice University, Houston, Texas; Chris Laplante, Texas State Library and Archives, Austin, Texas; Ralph Elder, Barker Texas History Center Archives, University of Texas, Austin, Texas; Waverly K. Winfree, Virginia Historical Society, Richmond, Virginia; Michael Plunkett and Barbara Bettcher, University of Virginia Libraries, Charlottesville, Virginia; D. L. Morecock, Virginia State Libraries, Richmond, Virginia; David Brown and Ms. Russell, William R. Perkins Library, and Mr. Cavanagh, Medical Center Library, Duke University, Durham, North Carolina; Ellen Neal, Dick Shrader and Drs. Carolyn Wallace and Issac Copeland, Southern Historical Collection and Ms. Long and Ms. Metter, Health Sciences Library, University of North Carolina, Chapel Hill, North Carolina; Ms. Yarborough, Department of Archives and History, Raleigh, North Carolina; Ms. Owens, South Caroliniana Library, University of South Carolina; Mrs. L. Helsey, South Carolina Department of Archives and History, Columbia, South Carolina; Barbara Davis, Medical College of the State of South Carolina Library, and Mrs. Cohen, South Carolina Historical Society, Charleston, South Carolina; Lilla M. Hawes, Georgia Historical Society, Savannah, Georgia; Kristin Feyling and Cynthia Wise, Robert Manning Strozier Library, Florida State University, Tallahassee, Florida; the staff of the University of Florida Libraries, Gainesville, Florida; and the staff of the Library of Congress and that of the National Library of Medicine, Washington, D.C.

Despite our research efforts in the South many volumes and articles were either overlooked or simply unavailable. For securing these studies as well as a wealth of current medical literature we are deeply indebted to Dawn McCaghy and Kausalya Padmarajan, of the Bowling Green State University Inter-Library Loan Department, who cheerfully processed literally hundreds of our requests.

It was during our stay at Duke University that we discovered Todd L. Savitt and his work and first learned that we were not the only ones interested in the history of Afro-American problems of health. Subsequent correspondence and discussions with Todd along with the appearance of his fine examination of *Medicine and Slavery* taught us much, as has his meticulous and often hard criticism of our own work, including various versions of this study. If we continue to disagree on certain points and therefore have not utilized all of his suggestions it is certainly not his fault. This is a much better book than it would have been had Savitt not forced us to make a number of significant corrections of both fact and interpretation.

Charles E. Rosenberg, Stanley L. Engerman, Ira Berlin, Nathan Irvin

Huggins, Peter H. Wood, Darrett B. Rutman, and Philip D. Curtin have also been critical of portions of this study, and while their criticisms did not always make pleasant reading they did help us think through difficulties and correct numerous errors. Indeed the kind but pointed comments of Professor Curtin spared us much embarrassment in Chapter 1. Moreover we are also particularly grateful to Professors Curtin and Rutman for words of encouragement which invariably seemed to arrive when we were the most discouraged.

For their contributions in time spent reading parts of the manuscript as well as their many splendid suggestions and criticisms, we are deeply indebted to Alfred W. Crosby, Jr., David Brion Davis, John Duffy, Eugene D. Genovese, John Haller, James Jones, Ronald Numbers, Gunter Risse, Anita H. Rutman, Edward Shorter, Kenneth Stampp, and Jerry Weaver.

We would also like to acknowledge our debt to Bowling Green colleagues Lawrence J. Friedman, James Q. Graham, Rachael Graham, Donald Rowney, and Bernard Sternsher who not only read and commented on various portions of the manuscript but were forced to "listen" to the book as it grew over the years. Additionally, Gary Hess, William Rock, and Lawrence Daly all as Chair or Acting Chair of the History Department at Bowling Green were superb in their efforts to provide free time and departmental resources while the book was being researched and written. Secretaries Phyllis Wulff, Judy Gilbert, and Connie Montgomery all exerted themselves in numerous thoughtful ways in our behalf; Connie in particular who almost without complaint typed numerous drafts of each chapter as well as at least two "final" drafts, and still lives in fear that "just one more draft" may be required. We wish also to express our thanks to editor Steve Fraser who had faith in this book.

Finally, we have an intangible debt to acknowledge – this to our two children Carrie and Graham. Both were born and grew from infants to youngsters in the midst of this project. Indeed Carrie was barely one month old when we set off on our second research tour of southern archives, and she spent much of her next three months in these archives wandering about and occasionally disturbing her strangely quiet surroundings. Earlier drafts of the manuscript bear the marks of Graham's first experiments with pencils, pens, and crayons, not to mention a game he played with typescript erasure fluid.

We hope that passing through an infancy and early childhood in which chaos was normal and travel frequent, surrounded by piles of papers, books, and preoccupied parents will not leave them with any lasting scars. But surely their contribution was an enormous, albeit involuntary one, and it is to them that we dedicate this book.

PART I

AFRICAN BEGINNINGS

INTRODUCTION TO PART I

And out of Darkness Came the Hands That Reach Thro' Nature
Molding Men.

Tennyson, *In Memoriam*

A specialist wrote recently that "the medical history of precolonial
Africa is still an almost entirely unexplored field."[1] To this it might be
added that the history of the colonial period is a barely explored field.
Recorded observation is frequently scarce, often defective, and it con-
sists almost exclusively of the observations of Europeans. The result is
essentially a Eurocentric view of West Africa and its disease environment, and this view, presented in Chapter 1, may project more of a
"dark continent" image than readers will care for. It should be noted at
the onset that our treatment is necessarily general and that important
exceptions do exist.

Yet much of the existing evidence suggests that many West Africans
were the product of a particularly hostile environment which consisted
more of deadly pathogens than nutritional plenty. As products of that
environment, West Africans necessarily developed genetically in ways
different from other peoples, and one of the purposes of this section is
to discuss those differences that science has identified (or thinks it has
identified) and the reasons why they came about.

Another purpose is to dramatize the extent to which the West Africans evolved defenses against some of the most deadly diseases of
their environment – a purpose accomplished by reference to the differential disease experience of black and white in West Africa. Finally the
nature of one set of black disease defenses – those against malaria – are
discussed in terms of epidemiologic and genetic knowledge. Even this
latter discussion, however, bristles with qualifications, indicative of the
infancy of the study of genetics within the context of disease immunities and susceptibilities.

What follows then is an attempt to unite ethnohistory and scientific
knowledge so as to better understand something of the West African's
biologic makeup on the eve of the black diaspora.

3

CHAPTER 1

THE BLACK MAN'S CRADLE AND
THE WHITE MAN'S GRAVE

Africa, the oldest home of man, is the home of the most dangerous of man's diseases.

C. D. Darlington (1969)[1]

Epidemiology at any given time is something more than the total of its established facts. It includes their orderly arrangement into chains of inference which extend more or less beyond the bounds of direct observation.

W. H. Frost (1936)[2]

I

The shores of West Africa were the point of embarkation for the bulk of the 10 million or so blacks who unwillingly left Africa to labor on the plantations and in the cities and mines of the New World.[3] Among these unhappy voyagers were the progenitors of today's North American black population. Yet although the black diaspora ceased long ago the West African homeland continues to exert an enormous physical influence on the descendants of the original migrants, both in terms of outward appearance and biochemical anomalies that have dictated a different black disease experience from the North American white.

West African climate, disease, and relative isolation are the three factors chiefly responsible for this influence. These factors combined and recombined over millennia to mold and shape the inhabitants. They were sheltered by the Sahara desert against easy access from North Africa and its succession of empires and emperors, while turbulent seas and contrary wind patterns discouraged intrusion from the South Atlantic. This is not to say that no caravans crossed the desert to West Africa or that no ships visited West African shores prior to the Portuguese explorations of the fifteenth century.

But contact with the outside world was limited even though regular trade routes did criss-cross West Africa and penetrate into the heart of the continent.[4] Likewise within West Africa relative isolation was a rule rather than an exception, with individuals contained in small

4

self-sustaining village states, enjoying little intercourse, social or otherwise, with even nearby countrymen. As a consequence, early European visitors could marvel at such strange phenomena as two tribes residing on opposite banks of the Senegal River: On one side the inhabitants were of "high stature and black," but across the river lived persons of "low stature" and a "browne or tawne" complexion.[5]

This is not to suggest that there was no racial blending of West Africans, but it should be noted that because its peoples were relatively isolated both externally from abroad and internally from one another, West Africa had long been a kind of genetic hothouse. West Africans experienced a long period of internal evolutionary development that saw generation after generation emerging from common breeding pools. The result was that while they demonstrated a considerable variation in physical types, they nonetheless came to share many common features including an overwhelming predominance of Negroid characteristics.

Certainly pigment is the most obvious characteristic; it is probably a function of climate, for dark skin keeps the body cooler in hot regions. Indeed it is generally believed (although not proven) that black skin evolved as a defense against damage from the West African sun, that is, "a compromise between the conflicting demands of protection from skin cancer and sunburn, thermoregulation and synthesis of Vitamin D."[6] Another characteristic is thick kinky hair that some are convinced serves as a sort of cap to protect the scalp from that same hot sun. In a similar vein, it is believed that hot humid air reaches lungs more efficiently through broad flat noses (as opposed to the thin nostrils of Caucasians that are credited with protecting lungs from frigid air), while the black's greater number of sweat glands supposedly operate to keep their bodies cooler. Other distinctly Negroid traits, such as a denser skeletal mass, narrower pelves, less muscular calves, smaller lungs, longer limbs, and shorter trunks, may well also be the product of the West Africans' long-term adaptation to their own peculiar environment – an adaptation that produced those broad characteristics usually thought of as racial.[7] But clearly the qualifications contained in the foregoing make speculative any explanation of how the black's outward or phenotypical characteristics came to be.

More is known, however, about other characteristics encouraged by that same environment which, although disproportionately present in blacks of West African origin, are not racial in nature. Rather, they represent more recent (and less permanent) genetic adjustments to environmental circumstances, which, in almost every case, relate to disease.

West Africa lies within the tropical belt. Its high average temperatures and lush vegetation make it a paradise for insects, many of them disease-bearing organisms that abuse humans on a year-round basis because they are free from those seasonal controls operative in more temperate climates. Indeed the tropical ambience is due to the location of most of West Africa well inside the line of forty-inch rainfall, and the interaction of these factors – high average temperature, heavy rainfall and an abundance of insects of myriad variety – gave birth to man's deadliest diseases.[8]

Yet humans continue to inhabit the region. Man has not been driven off or eliminated, because as a general rule "Nature prefers that neither host nor parasite should be too hard on the other. For Nature, survival of the species is all that counts and the norm, if there is one is that the host should not die and that his infection should be passed on to one new host individual."[9] Hence the very deadliness of these diseases summoned the mechanics of genetic selection in the inhabitants to erect defenses against them – not absolute defenses in most cases but rather defenses that guarded against pathogenic proliferation that would kill the host. Consequently, individuals endowed with traits limiting the extent of infection lived to reproduce, passing those traits along to offspring. Those that did not would die, and over time West Africans developed innate mechanisms of resistance to the major diseases of their environment. Thus, the diseases themselves elicited defensive traits in their host that certainly are genetic, but not properly called racial.

Malaria resistance makes a fine example. Unquestionably of all the world's infectious diseases "malaria has caused the greatest harm to the greatest number,"[10] and West Africa bids fair for first place as the world's malaria capital. It harbors some sixty of the world's 200 or so species of *Anopheles* mosquitoes, many of which carry and inject the malaria parasite into man.[11] The inhabitants of the region, therefore, seem to have been preyed upon by all four types of the disease (and their many strains) which parasitize the human species.[12]

To coexist with this disease, West Africans evolved hemoglobin defenses, which are blood abnormalities that resist malaria parasites and forestall their multiplication. Thus they grew relatively refractory to both the debilitating, but seldom fatal, types of malaria such as *Plasmodium vivax* and the frequently deadly *Plasmodium falciparum*.

West Africa is also inhabited by another small silvery pest, the *Aëdes aegypti* mosquito (a free translation would have it the "unpleasant Egyptian"), the most important vector of another great killer, yellow fever. Most epidemiologists think that West African forests were the birthplace of this disease, in part because of the omnipresence of that disagreeable bug but also because of the striking, still to be explained, ability of West Africans to resist yellow fever over the centuries – an ability notably lacking in Europeans, who became the disease's chief victims.

Still another example is transmitted by the tsetse fly (genus *Glossina*), a large biting fly that curses West Africa with twenty-two species, among them *Glossina palpalis* which imparts African trypanosomiasis – the African sleeping sickness – to humans.[13] Today, although the disease is endemic to the region, and although no permanent immunity seems to be bestowed upon its survivors, only a relatively small portion of exposed West Africans appear susceptible in the first place. Moreover, those blacks who do contract African sleeping sickness demonstrate a resistance to at least local strains, which has prompted the medical observation that the disease tends to be more acute in whites than in blacks.[14] Epidemiologists have still to account for this phenomenon, but a safe assumption would be that as in the case of yellow fever, while the mechanism of immunity is unknown, its presence is impressive testimony to the plasticity of man under environmental pressure.

High average West African temperatures also meant that little in the way of clothing or footwear was needed allowing the hookworm, which abounds in African soils, easy access to the human body. But again familiarity bred resistance, and as Rockefeller-funded researchers in the American South during the first decades of the twentieth century discovered, the black has somehow gained a relative immunity to hookworm infestations.

West Africans then were born into a world teeming with pathogens for which they developed a complex of defenses. Yet if they were equipped genetically to escape the worst of malaria, yellow fever, or hookworm disease, a bout with one or all was nonetheless something children could expect, and therefore child mortality was always tragically high as the cruel process of selection for protection continued.

There were, however, other diseases in West Africa to which the blacks seem to have been extraordinarily susceptible. Youngsters would normally contract yaws, for example, a disease transmitted by skin-to-skin contact that thrived among a people who required few clothes. In fact, if the child did not take the affliction at an early age, a fairly standard practice was for parents to "borrow the yaws" from an infected person – a process of innoculation which insured adult immunity.[15] European observers, who seldom suffered from the affliction themselves, believed yaws and also leprosy (which Europeans rarely saw anymore) to be "Negro diseases." The distinction between the two illnesses was never clear-cut.[16] West Africans were particularly susceptible to pneumonia, which proved inordinately fatal, and tetanus, which claimed countless lives, especially those of children.

Africa also harbored diseases that plagued that continent as they did Europe, treating black and white impartially. Smallpox put in frequent epidemic appearances, occasionally wiping out whole villages. Childhood diseases such as mumps and chickenpox made life as miserable for African youngsters as they did for European children. Tuberculosis and syphilis were well-known to Europeans but apparently strangers to West Africans until contact between the two facilitated their importation. Because of a lack of historical contact each of these two illnesses tended to run a more severe course in blacks than in whites.

To battle with this pestilential host in West Africa was the task of the African medicine men, who were the guardians of remedies handed down from generation to generation. Some of their cures took the form of magical rites. But for common ailments, they possessed quite an effective command of the healing properties of roots, herbs, and other vegetation. Indeed, recent work on West African healing practices leaves little doubt that African materia medica has important significance for today's medical world.

African and European doctors alike, however, have always labored under a serious disadvantage in West Africa, for their patients have invariably been malnourished and consequently more difficult to cure than healthy individuals. The most superficial accounting of West African nutrition shows a ledger heavy with starches on the debit side but light in protein credits. One reason for this is that most varieties of cattle (and horses and asses for that matter) did not develop the resistance to African trypanosomiasis that man did (it may be that the human variety is less deadly, representing an accommodation between host and parasite), and as a result those species of the bloodsucking tsetse fly, especially *Glossina morsitans,* sought out large animals so efficiently inside the forty-inch line of rainfall that cattle raising was usually unprofitable, if not always impossible.[17]

Hence, West Africans were limited to raising a few goats, chickens, dogs, and sometimes a pig, animals so scarce and highly prized that they were only slaughtered on special occasions. Animal protein then did not constitute an important item in the diet. Naturally bovine milk was excluded from that diet along with the other dairy products, and because of taboos against them, eggs were not normally eaten. Additionally, depending on the people and their customs, fruit consumption was frequently frowned upon as was the use of many vegetables.[18] Thus, in many cases, there were few dietary supplements to the starchy core of the West African diet, a core built around the principal crops of the region.

West Africa's most important cultivated plants have been imported, with its high-yield plants arriving only in the last few centuries from America. Prior to the sixteenth century (which saw the beginning of this introduction), the African diet centered on lower-yielding Asian imports of bananas, taro (often called the bull yam) and the small African yam, along with millet and rice.[19]

Because of the relatively poor yield of these crops, researchers have come to believe they barely sustained life, largely because of the tremendous multiplication of the West African peoples following the introduction of American plants, despite the heavy population drain of the slave trade. Cassava (manioc) and maize were the most crucial of these population stimulants.[20] Although high in carbohydrates, these plants offer little in the way of protein, and with very little animal protein in the diet, West Africans must have suffered from serious protein deficiencies. Moreover, this deficiency was even further compounded by the acidic character of some of West Africa's soils and the nitrogen deficient quality of most of them that meant a reduced protein yield of the vegetable crop. Additionally, those same soils were severely leached by heavy rains leaving them with a low mineral (especially phosphorus and calcium) content.[21]

Finally Africa's principal crops, which probably delivered a sufficient amount of some nutrients, such as vitamins A and B_6, would nonetheless have left consumers deficient in most of the other B-complex vitamins, vitamin C, calcium, and iron. Not incidentally these deficiencies, coupled with a want of animal protein, remain glaringly apparent in the West African diet of this century.[22]

Today poor nutrition in West Africa is considered that region's principal problem.[23] It is not so much that West Africans are undernourished as that they are badly nourished. The diet still tends to focus on a single starchy crop (cassava or maize) that provides carbohydrates in sufficient quantity to sustain life but is supplemented with little else.[24] Meat is still seldom eaten; the little that is eaten has a uniformly poor quality because West African animals, like their human owners, are also poorly nourished.[25] In addition, taboos remain that limit egg consumption, while milk products, vegetables (other than the principal crop), and fruits are not eaten with any regularity.[26] In short, the diets of yesterday and today seem to approximate.

The consequences of this regimen in the twentieth century are widespread anemia, kwashiorkor, and pellagra, which are all nutritional illnesses in their own right but also illnesses that leave the population susceptible to intercurrent diseases, such as pneumonia, West Africa's foremost killer today. Hence, all available information suggests that the nutritional status of those soon-to-be Afro-Americans who made the Middle Passage was determined by a diet overloaded in carbohydrates but, under the best of circumstances, low in proteins as well as many of the essential vitamins and minerals.

Moreover, West Africans had quantitative as well as qualitative nutritional problems to contend with. All too often rainy seasons alternated with droughts to make year-round agricultural activity difficult; famines therefore were not unusual occurrences. Consequently, not until the importation of cassava and maize from the Americas did a potential for resolving the quantitative difficulties even exist.[27]

Empiric evidence to confirm that blacks reaching the Americas were severely undernourished has been generated by research on the height of imported Africans as opposed to Creole-born slaves in the Caribbean. Data concerning the height of some 25,000 slaves in Trinidad reveal that new arrivals were significantly shorter than those born on the island.[28] Manual Moreno Fraginals[29] of Cuba has found the same to be true for that island. First generation Creole slaves were significantly taller than *bozales* (the freshly imported Africans). Not that taller is necessarily better, but this apparent rapid growth of American slaves over the course of a generation or so does suggest that even a slave diet in the New World was more protein-laden and probably of better overall quality than the West African diet.

Thus, at the risk of belaboring the point, West African nutrition was (and still is) poor. Moreover, the African was even further impoverished physically by his disease environment and paradoxically very possibly weakened as well by his defenses against that environment. By way of illustration, malaria creates anemia among its other depredations, but some of the blood abnormalities that protect against the disease are also suspected of producing other anemias, which may have aggravated that lack of protein inherent in the black diet. Likewise, the many worm-related diseases of the region must have eroded already depleted iron stores while also interfering with the metabolism of other nutrients.

Worms also share the host's protein intake which, if inadequate to begin with, means that he will have even fewer reserves for the production of substances crucial in the formation of antibodies. The result is a heightened susceptibility to invasion by other pathogens. Clearly, malnutrition and pestilence formed a grim partnership in winnowing West African lives.

But just as the West African evolved genetic protection against the diseases of his environment, he also seems to have made genetic adjustments to help him live with malnutrition. For example, some nutritionalists believe today that blacks require less iron than do whites.[30] And, perhaps because of a greater constitutional ability to absorb calcium, blacks seem to have a lower requirement for this mineral than whites.[31]

A grave difficulty with specialized adjustments to an environment, however, is that genetic assets can quickly convert to liabilities if that environment changes rapidly or if its inhabitants relocate to radically different geographic regions as was the case with West Africans suddenly bound for North America. In their homeland a more or less year-round supply of sunlight to activate the production of vitamin D was a crucial catalyst in the black's metabolic machinery. In a more temperate North America not annually blessed with abundant sunshine, however, pigment, protective against West African sun, now screened out much of that radiation that was so important to the black nutritionally. Several studies testify to the black's ability to better withstand heat than whites.

Conversely the latter respond more efficiently to cold; their metabolic rate is far ahead of blacks' when both are identically exposed. Hence, blacks are more susceptible than whites to cold injury and to some diseases common to cold climates (see Chapter 9).

Another trait harmless in West Africa, but one that would become troublesome in a temperate climate with a milk-drinking culture, is the high frequency of lactose intolerance that characterizes West Africans and their descendants, leaving them unable to consume much milk (see Chapter 6). This condition occurs when high levels of lactase enzyme (essential for breaking down milk sugars) fail to fully develop. In West Africa, of course, there was little encouragement for the enzyme to develop first because (unlike northern Europe) there was always abundant sunlight, and thus vitamin D, to facilitate the metabolism of calcium, and second because the tsetse fly made dairying unprofitable, therefore creating an historic situation of low milk usage.

The point here is that long-term adjustments to a West African environment held the potential for creating problems of health for blacks suddenly relocated in North America and in like manner for their descendants. Yet ironically, some of those adjustments were a major reason for that relocation with West African genetic and epidemiologic factors stimulating a lively demand for Africans in the New World.

That demand was due initially to the failure of American Indians to survive European diseases against which they had little or no resistance.[32] These included smallpox, usually regarded as their biggest killer, as well as "mild" diseases, such as measles and mumps, childhood afflictions for Europeans, but deadly plagues for the previously unexposed Indians.[33] Yet West Africans, already familiar with many of these Old World diseases, proved as resistant to them as whites. Consequently, as New World Indian populations declined, demand for black labor increased.

Its fulfillment, however, brought a second wave of disease to the Indians as African diseases such as falciparum malaria and yellow fever joined European pestilence in further diminishing the Indian ranks; once more the demand for black labor increased. Moreover, black refractoriness to these illnesses that struck as hard at whites as at Indians killed off any lingering possibility that Europeans might serve as a significant source of plantation labor. It was the African's ability to resist tropical as well as European disease that helped convince slaveholders, already impressed with his ability to labor in intense heat, that the black slave was a priceless gift from a thoughtful Creator.

Thus, those mechanisms for survival with which Mother Africa endowed her sons and daughters worked cruelly against her progeny by encouraging their enslavement. Exactly how potent these mechanisms were can best be appreciated by contrasting the experience of blacks and whites with yellow fever and malaria in Africa.

II

"Beware and take care of the bight of Benin. For the one that comes out there are twenty stay in." Although hyperbolic, this old chantey from the days of the slave trade suggests something of the price that Africa extracted from its European invaders, a price that established West Africa's reputation as a "White Man's Grave."[34]

Today we know men were not struck down by a hot West African sun but instead by the tiniest of organisms living under that sun: helminthic, protozoan, bacterial, and viral parasites. Yesterday, however, the sun got the blame. Since antiquity physicians had focused on the systems of patients with an eye to maintaining their "humors" (body fluids) in balance.[35] When those humors were thrown out of balance, as the African sun was said to do, disease resulted. Whites sickened and died; blacks did not, for obviously they could not suffer severe humoral dislocation caused by their own homeland. They were "acclimated."

Because of this static state of medical thought, the first centuries of Europe's presence on the coast saw little attention paid to precisely what was killing whites. It did not matter much anyway. Regardless of the symptoms, the cures – tinkering with the humors – were the same. Hence there was little incentive to sort out diseases, much less to distinguish what seemed to be uniquely African afflictions from that great body of illnesses that had traditionally bedeviled Europe. For this reason, although accounts of Europeans on the African coast assure us that they died in droves, the cause of mortality as well as the number and proportion of those who succumbed went largely unrecorded. It was a fatalistic age when no one bothered to keep score on "God's will."

But by the late seventeenth century, the Royal African Company started keeping score. Many slaving concerns did the same in the eighteenth century, and British army mortality records and accounts of exploratory journeys to the interior are available for the nineteenth century. These ledgers leave no doubt of incredible white mortality. The Royal African Company data indicate that during the late seventeenth and early eighteenth centuries fully *half* of the English merchants, soldiers, and officials connected with the company were losing their lives *within their first year of residence* on the coast, and only one out of ten ever made it back to England.[36]

Throughout the eighteenth century white crews on slaving vessels fared better only because their exposure to Africa was brief when compared with resident Royal African Company officials. A study of French slavers sailing from Nantes over a forty-year period during the last half of the eighteenth century reveals that crew mortality was upwards of an average 200 per 1,000 per voyage.[37] Late eighteenth-century British sailors out of Bristol and Liverpool encountered more dismal odds against survival with estimates of their mortality exceeding 200 per 1,000 per voyage.[38] In fact despite the well-known horrors of the Middle Passage for slaves, death claimed proportionately more of the white crew members topside than the black cargoes crowded below.[39]

Nineteenth-century statistics on British troop mortality in West Africa continued to reflect the same awful toll. The British discovered that the annual death rate per 1,000 soldiers stationed in the United Kingdom was 15.3. It ranged, however, between an appalling 483 and 668 per 1,000 mean strength annually on the African coast.[40] This deadly portrait of West Africa's disease environment was also painted by independent observers. One in Sierra Leone asserted that "the average tenure of office of the [British] officials, from the Governor downwards, was . . . less than twelve months; death or invaliding quickly claiming them."[41] A physician traveling in Africa published data that revealed that 10 out of every 16 whites in Gambia and 10 out of every 27 in Sierra Leone died annually during 1822–30.[42]

This spectacular rate of European demise was normally attributed to "fevers," although some physicians felt a professional call to be more precise and subsumed the bulk of the deaths under the rubric of "bilious remittent fever."[43] In reality, this "bilious remittent fever" for the most part described two diseases: yellow fever and falciparum malaria. That they were new diseases to Europeans against which they were relatively defenseless is well-illustrated by the way West Africans thrived in the midst of European death. An English physician marveled that despite "bilious fevers, of the most malignant kind . . . the natives appear to enjoy good health."[44] Then, with typical British understatement, he added that "the climate of Africa . . . has been generally found to be extremely prejudicial to the health of newly-imported Europeans."[45]

The full extent of this prejudice is reflected by the markedly different disease experience of nineteenth-century black and white troops serving the British Crown in West Africa. While whites were dying at a rate that skyrocketed between 483 and 668 per 1,000 mean strength annually, their black counterparts died at a rate of 31 per 1,000. Practically all the white deaths were a result of "fever," but few black deaths were attributed to this cause, even though the blacks themselves were recruited from all over West Africa and were not necessarily serving in their own region.[46]

This is not to say that being black automatically exempted one from the "fevers" under consideration, particularly if one were not born in Africa. Blacks, for example, recruited in the Americas for missionary work in West Africa reportedly perished from "fevers" at a very high rate.[47] Black immigrants from the United States to Liberia also sustained a high incidence of mortality from "fevers," the bulk of which may have been malaria.[48] Yet these are exceptions that remain to be explained. More typical is the story of Sierra Leone where African "fevers" harvested a heavy toll of whites, but were not major killers of liberated Africans.[49] Or again a near absolute black refractoriness to African fevers as well as a terrible white susceptibility can be seen in Europe's nineteenth-century effort to penetrate the interior of the continent, forging inland on what Michael Gelfand has termed the African "Rivers of Death." Of the 44 Europeans, for example, who accompanied Dr. Mungo Park on his second (1805) expedition to the Niger, 39 died of disease. Viewed in this light, Captain James Kingston Tuckey's expedition to the Congo River in 1816 was a salubrious outing, with only 48 percent of its members lost to "fevers."[50]

In addition to highlighting the deadliness of Africa, the expeditions served to remind whites that they were truly victims of disease discrimination. The great Niger expedition of 1841, for example, while not exacting a particularly heavy toll of whites (relatively) vividly demonstrated the superior ability of Africans to survive in their homeland. Among the 145 Europeans in the expedition, 42 (29 percent) died from fever. By contrast, all 158 of the "African and coloured men" survived.[51]

One obvious question arises. Why did Europeans continue to venture to West Africa in large numbers, given the suicidal odds against their survival? The answer is that the public was kept deliberately uninformed. During the seventeenth and eighteenth centuries, companies such as the Royal African Company were not anxious for it to be publicized that recruits for the coast had "three chances in five of being dead within a year" of their arrival.[52]

Therefore, as one student of the question has observed, "it is a moral certainty that the Company's recruiters kept quiet about them [the odds]."[53] Sailors, of course, were more aware of Africa's lethal reputation. Yet accustomed to braving exotic diseases in exotic places, they were on the whole a fatalistic lot. Finally, not all who reached the shores of West Africa did so voluntarily. Many sailors were crimped, while soldiers frequently "were recruited by allowing them to serve on the Coast in commutation of punishment in Britain."[54] Thus, West Africa was not lacking in a steady stream of potential fever victims.

III

Europeans who reached the coast were no strangers to malaria. They knew their "ague" intimately with its periodic visits of chills and fevers, nausea and sweating and aching. Indeed malaria was so prevalent in much of England that it was scarcely regarded as a disease. It was a nuisance, it made one "shake" from time to time, but seldom killed – seldom, but sometimes, as the ghosts of both James I and Oliver Cromwell could testify.

Most malaria types that occur around the world are similarly benign.[55] Of the four types of the disease that have been identified (each with many strains) as infecting man, three are rarely fatal.[56] Of these three, quartan malaria, caused by a parasite (protozoan) called *Plasmodium malariae*, and vivax malaria, caused by *Plasmodium vivax*, are of especial interest. The former protozoan, although not a complete stranger to the Western Hemisphere, has seemed far more at home in West Africa, while *P. vivax*, a universal parasite, the most widespread across the globe, has flourished in Europe, the Western Hemisphere, and Asia, yet in the recent past at least has been intriguingly rare in West Africa.[57] These malarial types are frequently enduring and often debilitating but not usually killers.

In West Africa, however, side by side with these relatively mild malarial types dwelled falciparum malaria, a deadly cousin. Even today falciparum malaria is the single most important cause of death in parts of Africa and other tropical regions. Although different malarial infections produce varying degrees of pathogenicity, only falciparum malaria is murderous because of the peculiar behavior of *Plasmodium falciparum*.[58]

In man, malaria infections begin with the injection of protozoa of the genus *Plasmodium* into the body by the mosquito. After circulating in the blood for a few minutes the parasites head for the liver to multiply for a few days. Then they are discharged into the bloodstream to feed on red corpuscles. At this point the body, aware that it has been invaded, marshals its defenses. White blood cells move in to capture and digest the parasites, and the spleen does its best to filter them out of the bloodstream. Soon outward signs of the battle within appear. The spleen increases in size, chills and fever rack the body as blood corpuscles break and disgorge the poisonous remains of dead parasites, and acute pains develop in the limbs.

These are the classic symptoms of a malaria attack. That *P. falciparum* attacks are frequently mounted with a lethal vigor derives from an imperfect host–parasite relationship in which the parasite, by killing off the host, engineers its own demise. Part of the nature of this imperfect relationship centers on the extent of parasitemia: The higher the parasite count in the host's bloodstream, the more intense the illness. In the case of the benign *plasmodia*, both *P. vivax* and *P. malariae* are self-limiting because of finicky appetites. *P. vivax* enters young erythrocytes (blood cells) almost exclusively, while *P. malariae* prefers mature erythrocytes. But *P. falciparum* invades both indiscriminately and consequently achieves a much higher parasite count.[59]

The second reason for the deadliness of *P. falciparum* is that sometimes these invaded blood cells develop an inclination to adhere to one another, to clump as it were. Clumps wandering around in the bloodstream of course often present a danger of blocking blood vessels leading to internal organs, with internal hemorrhage the usual result. This tendency to clump also endangers the brain where, if the flow of blood is sufficiently disrupted, the victim convulses, loses consciousness, and very likely dies. Still other complications from falciparum malaria include "bilious remittent fever" (from which stomach hemorrhage may result with the coffee ground vomitus frequently confused with yellow fever), cerebral malaria (with coma and convulsions normal), "algid" malaria (often marked by acute diarrhea) and blackwater fever (with the passage of urine ranging from a dark red color to black).[60]

This then is the damage that *P. falciparum* is capable of inflicting. The next concern is with how West Africans as a group managed to escape the worst of those damages. It should be stressed once more that much of the severity of any malaria attack depends on the extent of parasitemia – the higher the parasite count in one's bloodstream, the higher the likelihood of fatality. Refractoriness to falciparum malaria has nothing to do with an ability to escape parasite infection but rather stems from bodily resistance to the parasite after infection, a resistance which holds down the parasite count. This resistance is of two kinds: innate and acquired.

The difficulty with the latter is that for a number of reasons it is neither quickly acquired nor all that perfect after acquisition.[61] The immunity is acquired as the body develops an ability to produce antibodies that circulate in the bloodstream to combat the parasites and forestall their multiplication. But (and here is the problem) normally the body must endure a number of malarial attacks before it receives sufficient antigenic stimulation to produce enough antibodies.[62] Unquestionably in an area hyperendemic for falciparum malaria, such as West Africa, it was easy enough to contract the disease numerous times beginning with early childhood.[63] The trick was to survive long enough to "earn" one's immunity.

Another problem is that although immunity, once acquired, renders the host more or less refractory to a reinoculation with the same parasite (homologous acquired immunity), all strains of the same species (and there are many) are not immunologically similar. Therefore, despite premunition (immunity to a specific strain) one remains liable to infection by other strains, particularly those of a more virulent nature.[64]

Finally (and perhaps obviously given the foregoing), assuming that a person has acquired an effective degree of resistance to a particular type of malaria, he nonetheless exhibits little immunity to other types.[65] In other words, antibodies that are reasonably effective against *P. vivax*, are not effective against *P. falciparum*, as Europeans arriving on the coast soon discovered. For despite their long experience with vivax malaria at home, they died in vast numbers from falciparum malaria in Africa.

Europeans believed this was because they had not been "acclimated," observing that an old hand in the region had a far better chance of celebrating his next birthday than did a newcomer. Of course, if we read "acclimation" as acquiring immunity to *P. falciparum*, then the Europeans were correct in their assessment of the problem, or rather they were correct as far as their reasoning extended. They could not know, however, that compared with native blacks they were doubly disadvantaged in their chances of surviving falciparum malaria. Obviously, almost since birth natives had been in the process of acquiring immunity. But West Africans possessed more of a defense against *P. falciparum* than acquired immunity alone. Many of their defenses were innate.

The best known of these defenses is the sickling trait dramatically publicized lately because of the tragedy of sickle cell anemia.[66] Medical researchers, although cognizant of sickle cell anemia since 1910 (when the first clinical description of the disease appeared),[67] have only recently begun to grasp its etiology. Previously it was recognized only as a mysterious killer of the black young which medicine was helpless to prevent or cure.[68]

Gradually investigators closed in on the problem.[69] It was established that the sickle cell anomaly is the work of a single mutant gene that directs production of a type of hemoglobin differing in a number of important respects from normal hemoglobin.[70] Next it was discovered that so long as the possessor of this trait is heterozygous (inherits it from one parent only), he or she does not develop deadly sickle cell anemia. But of individuals whose parents both possess the trait, one in four is homozygous (inherits the gene from each parent) and develops the disease.[71]

Initially this was mystifying rather than clarifying, however, constituting a kind of genetic jigsaw puzzle with many missing pieces. For surely natural selection should not have permitted such a trait to endure, a trait which on the average shortens a lifetime by two-thirds. Because most victims die young, they are not likely to reproduce themselves. Therefore the trait should have died out. The mystery was that it had not.

As in any classic mystery there were clues. One was the high rate with which the trait occurred among blacks, reaching the 40 percentile range among some African groups.[72] Another was that it also appeared in parts of Greece and in populations of southern India.[73] Some tentative hypotheses were advanced associating the trait with malarial protection,[74] but it was not until 1954 that geneticist A. C. Allison[75] fully grasped the geographic significance of these clues, and correlated the sickle cell trait with areas where falciparum malaria is endemic. Finally, he offered the hypothesis that sickle cell provides protection against malaria infection, because cells that sickle are less easily parasitized by *P. falciparum* than normal erythrocytes, a hypothesis that has been sustained by an ensuing avalanche of studies and experiments.

Here then was the reason for the persistence of the sickle trait. Although sickle cell anemia kills homozygous individuals in early life, this disadvantage is balanced by the resistance that the trait affords heterozygous individuals to *Plasmodium falciparum*.[76] Those who die from the anemia pay the price for those who survive malaria. The genetic term for such a phenomenon is a *balanced polymorphism*.

Precisely how sickle hemoglobin resists the falciparum parasite is still unclear.[77] The anopheline mosquito which is the most common carrier (or to use the medical term "vector") of *P. falciparum* does not distinguish between sicklers and nonsicklers when looking for a blood meal but rather injects parasites into the bodies of both with hungry impartiality. Those parasites fail to thrive in a blood system composed of curved or sickle-shaped cells, however, whereas a system of normal cells often provides such a congenial environment that the parasites continue to feast and multiply until they kill both their host and themselves. For some reason then, bodies possessing the sickling trait reveal lower parasite counts when invaded by *P. falciparum* than those of nonsicklers,[78] and such deadly complications arising from the disease as cerebral malaria or blackwater fever seldom afflict them either.

Certainly there are many explanations for the sickle cells' ability to resist *P. falciparum,* ranging from the hypothesis that sickle hemoglobin is less easily digested by the parasite[79] to the suggestion of some kind of differential immune response between sicklers and nonsicklers.[80] The most generally accepted explanation is that the mechanism of resistance involves the ability of the sickle cell, when parasitized, to remove itself (and the parasite) from circulation.[81] Thus, while the exact nature of the relationship between sickle cells and parasites has yet to be determined, there is no question that S-hemoglobin is inhospitable to falciparum parasites.

Yet only a moment's reflection is required to see that a balanced polymorphism such as the sickling trait could hardly confer resistance to *P. falciparum* on an entire population, and in reality the frequency of the trait, even in endemic areas, usually averages less than 25 percent, although as earlier noted, frequencies as high as 40 percent have been found.[82]

Thus in retrospect, because West Africans as a group have proved so remarkably resistant to falciparum malaria, it seems inevitable that other defenses besides the sickle cell would be discovered. Indeed, following Allison's correlation of the sickling trait with regions of endemic falciparum malaria, the attention of his colleagues was riveted to Africa, suddenly seen as bristling with all sorts of answers to genetic riddles. Geneticists overnight turned malariologists and rushed about, needles in hand, uncovering more and more black hemoglobin abnormalities that were credited with malaria protection almost before those needles were dry.[83]

Among their findings were more sickling anomalies such as sickle cell hemoglobin C disease and sickle cell beta-thalassemia, both double heterozygous conditions resulting from the inheritance of the sickle cell trait from one parent and either hemoglobin C or beta-thalassemia genes from the other. Still, despite the correlation of the incidence of both diseases with malarial regions, additional proof is needed that they actually do afford protection against *P. falciparum*. If that proof is forthcoming, then the two abnormalities apparently have provided a less costly form of malaria resistance than the sickle trait alone, for the resulting diseases (particularly hemoglobin C), although similar symptomatically, are much milder than sickle cell anemia.[84]

Far more important than these sickling anomalies in terms of frequency is another less costly type of resistance to *P. falciparum* which, though a hemoglobin abnormality, is not a sickling disorder but a blood enzyme deficiency bearing the somewhat forbidding name of glucose-6-phosphate dehydrogenase deficiency, understandably better known as G6PD deficiency. Credit for suggesting that a deficiency of G6PD, like the sickle cell, owes its high frequency and geographic distribution to malaria selection belongs to Arno Motulsky and his colleagues who advanced the hypothesis in 1959.[85] Subsequent research appears to have sustained them, albeit not without debate, for G6PD deficiency does not appear to provide as strong a protection as the sickle cell, and consequently the evidence is less conclusive.[86]

G6PD is a complex enzyme whose deficiency receives greater expression in females than males. As in the case of the sickling trait many variants of G6PD deficiency (over 100) have been discovered with more turning up all the time, and again as with the sickling trait the nature of the malarial protection it affords is not fully understood.[87] Nonetheless some have held for over a decade now that G6PD deficiency inhibits parasite life by virtue of the role the enzyme plays in the formation of reduced (deoxidized) glutathione, a biochemical substance essential for preventing the oxidation of red cells. The hypothesis here would have a deficiency of G6PD responsible for higher levels of oxidized glutathione, so high that presumably parasite life is discouraged.[88]

As with the sickling trait, G6PD deficiency is one of the few polymorphisms for which there is definite evidence of stabilization by selection with geographic distribution of the trait pointing to malaria as the selective factor. It has a high rate of occurrence in blacks, but as with sickling disorders, is found in other peoples as well. The trait has been observed among Sephardic Jews, Greeks, Iranians, and other residents of areas in which falciparum malaria is (or was) endemic. It does seem, however, that blacks have had the longest historical experience with G6PD deficiency, because the variants that most of them exhibit produce fewer ill effects. They are therefore able to "live" with their anomaly more gracefully than do nonblacks with their variants.[89]

The G6PD trait today affects between 10 and 11 percent of American blacks (reaching 17 percent in the South), while in West Africa its frequency is between 8 and 24 percent.[90] The sickling trait also affects about 10 percent of the Afro-American population, and hemoglobin C and thalassemia traits are present in another 3 percent or so.[91] Hence roughly one-quarter of America's blacks still manifest blood abnormalities that would endow them with a considerable advantage over individuals possessing normal hemoglobin in areas of endemic falciparum malaria.[92] But because they do not reside in such areas, nor in most cases have their ancestors for many generations, these traits are slowly dying. In fact, their rate of demise (fall in gene frequency) is one more piece of evidence that implicates malaria as a major factor in their previous stabilization. The rate of decline correlates well with that which would be expected given certain assumptions regarding the incidence of falciparum malaria in this country, African genes mixing with white and Indian genes, and the fact of the Afro-Americans' removal from Africa for an average of twelve to fifteen generations.[93]

Conversely, judging from the frequency with which these traits are still manifested by blacks after some twelve generations in the United States, it can be calculated that at most half of the slaves imported from Africa were endowed with genetic protection of one type or another against falciparum malaria. This may imply that acquired rather than innate immunity was the West African's most important defense against the disease, and in actuality it has been hypothesized that the real importance of hemoglobin abnormalities was not to endow its carrier with lifetime protection, but rather to improve his chances for survival during those initial childhood assaults of *P. falciparum* and thus keep him alive long enough to acquire an active immunity.[94]

On the other hand, the imperfect nature of acquired immunity juxtaposed with the historical imperviousness blacks have demonstrated to the disease may suggest instead that more hemoglobin abnormalities which can be linked to malaria protection remain to be discovered. Indeed, researchers are now involved in precisely that process with still another hemoglobin characteristic of blacks, a characteristic which also serves to clarify a heretofore mysterious black refractoriness to the vivax type of malaria. On occasion it has been wrongly asserted that although they proved relatively refractory to *P. falciparum*, blacks were just as liable to vivax malaria (the most common in the Western Hemisphere) as anyone else.[95] This assertion no doubt derived from the previously mentioned axiom that there are few cross immunities between malarial types.

Yet that axiom was meant to apply to acquired immunities only, while the blacks' puzzling resistance to vivax malaria seemed to be very definitely innate.[96] Investigators have demonstrated that, unlike their white counterparts, blacks in the United States even today possess a remarkable ability to resist *Plasmodium vivax*. Experimental innoculation of whites and blacks with *P. vivax* over many years using several strains revealed that only 23 percent of the black volunteers became infected, although fully 96 percent of the whites developed the disease.[97]

This relative immunity for those of West African ancestry was as mysterious as it was disconcerting, not only because of the problem it posed regarding the nature of that immunity, but equally important because of the questions it raised regarding how they came about this immunity in the first place. A killer such as *P. falciparum* presumably wielded a power of genetic selection, which accounts for the defenses developed against it. But essentially benign *P. vivax* should not have had the ability to stimulate selection for defense mechanisms nor even the opportunity in the case of West Africans, given its previously noted infrequency in their homeland. Finally, sickling and enzyme deficiency genes provided no obvious explanation, for neither blood abnormality seems to discourage *P. vivax* in the slightest.[98]

Researchers were then left with an inexplicable resistance of blacks to *P. vivax*, viewed frankly by some as a "racial" immunity.[99] Others as well were far from satisfied that sickling disorders and enzyme deficiencies constituted the whole story of black refractoriness to *P. falciparum*, and they too suspected a "racial" factor working to defend blacks against malarial infection generally.[100] An exciting new discovery in malariology lends some credence to this view. As just noted, for the last four decades malariologists have been aware that most Africans and Afro-Americans are quite refractory to vivax malaria. But in addition, since the 1950s it has been known that the majority of blacks possess red blood cells without the Duffy group antigen determinants, Fy^a and Fy^b. This tendency to be Duffy-group-negative "is extremely rare in other racial groups without black admixture," although the frequency reaches 100 percent in parts of Africa.[101]

A study published in 1976 by Louis Miller and his associates has welded these two facts into the hypothesis that Duffy-negative erythrocytes are refractory to invasion by *P. vivax*, a hypothesis that they tested on volunteers. Eleven blacks and six whites were blood typed and then exposed to the bites of mosquitoes infected with *P. vivax*. Of the five blacks who had Duffy-negative determinants, none developed the disease. By contrast, the whites and the remaining six blacks, all of whom had Duffy-positive determinants, did contract vivax malaria.[102]

Certainly the size of the sample was small, yet subsequent studies employing larger samples have revealed findings consistent with Miller's hypothesis.[103] Researchers have also demonstrated that apes and monkeys who are Duffy-positive contract *Plasmodium knowlesi*, a simian malaria parasite, whereas those who are Duffy-negative are resistant.[104] Because the erythrocyte is the place where the malaria parasite reproduces, the researchers speculate that the Duffy-negative genotype may also have the ability to "reduce the reproductive potential of *P. falciparum*" – a frequently fatal potential as we have seen – in much the same manner as do other blood abnormalities.[105]

If proven true, then another sizable piece will fit into the puzzle of the blacks' resistance to falciparum malaria and perhaps also into the puzzle of the evolution of malarial types. We have mentioned that vivax malaria is both relatively benign and rare in West Africa, neither characteristic likely to encourage genetic resistance in a human population. But both do make sense if it is supposed that vivax malaria was at one time a far more virulent disease but, as so many other diseases, has evolved into a more benign form.[106] Therefore, long ago *P. vivax*, one could argue, did act as a selective factor in the process of biologic adaptation. Selection for the Duffy blood group genotype would have created a very refractory West African population, so refractory in fact that the disease disappeared from the region.

Suppose further (as many do) that *P. falciparum* is a relatively new, perhaps a newly evolved, parasite against which the blacks' old ability to withstand *P. vivax* proved somewhat prophylactic, but not sufficiently so. Thus a high frequency of other defense mechanisms were called forth by a novel and deadly parasite to supplement that original malaria protection, with the sickling trait the first response of man to a new parasite.

But the sickling trait was grossly inefficient because of the heavy price it exacted in sickle cell anemia victims, and consequently other hemoglobin abnormalities such as G6PD deficiency and milder sickling disorders represent an evolutionary effort to develop a better balance between protection against *P. falciparum*, on the one hand, and the least harm to the homozygous recipient, on the other.[107] In this case, West Africans would possess both an old protection (the Duffy blood group genotype) originally developed against *P. vivax* and defense mechanisms more recently evolved against *P. falciparum* with the former again accounting for the "racial" immunity some researchers have suspected.

Or again, it has been speculated that the key to this so-called racial immunity may lie in a kind of "additive effect" of genes for malarial resistance, including the sickling and enzyme deficiency genes, along with others at that time not correlated with malaria protection (such as the Duffy factor) and probably still others yet to be discovered, all of which contribute to a polygenic system that provides "natural" resistance to most malarial infections.[108] To date at least seven uniquely African genes have been isolated, some of which are explicable in terms of stabilization by malaria selection, while others have yet to be explained.[109] Finally part of the explanation for the differential treatment by race meted out by malaria may lie not with black immunities but with white susceptibilities. For it has also been hypothesized that some genes *increase* susceptibility to malaria infection.[110]

But whatever the final determination, it seems clear from both an historical and immunologic viewpoint that persons of West African ancestry were equipped by their environment to "live" with malaria, while those of European were not. Indeed it was European susceptibility to malaria and yellow fever (discussed in Chapter 2) that defended Africa for so long against the kind of intensive European colonization the Americas experienced from the beginning, all of which brings up some historical ironies. As Philip Curtin has suggested, Europeans may well have preferred to locate plantations in tropical Africa close to a seemingly inexhaustible source of cheap labor but were persuaded by the lethal nature of West African fevers to locate those plantations instead in the more salubrious New World.[111] Put plainly, they found the expense of transporting African workers across the Atlantic eminently preferable to challenging the odds against their own survival in Africa, which means Mother Africa forestalled European violation at the price of millions of her sons and daughters.

Again ironically, however, Europeans soon discovered that Africans and African fevers were not that easily divorced, and the trade that brought the former also carried the latter – diseases which in the New World promptly joined with European pestilence to profoundly influence the history of the Americas. Indian laborers were decimated and Africans, with resistance both to European and tropical diseases, became ever more highly prized. American plants such as cassava and maize traveled the other direction to swell West African populations and make still more blacks available to the New World.

But in addition to their disease immunities West Africans carried susceptibilities, wrought by that brace of realities we have already glimpsed, malnutrition and genetic adaptation to a hostile environment. The whole would soon combine to exacerbate for the Afro-American the two insuperable problems he has faced since arriving in this hemisphere: chronic ill health and an implacable racism.

IMMUNITIES: EPIDEMIOLOGY
AND THE SLAVE TRADE

INTRODUCTION TO PART II

In those slave ships came more than human cruelty and suffering;
there came, too, the seeds of terrible epidemics and pandemics.

Frank D. Ashburn (1947)[1]

In the ensuing section the focus shifts via the slave trade from Africa to
the West Indies and the southern United States, while it continues to
remain riveted on black resistance to yellow fever and malaria.

As mentioned previously, medical science has not acknowledged
that blacks were gifted with innate yellow fever protection relative to
whites. Yet that resistance is discernible in the vast epidemiologic laboratory of history, which Chapter II explores. It is not, however, always
clearly discernible, because acquired immunity to yellow fever sometimes camouflages innate protection. Therefore special (perhaps even
excessive) care has been taken in disentangling the two, so that the
statistical evidence upon which much of the chapter rests, evidence
generated in abundance by yellow fever's repeated assaults on cities of
the West Indies and the American South leaves no doubt of the blacks'
superior ability to host the disease and survive.

By contrast much of the reason why blacks have historically proved
resistant to malaria is known to medicine; yet, perhaps paradoxically, it
is much more difficult to spy this resistance at work than to detect
blacks' resistance to yellow fever.

Yellow fever's appearances were specific and limited epidemic events,
which means that differential morbidity and mortality by race are easily
linked to those appearances. But malaria fevers worked constantly, year
in and year out, quietly killing not only directly, but indirectly as well,
by weakening the victim, leaving him susceptible to the fatal effects of
intercurrent diseases.

Thus, although malaria was responsible for much more mortality
(and morbidity) than yellow fever, and in fact (epidemiologists assure
us) must have been the single most important cause of death in the
Old South, it did not leave behind the hard statistical evidence of its
discriminatory deadliness that yellow fever did. On the other hand,

white southerners, particularly physicians, needed no such data to know that blacks fared much better with malaria than they did, and Chapter 3 examines the opinions of those physicians who sought to explain why.

One overriding theme in both of these chapters is that black disease immunities contributed significantly to the ever-growing white conviction that blacks were a distinctly different species of man. This theme is expanded upon in Chapter 4, which briefly examines the development of racial thought among physicians confronted with the phenomenon of disease discrimination. Thus, as in Chapter 3, the evidence is impressionistic, meaning that most of it comes directly from the pens of southern physicians who published what they thought they knew about black disease immunities in the medical and agricultural journals of the region.

One might legitimately question the extent to which a small majority of articulate physicians reflected the thoughts of their profession as a whole, in which case our response is that the physicians in question were shaping, as well as reflecting, a burgeoning "scientific racism." How successful they were in this endeavor is a question taken up later.

The remainder of Chapter 4 is frankly (some may insist outrageously) speculative regarding the way yellow fever and malaria may have not only influenced the history of the South, Africa, the slaves, and slavery institutions in the hemisphere, but stimulated racism in the public mind as well. It could be argued with some justification that such speculations do not belong in a book such as this. On the other hand, precisely because the study of disease and its impact on man's affairs is in its infancy, such speculations seem justified if only because, by intriguing, they help to sensitize us further to the tremendous role disease has played on the stage of history.

CHAPTER 2

YELLOW FEVER IN
BLACK AND WHITE

I 'specks dat d'seze [yellow fever] don't hanker much after niggers,
kase he don't offen win de fite tell he gits a feller turned yaller, an'
niggers don't turn yellow wuff er cent; but whenebber he gits er
whiteman lyin' out lookin like er chromo of er mustard patch in
bloom, dere's gwine ter be er hole in de semeterry groun' nex' day,
sho!
"Old Si," Atlanta Constitution (1878)[1]

I

Unlike malaria, yellow fever has failed to stimulate genetic research,
even though historically the black has revealed an incredible agility in
sidestepping that plague's lethal scythe, a scythe which invariably
chopped a wide swath through whites.[2]

The disease is caused by a virus, injected into man by another kind
of mosquito, the female *Aëdes aegypti*. The victim's first signal that all is
not well is a general ill feeling; his features flush, he develops chills,
then a high fever and quite possibly a severe head- and backache add
to his distress. (Note that the symptoms to this point are sufficiently
similar to a malarial attack to explain why the two were frequently
confused.) Next the patient suffers through a restless, agitated two- or
three-day period of high fevers and then characteristically experiences
a remission.[3] If he is fortunate, he has enjoyed (relatively speaking) a
mild attack, and that is all there is to it.

If he is not fortunate, jaundice sets in a few hours later (hence "yellow" fever), the victim may hallucinate, internal hemorrhages occur,
and he begins vomiting black blood (thus the Spanish appellation "vo-
mito negro") which "seems to gush forth without any effort from the
patient."[4] Convulsions and coma usually come next, followed closely
by death due to damage to internal organs. Or again if luck is with
him, the patient might still recover during the second stage, although
in classic cases the odds were against this occurring.

Yet regardless of whether the attack is mild or severe, those who
recover can rest secure in the knowledge that they will not be called

upon to repeat the experience. They have acquired a permanent immunity to the disease in much the same fashion that immunity over the ages has been acquired to many other illnesses: by hosting the disease and surviving.

West Africans have generally been portrayed as essentially a population of survivors to account for their refractoriness to the disease,[5] and certainly many were. In West Africa, the disease was sufficiently omnipresent to warrant its description as endemic,[6] and like many illnesses it typically runs a much milder course in children than adults.[7] Hence yellow fever endemicity seemed to imply that children, although protected by their mothers' antibodies during the first months of life, could hardly have escaped the sickness during their first years of life. But when they contracted it, the disease would be at its most benign, and therefore an entire people became refractory without an undue loss of life. Of course by surviving the disease, whites reaching the African coast also could and did acquire immunities. Yet European visitors to Africa were invariably adults, and as adults did not fare well with yellow fever. Rather they succumbed in fearful numbers, leaving a vivid impression of black immunity and white susceptibility.

This method of accounting for black yellow fever refractoriness, however, has the appearance rather than the essence of a satisfactory explanation, for it contains a fundamental contradiction; if endemic yellow fever had produced a largely immune population of West African peoples, then the virus itself, with no host, should have disappeared (retreated to sylvan form). This in turn would have meant that following generations would not have had the opportunity to experience the disease as children, and consequently should have been ripe for yellow fever in epidemic proportions. Yet, whites in Africa reported no such epidemics and continued believing that the disease simply did not attack natives.[8]

Another difficulty with relying too heavily on acquired immunity to account for black refractoriness has to do with the failure of yellow fever to become endemic to much of the New World, where it was more or less epidemic depending on location and chance.[9] This failure suggests that no one group of people should have proven unduly resistant to the disease, for no one group had that much more of an opportunity than another to acquire yellow fever immunity. Yet wherever the disease made one of its dramatic epidemic appearances, whites, but not blacks, perished in wholesale numbers.

Of course, part of the reason for this was the result of the slave trade that would have constantly infused slave populations with Africans who had acquired immunity. Much of the slave population was Creole-born as well, however, and surely black refractoriness should not have been as absolute as the literature indicates if the black's only operable defense against the disease had to be acquired.[10]

But, in fact, the black did possess innate yellow fever immunities, immunities that medical science has yet to acknowledge let alone explain, but immunities that nonetheless are discernible within the history of black, white, and red men and the yellow plague.

II

Much ink has been lavished on the question of the origin of yellow fever. Paleontologic, archeologic, historical, linguistic, epidemiologic, and clinical evidence has been shuffled together like packs of cards to make a case for both an African[11] and an American[12] birthplace for the disease. Those who place it in the Americas rest much of their argument on the fact that the disease was first described and epidemics first recorded in the Western Hemisphere (Yucatan in Mexico, Cuba, and Barbados) in 1648, some 130 years before it was distinguished from malarial fevers and similarly described and recorded in West Africa.

By contrast, those who prefer Africa as yellow fever's homeland rely on immunologic evidence that seems to point steadfastly at that continent. American Indians proved very susceptible to the yellow fever epidemics that struck the Western Hemisphere from the seventeenth through the nineteenth centuries,[13] yet black Africans were not. The conclusion that flows from this observation is that native Africans had a much longer experience with the disease than native Americans, and therefore Africa must be the cradle of yellow fever. Corroborating immunologic evidence has been found in African monkeys, who reveal a tolerance for yellow fever infection, which South American monkeys do not.[14]

But questions remain. American Indian records along with later Spanish accounts have been scrutinized with an eye for evidence of yellow fever prior to 1648 or even prior to Columbus.[15] These efforts have revealed diseases that *could* have been yellow fever, but they *could* also have been any number of other epidemic maladies. Moreover, even if there was pre-Columbian yellow fever in the Americas, this still would not necessarily mean that the disease originated in the Western Hemisphere.

Archeologic findings since World War II have established some grounds for believing that there may have been Arab-African contacts with America as early as A.D. 900. Included in the evidence are records of westward voyages launched from Africa, possible pre-Columbian maize unearthed on that continent (America is the homeland of maize), Negroid skeletal remains in the West Indies of bodies interred prior to 1492 and other artifacts thought to be African that Columbus might have found had he been looking for them.[16]

The evidence of course is highly tentative. Thor Heyerdahl's rafting expedition from Africa to the West Indies demonstrated that such a voyage was within the realm of possibility,[17] and therefore pre-Columbian contacts between Africa and the Western Hemisphere could possibly have introduced yellow fever to the latter. It is possible but unlikely, for it is extremely doubtful that yellow fever could have arrived in America via a prolonged journey at sea. First, the vector as well as the virus had to make the crossing from Africa to the Americas. True, questions of the vector's origin in the past have been as hotly debated as those of the virus, but today it is generally agreed that "on etomological grounds the *aegypti* appears to be an importation to the New World."[18] In Africa, many species of mosquitoes are more or less closely allied to *Aëdes aegypti*, but no other member of the subgenus *stegomyia* is native to the Americas.[19] Yet the point is somewhat moot in terms of yellow fever's transcontinental migration, because the vectors' presence aboard ship (or raft) was absolutely essential for the survival of the virus. Unlike malaria, whose parasites can remain alive in the bodies of victims for years, yellow fever is only communicable for a very short span of time. In fact, the female *aegypti* must feed on a yellow fever victim when he has viremia (usually the first three to five days of the illness when the virus is still in the blood) in order to become infectious. Next, assuming the mosquito has imbibed the virus along with her blood meal,[20] she must survive for a period of twelve to eighteen days while the virus incubates. Only then is the mosquito able to transmit the disease.[21]

Aëdes can live (and therefore infect human beings) for up to seventy days, although its average life span is closer to a month. Among the parameters of mosquito survival, however, water is crucial, for *Aëdes* cannot live more than five days without it. Moreover, it becomes temperamental when the temperature drops, refusing to bite when the thermometer falls below 62 degrees Fahrenheit. Extended low temperature will send it into hibernation.

Given these complex factors, it is fascinating to speculate on the odds against yellow fever crossing the Atlantic in any vehicle short of a jet plane that could whisk an infected person from Africa to the Americas before he even realized he was ill, a possibility incidentally of no little concern to epidemiologists today given the heavy *Aëdes aegypti* population in much of the American Southeast.[22] But anyone embarking from Africa on a slow seagoing vessel with the yellow fever virus in his body would either have died or recovered long before that vessel made an American landfall. In any event, he was eliminated from the yellow fever equation. Dead he could no longer support the disease; alive he could not host it.

So the female *Aëdes* mosquito was a must for the journey. She may have been infected before she winged her way aboard or may have bitten an infected human on board. Providing that the human was in the early stage of the disease and providing that she survived the requisite two weeks or so, she then became infectious herself. But to have survived she would have needed water, and fairly clean (not too brackish) water. This probably eliminated bilge water leaving the water casks as her best bet.[23] Furthermore, because the duration of a rafting voyage or that of a sailing ship for that matter was probably going to exceed her lifetime, she had to produce offspring as well as other infected humans to continue the symbiotic host – vector – virus relationship. Naturally this meant male *Aëdes* aboard (although eggs can lie dormant for a year) and fairly calm water for eggs to hatch in.[24]

At this point the imponderables boggle the mind: mosquitoes breeding and biting and incubating the disease, humans transformed into carriers for a brief period and then into either corpses or immunes. Indeed presumably the legends of the Flying Dutchman and the Ancient Mariner derive from shipboard epidemics of yellow fever. According to John Duffy, "as early as the sixteenth century the disease was notorious among ships in tropical seas."[25] But despite the fury of such a shipboard epidemic, precisely because it was a shipboard epidemic (and therefore hosts were limited) most epidemics would have burned themselves out in the first part of the voyage, leaving the virus still weeks away from shore. Hence it is clear that, besides the vector, the two requisites for the yellow fever virus to make the American migration were a swift voyage and a good number of persons aboard as potential hosts. A raft meets neither of these requisites.

Early sailing vessels did not meet these requirements either. Not only were speedy crossings rarely accomplished by the ponderous craft of the sixteenth century, but vessels plying the routes from Africa to America were usually engaged in the slave trade, which meant many of the individuals on board (West Africans) were probably gifted with yellow fever immunity. Thus, the criterion of swiftness was not satisfied nor was that of an abundance of hosts.

Then too the vector would have encountered additional problems on slavers, including access to water. For good water was crucial to the life of both cargo and crew on a long voyage, and consequently one of the most important crew members was a cooper who knew how to seal water casks tightly.[26] Moreover, the virus traveling in a human carrier would most likely have been detected by sharp-eyed ship officers looking for signs of illness prior to sailing. Because they knew too well the horror of epidemic disease aboard ship, they had to remain sharp-eyed.

Finally once underway mosquitoes would have had some difficulty in gaining access to the white crew members of a slaver who, although presumably the most susceptible to yellow fever infection, as a rule lived, ate, and slept on deck because of the stench below. The deck, of course, was exposed to those same winds which propelled the ship, which gave the crew a good measure of mosquito protection.

It seems incredible then that yellow fever could have arrived in the Americas by raft and barely conceivable that it did so aboard early slavers. Yet assuming that it did, vector and virus were in for still more difficulties. Both were immigrants that had forsaken old haunts for a new and strange environment. Therefore, it has been suggested that a period of acclimation was probably necessary for the pair.[27] Additionally, survival in either case was dependent on the availability of sufficient human beings to harbor the virus, on the one hand, and supply blood meals for the vector, on the other.

In the latter case, the human beings must be fairly numerous and live in close proximity to one another because the range of the *Aëdes* is very short, seldom exceeding a few hundred yards.[28] In other words, yellow fever in the Americas was preeminently an urban disease, and prior to the middle of the sixteenth century few urban environments in the New World were capable of sustaining enough epidemics to maintain the virus on a continual basis. Thus even when beachheads were established by the disease such as that which occurred in Cuba in 1648 it soon died out for lack of hosts, which suggests that yellow fever was probably introduced and reintroduced many times before taking root in the Americas.[29]

Conditions improved for yellow fever after the mid-seventeenth century, however. Faster slaving vessels were sliding off the ways of shipbuilding yards; the tempo of the slave trade quickened under first Dutch and then English suzerainty, and as the Spanish monopoly on the Caribbean crumbled, other European nations staked claims to island real estate and the populations of the region swelled. Barbados, for example, by midcentury numbered over 30,000 souls packed to a density of some 200 per square mile.[30] Here was fine epidemic tinder, the slave trade was a lighted match and the rival European armies and navies criss-crossing the West Indies were the winds which spread the conflagration. Yellow fever finally achieved the status of a more or less permanent resident.

If indeed yellow fever was transplanted from Africa to the Americas, that is how it may well have happened, and at least the scenario does fit the facts of those first reported epidemics of 1648. An alternate possibility is that the disease much earlier had established itself in Brazil and was brought north on Dutch ships active in both Brazilian and Caribbean waters during the period in question,[31] while a third would have the disease already present in America in sylvatic form awaiting the importation of an efficient vector (the *Aëdes aegypti*) which by the mid-sixteenth century had become numerous enough and population had grown large enough that urban yellow fever could make an appearance.

But the latter is suggestive of an American or at least a dual African and American origin of the disease that brings us back to the problem of immunology. It bears repeating that African monkeys have proven far more resistant to yellow fever than American monkeys,[32] just as West Africans, as will be seen, were quite refractory to yellow fever. Conversely, American Indians succumbed to the disease as quickly as whites, all of which provides powerful evidence that Africa was the ancestral homeland of the plague.

Nor does the late reporting (1778) in West Africa of the disease in epidemic form constitute a very impressive counterargument. For one thing, we have already taken note of the conspiracy of silence on the subject of a white man's chances for a long life as opposed to a quick death in West Africa. Given that conspiracy, had such epidemics occurred knowledge of it would probably have been suppressed. But even more importantly, yellow fever was only one of a bundle of African diseases and not easily disentangled for identification from malarial attacks, let alone such illnesses as dengue, typhus, or even scurvy, all of which manifest some symptoms similar to those of yellow fever.[33] Yet significantly, yellow fever was quickly spotted as a new disease in the Americas which accounts for its detailed description, particularly in Barbados, where for some reason malaria either never established itself or disappeared early in the recorded history of the island.[34] Thus to turn an old controversy around, the early reporting of the disease in the New World becomes paradoxically additional testimony to its African origin, while the whole of the evidence suggests strongly that yellow fever was another tragic cargo of the slave trade.

III

Once established in the Caribbean sun, it was only a matter of time before the disease would visit North America. Endemicity there was, of course, impossible, because the seasonal onslaught of cold meant hibernation for the vector and hence no year-round means of transmission for the virus. But for a century, conditions were not hospitable for northward epidemic visits either. As had been the case with yellow fever's move from Africa to the West Indies, the disease presented very definite requirements. Not only did the plague have to await the growth of North American cities in order to flourish with any real vigor, but perhaps even more important, it was denied adequate transportation opportunities by the Navigation Laws. For those laws which severely restricted colonial commerce with the West Indies also had the prophylactic effect of sharply curtailing yellow fever's chances for northern visitations.[35] Moreover, those ships engaged in legal West Indian commerce were subjected by law to strict quarantine procedures that frequently must have left the yellow pestilence swinging at anchor in North American ports, unable to complete the last few hundred yards of its journey to the mainland.[36] There was, of course, also a brisk clandestine trade with the West Indies, but contraband traffic by its very nature was inimical to the diffusion of the disease. Small ships delivered their illicit cargoes at out of the way estuaries and wharves where yellow fever found few persons to abet its propagation.[37]

It is therefore ironic that the lowering of the Union Jack over North America signaled the elevation of the "Yellow Jack." In one convulsive effort, the American Revolution snapped the bonds of the Navigation Laws as well as British restriction on American commercial and territorial expansion. The country was opened to free trade and to a flood of immigrants from abroad. Cities grew and the tempo of trade quickened. Unlike their British cousins, impatient Yankees had little use for time-consuming quarantine procedures. Large ships cleared West Indian ports and hastened north to lie just a few days later, disseminating mosquitoes at wharves from water ballasts and water casks. New technology in the form of steam ships soon insured that these voyages were executed with such swiftness that often infected persons aboard ship were still able to communicate the disease after reaching North America.

Swollen, unplanned cities became swampy, mosquito-infested mudholes, and the pressure of population created impossible problems of sewage and drainage. And yellow fever came – in ripples at first, then waves, and finally in combers to batter at America's coastal towns. In the process, the yellow plague wrote a new and deadly chapter in the annals of North American disease.

IV

A source of no little irritation in those European courts with a stake in the seventeenth-century Caribbean region was the matter of "fevers." Not content with merely felling private citizens, "fevers" had become a major factor in foiling great plans of state. These great plans flowed from the new mercantilist *Weltanschauung* of Europe's maritime nations that prescribed state building atop colonial wealth, which was to come preferably at Iberia's expense; and Iberia was vulnerable. Spread thinly across the globe, Portugal had lost its grip on Africa, and Spain had lost the strength to maintain the Caribbean as a mare nostrum.[38]

Thus, the doors stood open to slave labor on one side of the Atlantic and to tropical islands for the employment of that labor on the other – a true mercantilist's dream. By occupying slaving stations in Old Guinea and islands in the West Indies, the Dutch were the first in pursuit of that dream. But their example was soon emulated by the English and then the French, each with their own "western design," and willy-nilly the Caribbean was "balkanized" with colonial powers determinedly hanging onto their own possessions while grasping for others.

The stage was set for a European game of "beggar-thy-neighbor" in the West Indies that would add a red tinge to Caribbean blue for a century and a half. Yet during those long decades of internecine warfare, the sum total of the carnage created by the world's greatest powers was minuscule when laid alongside the toll extracted by disease. For as navies and armies of vulnerable Europeans moved into a disease environment laden with African pathogens, pestilence, not military force, became paramount in the battle for the West Indies.

Of the 1,500 French soldiers who landed in 1665 to occupy Saint Lucin for example, only 89 survived a counterattack of disease apparently led by yellow fever. In 1693 Sir Frances Wheeler attacked the French in Martinique with a force of 4,500. The invasion collapsed in shambles as 3,100 men were wiped out by disease. Certainly the best known example in North America of disease carrying the day was Admiral Vernon's abortive assault on Cartagena during the war of Jenkin's Ear. He lost close to half of his original landing force of 19,000 men (including many Americans) to yellow fever.[39]

As the eighteenth century wore on and more and more unacclimated soldiers and sailors were sent out from Europe, physicians on the spot with a quantitative grasp of the horrendous morbidity and mortality armies were sustaining grew more and more alarmed. One such doctor grumbled about the "dreadful mortality" troops had endured "since Great Britain has been in possession of West Indian colonies" and doubted that they were worth the price.[40] Another pointed out that generally during the worst months a full one-third of the Jamaican troops were "unfit for service" at any one time.[41] Moreover, during 1782 when the island anticipated attack, of the 7,000 or so troops sent to Jamaica during the past three years, "there were not above 2,000 men fit for duty."[42]

A third observer bluntly spelled out the British military situation in the West Indies during 1796 stating that yellow fever was so pervasive that any campaign "is now considered as little better than a *forlorn hope*" (italics his).[43] And the dirgeful litany of military disasters grew still louder. Between 1793 and 1796 the British Caribbean Army saw disease thin its ranks by some 80,000 men of whom more than half were victims of yellow fever. Not to be outdone, the French threw armies into St. Domingue in an effort to reclaim the island from rebelling slaves. Within ten months after landing, French forces suffered a reduction of some 40,000 men by a coalition of black resistance and yellow pestilence, with the latter accounting for the lion's share of the dead.[44]

Nor was the military alone in its suffering, for despite near continual warfare West Indian civilian populations were growing. The Sugar Revolution further stimulated a demand for slaves, and this thriving traffic delivered African pathogens as well as African laborers. Burgeoning urban white populations provided fertile soil for yellow fever, and the disease – nurtured by increased military and commercial activity – grew ubiquitous. Indeed the tempo of its epidemics increased to the point where residents of major ports came to regard the arrival of yellow fever as they did the hurricanes of late summer: a seasonal occurrence. They grew inured to the creaking of carts piled high with dead trundling under their windows each evening and the stacked coffins at cemeteries awaiting the attention of exhausted gravediggers. But inevitably it was observed that only whites were doing the dying. Blacks by contrast seemed impervious to the yellow plague.[45]

This differential in black and white mortality was not lost upon West Indian military commands desperate for a remedy to the disease's heavy toll.[46] Furthermore colonists had begun to fear that at the rate white troops were succumbing to disease, Africans would soon control the Antilles by virtue of their resistance to fevers, on the one hand, and sheer numbers, on the other.[47] Thus physicians began to recommend the employment of black troops,[48] a suggestion the British acted upon. It was an experiment not without paradox, for as Francisco Guerra has pointed out, black soldiers quickly became crucial to British West Indian policy and thereby "set a practicable pattern of military establishment which furnished the means for a continuancy of slavery in the Caribbean, and of colonial dominion . . . for decades to come."[49]

From an English standpoint, however, the experiment was a resounding success.[50] The wisdom behind it was made apparent in an 1838 study conducted by the army that juxtaposed death rates for black and white troops stationed in the Caribbean. In the Windward and Leeward command during 1803–16, white soldiers perished at the rate of 138 per 1,000 mean strength annually.[51] Black soldiers by contrast died at a rate of only 64 per 1,000 mean strength. The years 1817–36 witnessed a substantial reduction in these levies with the white death rate lowered to 79 and the black to 40, but an enormous although explicable gap still existed between white and black mortality. Of the 79 white deaths per annum per 1,000 mean strength, fully 37 or about half of the deaths were due to "fevers." Yet less than 5 deaths of the black's average loss of 40 per 1,000 were fever-related. Therefore, if fever deaths could somehow have been eliminated, black and white would have died at almost exactly the same rate, a powerful testimony to the racial prejudices of falciparum malaria and yellow fever.

V

It is difficult to disentangle those malaria and yellow fever deaths placed under the rubric of "fevers" by the British army. But surely black immunities to malaria alone do not account for the imposing differential. Rather blacks must also have been able to resist yellow fever to an extraordinary degree, which implies something at work besides acquired immunity.

According to estimates made by Philip Curtin, Spanish America and the West Indies imported about 250,000 slaves between 1521 and 1650.[52] In other words, a quarter million blacks reached a New World that most authorities agree was still free of yellow fever. Thus, whether or not these blacks had acquired an immunity to the disease in Africa is irrelevant. What is relevant is the lack of an opportunity for their Creole-born descendants to acquire immunities in a disease environment that did not include the yellow plague. Hence when epidemics of the yellow plague did finally occur in 1648 a significant portion of the New World's black population should have proved susceptible to the disease. Yet as harrassed and envious whites were quick to observe, their black chattels seemed impervious to yellow fever's fatal march across the Caribbean.

Moreover from this point forward, while yellow fever made periodic calls on most coastal cities and towns of the West Indies, it did not really become endemic to much of the region (save perhaps Trinidad) but rather was frequently epidemic, depending on location and chance. Therefore, although as in Africa, blacks once more gained the opportunity of acquiring yellow fever immunity by experiencing it, and although the slave trade would have constantly infused slave populations with African immunes, black refractoriness relative to white susceptibility should not have been as absolute in the Caribbean region as the literature assures us it was, at least not if the blacks' only defense had to be acquired.

The seed of suspicion planted in West Africa as to the adequacy of the acquired-immunity-only argument, however, took root in a look at the blacks' West African experience with yellow fever and was nurtured by their continued refractoriness in the Caribbean. It only reaches fruition when the history of the disease in the United States is examined, particularly during the nineteenth century, when all the veils that thus far have concealed the full extent of innate black resistance to yellow fever are stripped away. First, there was no slave trade to provide a flow of theoretically immune Africans into the country; second, the disease was endemic to no part of the United States; and finally, because epidemic yellow fever visits were confined mostly to a few southern cities, only a fraction of the South's population, black or white, could have acquired immunity.

Yet, as will be seen, on occasion after occasion, although blacks proved by contracting yellow fever that they did not possess acquired immunities to it, they nonetheless displayed a remarkable ability to resist a fatal termination of the disease, an ability whites clearly did not have. The remainder of the chapter then, while acknowledging the importance of acquired immunity to yellow fever, will demonstrate that insofar as U.S. blacks were concerned, their first and most important line of defense against the disease was inheritable.

VI

It has already been stressed but bears repeating that yellow fever could not and did not become endemic to any portion of the United States, because its major vector, the *Aëdes aegypti* mosquito, does not winter well; therefore the virus faded as the first frosts arrived. The disease was consequently limited to short epidemic visitations after which a fortuitous combination of vector, virus, victim, season, and seaborne commerce was required for its reappearance. Moreover, any appearance or reappearance in strength was confined almost exclusively to towns and cities, again because of the vector. The range of *Aëdes aegypti* is very short, and it is necessarily dependent upon dense populations for blood meals.

Thus the yellow fever which made incursions into the antebellum South was strictly an urban disease and hardly the scourge of plantations it is occasionally represented to have been. Together then these factors that (1) denied the disease the status of a permanent resident and (2) confined it to urban areas meant very simply that only a tiny fraction of the South's black population could have acquired immunity to yellow fever, because slavery was overwhelmingly a rural occupation. Yet throughout the eighteenth and the first half of the nineteenth centuries, white physicians and laymen alike insisted that blacks did in fact possess an almost absolute immunity to the yellow plague.

It will be useful to glance quickly at those urban blacks along with their white counterparts who did acquire yellow fever immunity in order to appreciate how such a conviction of absolute immunity could gain currency. The individuals of whatever color who earned their resistance were the permanent residents of southern coastal cities ranging from Charleston to New Orleans, which witnessed numerous yellow fever invasions. Locals nicknamed the disease "stranger's fever" comfortably believing themselves safe because they were "acclimatized," while outsiders were not.[53] "Even the dogs, turkeys and chickens," they insisted, "have to undergo acclimation before they can do well here . . . hence the additional value attached . . . to the *acclimated* negro, horse, ox and milch cow."[54]

Today, of course, we can read acquired immunity for "acclimation" and wonder at the courage, or fatalism, of those thousands who deliberately faced yellow fever in an "unacclimated" state. But, throughout the nineteenth century, these cities abounded in transient victims for the disease. During Savannah's 1820 epidemic, "strangers" contributed about 80 percent of the death toll; only 20 percent of the 695 yellow fever victims were native Georgians.[55] Of the first 34 cases of yellow fever reported in New Orleans during 1848, none of the patients had been in the city over eight months. Similarly in Charleston during the city's ordeal of 1854, only 48 of the 612 whites dispatched to a yellow fever grave were native Charlestonians.[56] Fully 92 percent of the deceased had been outsiders.

The same had been true five years earlier when "strangers" were credited with practically all of the city's 109 yellow fever deaths. Fully seventy-six of the dead were Irish or German, another twenty-seven were foreigners from other countries or outsiders from other states, three were South Carolinians, but only three natives made the list of yellow fever casualties.[57] Foreign immigrants such as Charleston's Irish and Germans seemed particularly liable to the disease[58]; during the New Orleans outbreak of 1858, the Howard Association treated 3,414 cases of which 1,069 patients were German and 1485 were Irish. Only 409 of the patients were "natives of the United States."[59]

Nonetheless strangers whether of the foreign or domestic variety received little sympathy for absorbing the brunt of a yellow fever attack. Rather city fathers with an anxious eye on commerical health became downright abusive of foreigners and outsiders whose yellow-hued corpses were sullying their respective cities' reputations for salubrity. During the 1853 seige of New Orleans, newspapers repeatedly assured readers that outsiders were doing the dying, and they were mostly persons of the lower classes with "filthy habits."[60] The implication was clear that "clean living merchants" and others of substance had little to fear from yellow fever epidemics.

Savannah's leading newspaper imparted the same message in the wake of the 1854 visitation when it intoned: "It will be seen that the mortality has been much greater among our Irish population" and very "small . . . among acclimated persons."[61] Nor did Charleston's summary of two decades of yellow fever mortality entitled *Report on . . . Strangers Fever* leave any doubt as to the origins of those who monopolized that city's yellow fever death roles.[62]

However, and this is the important point, the death rolls make it clear as well that practically all of the victims, strangers or natives, were white. During the first six decades of the nineteenth century, while Savannah endured fifteen epidemics, Charleston twenty-two, and New Orleans earned its reputation as North America's yellow fever capital with at least thirty-three outbreaks,[63] blacks simply did not contribute significantly to the yellow fever dead.[64]

Illustrative is Charleston where the most complete differential mortality data were recorded and the black population outnumbered the white (whites equalled 43 percent of the population in 1820, 42 in 1830,

44.5 in 1840, and 46.5 in 1850).[65] Between 1817 and 1839, the city lost 1,145 whites to yellow fever and only 33 blacks.[66] By 1858, the toll had climbed (unfortunately these figures are only for those aged 18 years and over) to 2,885 whites but just 58 blacks.[67]

In the city of New Orleans a similar pattern is discernable. In 1820, although the races were exactly balanced, at least 84 percent of the individuals who perished (863) from the yellow fever of that year were white.[68] By 1849, despite the fact that whites now made up a large majority (77 percent) of the city's population, they constituted a far larger percentage (99) of the 769 yellow fever victims, and the following year they made it an even 100 percent of the 107 who succumbed.[69] Then in 1853 as New Orleans writhed under North America's most awful yellow fever epidemic, whites contributed 99 percent of the city's close to 8,000 (7,849) deaths.[70]

Of the "big three" yellow fever cities, statistics are the most meager for Savannah. But here too a dramatic black refractoriness to the disease is plainly evident. The year 1820, which found Savannah's blacks slightly outnumbering the whites, also found the city under yellow fever seige. During the epidemic months of July through November, 695 whites died from all causes (mostly from yellow fever), while about 200 blacks perished (mostly from other causes).[71] Again in 1854 during thirteen weeks of the yellow pestilence, 1,008 white deaths were recorded (whites now made up 55 percent of the population) of which 605 (but probably many more) were definitely caused by yellow fever. During this same period, by contrast, 95 black deaths were recorded of which yellow fever received credit for only 15.[72] Finally, although national mortality data are only available for the antebellum period during 1849–50 (a relatively light yellow fever year), the census listed 777 whites dead from the disease but only 8 blacks.[73]

The relative immunity of blacks to the disease is even more dramatically highlighted during those years in which rates of death are calculable.[74] In New Orleans during 1853, whites perished from yellow fever at a rate of 75 per 1,000; blacks at a rate of 3 per 1,000. In Savannah the following year, the death rates proved nearly identical to those of New Orleans: whites died from the disease at a rate of 72 per 1,000, blacks at a rate of only 2 per 1,000. In Charleston during 1854, the white death rate from yellow fever was 31 per 1,000, whereas the black death rate was statistically insignificant.

Moreover, even this differential does not fully disclose the magnitude of the blacks' invulnerability to yellow fever, for the rates are based upon the population supposed to be in the city. But as epidemics began, whites crowded every means of transportation in a headlong flight from the disease. Prior to Savannah's 1820 outbreak, the city contained about 5,000 persons. By the end of that epidemic the population was reduced to only 1,500 with 666 deaths accounting for only 20 percent of that reduction. Again in 1854 only one-third or so of the population remained throughout the epidemic, and this stampede of whites out of cities under yellow fever attack was repeated all over the South. Blacks, however (whether slave or free), constituted most of those who could not get away, and therefore the exposure rate of the black population was always much greater than that of the white.[75]

Antebellum physicians were abysmally ignorant of their pestilential enemy. They remained baffled by its etiology, bemused by its epidemiology, and bewildered by its malignance, yet their collective experience convinced them of one thing. Few would have disagreed with Dr. Samuel Cartwright of New Orleans when he pronounced Africans "perfect non-conductors of yellow fever."[76]

VII

The extent to which acquired immunity accounts for the remarkable "non-conductability" of blacks thus far is perhaps less important than the possibility that it could account for it and the black and white differential treatment meted out by the disease as well. It could be argued, for example, that the black populations of antebellum coastal cities were relatively permanent, consequently most had the opportunity to acquire immunity; the white population was largely transient, so most did not. But with the 1830s, many blacks also became transients as the westward movement of slavery accelerated, an acceleration that encouraged the growth of cities as well as the development of farms and plantations. Thus, the dense population so necessary for the Aëdes survival was provided, while the stimuli to the movement — technological advances in transportation, specifically railroads and steamboats – provided mobility for the virus. Not surprisingly then by the late 1840s, the tempo of yellow fever onslaughts against the South quickened, and numerous blacks with no previous exposure to the disease stood squarely in its path within the Mississippi Delta.

Thus it is paradoxical that at about the time Dr. Cartwright made his pronouncement, blacks began to demonstrate some "conductability." Following a yellow fever epidemic in Woodville, Mississippi, as early as 1844, it was noticed by a physician that despite the "vast disproportion between the number of [yellow fever] deaths in the two races . . . [seventy-two whites and twenty-seven blacks] I believe the negroes were no more exempt from an attack than the whites."[77] Dr. Fenner of New Orleans next called attention to the phenomenon during the 1847 epidemic, commenting that "all colored people recently settled in New Orleans were liable to have yellow fever, perhaps equally as much as white people."[78] He added, however, that from some cause or another "the disease is certainly much milder among them."[79]

The city's particularly virulent 1853 epidemic underscored this new piece of epidemiologic intelligence and impressed it firmly in the minds of physicians throughout the South. During those awful summer and autumn months the attention of the medical world was riveted on a beleaguered New Orleans, and then as frost arrived and yellow pestilence departed, eagerly awaited reports began filtering out. The world learned of the 8,000 deaths. It also learned that blacks had taken the disease in unprecedented numbers; in fact, the consensus was that it "affected unacclimated negroes . . . equally as generally as it did the white population."[80] Yet despite the virulence of the disease and the number of blacks who contracted it, "most physicians in the city never saw a fatal [black] case."[81] Unlike whites, "Negroes, whether natives of Louisiana, or 'non-creolized,' seldom died of the fever."[82]

An epidemic two years later in the Norfolk–Portsmouth area yielded data that documented, in terms of case histories, the observations of physicians in New Orleans on a differing black and white experience with yellow fever. During the siege in Norfolk, 143 white and 50 black yellow fever patients were admitted to the Howards Infirmary of that city.[83] For 46 percent of the whites, the infirmary was merely a place to die. By contrast, 94 percent of the blacks recovered. Similarly across the bay in Portsmouth, it was estimated that in terms of cases treated fully 42 percent of the whites, but only 5 percent of the blacks who contracted the yellow pestilence succumbed.[84] These data dovetailed remarkably with the Howard's experience in Portsmouth's sister city. Nonetheless, in Norfolk it was noted that "Very many colored people are down with the fever– [in fact] several hundred."[85]

Thus, the yellow-fever-ridden decade of the fifties had the effect of forcing the medical profession to reconsider old notions of absolute black immunity with a new tenet emerging that held that blacks as a general rule were equally as likely to contract yellow fever as whites but that they suffered much less from it, and far fewer died. Antebellum physicians in other words were now convinced that blacks had been somehow innately equipped to survive the disease, whereas whites were not; and the blacker the better. Mulattoes, experience had taught them, were more exempt than whites, and blacks much more exempt than mulattoes.[86] Dr. Nott of Mobile explained that never in his career had he witnessed "a single well marked [case] in a pure blooded negro."[87] "The smallest admixture . . . is a great, though not absolute protection against yellow fever . . . [but] I hazard nothing in the assertion, that one-fourth negro blood is a more perfect protection against yellow fever, than is vaccine against smallpox."[88]

Finally, a few physicians added to the medical opinion of black yellow fever susceptibility the suggestion that the more northward the disease traveled, the more liable were blacks.[89] But it remained for postwar years to put this hypothesis to the test.

VIII

During the war, the Crescent City found itself inundated by Yankees but free of the yellow pestilence thanks, ironically, to the detested federal blockade, which curtailed West Indian ship traffic.[90] Ironically, as well, this city, which had heretofore dreaded the onset of the yellow fever season, now saw "acclimatized" locals praying for the disease to arrive and kill the Yankees. Their wish was fulfilled too late, for yellow jack did not return until 1867. During the plague's absence, however, the city had filled with strangers, so fresh blood quite literally awaited yellow fever.[91] In particular, Yankee soldiers, both white and black, were exposed to the disease for the first time, and Army records provide excellent differential mortality statistics. White soldiers suffered a death rate of 256 per 1,000 average mean strength from yellow fever during the epidemic, while their black counterparts died at a rate of 73 per 1,000 mean strength.[92] Whites then proved some three-and-a-half times more liable to die from the disease than blacks, even though the death rate of blacks ran higher than ever before.

But still higher morbidity and mortality rates were to come as many blacks left the plantations that had quarantined them against yellow fever and moved to cities where they were certain to be exposed.[93] Thus, during Montgomery's 1873 epidemic, it was noted that "a remarkable feature [of the yellow fever outbreak] is the number of colored persons who were attacked."[94] Again following their 1876 epidemic, Savannah physicians discovered they had lost 114 blacks as well as 773 whites (blacks constituted 54 percent of the 1870 population) and puzzled over the contrast between the Negroes' previous immunity as slaves and their increasing liability as free men.[95]

This perplexity increased following the 1877 outbreak of yellow fever in the South Carolina Sea Islands. In tiny Port Royal, of the 137 blacks who did not flee the island, 87 contracted the disease. Whites as usual suffered more, with practically all of the 100 or so who remained taking the disease and one-quarter of those dying. By contrast only 1 black died, yet as a group Afro-Americans had actually seen an astounding 63 percent of their number contract the so-called saffron scourge.[96]

Unfortunately this high proportion of nonimmune blacks remained astounding only until the following year's yellow fever season, when the disease mounted a last full-scale assault on the U.S. mainland by raging up and down the Mississippi River throughout a long, hot, damp summer and autumn. At Memphis on the northern periphery of penetration, any lingering notions of an absolute black immunity evaporated during those terrible months of 1878 as 11,000 of the city's 14,000 blacks, along with almost all of the 6,000 whites who remained, played host to the virus.[97] And while the epidemic made it clear that blacks and whites without acquired immunity were similarly susceptible to the disease, the death rolls it precipitated laid a crescendo of emphasis on the vastly different manner in which yellow fever treated the two races. For although 78 percent of the Memphis black population was infected, only 9 percent of those infected died.[98] On the other hand, of the 6,000 white sufferers, 4,204 or 70 percent retched and hemorrhaged their way to yellow fever graves.[99]

The same phenomenon occurred in New Orleans where some 5,000 Negroes, constituting about one-fourth of its caseload, were treated by the Howard Association.[100] Again the number of blacks taking yellow fever was "unprecedented," yet again as happened throughout the Delta "the disease among them was of a much milder character than the whites, and their percentages of mortality very much smaller."[101] In Holly Springs, Mississippi, mortality data closely approximated that of Memphis with 72 percent of the infected whites failing to recover, while only 7 percent of the blacks succumbed.[102] In Grenada, Mississippi and other river towns, black and white mortality virtually duplicated that of Holly Springs leaving no doubt that in the face of "yellow jack" whites died and blacks survived.[103]

IX

The last decades of the nineteenth century found yellow fever hunters closing in on their quarry with the disease finally brought to bay in Cuba by Reed and his colleagues, who linked together work done by Ross, Finlay, and Carter. Thus by 1905, when the yellow plague paid a final visit to the United States, something of its etiology was known, and its epidemiology had ceased to be mysterious.[104]

For this reason, the comments of physicians in New Orleans (selected by fate appropriately enough to grapple with their old adversary this one last time) are especially germane because they were convinced that the epidemic that claimed only 19 black lives out of 434 dead[105] had proved "conclusively . . . that negroes are about as liable to contract the disease as whites, but that they have it usually in a remarkably mild form."[106] These physicians were saying then that acquired immunities were of little consequence in the differential reaction of whites and blacks to yellow fever since clearly if blacks contracted it, then they lacked these immunities. The important defense was represented by the blacks' ability to escape the virulent form of the disease that struck down whites with such terrible regularity.[107]

Perhaps it is belaboring the obvious to point out that this ability to "enjoy" the disease in "a remarkably mild form" must be the result of some innate defense mechanism developed by the human body to cope with endemic yellow fever in West Africa, a mechanism that permitted populations to survive the disease so that they could acquire immunities in large numbers. Indeed, without the word gene in their vocabularies, antebellum physicians were nonetheless grasping for a long-term environmental, or genetic, explanation when they credited the protection blacks enjoyed to prolonged residence in the "torrid zone," on the one hand, and found significance in the heightened susceptibility of mulattoes as opposed to "full-blooded" Negroes, on the other.[108] Certainly it is the existence of this mechanism that makes the changing experience of blacks with yellow fever in the South explicable.

The innate resistance is hardest to spy at work during the first decades of the nineteenth century, because relatively stable black populations living in areas where the disease was frequently epidemic could have proved refractory on the basis of acquired immunity alone. Native whites, of course, had also acquired immunities, but because the white population was on the whole far less stable than the black, the many deaths of nonimmune transients gave rise to the same notions of absolute black immunity that had long held sway in the West Indies and West Africa.

By the middle of the nineteenth century, however, blacks too were migrants of sorts, with many slaves traveling west by land and by sea via coastal cities, which frequently hosted yellow fever. Certainly it was no coincidence that New Orleans, the biggest western clearing house for these migrants, first saw blacks suffering from the disease in large numbers. Moreover, as cities grew, so did the mulatto population of these cities who proved far more susceptible to yellow fever than those of a darker hue. In fact by 1860, one of every four blacks living in a southern city was mulatto.[109]

Then with the close of the Civil War, blacks never before exposed to yellow fever became so in wholesale lots, as ex-slaves left rural residences for the cities. Hence physicians in many postwar southern communities saw a much higher incidence of yellow fever among blacks than had previously been witnessed with the 11,000 who contracted the disease in Memphis constituting the classic example.

Yet in every epidemic throughout the century, whether blacks hosted yellow fever in large numbers or not, their death rate was always amazingly low, relative to the white rate that was always appallingly high. Clearly those of West African descent possessed an ability to efficiently acquire a permanent immunity to the disease by experiencing it and surviving, while those of European descent quite inefficiently died.

X

As noted previously, specific genetic factors, such as those linking blood abnormalities with malaria protection, remain to be discovered in relation to yellow fever. Science has, however, been unearthing polymorphisms among black Africans that await explanation, the question of their importance typically shelved with the statement that "although the biological significance of this polymorphism is presently obscure, it seems likely that additional studies will clarify the nature of the selective factors which maintain this polymorphism."[110] Perhaps one or some of these newly discovered polymorphisms will reveal the answer to the question of black yellow fever resistance. Or maybe the answer is some other physiologic anomaly that remains to be detected. As mentioned in the last chapter, at least seven genes at present have been identified as "uniquely" African. Some have been stabilized and are explicable in terms of malaria selection. Others remain to be explained, perhaps within the context of yellow fever protection?

Tangentially, it may turn out that blacks were not usually resistant to the disease after all, but instead that whites were extraordinarily susceptible. Much has yet to be done on the complex problem of inheritable disease susceptibilities and immunities, but it may be that both might be the result of "many genes acting in concert, and some of these genes may form polymorphic systems" of their own.[111] Evidence that the Chinese generally had yellow fever in a mild form, as did blacks, can be gleaned from records of epidemics in Latin America.[112] Moreover, at least one epidemiologist at the turn of the century commented on a peculiar Chinese refractoriness to the disease[113] that, if true, becomes doubly intriguing because of the nagging epidemiologic mystery regarding why, to man's knowledge, yellow fever·has never penetrated Asia despite that continent's plentiful populations of the *Aëdes aegypti* mosquito.[114] If the Chinese were in fact as resistant to yellow fever as the West African, then of course the possibility of an innate European susceptibility to the disease is enhanced substantially.

But in any event questions left partially open early in the chapter can be closed at this point with some assurance now that the impressionistic evidence of differential black and white treatment by yellow fever has been confirmed statistically. The "acquired immunity only" argument made it difficult to comprehend how the yellow fever virus could have achieved sufficient successful crossings on a slaving vessel to establish itself in the Americas, given the numbers of supposedly immune black slaves, severely limiting potential hosts of the disease. It now seems likely, however, that blacks probably did host the disease in the holds of slave ships but escaped the notice of their white captors by experiencing the disease in a mild form, unrecognizable by the white crew. Hence if a portion of a slave cargo had no acquired immunity to the disease, the likelihood of virus, vector, and host maintaining a successful symbiotic relationship for the duration of the Middle Passage increases enormously.

Finally, the phenomenon of mild yellow fever in blacks also helps to provide one more answer for those who may still be wondering why yellow fever was seldom reported among Africans in West Africa. The answer is that it did occur and probably with some frequency, but again infected blacks simply did not display those "classic symptoms" whites had come to expect. Thus, even if Europeans had encountered a full-fledged epidemic on the Coast among Africans, they would not have recognized it as such. Surely it is not so strange that West Africans developed this ability to "live" with yellow fever, even if the nature of that ability is still unknown. In the words of Henry Rose Carter, one of yellow fever's conquerors, the blacks' "reaction to yellow fever is just what one would expect to have been evolved in a race for many generations in Africa subject to that infection."[115]

CHAPTER 3

BAD AIR IN A NEW WORLD

So little are they [Negroes] affected by that fell-destroyer of the white race, *malaria*, which kills more than war and famine, that they suffer in the Southern States more from disease of winter than those of summer.

Dr. Josiah Nott (1847)[1]

I

Because malarial parasites can remain alive in the body of a victim for years, malaria, unlike yellow fever, should have encountered no great difficulty in reaching the Americas. On the contrary, quite probably the disease entered the hemisphere from nearly all points on the compass, and (again unlike yellow fever whose vector required importation) most etomologists and malariologists agree that probably many appropriate species of anopheline vectors, especially *Anopheles gambiae* and *Anopheles funestus*, were on hand to abet its spread.[2]

Given these facts, one might reasonably expect a fairly straightforward account of malaria's arrival in and progress throughout the New World. Such, however, is not the case. It has been suggested (perhaps a bit naively) that malaria's distinctive symptoms should "mark it out sharply from other febrile illnesses," making identification of the disease in historical records a relatively easy matter.[3] But unfortunately malaria of the past is usually entangled in a bundle of fevers along with typhus, typhoid, even cholera infantum, and yellow fever, all of which are lumped together under the vague rubrics "remittent" or "intermittent" or "bilious" fever or a combination thereof such as "bilious remittent" fever connoting different ailments to different peoples during different periods.[4] For these reasons the date of malaria's debut in all of the Americas, and especially North America, has been the subject of not always cool and reasoned debate.

To date, full acceptance has eluded theories that place the disease in the New World prior to 1492, although the notion that malaria crossed the Bering Strait with the first Americans at one time enjoyed a brisk but brief currency.[5] Rather, the weight of opinion would have the

50

pre-Columbian aboriginal population troubled by mosquitoes (anopheline mosquitoes included) but untroubled by malaria until the transatlantic flow of European and African pathogens began. Since that flow was first directed at the West Indies and because the proper mosquitoes were present, there seems no reason to doubt that malaria spread as rapidly across the Caribbean basin as the early Spaniards.

One the other hand, much energy has been devoted to an old, but reoccurring, epidemiologic dispute over when and how "malaria" first reached North America.[6] Since it is generally agreed that pre-Columbian America was free of malaria, the debate centers squarely on the question of when it was imported and by whom.[7] Many have insisted that because the disease flourished in Europe, it must have arrived in the blood of Europeans from the very beginning and consequently established itself in all dawning colonies.[8]

But others have reasoned that because English colonists do not complain of severe malarial infections until the late seventeenth century after the slave trade had begun in earnest, the disease must have reached North America from Africa and was therefore a relative latecomer.[9] Assuming the eastern seaboard harbored some of those anopheline mosquitoes incriminated as malaria vectors, however, both sides are probably correct, and their quarrel has been essentially one of semantics.

It seems inevitable that *Plasmodium vivax* migrated in the bodies of the first Spaniards to set foot on Florida's soil. Certainly it arrived with settlers to Virginia and the Carolinas and quickly became part of the disease environment. Yet vivax malaria was such an old curse to Englishmen that it seems unlikely the infection would have elicited any more comment than the common cold.[10] But as Peter Wood points out, most assuredly the loud complaints of colonists in the late seventeenth century leave little doubt of a brand new disease experience.[11] Something had arrived in their midst that was described as malaria but was so "extraordinarie sicklie that sickness quickly seased many of our number."[12] Given this virulence one suspects that the sudden "seasing" of lives heralded the arrival of falciparum malaria, a suspicion considerably strengthened by the coincidence of the appearance of this new disease with the arrival of colonists from the West Indies and, even more importantly, with the real beginning of the African slave trade to North America. Hence "malaria" was both an early and a latecomer and of both European and African origin.[13]

Nonetheless, it was only with the tardy arrival of Africa's contribution that the halcyon days of salubrity in the colonies dissolved into a pottage of disease: the main ingredients of endemic malaria supplemented with epidemic seasonings. The frontier started its long westward march, and malaria kept pace taking root wherever clearings were made and mudholes of communities, plantations, and farms sprang up. It was noted that unusually wet summers invariably meant a profusion of "pestiferous gnats called moschetoes"[14] and a fine autumnal harvest of fresh malaria victims. People learned to pray for early black (killing) frosts that cut the "sickly season" mercifully short. Yet malaria grew more omnipresent and virulent with each passing year as more Africans, reservoirs of *Plasmodium falciparum*, were imported and more whites with no protection against the disease were on hand to host it.

II

By the turn of the nineteenth century, the cotton boom, a transportation revolution and the increasing mechanization of the English textile industry were acting in unison to lay open more and more of the South to agricultural exploitation, and as slavery expanded fevers followed that were constantly infused with new potency via an exuberant West Indian trade stimulated by the booming economy.

Virulent yellow fever filled the cemeteries and disrupted the commerce of major southern cities, while the countryside was sickly as never before. Some called their tormentor the slow fever, others the country fever; persons near rivers, lakes, and marshes knew it as river, lake, or marsh fever. When it was serious it was known as pernicious or malignant fever; when it was merely bothersome, people called it the chills or dumb fever or the shakes or the "auger"; however, physicians who disdained the vulgar, scientifically labeled it the intermittent, remittent, congestive, and/or bilious fever. It was ubiquitous; travelers took it for granted like "seasickness or mountain disease," and permanent residents after years of shaking did not even think of it as a disease.[15]

But wherever swamplands and "cricks" and marshes gave off those "noxious exhalations" the bad air reserved its worst poisons for white men.[16] Thus, along with refractoriness to yellow fever, black resistance to malaria was still one more medical phenomenon that set the black apart in the white mind throughout the antebellum period. Dr. Tidyman during the 1820s declared that "blacks suffer little, and are generally exempt from attack of intermittent and remittent bilious fevers, which prove so fatal to the white population."[17] Dr. Ramsay in the 1830s insisted that "Negroes are peculiarly exempt from miasmatic diseases."[18] Dr. Lewis wrote in the 1840s of the remarkable exemption of Africans from yellow fever, which, he said, "extends in a great measure to all the malarious fevers."[19] Dr. Ketchum in 1850 remarked that blacks "seem to be almost entirely exempt from the . . . fevers," while the well-known Josiah Nott of Mobile, Alabama, went further and declared that they were "exempt."[20] At their state medical convention, North Carolina physicians, although not so convinced of the black's

total immunity, nonetheless pronounced him much more "easily managed" if he did contract malaria.[21]

Certainly visitors to the South received a vivid impression of black
immunity to malaria. One traveler, for example, described a situation
on a Georgia plantation in which the house of the master and his
family stood on an "elevated area" with the slave quarters behind the
house and below it. Both were close to marshy lands and a "spring
bog." The whites were nearly prostrate with fever; the blacks were
"exempt" except for a single family "which lives apart from other
slaves" and none of whom were field laborers.[22] Solon Robinson of
Indiana made a simlar observation about the mosquito-infested rice
and sea island cotton plantations of South Carolina. "The whites," he
reported, "cannot live upon them, while the negroes remain perfectly
healthy," and indeed as John Duffy has pointed out, it was black
immunity to malaria that "made possible the development of rice plantations in South Carolina in the first place."[23]

Admittedly meager mortality statistics tend to bear out these impressions.[24] The city of Charleston mustered mortality figures for the years
1821 through 1858 revealing that white deaths from "fevers" exceeded
those of blacks by over a 5:1 ratio, with 3,948 whites but only 754
blacks succumbing to them.[25] Savannah too published data for 1815–23
that showed a great white mortality rate from autumnal fevers, prior to
the commencement of a dry culture for rice which would have cut
sharply into the anopheline mosquito population.[26] The fact that no
one bothered to include data on blacks suggests strongly that they
experienced very little malaria mortality. In New Orleans during 1850,
malaria death rates disclose whites dying from the disease at a rate of
190 per 100,000, yet blacks perishing at a rate of only 90 per 100,000. In
the Crescent City then, as elsewhere, malaria demonstrated a marked
color preference.[27]

Some southern physicians, however, believed that mortality did not
tell the whole story and consequently were not so convinced of an
absolute black refractoriness. A sharp-eyed South Carolina doctor
observed that although "fever is not the great outlet of life among
them," blacks nonetheless regularly contracted malaria.[28] A Charleston
colleague agreed that "Negroes are less liable to attacks . . . than
whites . . . but both classes are subject to it all their lives."[29] Dr. Pendleton of southern Georgia concurred that "the African is less susceptible to malarious influences than the white,"[30] a position neatly summed
up by the editors of the *New Orleans Medical News and Hospital Gazette*
who flatly stated that the black was hardly "exempt" from the disease.
Rather "malaria is certainly a *poison* to the negro as well as to the white,
but it is less deleterious to the former, and he more readily becomes
seasoned to it" (italics theirs).[31]

Once again there is statistical evidence – scanty to be sure – that buttresses this position. For certainly the account books and morbidity records kept by planters and overseers indicate many slave sick days lost to fevers and more than a few slaves down with the "fall fever."[32] Yet as one scrutinizes the argument between those who held the black to be almost absolutely immune to malaria and those who found him merely relatively refractory, it becomes clear that one of the variables, as in the case of yellow fever, was the degree of "blackness" one possessed. Dr. Arnold of Savannah, for example, wrote that on the basis of twenty-four years of practice in "malarial country" he could "corroborate the fact of the less liability of the Negro to all classes of our malarial fevers . . . but I cannot say that the Negro is exempt . . . still even when they do have it, they have it in a very light form and I do not recollect ever to have lost a full blooded African."[33] A Mobile doctor agreed that it was only "under extraordinary circumstances" that "full-blooded" blacks were sufficiently affected "as to cause death."[34]

Another of the variables had to do with the amount of "acclimation" one had received, a factor considerably clouded in malaria's case, for unlike a yellow fever attack, which left the patient immune to further attacks, the acquisition of malaria immunities was a slow and torturous process. Indeed, the process was so slow and long that many doubted the importance of a prolonged residence in a region. Dr. Nott, who for many seasons watched established white residents sicken while even newly arrived blacks remained untouched, was moved to declare that "there is no such thing as acclimation against intermittent or remittent fevers."[35] An Augusta, Georgia physician went further and suggested that longevity in an area actually militated against good health. The longer a person resided in a malarial region, the more liable he was to infection, a rule that went for Africans too.[36] The editors of the *New Orleans Medical News* took sharp exception to this position, calling it an attempt to "out-Herod Herod," while simultaneously seizing the opportunity to inform Nott that blacks and whites alike become acclimated.[37]

In light of today's knowledge, we can look back on the debate as one positing the virtues of innate as opposed to acquired malaria immunities. Southern physicians of course could not begin to fathom the complexity of acquired malaria immunity. Nonetheless, a few were remarkably astute in guessing the presence of some innate protective mechanism in blacks. A Virginia physician noted in his casebook the conviction that the disease ran a much different (and milder) course in blacks than in whites.[38] Another of his colleagues, who claimed to have treated 114 black and 400 white cases of malaria, saw the different course of the disease in terms of "the skins and surface glands of Negroes" which could better throw off the fever.[39]

Dr. Pendleton perhaps came closest to the truth by coupling his suspicion that the blacks' greater resistance to malaria stemmed from an ability to tolerate hotter climates with the acute observation that newly imported West Africans had always proved "immune" to the climate of the rice fields, but as the black became further removed from Africa in terms of generations, he frequently lost some of this immunity.[40]

Thus, southern physicians suspected both a kind of acquired immunity in Africans and an inheritable defense against malaria. But even when the doctors were able to grasp some of the principles at work in one or the other instance, neither explanation by itself was sufficient; hence the matter of black malaria resistance, although a subject of heated debate, remained mysterious and bewildering. A closer look at the intricate relationship between both types of immunities and the manner in which they combined to protect the slave in the American South reveals why.

The observation of medical men that malaria seemed to run a milder course in blacks was correct not because, as was theorized, their bodies threw off fevers more efficiently due to a better "ventilation" system but because of those previously discussed blood abnormalities that held down the level of parasitization and therefore the fevers. The Duffy-negative trait meant that most blacks would have been little annoyed by P. vivax, which was earliest to appear in the spring. This trait may also have frustrated falciparum malaria to some extent as well when it peaked in late summer and early autumn.[41] The Duffy-negative trait alone then may have provided blacks with some protection from early spring to late fall. Moreover, close to half of America's slaves had other defenses against P. falciparum (such as sickle trait and its variations, along with glucose-6-phosphate dehydrogenase deficiency), which made the latter months of the malaria season so "sicklie." For them a gentler bout with the disease was guaranteed (perhaps with few or no recognizable symptoms). Those reports that suggested that blacks seemed to be losing their immunities in proportion to their removal from Africa, however, indicated that some portion of the black population had been observed suffering from a much more rigorous encounter with malaria.

Yet, it would seem that the loss of immunities could not have been due to the disappearance of any of the aforementioned polymorphisms, for presumably they were stabilized by the presence of malaria in parts of the South, just as they had been stabilized by malaria selection in Africa. More importantly, even in those areas free from falciparum malaria, nature simply had not been given enough time to take much of an inroad in their eradication. It has been estimated, for example, that even today were genetic screening employed to assure the elimination of homozygous recipients of sickle trait, a century would be required to wipe out sickle cell anemia.[42] Thus, unless nature had received assistance, most of the blacks' malarial defenses brought from Africa should still have been intact.

Nature did receive some assistance, however, and assistance of the kind that permits a guess or two as to both the identity of the chief black malaria sufferers and why they were suffering. By the late 1840s when Dr. Pendleton made his observations, the South had seen few slave imports for over a half century. Indeed it has been estimated that as early as the 1770s about 80 percent of the blacks in this country were native-born.[43] Consequently, almost all slaves were a number of generations removed from their mother country, and frequently no one, neither slave nor owner, knew a slave's family tree or the arrival date of his original African progenitor. As a rule of thumb, therefore, degrees of blackness were employed by planters to estimate time away from Africa. Since the eighteenth century had witnessed a good deal of miscegenation, that general rule was not a bad guide. Very black Afro-Americans, in other words, were believed to be closest to their homeland, whereas mulattos came from older American families.

Hence physicians who drew attention to the relationship between black malaria susceptibility and prolonged North American residence were in effect making the same point that other doctors were making when they suggested that the lighter the complexion the more liable to malarial fever one became. This is the same phenomenon, of course, that was observed in black immunity to yellow fever.

Today geneticists would agree that an infusion of Caucasian genes could have hastened the end of malarial protection for some, and the 1860 census indicated that enough of these genes were present in 10.5 percent of America's slave population for them to be classified as mulatto. Yet even here the importance of acquired immunity or, better, its absence cannot be overlooked. For the lighter blacks invariably were heavily represented on the planters' household staff and actually swarmed in the cities. In fact, by 1860 mulattoes constituted 39 percent of the freedmen in southern cities and 20 percent of the urban slave population, but less than 10 percent of the rural workers.[44]

Therefore whether house slave, urban slave, or urban freedman, these blacks, because of less exposure, would have been less likely than field hands to have maintained immunity by enduring periodic malarial attacks. They would also probably have been less likely to possess the protective polymorphisms because of their greater percentage of Caucasian genes. Hence, with less in the way of both genetic and acquired immunities, they inevitably would have suffered more from malaria when infected.

Moreover, the condition of insufficient acquired immunity is also a factor on the white side of the white–black susceptibility coin. Many whites by their own habits left their bodies relatively defenseless against malaria when they did contract it. This is because those permanent residents, who could afford to, avoided the "sickly season" religiously. Many planters in Georgia and the Carolinas maintained summer homes on the beaches and islands off their respective coasts or on high pinelands inland where the "auger" did not often visit. But even planters in straitened circumstances "who could borrow the price of an overseer" fled during the malaria season.[45]

They sojourned in the North or otherwise absented themselves with the result that when they did sustain an attack of malaria (as they usually did because they could not dodge infestation forever, despite all their precautions; physicians thus warned them against returning even for a single night), they suffered far more intensely than those who regularly experienced the disease and therefore maintained some degree of immunity against it.

In this latter category, fell individuals such as the white overseers, who remained behind to run plantations after the seasonal exodus of the planter and his family. It was well known that as a group they were "less liable" during the summer and autumnal months than other whites, who were less often exposed.[46] Yet their habits too may have retarded the process of acquiring immunity, for as one medical man advised, whites should take a lesson from blacks and shed their fear of the outdoors. He pointed out that blacks spent warm nights sleeping in the open air, whereas whites shut themselves up tightly in houses. Despite this "precaution," whites nevertheless had double the amount of sickness.[47]

Finally again as with yellow fever, the impression of extreme white liability was accentuated by the steady stream of outsiders and immigrants, particularly Irishmen who entered the South with bodies defenseless against malarial parasites. Newcomers, of course, were soon initiated by the trial of "acclimation" and those who survived did acquire some immunity against future attacks. But in the meantime, their experience tended to reinforce the notion of white susceptibility to and black immunity from malarial fevers.

Thus medical men were presented with a set of peculiar circumstances that tended to exaggerate the extent of slave refractoriness to those "mysterious emanations of swamps." In addition to possessing innate defenses against the disease, most slaves were also in constant jeopardy from infected mosquitoes and therefore maintained a high level of acquired immunity as well. Whites, who suffered from the disease, on the other hand, were in many cases newcomers or permanent residents, who had for a time successfully avoided infection (and thus the process of acquiring immunity) only to have the disease finally catch up with them and extract a heavy price for that temporary success.

It was a combination of factors then – the black's innate malarial defense, his greater exposure to the disease, white immigration, and the white habit of fleeing the disease – that all combined to create a vivid impression of black refractoriness to malaria as well as yellow fever. Unhappily as we will see, successful physiologic resistance to these two tropical killers carried with it an enormous social price.

CHAPTER 4

TROPICAL KILLERS, RACE, AND
THE PECULIAR INSTITUTION

The misunderstanding of the medical men came ultimately to be
enshrined at the core of scientific racism.

Philip Curtin (1964)[1]

I

European physicians on the coast attempted early to understand why
their compatriots failed so miserably to survive those "fevers" to which
the black seemed impervious. Unfortunately, their devotion to epidemiologic thought, aged some one-and-a-half millennia, yielded the explanation that the West African sun unbalanced humors in European
bodies. Worse, their efforts to correct humoral imbalances in fever-
stricken victims by draining the body of blood and bile must have
contributed heavily to the mounting European death toll. Doubtless
many would have survived these dehydrating illnesses had not physicians joined pathogens in depleting body fluids.

Yet not all medical knowledge derived from the ancients was without
value. In his classic scrutiny of *Airs, Waters, and Places*, Hippocrates had
speculated that "bad air" might carry disease. Although established in
antiquity, this notion had never firmly embedded itself in European
thought; continental physicians preferred to rely on Galen. After yellow fever and malaria managed their respective migrations to the
Americas and embattled physicians proved helpless against the pair on
both sides of the Atlantic, however, the hypothesis began to receive
some serious attention.[2] Galen's long reign was at last threatened by
changes in medical thought quite literally in the air, and a new empiricism began to permeate the medical profession.

The great English physician Thomas Sydenham (1624–89) was an
important figure in this movement urging colleagues to abandon the
theoretic for empiric observation, while the migration of Europeans to
the Americas under the stimulus of colonization and tropical wars provided a new generation of physicians with bountiful opportunities to
observe the mayhem wrought by these diseases firsthand.[3] The fevers,
they noticed, were mostly contracted in low-lying marshy areas, where

58

water was stagnant and air fetid, or around waterfronts, where the air was absolutely alive with unpleasantness. Hippocrates had been right, and in the language of the period, medical wisdom held that some kind of "poisonous effluvium" emanating from these areas, laden with "morbific and pecant" matter, was triggering the fevers.[4] Thus, by implicating the air, physicians took a seemingly large stride toward pinpointing mosquitoes as the real villains.

Also on the positive side the new empiricism did work improvements in medical treatment and disease prevention. Under the influence of the towering figure of Sydenham, the use of the chinchona bark of the Incas (from which quinine was later extracted) spread widely and was regularly effecting miraculous cures in malaria cases by the end of the seventeenth century, even if it proved a disappointment in revivifying yellow fever and typhoid victims.[5]

Progress was made as well in the area of preventive medicine as cleared areas, particularly those in North America, were identified as healthier than uncleared areas. Cutting down tall trees to admit sunlight and purify air was obviously a good idea. Standing water in cities and surrounding swamps often became the object of energetic sanitation proposals that were sometimes even adopted. Sailing men discovered that shipboard epidemics that broke out in tropical waters could often be extinguished by sailing for a cold climate, if they could only sail fast enough.

But unhappily, despite the flood of empiric data, which increasingly intruded on the comfortable and gentlemanly practice of speculative medicine, the new "miasmatic" theory did little to sidetrack humoral practice. Moreover, although miasmatic theory has been viewed as "novel" and "revolutionary," and even hailed as the forerunner of germ theory, in the field of tropical medicine it seems not to represent a radical change in thinking so much as merely a change in emphasis – and not all that much of a change at that.[6]

Previously the sun had been indicted as the culprit, knocking humors out of balance, because persons acquired fevers more readily in tropical and subtropical climates. Yet even now with the brooding, suspicious gaze of medical men deflected to the air around them, they kept the sun in one corner of their eyes, because a serious flaw in the miasmatic theory was its failure to account for the racial preferences of the fevers in question.

Presumably "poisonous effluvium" was poisonous to everyone – black and white – which did nothing to clarify why blacks escaped fevers that cut down whites. On the other hand, humoral theory did offer an explanation. Blacks were accustomed to a hot sun that produced no ill effect on their humors in either tropical Africa or tropical America. The result of this inconclusive note was that sun and air were fused into a new lodestar toward which medical eyes turned for etiological guidance, and science backed away from avenues that might have led more quickly to those epidemiologic breakthroughs that only came with the turn of the twentieth century. Moreover, despite some clinical advances fostered by the new empiricism, physicians continued attempts to balance blood and bile and even redoubled those efforts as they entered the "Heroic Age" of medicine although these efforts were often more effective in killing than in curing.[7]

II

West Indian warfare of the latter eighteenth century placed physicians under pressure from governments to *do something* about the fevers that were decimating troops and deciding battles. Their solution, as we saw, was to surrender to Nature and recommend the employment of black troops. Accompanying the white flag was a new means of accounting for black fever resistance. The sun, air, and humors were all folded neatly into a new and more comprehensive "acclimatization" theory that held rightly, for the wrong reasons, that the sustained residence of a people in a tropical or subtropical region was a necessary precondition for the enjoyment of good health within that region.

Yellow fever susceptibility was conceived of as "the effect of climate, operating upon exotic bodies," those exotic bodies being colored white.[8] Blacks then, who were not exotic in the tropics, suffered no humoral dislocation when moved from tropical Africa to the tropical areas of the Americas. Hence it followed that acclimatization in one region must work for another, since in either region black humors remained placidly in balance. But while the recognition that whites could also become acclimatized simply by surviving for a year or two squared with acclimatization theory, the observation that for some reason or other black immunities were always more certain continued to nag at the medical mind.

Had physicians remained with their environmental (i.e., acclimatization) explanation for black refractoriness to yellow fever and malaria, nineteenth-century American racial thought might have avoided a nasty turn, which ultimately led to a medical portrayal of the African as an inferior species of man. But the desires of physicians to explain the mechanics of this refractoriness opened a Pandora's box of scientific and racial riddles that, because they could not be resolved with existing anthropomedical knowledge, stimulated the wildest and most destructive sort of theorizing about the black.

Early in the nineteenth century, southern physicians merely noted a black resistance to yellow fever that although inexplicable was nonetheless to be expected in the natural order of things. Typical was one physician's comment that "Nature has, with a special regard to the safety of blacks, rendered them almost proof against the insidious attacks of this terrible disease."[9] Those who attempted to account for this phenomenon did so on the basis of prolonged residence in the "torrid zone," their "natural place of abode."[10] But then physicians grew restive with their own vagueness and became bolder with specifics. It was declared that the "negro was destined by nature to live under the vertical sun of the torrid zone;" his skin, hair, and indeed all his phenotypical characteristics permitted him to resist atmospheric heat and therefore afforded him a protection against fevers.[11]

Clearly the theorizing was beginning to drift away from an environmental mooring, whereupon a strong racial current seized it with such observations as dark skin keeps its owner cooler, the African's capacity for perspiring is greater than that of whites, and his body odors are different from those of whites.[12] These factors, it was suggested, indicated that the slave had a built-in ability to throw off those foul vapors that brought on fevers so deadly to his master.[13]

After further probing and poking, it was determined that the black's lungs and heart were smaller than those of whites.[14] This it was suggested, combined with an overabundance in the black's bloodstream of "lymph, phlegm, mucus and other humors," rendered him deficient in "red blood."[15] The result was "molasses blood" that might protect him against fevers.[16] Additionally his liver, glands, and kidneys, larger than those of whites, might also be responsible.[17] Then some physicians began to hold that fevers were actually excitements of the brain, and it was "discovered" that blacks had smaller brains than whites as well as less developed nervous systems.[18] Here then was the real reason for different racial fever susceptibilities. Whites were in far more danger than blacks because of their intellectual activity.[19]

Hence the Afro-American started paying a stiff price for his freedom from malaria and yellow fever at the hands of some antebellum physicians. For along with thicker blood; smaller brains, lungs, and hearts; larger livers, kidneys, and glands, which set him apart in the medical mind, came the conviction that these attributes made the Negro sluggish, dull in mind and body, weak willed, and so mentally inferior that no education can be of help, in fact "the most complete dolt on earth."[20] On the other hand, his perceptive facilities were much keener than those of the Caucasian, indeed they were those of "the lower class animals."[21]

Thus under the spur of white and black differential fever mortality, racial differences – both real and imagined – became the subject of intense medical speculation,[22] and as science continued the project of classifying and linking together the "great chain of being," questions of "race" loomed larger and larger. The black's disease immunities, as much as his phenotypical characteristics, implied to southern physicians that Africans were of a different species than the Caucasian, and an inferior one at that.[23] Those immunities must also have helped to shape the white public's attitude toward the black.

III

Among the first yellow fever epidemics in North America to involve any great number of blacks, the most extensive occurred not in the South but rather in the Philadelphia of 1793, then the nation's capital.[24] This particular yellow plague had already won a malignant fame first for the manslaughter it committed on refugee settlers crossing from the island of Bulma on the African coast to Grenada in the Caribbean, and then for a lethal tour of the latter region, spreading "so rapidly that every military doctor in the West Indies had the opportunity to see hundreds of cases."[25]

The same opportunity befell Philadelphia physicians as the disease, apparently arriving with refugees fleeing the St. Domingue slave revolution, burst on the city with a fury that left 5,000 dead in its wake.[26] Few of those dead were blacks, however, and it was there in Philadelphia that American physicians came face to face with the phenomenon of black resistance to yellow fever.

Indeed, at first, all of the city's 2,500 blacks seemed immune, so immune in fact that some viewed them suspiciously as carriers of the disease.[27] Nevertheless, blacks suddenly found themselves eagerly sought after as nurses for the sick, not only because of their resistance to the scourge but also because many whites who had not fled the city would not dream of approaching the bedside of an infected person, not even that of a spouse or child.[28] One suspects that it was envy of black immunities as well as white cowardice in the face of the pestilence that gave birth to a bitterness against blacks that swelled in the aftermath of the pestilence and triggered an animosity that continued to echo throughout succeeding yellow fever epidemics until the disease itself was conquered.

Blacks were accused of exploiting their immunity by "extorting two, three, four, even five dollars a night for attendance" on the sick.[29] They also suffered from charges of looting the homes of the sick and the dead. Some of the city's physicians were vehement in denouncing bad black behavior.[30] Others, however, led by Benjamin Rush,[31] sprang quickly to the black's defense. Rush in particular was effusive in the compliments he paid to his "african brethren." It was pointed out that under the leadership of the Reverend Absalom Jones and Richard Allen, Philadelphia's African Society had voluntarily assumed the most onerous and disgusting burdens of the epidemic – treating the sick and carting and burying the dead – and had managed to bring some order to a city collapsing in shambles.[32] Practically lost in this controversy was that blacks had not proven all that immune to yellow fever. Rather they had contracted the disease later than most whites, coming down with it after the epidemic had already raged for a month or so, and their cases were lighter because they never hemorrhaged, which meant that relatively few died.[33] Nevertheless the bitterness remained, the myth of absolute black immunity burgeoned, and rumors of sinister black intentions broke out simultaneously with yellow fever in community after community throughout the nineteenth-century South.

Rumors! Epidemics started with them and ended with them, rumors which spread faster than the fever. A vessel would put in, as did the steamer *Ben Franklin* at the start of Norfolk's 1855 epidemic, from some yellow fever plagued island, in this case St. Thomas.[34] Soon whispers would circulate of nightly excursions from the ship. They were burial parties some murmured. Then a rumor circulated of a corpse with "orange-hued hands" washed up on the beach. Yet when questioned the captain "blandly demured" the presence of yellow fever aboard his ship. Next came the rumor that two terrified passengers had jumped overboard and swam ashore. A few days later some cases of severe "bilious remittent" fever were reported. The newspaper flatly denied any yellow fever threat. Still the exodus of whites was underway.

Blacks by contrast remained. Slaves stayed because they were so ordered and free coloreds because they had no place to go; soon only black people frequented the streets. "You may walk the streets all day long," wrote one of Portsmouth's first ladies during the epidemic of 1855, "and you will not see a dozen white persons."[35] Even Creole whites, who spoke so confidently of "stranger's fever" took few chances on venturing out of their homes, although city officials might rush out from time to time to burn animal skins or blast the heavens with cannon fire in efforts to cleanse the air of those noxious influences that were doing all the killing. But for the most part whites huddled indoors armed with bits of garlic deposited in their clothing, doused themselves with camphor, breathed through vinegar-soaked rags, chewed chinchona bark, and prayed.[36]

And to no avail. Yellow fever unerringly sought out the susceptible and a pall of death settled over stricken cities. "Upon arrival at Mobile," wrote a witness to the 1834 carnage, "the first sad object that had saluted me was a bier bearing a dead body to its final resting place. I went into town this morning and found everything as desolate as you can well imagine." The only persons to be seen on the streets were Negroes, their voices and footsteps drowned out by "the solemn rumbling of the death carts."[37]

Whites became utterly dependent on black servants who ran errands, nursed the sick, buried the dead, and brought news to the living. With dependency, however, came fear, and as in Philadelphia black immunities provoked hostility and suspicion. There was always the dread of slave conspiracy to haunt already troubled white minds such as that reputed to have occurred in Mobile during the 1839 epidemic. While whites were prostrate with the calenture, a series of fires demolished a good portion of the town, fires that rightly or wrongly were credited to slave plotters.[38]

Of course, anything missing from shops and stores reopened after the plague had passed was invariably blamed on blacks. But perhaps the worst stigma to attach itself to blacks by virtue of their resistance to yellow fever is not so tangible. Slaveholders might express relief during epidemics that at least their servants were safe. Yet whites who frantically tried to immunize themselves only to see loved ones struck down by disease, to watch them writhe under the effects of "cures" such as jalap and lead and calomel and turpentine, to witness their suffering from the pains of lancing, blistering, bleeding, and sweating before finally being carted off to yellow fever graves must have felt more than mere envy of black imperviousness to the disease. To be sure, some at least must have grown to actively resent the race that Nature seemed to be letting off so easily.

IV

The full impact of malaria and epidemic yellow fever on slavery, on the black, and on the South generally can only be speculated upon, for the evidence is skimpy, the variables many, and the questions – those of the relationship of disease to culture, society, and human behavior – enormously complex.

Yet having already taken a tentative step in a speculative direction, it is difficult to resist a few more. First, the manner in which yellow fever and malaria dealt differently with the two races in the South should prove of interest to those who are concerned with differential black and white mortality statistics for the antebellum period. Their collective wisdom at this point would have the life expectancy of slaves only slightly below that of white southerners, which has been interpreted as suggestive of a relatively full life for slaves in a material sense. It has been estimated, however, that yellow fever killed 500,000 North Americans alone, with most of these deaths occurring in the nineteenth-century South.[39] And while malaria's toll will never be known, it was unquestionably the single most important cause of death in the region; its endemic harvest in lives exceeding in gargantuan proportions that of sporadically epidemic yellow fever.

The point here is quite simply that blacks were resistant to both tropical killers that regularly winnowed the white population, yet their life expectancy was nonetheless *below* that of whites. Thus, if the counterfactual is entertained for the moment – had there been no malaria and yellow fever stalking the whites of the South – then their life expectancy might well have been *substantially* above that of their slaves instead of just slightly. If true, this may imply that the material conditions of slave life were somewhat worse than they have been portrayed by many; at least those material conditions that affected life expectancy. On the other side of the demographic coin, researchers have found slave fertility somewhat higher than that of white Southerners[40]; a phenomenon which has also lent itself to interpretations of good material treatment while enhancing the image of the paternalistic (no pun intended) planter.

But some part of the explanation for higher black fertility may be a result of malaria's pervasiveness in the South and in the physiologic changes that a malaria attack can produce. It has been discovered that possessors of the sickling trait have a significantly higher rate of fertility than nonsicklers in malarial regions ranging from the Congo to the Caribbean.[41] Yet the most sensible hypothesis to account for this does not have the trait encouraging fertility but rather its nonpossession discouraging fertility. Put succinctly, malaria attacks elevate male scrotal temperature, and the higher temperature destroys sperm; for some two months following a bout with malaria, a male's sperm count, although gradually increasing, is nonetheless considerably reduced. Thus because two malarial attacks yearly were not unusual, individuals with little or no resistance to the disease might well have been infertile for up to one-third of that year, and to this infertile period must also be added the time actually spent under attack when presumably sexual activity would have been close to the bottom on one's list of priorities.

Sicklers, however, even when attacked have a much shorter duration of fever and consequently less reduction in sperm count. Yet if this hypothesis contains some truth, then it should not apply to just male possessors of the sickle cell trait but to all males endowed with some form of malaria protection as against those without protection, and it should apply not just to falciparum malaria but to all forms of malaria. Because whites were the chief malaria sufferers in the South, then clearly their fertility *should have been lower* than that of blacks.

Malaria and yellow fever have probably shaped the history of the South in many other ways that we have been slow to recognize. For example, traditional historiography holds that the presence of unfree labor in the South was an important factor in disuading free laborers from immigrating to the region. The impact of little immigration was to further enhance the value of slave labor and retard the South's economic and industrial growth vis-à-vis a slave-free North.

Doubtless this is all true, but should not pathogenic barricades share some of the blame for discouraging immigration? It was certainly no secret that the North enjoyed much more salubrity than the South, and given the number of the immigrants who did head southward only, as we have observed, to falter in the yellow fever/malaria gauntlet awaiting them, surely word must have gotten about to avoid the region. In fact, Darrett Rutman believes that the "word" was first circulated by William Penn who began introducing anti-Virginia material in his pamphlets of the 1680s.[42] Certainly later complaints by individuals such as Hume, who lamented that outsiders were afraid to settle in Charleston, suggest that the word was out.[43]

An argument against this, however, is that following the Civil War the South did experience considerable migration from the North despite its reputation for insalubrity. In part, one suspects this was a function of anticipated profits being worth the risk. But also the risk was somewhat minimized. As previously noted, the federal blockade had kept the South virtually yellow fever-free during the war, while the use of quinine was becoming widespread and its effectiveness against malaria well-known.

But to return to the antebellum period, bad as southern fevers were, the climate at least offered more seasonal relief to the inhabitants than West Indian residents received from the fevers which infected them. This may explain also the differing patterns of slave treatment in the Caribbean as opposed to North America. Despite the crossfire of debate that occasionally erupts on the subject, most contributors to the historiography of slavery today are in agreement that West Indian slaves, regardless of the nationality of their masters, did not live as long or as well as their North American fellows. Interpretations to account for the differential range from the cultural to the economic, with the latter clearly the front runner.

One "social" difference between the American and West Indian peculiar institutions that receives repeated comment, however, is the factor of absentee ownership in much of the latter region, particularly in the British and French islands. Another difference is the careless attitude of West Indian planters toward life itself. They "lived fast, spent recklessly, played desperately, and died young."[44]

But, might not disease (yellow fever and malaria) have been an important determinant in both the absenteeism and in a frenetic fatalistic West Indian life style?[45] For although blacks were mostly immune to these diseases, their masters were frequently not. Surely then those who could afford to absent themselves from the islands for extended periods of time would have done so for health reasons alone, while those who could not may well have sought refuge in dissipation.

Either way the slaves were the losers. If their owners fled the islands, they fell under the supervision of an overseer often more interested in a good crop than the welfare of his charges. Yet, even if the owner remained on the plantation, an individual who "lived fast" and expected to "die young" would hardly have been overly solicitous of the lives of his slaves.

In the American South, the stereotypic planter is also one who played life "fast, loose, and openhanded" albeit not to the extremes of his West Indian counterpart. But neither were malaria and yellow fever in the American South so extreme a problem as in the Caribbean region. Thus, while still something of a fatalistic lot, southern planters were nonetheless able to take a longer view of their own lives and consequently of their economic future, which depended upon their slaves. North American bondsmen were therefore assured better treatment and a concomitant longer expectation of life than blacks in the West Indies.

Finally there is a matter of how West African immunities to yellow fever and malaria worked so cruelly against the black. We have already noted that these diseases slew whites and Indians with such a vigor that the black with his ability to survive them became crucial to the colonization of tropical America and absolutely indispensable in the white mind.

Employing the counterfactual again for a moment, what if blacks had not been gifted with this disease resistance? Then how many thousands or millions fewer blacks might have been uprooted from their homeland and resettled in the Americas? Or to sketch a scenario suggested by David Brion Davis, what if the African and American disease environments had been reversed. Then "West Europeans might have colonized West Africa and stayed clear of the ravages of the North American Coast!" Going further "one can imagine West Africans dying off in vast numbers and being replaced by Amerind slaves transported eastward across the Atlantic."[46]

The point of this fantasizing is to underscore the crucial importance of black immunities to diseases in black victimization. Moreover, those immunities served not only as a spur to the Atlantic slave trade but also functioned prominently in an apology for the peculiar institution, particularly in the United States where white southerners felt increasingly compelled to defend it during the nineteenth century. For them the fact of black immunity to tropical fevers was demonstrable proof of the Creator's divine intention that blacks should hew the wood and draw the water in the world's hot regions.

"White men," wrote one southern physician, "will never be able to be substituted for negroes as field laborers; for . . . overseers invariably get sick – their children also, who are born on these plantations seldom or ever escape having fever, when the negroes around them are perfectly healthy."[47]

Yellow fever deaths among Irish laborers in New Orleans were interpreted by a local physician as "proof" that nature had ordained that blacks do the manual labor in hot climates, while whites should not. And those who died seeking to supplant the African as a laborer, got what they deserved for going against the natural order of things.[48]

Thus during the last days of slavery as planters sought desperately to convince others as well as themselves of the correctness of their course, southern agricultural journals cried out that

The white man will never raise – *can* never raise a cotton or a sugar crop in the United States. In our swamps and under our suns the negro thrives, but the white man dies. Without the productive power of the African whom an 'all-wise Creator' had perfectly adapted to the labor needs of the South, its lands would have remained 'a howling wilderness'.[49]

Black disease immunities then constituted a kind of double-edged sword, with both edges wielded against the possessor. For in the hands of white slaveholders, those edges were respectively a reason for and a rationale of slavery.

SUSCEPTIBILITIES

INTRODUCTION TO PART III

Epidemiology is, more than any other branch of medicine, unable
to rely exclusively on the laboratory and can still learn much from
the records of history's cruel and gigantic "experiments."

Erwin H. Ackerknecht (1945)[1]

This section dealing with black-related disease susceptibilities is the
core of the book. One argument that permeates its six chapters should
be a familiar one by now, namely that black disease susceptibilities,
like immunities, did much to inculcate in physicians, slaveholders, and
some unmeasurable portion of the literate public the idea that, from a
scientific standpoint, blacks were indeed a different breed of man. At
this point, however, a few words about the evidence that supports this
argument seem appropriate.

Unquestionably, a good deal of the medical literature concerned with
the health differences of black and white was produced in the sectional
heat that led to the Civil War – produced, in the words of Todd Savitt, by
physicians who . . . "were writing for an audience who wished to hear
that blacks were distinct from whites. This was, after all, a part of the
proslavery argument,"[2] and incidentally a part we treat in Section IV.

Yet, just because some physicians who wrote about black health
differences were committed to the southern cause, it does not necessarily follow that they themselves were not convinced of that distinctiveness, nor that they failed to convince others. Moreover, there was also
much antebellum medical literature on the black written long before
the Civil War that contains no trace of political taint. Finally in this
connection, notions of black–white medical differences hardly originated in North America. Rather, as we have already seen, physicians
in Africa and the West Indies were aware of and writing about racial
dissimilarities in disease susceptibilities long before white Southerners,
physicians included, felt compelled to wield a pen in slavery's defense.

Indeed Part III begins with a survey of black disease susceptibilities
as they were described by West Indian physicians who "pioneered" in
the field of slave medicine and consequently were read widely by latter-

71

day antebellum counterparts. One could of course argue that pioneers in slave medicine also had a vested interest in identifying distinctive black susceptibilities, but this begs the question. Today medicine is aware of the phenomena of black-related diseases. Yesterday, physicians most of whose patients were black were perhaps even more sensitized to this problem, and merely because they may have used distinctive black health differences for political or economic ends does not mean that the differences did not exist, were not widely understood to exist, and did not influence white attitudes toward the black.

Conveniently, mention of the West Indies leads in roundabout fashion to the central theme of this section: poor slave nutrition was at the root of many of these slave diseases. In fact, recent scholarship on the West Indies makes it clear that many of the health problems of slaves in that region clustered around malnutrition.[3] There is, however, no such agreement for slaves and their illnesses in the southern United States, largely one suspects because the slave diet appears on the surface to be neither all that bad nor all that different from the diet of whites.

The hypothesis, however, that we advance is that the black genetic heritage coupled with the kinds of foods available to slaves meant a diet that for whites may have been nutritionally adequate, but that for blacks failed to deliver sufficient usable quantities of a number of important nutrients.

This hypothesis is explored and tested in a number of ways. First an effort is made to determine which foods (and in what quantities) constituted the basic diet of most slaves. Second, the nutritional yield of these foods is examined within the context of the blacks' ability to metabolize and/or mobilize those nutrients, as indicated by a sizable body of nutritional, biochemical, and genetic findings that bear on the subject. Third, in the case of suspected deficiencies established by the foregoing, an effort has been made to discover the diseases these deficiencies might produce and the symptoms of those diseases. Armed with this information the antebellum literature on the so-called Negro diseases has been examined with an eye to matching deficiency and disease.

This procedure frequently takes us across uncharted and sometimes treacherous terrain. Nutritionists, geneticists, and biochemists disagree with as much enthusiasm as social scientists and just as rarely achieve a consensus. Nonetheless, we have tried to avoid presenting arguments that cannot be supported by studies representative of a substantial body of evidence frequently tending toward consensus. In the few cases where this is impossible, yet the argument seems important, we warn the reader of its tentative nature.

Another difficulty is the risk of diagnosing yesterday's ailments on the basis of incomplete descriptions, imprecise symptoms, and less than satisfactory morbidity and mortality data. Obviously no technique for attacking a problem of this complexity is going to be foolproof; yet the one we employ is intended to minimize the risk involved. First, in most cases we do not pursue nutritional deficiencies unless analysis has revealed them to be glaring deficiencies. The next step has been to examine genetic and environmental circumstances that may have either mitigated or complicated that deficiency. Then the list of antebellum Negro diseases is consulted in a search for an illness whose symptoms appear to have been the product of the deficiency in question.

Finally, morbidity and mortality data are consulted to see whether the particular disease did in fact fall with heavier weight on black people than on whites. We feel justified in claiming a probable "match" between deficiency and disease if it turns out that the deficiency is one that whites did not share, if the deficiency is known to produce a certain set of symptoms, and if these symptoms were manifested by blacks with a far greater frequency than whites. One problem with this technique is that it can lend itself to circularity, that is, if the deficiency then the disease; if the disease then the deficiency, and in fact this occurs on occasion. For example, nutritional analysis suggests that some slaves were probably vitamin A deficient; some nightblindness, a classic symptom of Vitamin A deficiency was found among the slaves; thus the suspicion of a vitamin A deficiency for a portion of the slave population is strengthened.

Again in a broader context circularity may be seen as something of a check on the entire question of slave malnutrition. In Chapter 9, infectious diseases come under scrutiny, and as a general rule badly nourished peoples suffer a greater frequency of these diseases than do the well-nourished. Thus, because slaves did experience a much higher rate of mortality from a group of these infectious diseases, this might be taken as still one more indication that slaves were in fact malnourished.

True, other factors may have predisposed blacks to some of these illnesses and these factors are explored. Nonetheless poor nutrition, which diminishes the body's ability to fight off infection, also must have played an important if unmeasurable role in this set of disease susceptibilities as well.

The section concludes with a look at the manner in which epidemic cholera treated blacks more severely than whites for reasons epidemiologists have yet to explain. Perhaps because it has become almost a conditioned response by this time or perhaps it is only because of frustration after examining a number of unsatisfactory explanations, but in any event we cannot resist smuggling in the suggestion that malnutrition may once again have been at fault. This, however, is a gratuitous guess.

CHAPTER 5

"NEGRO DISEASES": AN INTRODUCTORY GLIMPSE

After having noticed these strongly marked differences [in disease susceptibilities], we are naturally led to the question, do these races of men spring from the same original stock?

W. G. Ramsay (1839)[1]

I

Negro susceptibilities to diseases, perhaps even more than their immunities, were instrumental in branding blacks as an exotic breed in the eyes of physicians, planters, overseers, and others in intimate contact with them. Many of these susceptibilities first came fully to light on West Indian plantations where the climate, as in West Africa, was tropical, and a lively slave trade was able to supply fresh pathogens as well as fresh bodies for the cane, coffee, and tobacco fields.

If physicians in Africa were appalled by the loathsome "morbid afflictions of the skin" such as "lepra psoriasis," "scabies," and "frambesia" that blacks manifested,[2] West Indian doctors were no less repulsed by them. Frambesia (yaws) blossomed on black bodies in the warm and humid islands becoming "one of the greatest evils to which negroes are subject."[3] Leprosy was another hideously disfiguring disease brought by the blacks from West Africa and another that physicians believed blacks were far more "subject thereto."[4] Called "cacabay" (coco bay) in some islands and the "joint evil" in others because the victim's toes and fingers tended to drop off at the site of the "evil," the disease not infrequently deprived slaves of essential appendages which in turn deprived masters of their slaves' services.

Perhaps, however, the affliction that physicians and planters found most morbidly fascinating in the islands was the black propensity for consuming nonfoods, particularly earth. The habit of chewing small amounts of clay was not unusual in West Africa yesterday (nor is it today), but it frequently became transmuted in the slave quarters from a gentle habit to a raging compulsion.[5] Called alternately the "mal d'estomach," "hati weri," and just plain "dirt-eating," the victims who began by nibbling "particular kinds of earth" in the end would "eat

74

plaster from the walls, or dust collected from the floor, when they can come at no other."[6]

Stomach pains, depression, swelling of the tissues (dropsy), a bloated face, ashen complexion, a failing appetite, vertigo, palpitations of the heart, and shortness of breath were all signals to the planter and physician that they had a possible dirt-eater on their hands. These signals terrified them, because the practice had the reputation of spreading rapidly through the slave force. On some estates, it was reported to cause at least half of the deaths annually."[7] Physicians continuously warned planters and each other about the secretive nature of dirt-eating and its insidious contagion, and all kept a sharp eye out for symptoms.

Once discovered, a dirt-eater was at risk of being outfitted with an iron mask to assist him in breaking the habit. Doubtless this helps in part at least to explain his secrecy in the first place. Another reason for secrecy was that many of the victims believed themselves to have been poisoned or cursed by an obeah man.[8] Some whites, on the other hand, believed that the practice might well be hereditary. Most noticed that, although it was "common at all ages," it was most likely to afflict children and pregnant women.[9]

Blacks also were far more susceptible than whites to tetanus. Indeed if a slave was badly injured in the West Indies, physicians expected that he would die of the "jawfall" (as it was called). But often the malady appeared in persons without a history of a wound. In many cases, this was probably due to the slave habit of walking barefoot thus offering an easy target for the chigger, a "pathfinder for tetanus."[10] Yet so many more blacks than whites developed the disease that it was known in the islands as a peculiarly black affliction.[11]

When the disease occurred in babies it was diagnosed as trismus nascentium, and when it occurred within a few days after birth it was known as the "nine day fits." In his eighteenth-century *History of the West Indies*, Bryan Edwards identified trismus nascentium along with the "mal d'estomach" as the two greatest slave killers in many of the islands, and there seems little doubt that the toll of infants claimed by the disease was terrible.[12]

In some cases, the diagnosis of nine day fits may have cloaked infanticide, for during the first nine days of life "African infants were regarded as not yet fully part of the terrestrial world."[13] A more likely cause, however, was an infected umbilicus. Physicians at that time, had little notion of antiseptic procedures, and the African custom of shaking ashes on or packing the umbilical stump with mud hardly improved an infant's chance of escaping infection. Regardless, the proportion of black infant mortality from "jawfall" so overshadowed the white that, like its adult counterpart tetanus, trismus nascentium too was viewed as a peculiarly black malady.[14]

Black youngsters in the West Indies also apparently had many more "teething" difficulties than white children; "purgings, fevers and convulsions" were the most common complaints. Yet because of the malignancy that "teething" complications frequently assumed, especially the complication of "convulsions," many black toddlers successfully dodged the "jawfall" only to be felled by this illness.[15]

Ranking alongside tetanus and dirt-eating as a major killer of West Indian slaves was "worms" which, according to one eighteenth-century British physician, "kill[ed] more people in the West Indies than all other diseases, the [bloody] flux only excepted."[16] But worms may have also caused the bloody flux. Although doctors of the period were unaccustomed to classifying helminthic pathogens, they did identify both the guinea worm and tapeworm as particularly active culprits in the ravaging of black bodies. Diarrhea, dysentery, and the flux were all complaints that proved proportionately far more fatal to black than to white West Indians. In fact one physician writing with what was perhaps a misplaced sense of humor reported that in the Caribbean "the seat of the greater part of negro disorders . . . is in their bowels."[17]

The lungs too, however, were an important "seat." In the winter months, the islands saw much black mortality from "epidemic catarrh," and even more from pneumonia. Consumption (tuberculosis) also plagued the Caribbean slave population, and the black was regarded as far more susceptible to both of these illnesses.[18] Another epidemic disease believed to favor blacks was the "putrid sore throat" (diphtheria) that tended to afflict mainly women and children. "Indeed they are almost its only victims," observed a physician in Jamaica, "for, though men do not entirely escape, they are much less apt to perish under the disorder."[19] Whooping cough too was an ailment that struck hard at black youngsters while seeming to avoid white children.

Asiatic cholera invaded the western hemisphere for the first time in the nineteenth century where it quickly established a reputation for a particular hostility toward blacks. It swept through the island of Cuba in 1833, leaving some sugar plantations with 20 to 50 percent fewer hands.[20] The plague returned again in the 1850s, wiping out 10 percent of Puerto Rico's already dwindling slave labor force and causing so much slave mortality in Cuba that planters began to seriously consider abolition because of losses from slave deaths.[21] Following these two disastrous epidemics, it would have been difficult indeed to convince a Cuban planter that blacks were not somehow extraordinarily susceptible to Asiatic cholera.

West Indian slaves were also harrassed by a host of normally nonlethal, but nonetheless debilitating, illnesses. Rheumatism and "bone-ache cases" were common in blacks (as opposed to whites), while doctors commented that slaves suffered much more from dental caries.[22] "Sore eyes" posed such a serious problem among slaves that island physicians devoted whole sections of books to the malady, and invariably within those sections much space was devoted to "nyctalo-pia," as night blindness was termed, a "disease which is so frequently seen among the Negroes."[23] Additionally, scurvy and pellagra were not uncommon among slaves, while beriberi seems to have been a problem as well.[24]

Most of the aforementioned diseases came to be known as black-related or peculiarly "Negro" diseases requiring specialists, and physicians in the West Indies grew rich serving slave plantations. In the process, the doctors convinced themselves that the black was a different specimen demanding different treatment than whites. However, the differences between black and white, lamented one physician, were such that "the knife of the anatomist" was not able to reveal them.[25]

II

West Indian physicians/authors, particularly the British, passed along their experience with black-related disease immunities and susceptibilities to North American colleagues, who were therefore alerted to certain problems of slave health. But it was not until the first decades of the nineteenth century that antebellum doctors began constructing their own "package" of essentially "Negro" diseases, and by this time the Atlantic slave trade had ceased.

Thus, they saw nothing of diseases such as the African sleeping sickness, which had reached the New World in the bodies of infected persons, but because the vector *glossina* was an unsuccessful migrant, this dangerous affliction could not be transmitted to new victims. Similarly, they saw little of diseases such as yaws or leprosy, which did not flourish with vigor in the more temperate latitudes of the American South, as they did in the West Indies and therefore had required a constant stream of fresh infection from West African reservoirs via the slave trade for survival.

On the other hand, North American slaves suffered from a great many diseases common to their West Indian brothers.[26] Adults, for example, sustained a high incidence of tetanus in the American South, and youngsters perished at a high rate from trismus nascentium or the nine-day fits. As in the Caribbean, slave children had more fatal difficulties with teething than white, and they died by the thousands from worms, diphtheria, and whooping cough. Child and adult alike succumbed to catarrh, pneumonia, and bowel complaints, while physicians in North America too found themselves alternately fascinated and repelled by the black habit of consuming dirt. Southern plantations also saw more than their share of eye complaints including partial and total blindness; rheumatism was frequent as were skin afflictions and dental problems.

In addition, some slave diseases seemingly peculiar to North America were rare or unknown in the West Indies. Adults were particularly liable to "scrofula," seldom described among West Indian slaves. Black children, far more than white, succumbed to convulsions and "fits and seizures," while "smothering" was also an important cause of death among the very young slaves. These diseases then constituted the Negro disease "package" of the American South, put together by antebellum physicians who bound that package with much ethnologic nonsense.

Perhaps because of the latter this group of black susceptibilities (in many cases fatal) compiled by southern physicians has received little attention from scholars,[27] when noted, more often than not their collective opinions have been brushed aside as originating from medical incompetents, and racist medical incompetents at that.[28] The incompetency complaint, however, suggests only that differences in the medical care of black and white will not explain differential morbidity and mortality (unless, of course, it can be shown that blacks received considerably *more* medical attention than whites),[29] while the racist charge seems irrelevant, because no one really believes that southern doctors deliberately dispatched slave patients.

Thus, it remains that although physicians were not always adept at curing they could hardly avoid observing, and their collective opinion was that slaves were experiencing a much higher mortality rate than whites from infectious diseases, slave youngsters were sustaining a high level of infant mortality, and all were subject to an unusual frequency of dental caries and eye, bone, and skin complaints. Taken together, this portrait of morbidity and mortality seems suggestive of widespread nutritional deficiencies, inheritable disease susceptibilities, and genetic anomalies, all of which form the burden of the remaining chapters of this study.

CHAPTER 6

NUTRIENTS AND NUTRIMENTS

Nigger make de co'n; hog eat de co'n and nigger eat de hog.
An ex-slave[1]

I

One of the many controversies touched off by Robert Fogel and Stanley Engerman's "cliometric" examination of the peculiar institution concerns slave nutrition. The cliometricians portrayed the slave diet as not only substantial calorically but as actually exceeding "modern (1964) recommended daily levels of the chief nutrients."[2] This portrayal stands in sharp contrast to a more accepted view that has also found "cliometric" support.[3] Richard Sutch,[4] after reworking the Fogel and Engerman calculations, concluded that *Time on the Cross* claimed too much, that the caloric intake of slaves was "neither excessive nor generous," and the diet, far from being balanced, was dangerously deficient in many of the chief nutrients.

This clash of cliometricians over nutrients and nutriments has had the heuristic effect of introducing students of the South to such novel preoccupations as livestock slaughter rates and conversion ratios, the kinds of sweet potatoes consumed, and even the proper way to cook cowpeas. As in so many areas of the study of slavery, "cliometrics" (in this case cliometric calorie counting) has brought a new sophistication to an old argument, and we are satisfied with the Fogel and Engerman findings regarding the kinds and quantities of foods generally available to slaves. Indeed, we have accepted these findings, modified them with assumptions suggested by antebellum literature and black genetic circumstances and then used the amounts of foods in question as the basis for a chemical analysis of the slave diet with an eye to ascertaining its quality. It is only here with the matter of quality that we find ourselves most sharply in disagreement with the cliometricians; not because of any specific errors they have made, but rather because the question we pose is not whether the slave diet was qualitatively adequate, but whether it was qualitatively adequate for persons of West African descent.

79

The question, of course, is novel, while the relationships between nutrition, genetics, and physical environment are complex. Moreover, the medical and nutritional literature upon which our analysis rests is in itself occasionally novel, complex and (in some cases) controversial. With this word of caution, let us begin with the quantitative aspects of slave comestibles.

II

Prior to the Fogel and Engerman study, a major difficulty of coming to grips with problems of what the slaves ate and how much was that the sources simply did not agree. In quantitative terms, one ex-slave gloomily recalled that there "never was as much [food] as we needed" and "we prayed that us niggers could have all we wanted and special for fresh meat."[5] Another, however, claimed that "we had plenty to eat. Whoo-ee! Just plenty to eat."[6] A frequent visitor to the antebellum South agreed that indeed "the slaves have plenty to eat; [they] probably are fed better than the proletarian class of any other part of the world."[7] But still another sojourner in the region confessed to his diary "it was not a pleasant thought, that while such unlimited profusion reigned on [the] table of the master, a large portion of his slaves rarely tasted flesh" and "generally the fare of plantation slaves is coarse and scanty."[8]

Planters themselves, writing for regional journals, managed to convey the impression that their own slaves were absolute gourmands enjoying the utmost variety in foodstuffs, while simultaneously insinuating that other slaveholders were not so open-handed.[9] But plantation records alone indicate that the slaves subsisted for the most part on fat pork and corn or rice, with an occasional dollop of molasses to enliven drab fare.

The nutritional problem then becomes one of variety. "We wasn't allowed to eat all the different kinds of victuals the white folks ate,"[10] stated one ex-slave, while another explained that "Marster would buy a years ration on de first of every year and when he git it, he would have some cooked and would set down and eat a meal of it. He would tell us it didn't hurt him, so it won't hurt us. Dats de kind of food us slaves had to eat all de year."[11]

U. B. Phillips[12] found from many years of sifting plantation documents that "the basic food allowance came to be somewhat standardized," with the slaves receiving "a quart of cornmeal and half a pound of salt pork per day for each adult and proportionably for children, commuted or supplemented with sweet potatoes, field peas, sirup, rice, fruit and 'garden sass' as locality and season might suggest." Yet in an age increasingly aware of nutrients, scholars have become concerned that not all that much commuting and/or supplementing took place and have pronounced the slave diet quantitatively satisfactory ('of sufficient bulk') but qualitatively deficient ('of improper balance').[13] In fact, many would agree with Eugene Genovese's assertion that this qualitative inadequacy produced "specific hungers, dangerous deficiencies, and [an] . . . unidentified form of malnutrition" that meant a substantial number of slaves who were "either physically impaired or chronically ill."[14]

Fogel and Engerman, however, who made the first serious effort to resolve questions of slave nutrition, found the slave diet to be both quantitatively and qualitatively satisfactory. Sections III through VIII, divided by categories of foods consumed by slaves, present their findings and our modifications.

III

Planters, large and small, across much of the South and particularly in the cotton belt consistently claimed that they issued an average of about three pounds of pork "clear of bone" per week per working slave. In fact, this allotment has been confirmed by students of slavery so often as to become a truism. Fogel and Engerman, on the other hand could only feed a slave 88 pounds of pork annually on the basis of their "systematic data" drawn from the 1860 manuscript censuses.[15] There are problems with these "systematic" data where pork is concerned, however, that suggest that their estimations may considerably understate slave pork consumption. First, the manuscript census schedules Fogel and Engerman consulted for the number of hogs per plantation do not reveal that swine were permitted to run "wild" on most cotton belt plantations.[16]

Thus owners had only a vague notion of how many they "owned." Although plantation records of the region usually distinguish between "tame" and "wild" pork in the storehouse awaiting consumption, it seems highly probable that many planters when counting live swine for census purposes thought only of those which were penned up for fattening.[17] Second, slaves themselves were often permitted to raise hogs, which they frequently sold to their masters, and it is doubtful that the number of slave-owned swine on a plantation are reflected in the manuscript census. Third, and most important, cotton belt plantations were scarcely self-sufficient manors, and outside purchases of pork were considerable for many, if not most, planters.[18] For these reasons, there seems little cause to doubt planter claims that working slaves received on the average the 3 pounds of pork weekly.

By contrast, there were sufficient cattle on the plantations of the South to permit the Fogel and Engerman assumption that slaves enjoyed a fairly high level of beef consumption. Yet much literary evidence contradicts this assumption. A Yankee agronomist, Solon Robinson, put it clearly enough while visiting cotton belt plantations. He discovered that on many of them pork production was insufficient to feed the slaves without outside purchasing yet observed that the plantations also possessed many cattle. "Well, if you can't raise pork, why not feed your negroes on beef?" was the query, and the reply: "Simply because it would raise a revolt, sooner than all the whip-lashes ever braided in Massachusetts. Fat pork and corn bread is the natural aliment of a negro. Deprive him of these and he is miserable. Give him his regular allowance and the negro enjoys . . . 'heaven on earth.' "[19]

Perhaps slave preference for pork might have been overcome were it not for the inferior preserving qualities of beef. Unlike pork, it neither pickled nor smoked well; dried it was extremely unpalatable.[20] Therefore, when beef was served on the plantation it was served fresh. This occurred, however, on special occasions only and usually in the winter months, because the cold retarded spoilage. Thus, for some slaves, at least, beef consumption was limited to the holiday season around Christmas time.[21]

Another problem with beef was that planters on the whole were very skeptical of fresh meat, believing that it caused sickness among the blacks (which it undoubtedly did when it was not all that fresh). In fact, in much of the South, whites also feared fresh meat and continued to do so even after it was readily available, and they had facilities for refrigeration.[22]

But in addition to slave preference for pork, there was also the planters' conviction that hog was the only proper meat for laborers.[23] A physician, writing in 1859, clearly articulated the planters' belief that "fatty articles of diet are peculiarly appropriate on account of their heat producing properties" and "fat bacon and pork are the most nourishing of all foods for the Negro."[24]

Earlier in the century, the conviction had been the same. Bacon was the proper "nourishment" for slaves, and "a pound goes as far as three pounds of beefsteak."[25] During the intervening decades, planters and physicians lost few oportunities to remind one another in agricultural and medical journals of the efficacy of pork. Fresh beef might be served on occasion, but pork was the fuel upon which the efficiency of labor depended.

So why all the plantation cattle? The answer, it seems, is that cattle (as opposed to hogs) "were maintained primarily for manure and only incidently for meat and milk."[26] The notion of cattle raising as a profitable enterprise *per se* was dismissed by planters, who made little effort to improve their breeds and permitted cattle, like hogs, a semiwild existence foraging in fallow fields for themselves.[27] When the cattle became too numerous, their superior traveling powers (over swine) made it relatively easy for them to be driven to towns and cities. There fresh beef could be marketed quickly thus avoiding the problems of beef's inferior preserving qualities and the absence of a packing industry in the South.[28]

To summarize then, slave meat preferences and planters' notions regarding black health combined to suggest strongly that cattle were employed mostly as fertilizer producers. They may eventually have wound up in the market place but, except for the occasional barbecue or holiday feast, not in slave stomachs.

IV

A shift from one product of cattle to another brings up the problem of plantation milk consumption. As with beef consumption, one might conclude on a priori grounds that the presence of many cattle on the plantation meant an abundance of milk for the slaves. This is incorrect, however, for reasons that fall alternately under the headings of milk production and black biology.

To begin with, the antebellum South was notorious for low milk production. Travelers crossing the Mason-Dixon line on a southward trek reported that milk was fairly plentiful in border states such as Kentucky yet "a great rarity" in the Deep South.[29] Part of the reason was that cattle, like hogs, were not usually penned up but rather permitted to run wild and forage for themselves. The result was that they were frequently too wild to be milked.[30]

Another reason was the poor quality of the animals themselves. For example, a traveler reported that southern cows did not calve more than once in two years and that even when they did give milk, the yield was "far less in quantity" than that produced by northern cows.[31] Hence the classic plight of the South Carolina planter whose cattle were such bad "milkers" that he and his family were forced to rely on goat milk for coffee.[32] Still one more difficulty was the poor quality of southern milk described by one unenthusiastic visitor as "blue and watery."[33] The butter churned from it was routinely denounced as "sickly looking,"[34] while that inveterate observer of things southern, Frederick Law Olmsted, complained more than once of "what to both eye and tongue seemed lard,"[35] but what was termed butter. Apparently then only the more progressive plantations saw much in the way of milk, and this usually was of poor quality. Still, even on these units it was only available on a seasonal basis, limited to the warmest months of spring and summer which of course presented many spoilage problems.[36] In part then, because of scarcity, milk, when produced, went mostly to the white population and it became "customary" to not "feed dairy products to slaves."[37] Where a small milk surplus was produced, it usually went to the slave children.

Yet what appears to have been a slovenly southern attitude toward milk production may well have had an important rationale behind it, for a good portion of the South's population–the blacks–could not drink much of it in the first place and planters knew it. Today it is estimated that somewhere between 70 and 80 percent of the adult Afro-American population is lactose intolerant as opposed to 5 to 19 percent of their white counterparts.[38]

This phenomenon of lactose intolerance is not fully understood. All infants are obviously lactose tolerant, else they could not live.[39] But sometime after weaning, a majority of the world's population loses the ability to digest milk, meaning the level of the lactase enzyme that metabolizes milk's lactose into absorbable sugars decreases. When this occurs and the individual persists in drinking milk he is rudely rewarded with abdominal cramps, bloating, and diarrhea. Sooner or later he connects milk with the problem and eliminates it from his diet. A study has found that 72 percent of lactose intolerant Americans stop drinking milk completely because of the complications that result.[40]

Most persons of northern European descent as well as some other peoples scattered around the world, however, do not lose the lactase enzyme. This means that milk remains a regular part of their dietary regimen throughout a lifetime. A sensible hypothesis advanced to account for the development of lactose tolerance, at least its development among northern Europeans, is that the lactase enzyme was genetically encouraged among ancient residents because of the prevalence of rickets and osteomalacia caused by a lack of sunshine. The result would have been many pelvic deformities among females and consequently a reduction in their reproductivity. The lactase enzyme was therefore encouraged because milk provides its consumer with both a rickets preventative (calcium) and a substitute for vitamin D (lactose) to facilitate the absorption of that calcium.[41]

By contrast in West Africa there was no lack of abundant sunshine. Moreover, the presence of the tsetse fly made the raising of cattle virtually impossible, effectively discouraging the development of a milk-drinking culture.[42] These twin factors were instrumental in creating a historical situation of low milk consumption with no need for humans to develop high levels of the lactase enzyme.[43]

Yesterday on the plantation the rate of lactose intolerance was probably even higher than that of today, perhaps even approaching 100 percent by the time adulthood was reached. With blacks, the problem begins soon after infancy,[44] and the level of intolerance increases with age; whereas with whites the difficulty remains constant with age. Thus, studies have revealed that by age eleven at least 40 to 45 percent of black youngsters exhibit symptoms of lactose intolerance, about 60 percent of black teenagers manifest symptoms,[45] with the rate reaching the 70 to 80 percent range for adults.[46]

No wonder that when milk consumption is mentioned in connection with the plantations it is invariably the children who are doing the consuming. Yet it seems that even many children were noticeably lactose intolerant, for planters warned one another that they "should have no sweet milk"; "none but sour, or buttermilk," advised one perceptive master.[47] Planters could not know that the souring process converted the lactose to lactic acid, which made the milk more digestible. But in a very real way they may have pioneered in the treatment of lactose intolerance.

In summary then, slaves consumed very little milk, first because the South produced little of it, and second because they could not drink it. Ingestion of as little as one eight-ounce glass of milk will trigger symptoms in the lactose intolerant.[48] So even where milk was available consumption was probably limited to a daily dollop in their coffee. For children, milk was sometimes available, but on a seasonal basis only. Thus, in the words of one student of southern foods, "although the food habits of whites and slaves were similar in many respects, one of the greatest differences was in the relative amount of dairy products consumed."[49]

V

Cowpeas and sweet potatoes are considered together because questions of the quantities consumed hinge on amounts fed to livestock and problems of storage. Unquestionably both were grown in large quantities on southern plantations, and superficially a glance at the manuscript census schedules would convince one that at least these two items appeared on slave tables in profusion.

Yet in the case of the cowpea (the black-eyed pea, field pea, crowder pea, etc.), one should not make the assumption that slaves desired or even ate them if offered. Today cowpeas are viewed as the quintessence of southern dining (particularly by Yankees) and the "soul" of soul food. As late as the eve of the War Between the States, however, most Southerners, black and white, regarded these legumes as "fodder" which was by far their major use. The herbage was used as forage, while the seed of the plant was a "major source of food for cattle, horses, mules, and hogs in all cotton and corn growing areas."[51] It is true that some planters who found blacks to be "fond" of the "common field pea," delightedly advised one another of this cheap source of slave food and even suggested drying them and putting some aside for later consumption.[52] Still, the very fact that a few planters were exhorting others to dry and store cowpeas suggests that the vast majority of the slaves did not enjoy them on a year-round basis. Rather most of the slaves who were fond of cowpeas and whose masters made them available consumed them for a few weeks only while they were in season.

A similar problem exists in the case of sweet potatoes, which manuscript census data on southern production indicate were piled on slave tables to the extent of 318 pounds annually per male aged 18 to 35.[53] But to have apportioned sweet potatoes in this manner meant that livestock went hungry. For sweet potatoes were "frequently employed to supplement corn in the fattening of stock" and often left right in the fields for the animals.[54] In fact, sweet potatoes were regarded as the best and quickest means (when boiled) of fattening hogs for the winter killing season and were often employed lavishly for this purpose.[55] This does not mean of course that slaves did not eat sweet potatoes. Indeed some planters stored them for year-round consumption; however others, perhaps most, regarded them as a seasonal food and encouraged the slaves to feast on them while they lasted.[56]

Moreover, those planters who did store sweet potatoes expected some loss from rot no matter how well the pile was ventilated. And the standard method of cooking sweet potatoes – tossing them into a fire or popping them into the coals of a cookstove – meant a good deal of waste. When done, the sweet meat of the center was extracted and the charred husk thrown aside. Thus, after the sweet potatoes were shared with livestock and storage and cooking losses are subtracted, it would seem likely that only a portion of the sweet potatoes produced on the plantation actually found their way into slave stomachs.

VI

Planters claimed, and their records bear them out, that it was practically a tradition to allot one peck of cornmeal weekly per slave which translates into something over one pound daily. Yet, probably most did not consume all of this large ration. On plantations that permitted slave enterprise, bondsmen frequently fed a portion of their rations to the family hogs and chickens, which were raised to procure tobacco, liquor, and Sunday clothes. On other plantations, it was customary that slaves exchange surplus cornmeal for these luxury items. Cornmeal also served as food for the family dog(s) that few slave cabins were without.[57]

Finally, as was the case with sweet potatoes, often a great deal of cornmeal was lost in cooking methods. So long as cornbread was prepared in the plantation kitchen in pans, no particular loss occurred. A favorite method of preparing "pone" or hoecakes or cornash cakes, however, was "to mix the meal with a little water, then lay the mixture in the fire to bake," perhaps on a hoe.[58] "When it is 'done brown,' the ashes are scraped off," and a good deal less meal was consumed than went into the fire.[59]

VII

Undoubtedly because of biscuits, another perennial frontrunner in southern cuisine, the assumption is sometimes made that wheat flour was plentiful in the South.[60] Most of the South, however, lies outside of the wheat region. Thus, in the Deep South states of Georgia, Alabama, Mississippi, and Louisiana the 1860 wheat production would have yielded only 57 pounds of wheat flour per man, woman, and child – slave and white combined – [61] so of course whites, not blacks, were the big consumers of wheat bread.[62]

Actually, even in a state such as Arkansas where the yield of wheat per person was twice that of the Deep South, it is still "unlikely that slaves ate wheat bread to any great extent. The high prices of wheat flour as compared to corn meal prevented the widespread use of wheat bread for slaves, as well as for many of the white people of the period."[63] Rather, the only way that wheat flour found its way into the slave diet on most cotton belt plantations was in the form of those cherished biscuits served occasionally on Sundays and/or holidays. As with cattle, the bulk of the little wheat raised on plantations seems to have been intended for the market and not for local consumption.[64]

VIII

There remains the question of the extent to which the basic hog-and-hominy core of the slave diet was "commuted and/or supplemented" with comestibles other than those already mentioned, a question that defies any ready answer. The evidence suggests that a majority of slaves was permitted to raise produce, poultry, and pigs, but a sizable minority was not.

Moreover, many ex-slaves testified that they did not care for green vegetables of any kind. Rather they only became a standard part of black fare following the Civil War. Thus, pin money, rather than a variety in viands, was frequently the chief motive in slave enterprises such as gardening as well as hog and chicken raising. Fish and game, including the oft-mentioned possum, undoubtedly graced some slave tables. But on how many tables, and how frequently did these supplements appear?

A few planters seem to have made heroic efforts to grow and stockpile sufficient vegetables for year-round slave consumption,[65] but others apparently begrudged their slaves even basic meat and meal provisions and attempted to stint on them.[66] There were those who believed (correctly) that molasses was healthy for slaves and issued it liberally,[67] yet there were others who feared that molasses, at least in the diet of children, would lead to dirt-eating.[68] Still others issued molasses in lieu of meat, and there were those who presumably found molasses too expensive to serve or too bothersome or both.[69] Many planters appointed individuals to cook for the slaves in an attempt to insure that they received variety in their victuals. Many more, however, expected the slaves to cook for themselves, and all too frequently after the blacks had spent a long and wearisome day in the fields that cooking was badly done.

IX

Although evidence was presented to suggest that in many cases slaves did not consume foods in the quantities the Fogel and Engerman estimates might indicate, we certainly do not mean to imply that slaves in the American South were on the verge of starvation. Rather, it seems a safe assumption that some slaves enjoyed a wide variety of foods; others suffered from a seldom if ever supplemented hog-and-corn routine, while most existed on a basic meat-and-meal core with some supplementation, including the fish and game they provided for themselves. Unquestionably, the core itself supplied enough in the way of calories. Calculations by the United Nations Food and Agriculture Organization suggest that the caloric requirement for a medium-sized male in his mid-twenties performing moderately heavy agricultural labor for ten hours is between 3,200 and 4,000 calories daily.[70] If something approaching a pound of the cornmeal ration were converted into cornpone and consumed along with the half pound or so of pork allotted daily and a sweet potato or two, this caloric requirement would have been met. Whether the diet was nutritionally adequate for the slaves, however, is another question entirely.[71]

Sections X through XIV present an analysis of the chief nutrients in the slave diet: protein; vitamins A, B_1, B_2, B_3, C, and D; calcium; and iron.

X

A high quality protein is one that contains all eight essential amino acids in sufficient amounts to support and sustain life. Thus, the value of any protein depends on the various amino acids it contains. Methods have been devised to give protein a chemical score ranging from high (animal protein) to low (vegetable protein), although two foods of relatively poor values when combined may constitute – depending on their amino acid pattern – a good protein.[72] For example, cowpeas do not offer a complete protein. On the other hand, they are high in tryptophan and lysine, precisely those amino acids in which corn is deficient.[73] Thus, those slaves whose masters did dry and store this legume for serving on a year-round basis would (if they consumed them with corn) have received a good amount of fairly complete protein.[74] Yet earlier we asserted that this was hardly common practice, and therefore corn alone, the slaves' biggest source of protein, would have left them with an apparent protein deficiency.

Now had the slaves eaten a half pound of pork daily consisting of a composite of trimmed, lean cuts (ham, loin, shoulder) which averaged 78 percent lean and 22 percent fat they would have derived much of what today would be their recommended daily allowance (RDA) of protein (36 of a RDA of 56 grams).[75]

Slaveholders, antebellum physicians, ex-slaves, visitors to the South, and students of slavery alike, however, made no mention of slaves dining on hams or loins, except, of course, those stolen on occasion from the master's storehouse. Rather, they unanimously set slave tables with fat pork and fat bacon, in part because it was inexpensive, and in part because of a planter conviction that "fatty articles of diet are peculiarly appropriate on account of their heat-producing properties," and for hard-working slaves "fat bacon and pork are the most nourishing of all foods."[76] Therefore, a medium-fat class of pork, with cuts consisting of bacon or belly and backfat, probably more closely approximated the quality of pork consumed by the slaves, and this would have yielded about a third (18 grams) of their daily protein requirements.

A pound of cornmeal contains about 41 grams of protein, the meat ration about 18 and a couple of good-sized sweet potatoes another half dozen or so which put the slave close to his RDA for protein (and doubtless other comestibles consumed actually put him over).[77] Nonetheless about three-quarters of that protein (sweet potatoes also yield an incomplete protein) was of low quality.

XI

Superficially it would seem that slaves derived a fair amount of vitamin A from corn. This is not true, however, for it was white corn, not yellow, that was normally raised for human consumption in the South,[78] and white corn contains absolutely no vitamin A.

Some sweet potatoes, on the other hand, yield a great deal of this vitamin, as evidenced by the orange hue of the flesh. Yet there are sweet potatoes, and then there are sweet potatoes, with the nutritive values of vitamin A varying depending on the kind from less than 0.1 per 100 grams to 4.1.[79] Put another way some kinds of sweet potatoes contain forty times more vitamin A than others. Of the varieties grown in the antebellum South, Richard Sutch has unearthed evidence to indicate that the colors of their flesh ranged from a "yellowish tint" to "very white"; the light colors suggesting that the varieties of antebellum sweet potatoes to which slaves had access were not high in vitamin A.[80]

Fresh cowpeas contained some vitamin A (a cup would have provided about one-tenth of the daily RDA), and because the vitamin can be stored by the body[81] (even though fresh peas were only consumed seasonally) they would also have made a contribution toward an adequate year-round supply.

Vitamin C cannot be stored, therefore, the ascorbic acid yielded by fresh cowpeas and sweet potatoes, constituting the only vitamin C in the core diet, would have been of temporary benefit only. Those who ate garden greens or fruit also would have benefited from a seasonal dose of this vitamin. Yet the testimony of ex-slaves indicates that many did not care for vegetables or fruit; planters frequently considered fruit a source of slave disease, and one visitor to the South summed up the general attitude toward vegetables in Mississippi by suggesting tongue-in-cheek that they were "forbidden by law."[82]

Thus, for many slaves their vitamin C intake seems to have been a matter of a haphazard seasonal injection only, and many were without the vitamin for a good portion of the year. Moreover, greens and fresh cowpeas were normally subjected to thorough cooking (a lamentable southern practice that persists today), and as is well known heat destroys ascorbic acid; consequently something between 15 and 40 percent of the potential seasonal offering of vitamin C was probably lost.[83]

Much vitamin C as well is lost in sweet potatoes when stored; conversely the vitamin A content increases slightly during storage but not enough to have made any appreciable difference.[84] There is, however, a good reason for suspecting a substantial loss of vitamin A. Much mention is made of rancid fat pork and cooking fat on the plantation. Vitamin A is a fat-soluble vitamin meaning that it is rendered usable by fatty acids. But if that fat is rancid, the solvents it contains destroy, rather than dissolve, the vitamin.[85] Additionally, research suggests that the body must have sunlight to release the bulk of its vitamin A that is stored in the liver.[86] Hence those slaves whose masters either did not keep sweet potatoes for the winter months, or ran out early in the winter, would not have enjoyed the full benefits of the vitamin A their body had stored. Finally, the low serum level of vitamin A (despite a normal level in the liver) in black subjects has led at least one group of researchers to hypothesize that their ability to mobilize this vitamin may be impaired.[87]

Given all of these factors then, it would seem that most slaves were somewhat vitamin C deficient for much of the year. By contrast vitamin A may have been sufficiently supplied to the majority of the slaves. Yet variables such as the kinds of potatoes consumed and the complexity of vitamin A's utilization caution that others may have actually been vitamin A deficient as well.

XII

Raw dried peas furnish almost twice as much thiamine (B_1), riboflavin (B_2) and niacin (B_3) as fresh cowpeas, so once more those slaves with progressive masters would have fared far better nutritionally than those forced to consume only what the season had to offer. But even for these individuals the remainder of their core diet was dismally deficient in the B complex, save thiamine. Corn is notoriously lacking in B_2 and B_3, and with even a full pound of cornmeal supplying only one-quarter to one-half of the daily RDA, slaves would have been hard pressed to make up the remainder. Consuming betwen ten and twelve good-sized sweet potatoes, for example, would have done it, but in this case plantations would have produced more pudgy thralls than cotton.

The ration of fat pork would have been little help because it was largely fat, producing only 16 percent of the niacin and 15 percent of the riboflavin requirements. Thus, slaves were receiving little of vitamins B_2 and B_3. Moreover, the apparent satisfaction of the B_1 requirement is deceptive because the more carbohydrates in the diet, the higher the requirement of thiamine.[88] Similarly, the deficiency of vitamin B_2 is more serious than one might suppose because its requirement is linked to the fat content of the diet: the more fats, the more riboflavin required.[89] Again the requirement for niacin is based on calories (with which the slave diet abounded): the more calories the greater the demand for niacin.[90]

Additionally, cooking losses must be considered in the original supply of the B complex, particularly given the great amount of boiling and frying that took place in the slave quarters. Fully 25 to 50 percent of vitamin B_1 in pork is lost in cooking along with significant amounts of vitamins B_2 and B_3.[91] Finally, in the case of niacin, the whole of the slave diet concealed another adverse effect. For although the amount of niacin in the slave diet was very low, the body might have produced niacin by converting what little tryptophan the diet did yield.[92] Yet because that diet (because of cornmeal in particular) also contained an excess of leucine, the body's niacin production was inhibited.[93] Similarly, vitamin B_2 is crucial in the conversion of tryptophan to niacin,[94] but the slave comestibles were deficient in riboflavin. The absence of sufficient niacin in turn suggests that the slaves were unable to properly metabolize the carbohydrates, fats, and proteins in the diet, which means they could not possibly have received the full benefit of those nutrients.[95]

XIII

Vitamin D exists in several forms, but, because it is naturally present in few foods, most of it comes from cholecalciferol (D_3) which is obtained by irradiation on the skin from a chemical precursor present in living skin cells called 7-dehydrocholesterol. Season changes and different geographical regions affect vitamin D levels in individuals. The darker pigmentation of the black protected against sun damage in Africa. His black skin, however, transmits ultraviolet radiation only one-third as well as white skin.[96] Thus, it is believed that pigment reduces the synthesis of vitamin D by the skin.[97] And therefore the black transplanted to more northerly latitudes found himself low in vitamin D, especially during the winter and spring months of pale sunlight, shorter days, and overcast skies. Whites, in other words, because of a lack of pigment, have access to sufficient vitamin D in North America; blacks frequently do not.

Vitamin D is crucial in the intestinal absorption of calcium, but it is also important for normal growth and skeletal development and the bone mineral mobilization process, a process that could have replenished the dangerously low serum calcium levels, which for the following reasons were undoubtedly characteristic of the slaves.[98]

First, the core of the slave diet was composed of fat pork and cornmeal. The yield of phosphorus from this core, while not extraordinarily high by itself, is overwhelmingly high in relation to the low calcium offering of the diet. Lactose-intolerant slaves would have derived little calcium from milk, while the greens, sweet potatoes, etc., which supplemented the core, although a source of some calcium, could not have provided enough to overcome a year-round imbalance because of their seasonal appearance on tables. This excessive amount of phosphorous in relation to calcium in turn would have hindered the absorption of the little calcium the slaves did receive, and therefore increased their requirements. Similarly, the fatty acids flowing from fat pork also interfered with the bodily absorption of calcium, as do the oxalic acids contained in greens that form insoluble salts to impair absorption of the pair of minerals in question.[99]

Second, if calcium did not already have a difficult time playing a proper nutritional role in the slave regimen, it was further frustrated by the peculiar nature of the proteins inherent in that regimen. High-quality protein promotes efficient absorption of calcium.[100] Yet high quality protein content was not an outstanding feature of the slave regimen. Clearly then, many circumstances combined to deny calcium a full nutritional participation in the slave diet, yet even at this point these circumstances might have been at least partially overcome had it not been for two more factors that were also hostile to calcium absorption.

An adequate source of vitamin C also would have increased the absorption of what calcium was available; conversely, vitamin C is so crucial to calcium accumulation that its deficiency can cause calcium deficiency.[101] Yet ascorbic acid cannot be stored by the body,[102] and no one seriously argues that slaves received a year-round supply of this vitamin. Finally, the two remaining factors that could have enhanced the absorption of calcium are lactose and vitamin D (the reason milk is fortified with this vitamin today),[103] but as already noted pigment that was kindly to blacks in their West African homeland militated against an adequate year-round supply of this vitamin in temperate North America. Thus, even if one's calcium intake is adequate (the slaves' clearly was not), it will be very poorly absorbed if one's vitamin D levels are inadequate (which the slaves' doubtless were for at least a portion of the year).

XIV

Iron presents very much the same situation. Its absorption is aided by ascorbic acid and lactose, and it is more than doubled if eaten with animal protein. But all of the above were deficient in the slave diet.[104] Absorption is decreased by phosphorus (because phosphorus competes with iron for metal-binding sites in the intestinal mucosa) which, of course, was very much present in that diet and by an inadequate supply of amino acids, lysine and tryptophan, both of which were undersupplied.[105] Moreover, iron absorption from carbohydrates appears to be affected by the type of carbohydrate. Experiments on animals have indicated that minimum retention takes place if 60 percent or more of the carbohydrate is a starch, more is absorbed if 60 percent is sucrose, and maximum retention is achieved from lactose.[106] Therefore, although iron abounds in cornmeal (the slave's biggest source), most of it probably was not absorbed, and in fact only about 4 to 5 percent of the iron in the cornmeal normally is absorbed.[107]

XV

At least two other genetic factors may have affected the blacks nutritionally. The first has to do with the previously discussed hemoglobin anomolies such as glucose-6-phosphate dehydrogenase deficiency and various sickling disorders. Despite the explosive development of knowledge regarding inherited abnormalities of hemoglobin synthesis, much has yet to be done regarding their effects on the heterozygous recipient.

Suggestions have been made that possession of these traits alone may occasion a mild anemia,[108] while accumulating evidence leaves little doubt that hemoglobin abnormalities are probably not as benign to the heterozygous recipient as once was believed. For example, viral and bacterial infections are apparently more likely to produce a serious anemic condition in carriers than in noncarriers of the traits.[109]

Second, and this regards calcium, persons receiving little of the mineral in the diet seem able over time to make an adjustment to lower calcium requirements. So it may be that blacks, who seem to have lower levels of serum calcium, possibly because of a history of centuries of relative calcium deprivation, may, in fact, have lower requirements.[110] Yet again, even these lower requirements may not have been met in North America, in part because of a low level of vitamin D coupled with all the other dietary impediments to calcium absorption, and in part because of the loss of calcium due to hard labor. Experiments have shown that the loss of calcium through perspiration during a day's labor in 70 degree weather is 22 percent, at 86 degrees 25 percent and at 100 degrees 33 percent.[111]

To summarize then, West Africans were marvelously adapted for survival in their homeland. These mechanisms contained the potential for provoking severe nutritional difficulties, however, once their possessor was removed from West Africa's specialized environment. This potential should have been realized after the blacks' forced migration to North America. To repeat ourselves, therefore, the important question concerning slave nutrition that we are posing is not whether the slave diet was adequate, but rather, was it adequate for persons of West African descent? Nutritional analysis thus far suggests not. As we have seen, the core of the slave diet consisted of hog and corn, and anyone black or white whose diet was confined largely to this core along with the other foods analyzed would have suffered the consequences of the peculiar chemical nature of a regimen that was deficient to a greater or lesser extent in all of the chief nutrients: extremely so in calcium, vitamin C, riboflavin, and niacin; seriously so in protein and iron (especially the diets of females); and seasonally so in vitamin A and thiamine. Given the difficulties with vitamin D created by their darker skin in temperate climates, however, combined with their high frequency of lactose intolerance, blacks would have suffered far more than whites on the same diet from calcium deficiencies; abnormal hemoglobin may well have elevated their nutritional requirements for protein and folic acid (a B vitamin), while these problems combined would have impaired their ability to fully utilize still other nutrients.

At least this is our hypothesis that admittedly requires scrutiny under strong light. We expect that a look at the aforementioned peculiarly "Negro diseases" will help to shed that light. Diet is important because it speaks to the larger question of slave health. Conversely, slave health speaks to matters of nutritional adequacy, which suggests the fallacy of considering either in isolation. Examined in tandem, the one should always act as a check on the other. If blacks were well-nourished, then diseases with a nutritional etiology should be conspicuously absent in the slave quarters. If, on the other hand, specific nutrients were lacking in the slave diet, then diseases whose etiologies include these dietary lacunae should be in evidence and perhaps a "match" of deficiencies and diseases can be achieved.

The following chapters then will search for such matches beginning with the diet and diseases of slave children whose physical well-being should be indicative not only of the level of health and nutrition of their own generation but reflective of their parents' generation as well.

CHAPTER 7

THE CHILDREN

The children must be particularly attended to for rearing them is
not only a duty, but also the most profitable part of plantation
business.

Andrew Flinn (1840)[1]

Children came hard because of high mortality, and those who survived were the more precious because of it.

Nathan Irvin Huggins (1977)[2]

I

That the rate of slave child mortality was high both absolutely and
relative to the white rate no one disputes. But for historians bent on
portraying slaveholders as "economic men" the phenomenon has precipitated much teeth-gnashing, for it confronts directly "the strange
paradox" of economic men apparently not, for a change, in pursuit of
their own best interests.[3] Nor for that matter is the image of the
benign, paternalistic master enhanced by the possibility that his plantation graveyard was dominated by plots containing little black
bodies.

The planter did not know biology, nutrition, and disease, however,
as he knew cotton, sugar, and rice. Doubtless he could have prevented
some deaths by improving the physical environment of the slaves. Yet
the thrust of this chapter is that much slave mortality stemmed from
nutritional difficulties that the planter was not able to understand, let
alone correct.

II

A case has been made that because of such difficulties as lactose intolerance, problems with vitamin D, and other genetic factors, a significant portion of the slave population was seriously deprived of calcium
and iron. If true, then many slave children were in severe nutritional
straits, in some instances even before birth. It is true that the fetus is

96

parasitic for these minerals, meaning that even if the mother is deficient, it will do its best to satisfy its own needs by drawing on her stores.[4] But assuming a deficiency to begin with, the high fertility of many slave mothers would have meant something akin to bankruptcy of those stores long before they produced their last child, unless they received a special diet to replace depleted mineral supplies – an unlikely event on the plantation.[5] If, on the other hand, multiparous mothers tried to "eat for two" while pregnant, the result would have been an even higher intake of carbohydrates and fats, which would have further increased bodily needs for minerals (and vitamins) already in dangerously short supply. Some slave babies then entered the world with nutrient deficiencies.[6]

The baby began his dietary routine normally enough at his mother's breast, but the same factors which created vitamin deficiencies (especially ascorbic acid and B vitamins) for the fetus imply that in some cases the infant's sole source of nourishment, his mother's milk, would perpetuate these deficiencies.[7] Thus the first opportunity to correct them would come with weaning, which seems to have occurred between ages nine months and one year.

The quality of a mother's milk is dependent on her nutritional status. Moreover, even the finest mother's milk loses much of its value after six months. It no longer contains protective antibodies, but most importantly, the child's protein needs are no longer met if the breast milk is neither replaced nor supplemented with a rich source of protein.[8] Thus, because human milk contains very little iron, prolonged nursing could also easily have meant anemia for the youngster. The iron stored by the fetus combined with the small amount contained in the milk provided the baby should have lasted the infant about six months. But if the mother's iron stores were inadequate, the baby was born prematurely, or, if iron-containing foods were not introduced into the baby's regimen, anemia would inevitably have resulted.[9] The point here is then that by the time weaning took place (usually at about one year) many slave infants were quite conceivably suffering from nutritional deficiencies because of the mother's status. Thus, the introduction of solid foods should have had an important positive effect.

Unfortunately, weaning for many was a giant nutritional step backwards, because planters were uniformly convinced that the proper diet for children consisted mostly of cornbread, hominy, and fat. In other words, slave babies were weaned to a diet even higher in carbohydrates and lower in protein than that of their parents. Wanting "de chillun to hurry en grow," planters gave them plenty of bread and hominy.[10] Some thought vegetables "not proper for them." They also believed that "clear" meat (as opposed to fat) would "debilitate" children and "until puberty meats should not enter too much into the diet."[11]

Slave children who were the victims of this sort of nutritional theorizing consequently would have continued to be iron deficient[12] with bovine milk their only important potential source of calcium and magnesium. Because the level of lactose intolerance among blacks increases with age, proportionately more slave children than adults would have been able to use milk. But, as previously discussed, today as many as 40 percent of school-age black children exhibit lactose intolerance symptoms. In fact, lactose intolerance may start as early as the first six months, and often does in the first four years. Experiments have shown, for example, that lactase levels in Baganda babies commonly fall during the breastfeeding period, causing malnutrition problems in the first year of life.[13]

The seasonal vagaries of southern milk production, however, meant that even those youngsters who could use milk probably had access to it for a portion of the year only. Yet assuming that a child did receive substantial quantities of bovine milk, his mineral deficiencies may still not have been "cured" because first, a child must consume three times more cow's milk than human milk to absorb the same amount of calcium[14]; second, the high fat content of the slave child's diet would have further impaired the utilization of this mineral[15]; and third, those children who were losing the lactase enzyme could not have properly metabolized the milk sugars, which means that continued consumption would have hindered the absorption of other nutrients.[16]

Thus, those slave children with calcium, magnesium, and/or iron deficiencies early in life could expect little from the fare to which they were weaned – a diet more likely to occasion these deficiencies than to cure them. In fact, because the slave regimen was more nutritionally disastrous for children than it was for adults, one is tempted to castigate southern planters for meanness, particularly because the child's victuals appear suspiciously inexpensive.

But most masters appear to have been quite solicitous of the health of their burgeoning assets, and ironically the rations served were believed to be the healthiest possible. Planters were convinced "that negroes and white people are very different in their habits and constitutions, and that while fat meat is the life of the negro it is a prolific source of disease and death among the whites."[17] For slave children, fat and corn were "peculiarly appropriate"[18] and "negroes who are freely supplied with them grow plump, sleek and shiny."[19] Masters on the whole seem to have taken as much pride in the "fat and shiny" pickaninnies as they did in their "carriage hosses."[20] As will be seen, however, they were often deceived by this "plumpness" that can be as symptomatic of bad nutrition as it can good nutrition. Indeed a regimen high in carbohydrates and low in proteins will produce precisely this kind of physical appearance, which to the twentieth-century medical eye spells protein–calorie malnutrition.

III

If slave children were severely deficient in calcium, magnesium, and iron, then evidence of this ought to be contained in antebellum records. More specifically, black children should reveal a much higher incidence of morbidity and mortality than whites from diseases with an etiology that includes these nutritional deficiencies. Not that all white children enjoyed a diet substantially different or superior to that of blacks, although many undoubtedly did because of planters beliefs regarding "Negro nutrition," and because the circumstances of slavery often dictated a circumscribed regimen. But our basic contention is that, even if white children were fed the same diet as slave children, the latter would have evidenced symptoms of malnourishment to a greater degree for biologic reasons already discussed.

Our evidence from antebellum sources is both statistical and impressionistic. Most of the impressionistic evidence comes from the pens of those southern physicians who, as a group, entertained a belief in a "package" of largely "Negro diseases" that blacks were far more likely to contract and die from than whites. Much of this "package" is composed of children's diseases, and clincial descriptions of these ailments become extremely valuable when trying to match deficiency with disease.

Statistical data have been drawn from various state manuscript census schedules of mortality for the year 1849–50[21] and DeBow's *Mortality Statistics* of the 1850 mortality figures done in 1855.[22] Unfortunately, the practice of compiling and publishing extensive mortality statistics in 1850 was not followed during the next decennial census, and those published data that are available for 1860 are of little worth for our purposes.[23] The 1850 data are not as complete as one might wish,[24] and despite their invaluable nature as one of the few available comprehensive sources on the causes of slave deaths, any rates derived from them are invariably going to be low.[25] Most authorities, in fact, would probably double the infant mortality rate of both white and black.[26] In this case, however, the fact of black and white differentials is more significant than the actual rates.

The census of 1850 revealed a black population in the United States of 3,638,808. Of these, 2,539,617 or about 70 percent resided in the seven states of Virginia, North Carolina, South Carolina, Mississippi, Georgia, Alabama, and Louisiana, which constitute the seven-state sample from which mortality data have been drawn for this study. About 31 percent (786,404) of that population was aged nine and under. The whites residing in these states by contrast numbered 3,221,686 with 34 percent of their numbers (1,084,486) falling into the nine-and-under category.

A nine-and-under age grouping is of course an actuarially perilous

Table 1. *Age-specific death rates by race per*
1,000 persons, seven-state sample, 1850

	Age (yr)			
Race	0–1	1–4	5–9	0–9
White	61.4	11.8	5.0	12.9
Black	137.2	27.7	6.8	26.3

Source: Computed from data contained in J.D.B. Debow (ed.), *Mortality Statistics of the Seventh Census of The*
United States (Washington, D.C., 1854).

category. Yet it was far more hazardous for black children than for
white. Black children in this cohort accounted for fully 51 percent of all
Negro deaths, while white children contributed only 38 percent of the
white deaths during the year 1849–50. Table 1 presents the age-specific
death rates for our seven-state sample. Clearly the disproportionate
number of deaths of black children in the 0- to 4-year age group accounts for much of the black–white differential. Black youngsters in
this cohort died at a rate more than double that of their white counterparts. A glance at the diseases that caused these deaths reveals that out
of a possible 120 or so lethal afflictions contained in the census there
were 6 maladies to which slave youngsters proved extraordinarily susceptible. Indeed "convulsions," "teething," "tetanus," "lockjaw,"
"suffocation," and "worms," were listed as the cause of almost one-
quarter (23 percent) of the black deaths for which a cause was given in
the 0–9 age group, yet they accounted for only 12 percent of the white
deaths exclusive of "unknown" causes in the same age cohort.[27] By
total population, the differential is even more impressive. Fully 450 out
of every 100,000 black children in the 9-and-under age group could
expect to die from one of these illnesses, while only 110 white youngsters per 100,000 faced the same prospect. Hence a black child's risk of
dying from one of these six diseases was more than four times that of
his white counterpart, which calls for a close examination of each of
these fatal maladies in an effort to discover the reasons behind this
deadly color preference.

These causes of death, of course, were determined on the basis of
symptoms that could spell many diseases and consequently are treacherous evidence. Therefore, much of the examination that follows must
necessarily be speculative. Against this, however, is the substantial
black and white difference in experience with the diseases in question.
Moreover, as will be seen, these symptoms do dovetail with those that
should have been produced by the aforementioned black nutritional
deficiencies.

IV

Medical science in this century has grown increasingly aware that calcium, magnesium, and vitamin D deficiencies, singularly and in combination, play an important part in the etiology of the long misunderstood children's disease called *tetany*, an affliction characterized by hyperirritability of the neuromuscular system, whose symptoms include convulsions and spasms of the voluntary muscles.[28] Calcium and magnesium are essential to the proper contraction and relaxation of these muscles, and vitamin D is essential to the absorption of both minerals; thus, a severe deficiency of any one may produce those tetanic symptoms, including convulsions, which can lead to death.[29]

Because of factors discussed in the previous chapter, a vicious cycle of calcium–magnesium deficiency must have been inevitable for many slave families. It began with a deficient mother undergoing multiple pregnancies and her maternal serum calcium falling with each suceeding pregnancy until she herself became a candidate for maternal tetany. Simultaneously, each successive fetus whose own bone development is dependent on its mother's mineral supply was progressively more deprived. Today this vicious cycle is known to account for the positive correlation between frequent pregnancies, maternal dietary deficiencies, and hypocalcemic or hypomagnesic convulsions in infants.[30]

A shortage of vitamin D would have compounded the problem for the fetus of a slave mother. This shortage was occasioned not only by his mother's pigmentation but also by the practice of "lying in" which meant little exposure to the sun during the last weeks of pregnancy.[31] The fetus is unable to metabolize vitamin D independently, hence the passage of the vitamin through the placenta from mother to fetus imposes an increased demand on her stores. A strong correlation between maternal 25-OHD (25-hydroxyvitamin, a form of vitamin D) and umbilical cord levels of the vitamin in the newborn has recently been discovered. Hence all infants with mothers of low 25-OHD are low themselves for "significant periods" of time.[32]

Black Americans, it seems, have "significantly" lower levels of 25-OHD than whites, with this level dipping even further during the winter months.[33] Because pigment causes a decreased transmission of ultraviolet radiation that results in a reduced amount of vitamin D production, it is assumed that this is the major explanation for lower levels of 25-OHD among blacks. Thus the unborn child slave may easily have become vitamin D deficient and unable to utilize minerals it did draw from its mother's skeletal structure. Some slave babies, therefore, must have developed tetany while still in the womb.[34]

After birth, because the infant was still dependent on the extent of its mother's mineral stores, nursing may not have cured the problem, while weaning to a high carbohydrate–low protein diet would certainly have exacerbated it for the reasons already stressed. Finally, even those slave infants given a plentiful supply of bovine milk could not be considered safe from tetany, for the high phosphorus content of undiluted bovine milk has been indicted as an important factor in the disease.[35] Indeed, a diet low in calcium relative to phosphorus as was the slave child's regimen with its heavy dose of cornmeal may well have been tetany producing.

In short, reason for suspecting tetany among the slaves abounds, but because it was not recognized as a disease during antebellum days, all children's ailments characterized by its symptoms demand scrutiny. Three likely possibilities are "convulsions," "teething," and "tetanus," all of which antebellum physicians held responsible for a substantially higher incidence of black as opposed to white infant mortality.[36] This collective opinion is buttressed by mortality statistics generated by the seventh census which indicate that black children were unquestionably the chief victims of the diseases in question.

The lethal trio killed 2,419 individuals during the year 1849–50 in the seven largest slave-holding states, with blacks constituting 66.5 percent of the victims. Fully 205 blacks per 100,000 live population aged nine-and-under could expect to die from one of the three diseases, as opposed to only 75 per 100,000 white youngsters. Supporting data confirming the discriminatory nature of these diseases come from the city of Charleston, where during the years 1822–48 they killed 2,401 individuals. Of that total, 72.4 percent were black, although the white population exceeded the blacks throughout much of that period.[37]

"Convulsions" of course are symptomatic of many maladies, but they do describe precisely those symptoms of nutritional tetany for which we are searching. Teething is suspect because nineteenth-century physicians observed that the convulsions which ravaged babies often occurred during the teething period and concluded that the sprouting of teeth was somehow responsible, hence "teething" as a cause of death.[38]

Infants do not die, however, simply because their teeth make an appearance.[39] Rather it is at this point that some mothers, who had not yet weaned their babies, decided (often hastily) to do so, and in the process quite possibly deprived the child of his sole source of calcium. At the same time, the high phosphorus content of bovine milk abruptly introduced is known to trigger convulsions.[40] Confirmation that "teething" deaths frequently represented tetany cases may be found in nineteenth-century clinical descriptions of the problem. The symptoms – hurried "crouplike" breathing, crowing cough, convulsive movements of the body, constant frowning ("carp mouth"), wrist and ankle joints drawn inward and head drawn back – depict tetany in its classic form.[41]

Tetanus presents a somewhat different problem of linkage with tetany. Convulsions and teething were not diseases by themselves but rather (it has been argued) frequent symptoms of a disease whose nutritional origins became widely known only in this century. Yet during antebellum days, tetanus was understood to be a disease, was associated (albeit imperfectly) with wounds, and appears as a cause of death in the mortality schedules of the census of 1850. "Lockjaw," however, also appears as a cause of death which suggests (as do the categories of "convulsions" and "teething") both a fondness of medical men for symptomatic appellations and a reluctance, despite the urgings of specialists, to regard lower jaw rigidity of the muscle and tetanus (without trismus) as one and the same.

Although erroneous, the distinction made is useful. For the outward symptoms of tetany and tetanus are nearly identical, and as the former was for all practical purposes unknown during the nineteenth century, it would doubtless have been diagnosed as the latter. Had patients uniformly displayed a history of wounds, one could be more certain that the statistics were speaking of tetanus, not tetany, yet physicians often pondered the mystery of tetanus without wounds.[42] Moreover, it was noted that tetanus "epidemics" occurred among southern blacks during the late winter months when milk and sunshine were in short supply.[43] Today tetany deaths peak during the same months,[44] all of which suggests strongly that tetany may often have been diagnosed as tetanus,[45] thereby explaining our lumping of tetanus deaths with convulsions and teething for purposes of analysis.

That we also included "lockjaw" by subsuming it under tetanus requires even more explanation, for in this case at least it might be surmised that one is confronting bona fide cases of tetanus. Yet it is an uneasy confrontation, again because of the uncanny awareness of color and youth that "lockjaw" revealed. Of the 398 reported victims of fatal "lockjaw" within our seven-state sample, 265 or 67 percent were blacks, while 308 of the victims or 77 percent were under the age of five.

Common symptoms of tetany are severe and prolonged spasms of the larynx (often to the point of suffocation) and a rigid face characterized by "carp mouth" in which the corners of the mouth are turned down, causing difficulties in speech or swallowing.[46] The whole, in the words of an antebellum physician, created "an expression so peculiar and characteristic as never to be forgotten when once seen."[47] Certainly these symptoms may have been confused with lower jaw rigidity (particularly in the case of infants) by almost all laymen and more than a few antebellum physicians. In fact, nineteenth-century doctors referred to lockjaw as being "traumatic" or "idiopathic." The former was caused by an injury, but the latter was of a chronic nature due to "general causes" that affected the larynx muscles causing voice changes, a stiff neck and jaw, distended limbs and "violent spasms."[48]

This is not to say that a high incidence of tetanus among southern infants would be surprising, and we are certainly not arguing that all "lockjaw" deaths were tetany. Tetanus thrives best in agrarian areas where persons go barefoot, and sterile medical procedures are absent. Moreover, historically the disease has revealed a special affinity for infants, whose umbilicus proves particularly liable to infection. Indeed, a few physicians (correctly) thought umbilicus infection an important factor in what they termed trismus nascentium and what midwives called the "nine-day fits."[49] Others were close to the mark. One doctor believed that if the bandage wrapped around the umbilicus was dampened by urine and not changed that a "cold" would be precipitated leading to the infant's death,[50] while others claimed they avoided the onset of the disease by painting the umbilicus stump with turpentine.[51] Many physicians, however, ignored umbilicus infection as a factor. One, for example, insisted that he prevented trismus nascentium among Negro infants by purging them from birth, and another pair of physicians explained that the disease was caused by smoke from burning wood and that those Negroes whose houses were chimneyless were the most susceptible.[52]

The fact that antebellum physicians were far from unanimous in believing the nine-day fits stemmed from umbilical infection may be testimony only to the state of their art; or it may be that they were up against more than one disease manifesting similar symptoms, with tetany at least one candidate for that other affliction. Surely umbilical sepsis does not seem to have been the only cause of the "nine-day fits." More than one doctor reported, as did Dr. Dugas, that "I have examined a number of these children" [who died of trismus] but found "nothing wrong about the umbilicus."[53] Moreover, the question remains of why, in an age with little thought given to antiseptic procedure, the disease sought out only black babies,[54] a problem that baffled one experimentally inclined doctor who used both rusty and clean scissors on the umbilical cords of black and white alike, yet saw only blacks contract "lockjaw."[55]

V

Rickets, a usually nonlethal childhood disease of the growing skeleton, would not normally be included in a discussion of child mortality. Rickets and tetany share similar etiologies, however, and a high incidence of the former among a population is usually prima facie evidence of the presence of the latter. Thus, if a high frequency of rickets can be discerned during the slave days, the case for nutritional tetany as an important killer of slave youngsters will be immeasurably strengthened.

Rickets is a disease characterized by defective bone growth, with its most common cause a vitamin D deficiency, which can arise from a lack of dietary vitamin D_3 or inadequate exposure to the sun. But rickets can also develop in a youngster enjoying plenty of vitamin D if he is deficient in calcium and/or phosphorus.[56]

As with tetany, maternal vitamin D deficiency can lead to rickets even before birth.[57] Essentially a disease of children, symptoms include pain in the abdomen or legs but especially in the joints and muscles. The long bones bend creating "bowlegs" that can make walking difficult. Nodular enlargements at the ends of the chest ribs are responsible for the classic symptoms known as the "rachitic rosary." Convulsions of tetany (due to hypocalcemia) are an early sign of rickets; and in severe cases, the softening of the rib cage triggers internal problems including the degeneration of the liver and spleen and pulmonary infections known as "rachitic lung."[58]

Once again, the often mentioned factor of black pigmentation is held responsible for the black's special vulnerability to the affliction, for his skin transmits only one-third of the antirachitic ultraviolet radiation that white skin does.[59] Thus, although the black was well adapted to the West African environment (where rickets is rare), in North America without a dietary source of vitamin D he must have been rickets prone from the beginning.

Spying the affliction on the plantation, however, is another matter, because while not unknown in antebellum times, its seldom fatal nature facilitated its escaping both statistical and medical attention. Indeed writing as late as the 1890s, a specialist complained that rickets was seldom diagnosed unless very severe and was unrecognized by most doctors in its early stages.[60] In terms of mortality even in this century, when the disease was found to be widespread and regularly diagnosed, deaths attrbuted to rickets since 1910 averaged only 280 per year for the next half century throughout the United States.[61] Furthermore, perhaps because of general malnutrition a history of pica and worms is commonly associated with the disease; thus, a death from rickets particularly in the antebellum South may often have been disguised as one of the former.[62] A case for its frequency among slaves, therefore, must be largely inferential.

The "hardest" data come from the seventh census that revealed 25 deaths from rickets during the year 1849–50 in our seven-state sample. Eighty-four percent (21) of the victims were black children. Numerically, the number of deaths seems insignificant, but because rickets is rarely fatal, 25 deaths does suggest a fairly high incidence of the disease. Certainly its attraction to blacks is obvious.

A high frequency of childhood rickets is also indicated by runaway slave advertisements culled from newspapers ranging geographically from New Orleans to Charleston to Memphis which frequently mention deformed bones.[63] Descriptions identifying a runaway as "bowlegged and lame," "slightly bandylegged," "very knock-kneed," "slightly knock-kneed," and "much knock-kneed" appeared so often in antebellum newspapers that they could not have been very useful as a distinguishing characteristic. Bowlegs and knock-knees, of course, are the most obvious signs of a bout with childhood rickets.

Finally, at the turn of this century as the medical profession became far more concerned about the problem of rickets, such a high frequency of the disease among blacks was discovered that physicians came to believe that *all* black children in the cities of Washington and New York suffered from rickets,[64] while a study during the 1920s revealed that 88 percent of the black children in Memphis were rachitic.[65] In North Carolina, a prominent physician claimed that "nearly all negro babies are bow-legged" as a result of rickets.[66]

In 1917, Dr. Alfred Hess, one of America's foremost authorities on the disease announced that 90 percent of all Afro-American children were cursed with an "inherent racial tendency" to the malady.[67] It is important that this group of physicians who "discovered" an overwhelmingly heavy incidence of rickets in black children also asserted that the disease must have been widespread on the plantations as well. [68] If true, then nutritional tetany must also have been widespread and consequently responsible for many of those previously discussed child deaths.

VI

The link between calcium, magnesium, and vitamin D deficiencies among slave children, on the one hand, and nutritional tetany, on the other, represents the beginning of a chain to which other nutritional diseases may possibly be joined, among them that mysterious killer of slave children: *smothering.* Everyone familiar with the subject of American Negro slavery has encountered and perhaps puzzled over the appalling number of instances of parents having supposedly "overlain," "smothered," or "suffocated" their child while sleeping and the concomitant planter disgust at the carelessness of slave parents.[69]

Superficially it would seem that planters most certainly did have reason for disgust. Of the 723 deaths from suffocation recorded during 1849–50 in the seven largest slaveholding states, 666 or fully 92 percent of the victims were black. In terms of live population under one year of age, the differential is even more staggering. For every 100,000 blacks aged one and under, 1,085 could expect to succumb to "suffocation," yet only 64 white infants per 100,000 would perish from the same cause. Smothering, however, was not the real cause of death.

In the past, when youngsters often slept with parents, it is understandable that the latter believed they had accidentally "overlain" a child found dead in the morning. But experiments have demonstrated the near impossibility of an infant smothering so long as any circulating air reaches him,[70] and today, although babies seldom sleep with parents, infant deaths continue at a rate of a least 1 out of every 350 births, which makes it collectively the major killer of babies aged one week to twelve months, claiming some 10,000 lives every year in the United States alone.[71]

Contemporary appellations for the disease (or diseases) in question are crib or cot deaths or, more scientifically, the sudden infant death syndrome (SIDS), and there is good reason to believe that the "smothering" deaths in the slave quarters and the crib deaths of the present stem from the same cause or causes. True, antebellum literature is replete with references to careless or tired parents overlaying their infants at night. The ex-slave John Brown, for example, reported that "numbers of negro infants are overlaid and smothered by mothers at night, in consequence of their having been overworked in the day,"[72] and as late as 1969 references were made to the "overlaying" of slave babies by "weary, exhausted mothers."[73] After studying the problem for Virginia, however, Todd Savitt has reported that there exists not only a compelling descriptive similarity between the "smothering" deaths of slave infants and modern day crib deaths, but that there is also "a remarkable epidemiological correspondence, both in age and seasonal variation between the two."[74]

More than half of crib deaths occur during the coldest months of the year, with the majority of the victims aged between two and eight months.[75] Mortality figures from our seven states coincide with these findings by revealing that some 58 percent of the smothering deaths occurred during South's chilliest months, while fully 82 percent of the smothering victims were less than one year of age.

Hypotheses to account for this aptly described "disease of theories" have ranged from the implication of foreign proteins in bovine milk[76] to low blood sugar,[77] whiplash from spinal injuries,[78] airway obstruction,[79] botulism,[80] immature neural systems,[81] fluoridation of water, the rejection of a mother by her baby, use of bleach in the diaper wash water,[82] and congenital anomalies of the parathyroids[83] to anaphylaxis by the house dust mite.[84] Yet none individually have proven sufficiently inclusive to account for all of the factors in the syndrome, while others are so contradictory as to constitute mutually exclusive explanatory efforts.

Indeed data generated by small experiments and questionable samples have yielded findings which vary so wildly it is surprising that, in addition to the aforementioned age and seasonal factors, even the following broad generalizations regarding the syndrome have been agreed upon: (1) the disease kills from two to three times as many blacks as whites in proportion to their respective populations[85]; (2) a significant percentage of the victims are born prematurely or weigh under five-and-a-half pounds a birth[86]; (3) although most SIDS victims die suddenly from no apparent cause, a common thread of respiratory infections and convulsions seems to link those who manifested some premonitory signs prior to death, while autopsies performed on SIDS youngsters have revealed signs of respiratory distress and circulatory collapse before death[87]; (4) mothers of SIDS babies are twice as likely to be anemic as their more fortunate sisters whose infants do not become SIDS statistics[88]; and (5) babies born closely on the heels of an earlier pregnancy are at a much greater risk of SIDS.[89]

Doubtless when the puzzle of SIDS is finally resolved, no single cause but rather an accumulation of factors will be found at fault. This accumulation will probably accomodate many of the myriad hypotheses already advanced and the many more still to come. There does seem to be, however, one common denominator that has thus far been largely overlooked. Medical researchers seldom search for nutritional etiologies, on the one hand, and seldom adopt a historical viewpoint, on the other. Yet the generally agreed-upon SIDS factors do make sense for the slave quarters if a nutritional etiology is assumed.

It has already been argued that the slave diet would have meant malnutrition for some, and it has been argued that given the blacks' genetic differences the diet would have worked a greater hardship on them than on whites. Furthermore, it has been seen that blacks constituted an overwhelming majority of "smothering" deaths, the bulk of which were probably SIDS fatalities. Granted, a black slave infant who died would have been more likely to have its death listed as "smothering" than a white child, and the fact that blacks appear to have succumbed to "smothering" at a rate seventeen times greater than that of white children suggests a blatant bias in the figures. Nevertheless, because overall black infant mortality was far heavier than that of whites, it can be assumed that, despite the skewed nature of the data, blacks did die at a far greater rate from "smothering" (SIDS) than whites, exactly as they do today.

Nutritional reasons may provide at least a partial explanation. Most "smothering" deaths occurred during the coldest months of the year, when blacks would have had their most serious vitamin D difficulties. Thus, a mother whose fetus had depleted her calcium stores and whose diet provided little calcium (fresh vegetables and milk were in short supply) may have been unable (because of an absence of vitamin D) even to absorb the little calcium that her diet did yield during these months. The result then may have been the birth of a calcium- (and/or magnesium-)deficient baby. Second, mothers of victims of SIDS are twice as likely to be anemic than mothers of "normal" babies, and the slave regimen, low in both iron and protein, was very likely to produce anemia. Third, a high percentage of SIDS victims are born prematurely or are low-birth-weight (LBW) babies. Anemic mothers are much more likely to bear a premature infant or LBW baby after full term. Moreover, hypocalcemia (low serum calcium levels) has been detected in LBW babies suggesting strongly that the mother was also hypocalcemic.[90]

Fourth, an infant with a poor nutritional heritage (which certainly includes many LBW babies) would be more susceptible to disease generally than his luckier fellows and to those respiratory difficulties that form another common denominator. Additionally, we should remind ourselves that blacks have historically been more liable to respiratory ailments than whites.

Fifth, black fertility was apparently higher than white fertility which suggests a higher frequency of pregnancies.[91] Hence black babies would have been more likely than their white counterparts to have followed a recent pregnancy. Multiparous mothers in turn are more prone to calcium depletion and anemia.

In addition to these points, there are other general nutritional factors that demand consideration. Researchers are now convinced that victims of SIDS, at least as a group, are not, as until recently believed, completely "normal." Rather specific neurologic tests have indicated that potential SIDS victims have less ability to adapt to physiologic challenges, for example, such newborns respond inadequately to nasal obstructions. Thus, if the nose is blocked, by a swelling of the nose lining for example, some babies may die rather than breathe through their mouths.[92] Moreover, their growth and development is slightly below "normal" standards.[93] Their poorer autonomic control has led researchers to suspect that some subtle congenital defect, combined with developmental, environmental, or pathologic stresses, cause a breathing deficit that can result in death.[94]

One proponent of this school holds that during sleep the autonomic inspiratory–expiratory rhythmic cycle is disrupted by recurrent periods of apnea (the cessation of breathing for at least two seconds). Short apneic periods are considered normal in babies as well as adults. But a small percentage of newborns, and perhaps 20 percent of LBW babies, enter the world with an abnormality of the respiratory control center in the lower brain stem region. These are the babies in the high risk group for SIDS. They experience more prolonged apneic periods (sometimes over fifteen seconds) and a higher rate of episodes while asleep than normal babies; consequently, gas exchange needs are threatened, followed by anoxia, cyanosis, the elevation of blood carbon dioxide and finally cardiac arrest. If the prolonged episode is interrupted by arousal or resuscitation, the baby will immediately return to a healthy condition, but within a few weeks at least one-fifth of such "near-miss" babies will succumb to SIDS. High-risk infants, it is therefore believed, can be identified on the basis of a marked tendency toward apnea.[95]

Significantly a high correlation between hypocalcemia, recurrent apnea, and LBW babies has been found.[96] Hypocalcemia predisposes to tetany which, it has been observed, should have been a serious problem of many slave youngsters and may account for the convulsions spied in modern SIDS cases as well. The nutritional experience of the slaves then, especially their calcium deficiency, linked with their apparent high incidence of SIDS, suggests strongly that hypocalcemia be given a more energetic investigation by SIDS researchers.

In addition, Dr. Joan L. Caddell has pointed out that the magnesium deprivation growth syndrome that has occupied her attention for several years closely approximates SIDS.[97] She argues that premature or LBW infants who tend to double their weight in the first three to four months of life (in contrast to the normal baby who doubles his weight in about six months), or are born to young and/or multiparous mothers whose magnesium stores have been diminished or whose diet is poor in magnesium relative to calcium, phosphorus, and protein (which increase the requirements for magnesium) are all quite vulnerable to SIDS.

A female can become magnesium deficient if she must support the increased magnesium requirements of pregnancies with only short intervals in between, particularly if, as in the case of a young woman, her own anabolic (body building) requirements are high. Whether a woman remains in magnesium balance throughout these pregnancies depends upon her diet. The low-income urban American mothers observed by Caddell et al. were generally magnesium deficient. They often lived on a magnesium-poor diet of overmilled flour products, potatoes and fatty meats.[98] The best sources of magnesium are shellfish, nuts, whole grains, and green vegetables, foods least available in cold months when crib deaths have the highest incidence and not particularly prominent in the diet of the slaves yesterday or blacks today.

Moreover, magnesium deficiency was often found in one- to six-month-old infants studied who had experienced sudden life-threatening episodes characterized by the pallor of dusky skin color, rigidity, apnea (cessation of breathing), an irregular heartbeat, rigidity, and sometimes convulsions. These symptoms are also considered to be premonitory signs of SIDS.[99]

Caddell's hypothesis is that histamine and other neurochemicals that are normally present in the body may be suddenly released in the magnesium-deficient infant by some as yet unknown mechanism. It is known, however, that this phenomenon will produce premonitory signs of SIDS, if mild, and a potentially fatal shocklike state if severe. This shock is similar to anaphylactic shock except that it is not associated with allergy. Significantly, the findings at death are similar in both the magnesium deficiency syndrome and SIDS. They are chiefly internal and include blood spots on the surface of the organs of the chest; the heart and lungs are heavier than normal; the blood in the heart is fluid; and the lungs show varying amounts of edema (accumulated fluid), congestion of blood, and hemorrhage.[100]

Although it must be tested further, Caddell's hypothesis is compatible with the facts known about SIDS[101] and the impaired nutritional circumstances of the plantation.

VII

The practice of weaning plantation infants to a diet high in carbohydrates and low in proteins should have resulted in a fairly high incidence of *protein–calorie malnutrition*. Moreover, this problem may have
been exacerbated considerably by lactose intolerance, which some
black children develop during the first year of life, because the lactase
enzyme is important not only for the metabolism of the milk sugar,
lactose, but indirectly for all carbohydrates. Studies of African populations for example reveal a high correlation between infant malnutrition
and tribes characterized by low lactase levels. In fact, it has been hypothesized that lactose intolerance can be a predisposing factor to
kwashiorkor.[102]

Kwashiorkor is one of the most prevalent types of protein–calorie
malnutrition whose sufferers are normally children in the five-and-
under age group and whose symptoms in extreme form include those
distended bellies with which the entire world has become heartbreak-
ingly familiar since World War II. Not until 1956, however, when
enough information had accumulated on kwashiorkor's etiology, was a
protein-deficient diet established as the culprit. The disease was first
observed clinically on the Gold Coast (now Ghana), hence the Ga word
which means "the sickness of the deprived child."[103]

In this sense of the word, antebellum plantations probably abounded
with somewhat deprived children who exhibited mild cases of kwashiorkor. Their diet was not completely devoid of protein but was seriously deficient because it (1) centered around corn, a low-quality protein, and (2) contained too little protein in proportion to total caloric
intake. Either or both of these conditions can be responsible for
kwashiorkor.[104] Classic symptoms include skin lesions, apathy, anemia,
coldness of the extremities, muscular atrophy, diarrhea, "moon face"
(blubbery cheeks), an enlarged fatty liver, and edema.

But it is estimated that for every classic case of kwashiorkor, there
are ninety-nine subclinical cases whose victims are in a mild incipient
stage of kwashiorkor, designated as "infantile malnutrition" which occurs after a child is weaned to a protein-poor diet.[105] The chief outward
characteristic of such a condition is slight edema and the little pot
bellies carried by children, which unfortunately are still seen in this
country and are extremely common in Africa among children between
the ages of nine and thirty-six months.

This prekwashiorkor state is dangerous because severe protein–calorie malnutrition can develop if stimulated by an intercurrent disease
such as respiratory infection, with concomitant effects ranging from
stunted bone growth and psychomotor retardation to permanent brain
and liver damage, to death.[106] Furthermore, it predisposes to infections
such as bronchopneumonia, the most frequent cause of death in kwashi-

orkor cases.[107] Either way the disease is so camouflaged that it is difficult
to spy in antebellum statistics on child morbidity and mortality although
not impossible, for manuscript censuses list "dropsy," "swelling," etc.
as the cause of death for many youngsters.

Ironically evidence very suggestive of mild kwashiorkor comes from
the testimony of slaves whose self-satisfied masters took pride in the
sleek plump pickaninnies of their plantations. "Marse like to see his
slaves fat and shiny, just like he wants to see de carriage hosses slick
and spanky," asserted one ex-slave.[108] "Marster . . . kept his niggers
fat, just like he keep his hogs and hosses fat, he did,"[109] reported
another, while a third remarked that the children "stayed so fat and
sleek that the Negroes called them Marster Majors little black pigs."[110]

Further evidence comes from the pens of travelers who accepted the
sight of pudgy youngsters as evidence of planter largess. William Russell, for example, commented on pickaninnies in Louisiana with their
"glistening fat ribs and corpulent paunches."[111] By contrast Fredrika
Bremer encountered more serious cases of edema such as the "young
lad very much swollen as if with dropsy."[112] Moreover, physicians
were not fooled and pondered at some length the phenomenon of the
distention of slave children's stomachs.[113]

Another form of protein–calorie malnutrition symptomatically on the
opposite pole from kwashiorkor is marasmus, which is quite simply
starvation. It is caused by an inadequate intake of calories, with a
resulting general emaciation and growth retardation. In this case, victims did not belong to planters who believed (even if they were in
error) that they were feeding children properly, but rather to mean and
stingy planters who deliberately neglected slave offspring. Men of this
ilk may have been comparatively rare among slaveholders but not so
rare that references of negligence cannot be found.[114] Physicians complained from time to time of slave children who were "*not thriving*" and
suspected some lesion of nutrition if not outright "starvation."[115]

A Mississippi doctor writing on "The Negro and his Diseases" described marasmus vividly in 1853 as one "to which negro children are
liable between the second and fifth year . . . . It is literally a 'wasting
away' – *a tabes* . . . styled provincially [as] 'the drooping disease of negro children.' " It began with "languor, fretfulness and loss of strength.
The child gradually becomes emaciated . . . diarrhea supervenes . . .
[soon] fever complicates the case" and perhaps "convulsions."[116]

Both kwashiorkor and marasmus puzzled physicians, who blamed
them alternately on prolonged lactation and premature weaning (in
many cases these were probably correct assessments), and on unsanitary conditions, diet, worms, and dirt eating. This shotgun approach
pathologically may have scored important hits, for a diet that produces
kwashiorkor or marasmus in children will also create problems with

worms, and very possibly a craving for pica all of which suggests an examination of the latter two disorders.

VIII

Cachexia africana and dirt eating were two of the most common antebellum sobriquets for *pica,* an exotic disease which fascinated physicians and terrified planters because it seemed to appear almost solely among blacks.[117] "Pica" comes from the Latin for magpie, a bird who will eat anything, and certainly our seven-state sampling of mortality statistics from the 1850 census confirms the predilection of Africans for geophagy, while at the same time suggesting the normally nonlethal nature of the malady. For despite the fearsome reputation of dirt eating, only 86 deaths were attributed to it. Yet almost all (83) of the victims were black.

Symptoms of adult dirt eating first manifested themselves as dyspepsia, then acute diarrhea, heart palpitations, and a jaundiced or ash-colored skin. Advanced cases caused emaciation and anemia, swellings and "dropsical effusions."[118] Children, on the other hand, often developed only edema, as in the case of kwashiorkor.

More will be said about dirt eating in the following chapter which discusses adult diseases, but the habit among slaves does seem to have been symptomatic of mineral deficiencies, particularly in light of the evidence that indicates a dietary lack of iron, calcium, and magnesium, the minerals most often associated with the practice. Interestingly such a possibility did not escape antebellum medical authorities,[119] some of whom observed that better, more varied slave diets constituted the best insurance planters could have against pica outbreaks on their plantations.[120] Significant also is their collective warning that youngsters and pregnant and lactating women were most liable to acquire the pica habit, precisely those groups with the highest requirements for iron, calcium, and magnesium.[121]

IX

Worms proved extraordinarily deadly to the under-ten-year-old age group of the slaves. Of 1,709 deaths due to worms recorded during 1849–50 in the seven-state sample, 77 percent of the victims were listed as black, while 96 percent of the total were aged nine-and-under. In terms of live population, 168 out of every 100,000 black youngsters under ten years of age could expect to die of worms as opposed to only 36 out of every 100,000 white children. Small wonder that antebellum authorities viewed worms as one of the most terrible maladies to affect the slave population.[122] What they could not know is that the high incidence of worm mortality among slave children is itself potent evidence of serious malnutrition.

The roundworms *Ascaris* and *Trichuris* were a special scourge of southern slaves,[123] while today black children still suffer more from greater infestations of the roundworms than white children.[124] This may suggest a special susceptibility, since different worms do treat peoples differently (for example, blacks' relative immunity to *Necator americanus* or hookworm).[125]

Worms should present few problems for the well-nourished person, yet they obviously gave slave youngsters problems of a serious and frequently fatal nature. As Professor Josué de Castro put it, with perhaps more poetry than worms deserve: "There can no longer be any doubt that, with good nutrition . . . worms become quite inoffensive, sharing the regime of abundance like peaceful fellow boarders. They become quiet domestic animals, like any other . . . . All that is necessary is to furnish enough food for both man and worm."[126] That food should include particularly substantial doses of proteins, iron, vitamin A, and the vitamin B complex. Only when enough of these nutrients are not forthcoming do worms abuse their host by interfering with the digestion and absorption of those nutrients they do encounter.[127]

Signals of this abuse are manifested in abdominal pains, diarrhea, and lethargy, symptoms with which planters and doctors were all too familiar. In the more chronic stages, the spleen enlarges while the liver shrinks, the abdomen bloats, and convulsions may result. The roundworms were undoubtedly responsible for causing iron deficiencies and anemia in the slave (as well as protein malnutrition in the child), for a synergistic interaction exists between worms and malnutrition. The worms influence the host's nutritional status, while malnutrition decreases the host's ability to withstand worm invasion. The result can be a dangerously decreased resistance to infection as well as underdevelopment in the child. Studies have demonstrated a positive correlation between worm infestation and below normal heights, weights, and skinfold measurements.[128] Conversely, as was pointed out, large amounts of iron, vitamins, and protein actually create a partial immunity, that is, they can prevent or cure worm damage.

The ascarid infestation was probably the most common among slaves, frequently interfering with both their digestion and absorption of nutrients.[129] Additionally, the worm secretes enzymes that cause protein losses.[130] Indeed just a few worms in one child can cause a 10-percent loss of protein (and losses of vitamins A, C, and B complex), which is particularly serious in youngsters, for their protein supply is crucial to adequate brain development.[131] Another loss that results from these raids on protein reserves is the ability to produce new gamma globulin in the form of antibodies. The ensuing lack of immune responses leaves the host highly susceptible to infections.[132]

Worms also have a synergistic interaction with iron. Even a very light load of worms can cause the loss of some 10 percent or more of one's RDA of iron (obtained by few of the slaves anyway).[133] Whether or not iron deficiency anemia results from these worms depends upon the balance between dietary iron absorption (taking into account such factors as the source of the iron and phytate consumption) and iron losses due to infestation.

X

Protein–calorie malnutrition, pica, and worm ravages are so interrelated as to constitute their own syndrome, and jaundice, edema, anemia, diarrhea, and apathy are all symptoms of the three afflictions. The poor quality diet that begets kwashiorkor or marasmus may also stimulate an impulse to fill the hungry stomach with nonfoods. It can also breed specific hungers. For example, if a diet is low in protein, it is very difficult for the body to satisfy its iron requirements. Hence again the pica impulse although this time for specific materials containing iron, calcium, or magnesium, and so forth.

Pica, on the other hand, while frequently the result of mineral deficiencies, is also capable of generating these deficiencies, both by decreasing the practitioner's interest in real foods and, it has been theorized, by actually binding minerals inside the body, thus making them unusable.[134] Finally, of course, pica usage can add worms to the body. When forced to share a diet sufficiently low in quality to produce protein–calorie malnutrition, worms in turn are harmful to their hosts, and their abuse very often results in iron-deficiency anemia that heightens the pica craving.

Because of these disease interactions, it can be assumed that slave children were not infrequently victims of all three. The net effect was not only to increase their chances of dying from one of them but also to leave their bodies depleted and consequently raise their susceptibility to infectious disease as well.

XI

Slave infant and child mortality was considerably higher than that of whites in the antebellum South. Doubtless some of the differential can be blamed on circumstances of slavery, which produced everything from planter neglect to slave negligence. Yet there does seem to be significance in the fact that black youngsters died at a much higher rate than whites from a few specific diseases, whose symptoms can be triggered by precisely those nutritional deficits most likely to have been occasioned by a combination of the slave's diet and his genetic heritage. Certainly not every death from convulsion was a case of tetany nor every child's pot belly evidence of protein–calorie malnutrition. On the other hand, some undoubtedly were. We feel many were in part because of the correlations established between the slave diet and the diseases that were killing the slave young, and, in part, because, as will be seen in later chapters, in the decades following slavery (and even today) black youngsters continue to die at a much higher rate than their white counterparts from many of these same symptoms. Granted today, as yesterday, the blacks' physical environment is inferior to that of whites. But constant also is climate and the black genetic heritage. And the black diet is still extraordinarily low in calcium and iron and terribly high in carbohydrates and fats.

CHAPTER 8

ALIMENTS AND AILMENTS

Corn, abounding as it does in oily matter is also a heat-producing agent, acting precisely like fat meat; and in addition to this its other elements render it a valuable muscle producing food. How fortunate that pork and corn, the most valuable of all articles of diet for negroes, may be readily produced throughout the whole region where slaves are worked.

John S. Wilson (1859)[1]

I am persuaded that they [planters and overseers] can do much to promote the health of their negroes by timely care and attention, and thus avoid, in some measure, what I have often heard them say gives them the greatest trouble in the management of their plantations, namely, *the sickness amongst the negroes.* (italics his)

Ralph Butterfield (1858)[2]

I

Descriptions of runaway slaves are replete with references to crooked or bandy legs, knocked-knees, stooped shoulders, jaundiced complexions, splotchy skin, inflamed and watery eyes, partial blindness, speech impediments, and rotten, missing, or buck teeth.[3] Moreover, the records of over 100 estates ranging from Louisiana to South Carolina and from Florida to Arkansas suggest that the afflictions of the runaways were hardly atypical, for these data also point to a high incidence of blindness, lameness, deformed bones, skin lesions, and dental problems.

All of this is indicative of primary nutritional problems among the bondsmen.[4] Of course nonnutritional problems were doubtless at the root of some of these difficulties. Nonethless, the frequently mentioned bone maladies point to an absence of sufficient calcium, ascorbic acid, magnesium, and/or vitamin D in the diet, while the skin, teeth, and eye complaints suggest a multiple deficiency including vitamins A, C and the B complex – in every case vitamins and minerals in which the slave diet was most likely to have been deficient.

117

II

Millions of individuals around the world today are either partially or totally blind because of acute vitamin A deficiency. The fact, therefore, that yesterday antebellum physicians reported an inordinate amount of blindness among slaves sharpens the suspicion that the diet of some was indeed deficient in this vitamin.[5]

More prevalent than blindness were complaints of "sore eyes" and "stinging eyes" which "did not go away for days or weeks, if then."[6] These symptoms indicate an absence of vitamin A, for when the nutrient is not forthcoming from the diet the eye dries and cracks, collects dust or dirt and becomes infected. Mild infections were manifested in the "sore eyes"; the more severe infections resulted in partial or total blindness. Perhaps many slaves did not enjoy the profusion of sweet potatoes others have urged that they did, or perhaps the sweet potatoes in question were of the white variety containing little vitamin A.[7] Alternatively, an absence of riboflavin in the diet can produce visual fatigue, and because inflamed eyes are also symptomatic of pellagra (see below) and the slave diet could have been pellagra-producing, it seems likely that a shortage of the B vitamins may also have contributed to the eye difficulties of slaves.

III

The regularity with which slaves exhibited bad and deformed teeth points to deficiencies of vitamins D and C and calcium. The high frequency of "buck teeth" and crooked teeth that runaway slave advertisements highlight has been noted. Bad teeth were also common. Antebellum physicians stated flatly that "the teeth of negroes . . . decay more rapidly than those of white people,"[8] and "you will find but few negroes who are not subject to tooth-ache."[9] Indeed "an examination of the physicians' accounts reveals that a large portion of their practice was extracting teeth."[10] Clearly the stereotyped picture of slaves flashing white toothy grins demands considerable retouching to show the many gaps in those grins.

The same deficiencies that produced dental problems in slaves may also bear responsibility for the high incidence of deformed bones that, as already mentioned in the discussion of childhood diseases, must in many cases have been the work of rickets. Also to be blamed on rickets is the high frequency of pelvic deformities with which "the slave population in the South was particularly affected."[11] In fact, it was by experimenting on the many cases afforded by slave women that southern physicians learned to perform the cesarean section. A Georgia doctor pondering the difficulties of black parturition wrote in 1849 that "reasoning a priori, one would have supposed that the delicate white female would have had a much oftener demand for the physician than the coarse muscular negress. But such is not the fact."[12] Physicians for the most part spoke gingerly and vaguely about "infirmities peculiar to women" of which slave women suffered to a much greater extent than whites.[13] But they were sufficiently succinct to make it clear that many of these problems were related to deformed pelves wrought by rickets, a problem that was to continue for over a century. As late as the 1950s black women still suffered from deformed pelves, as a result of childhood rickets, at a rate seven-and-a-half times that of their white sisters.[14]

IV

The train of symptoms [wrote a physician in 1833] that progressively arise from . . . dirt eating are indigestion and emaciation; a bloated countenance; a dirty-yellow tinge in the cellular tissues of the eyelids; paleness of the lips and ends of the fingers; whiteness of the tongue; great indolence, with an utter aversion to the most ordinary exertion; palpitation of the heart; difficult, or rather frequent and oppressed, respiration, even during moderate exercise, which never fails to induce a rapid pulse; habitual coldness of the skin; and occasional giddiness of the head, attended with a disposition to faint, sometimes causing a state of stupor.[15]

Although physicians throughout the South who wrote about dirt eating chanted the symptoms to one another, almost everything else about the disease then, as now, was shrouded in contradiction. Its alleged malignancy provides an example. Antebellum planter and modern historian alike have reported that many slaves ate dirt and that "practically all dirt eaters died."[16] As previously noted, however, during 1849–50 only eighty-three black deaths were attributed to the practice, and although there is the testimony of an antebellum physician to assure us that death from pica was frequently attributed to the heart,[17] it is difficult to believe, at least on the basis of the 1849–50 schedule of mortality, that dirt eating lived up to its reputation as a major killer of slaves. Perhaps the year in question was an unusually healthy year for dirt eaters. But there is also the possibility that physicians exaggerated the malignancy of dirt eating in their writings, that literature revealing an utter confusion regarding pica's etiology.

Yet while baffled by the origin of pica, southern physicians were no more or less perceptive than other authorities concerned with the African's propensity for nonfoods; authorities are still puzzling over it today. Three schools of thought have existed on the subject, each with loud advocates. Some, for example, have believed that pica was a response to hookworm infection,[18] others have insisted that clay eating was essentially a cultural trait or habit passed along from generation to generation;[19] while still others have argued that geophagy implies certain lesions of nutrition.[20]

Of the three, the hookworm theory is the most dubious because a number of studies appearing since the 1930s have demonstrated in convincing fashion that blacks as a group possess a relative immunity to the ravages of hookworm.[21] On the other hand, the culturalists are still very much in the running. During the first centuries of slavery in the Americas pica was frequently observed among blacks with the prevailing opinion being that it was a habit acquired in Africa which would disappear when the slave trade disappeared.[22] When clay eating survived this disappearance, many antebellum physicians viewed it as a residual African habit of "idopathic" origins reacquired by each generation through imitation, thus arming themselves with a plausible explanation of pica's epidemic-like appearance on unfortunate plantations.[23]

Subsequent variations[24] on this theme have been sounded. One of the most recent theories advances the interesting analogy that pica begins as an experiment, with youngsters nibbling clay just as they might puff on cigarettes, and, like smoking, becomes "a habit difficult to break despite occasional serious harm to the body."[25] Pleasure derived from the taste ("slightly bitter-sour"), relaxation, and oral gratification are the chief benefits derived from the practice. Other benefits of a psychological nature also accrue to the user, for as the practice is handed down by example from generation to generation, so too is lore that would have pica important in the male's sexual performance as well as the female's ability to produce a healthy baby. Finally, it is argued that no link between pica and nutritional deficiencies has been proven, and consequently the practice indulged in by multitudes of southerners in the past, and not a few today, must have a cultural origin.[26]

The difficulty with this ably argued thesis is that it tells only half of the story (and in our opinion the weaker half) while taking the cultural argument much further than most culturalists prefer to go. Indeed as a group they readily concede that nutritional deficiencies play an extremely important part in the etiology of pica but maintain that culture also has an important role.[27]

It is no longer true that no connection has been established between the dirt eating and nutritional deficiencies. On the contrary, an impressive number of both statistical and clinical studies testify to precisely this connection. Major conclusions may be categorized and summarized as follows:

1. Geophagy is practiced, with few exceptions, by the malnourished.[28]
2. Their nutritional deficiencies commonly include vitamins B_1 and B_3 and protein but especially the minerals calcium and (most especially) iron.[29]
3. The soils consumed by pica users have been analyzed and often found to contain high concentrations of these minerals.[30]

4. Treated clinically with the minerals in question dirt eaters have lost interest in "substitute" or nonfoods, while control group recipients of placebos (instead of mineral supplements) did not abandon "nonfoods." Those who were "cured" usually remained so as long as mineral treatments continued; when treatments were terminated, so was pica abstinence.[31]

5. Babies and animals deprived of certain nutrients will, given the choice, instinctively select the foods containing those nutrients.[32]

6. Animal studies reveal that not all nonfood is consumed for its direct nutritional value. In fact, in some cases the nonfood provides no nutrients but nonetheless does stimulate the bodily production of certain nutrients.[33]

The foregoing should not be constituted as a blanket denial that cultural factors are important in the etiology of pica, but it does suggest reasonable grounds for believing that, given the apparent deficiencies in the slave diet of protein, B_1 and B_3 as well as calcium and iron, dirt eating among slaves may well have had a nutritional etiology. Not incidentally this possibility did not escape some antebellum medical authorities, who argued vigorously that a better slave diet would prevent pica outbreaks on plantations.[34]

Equally significant is the linking by other antebellum physicians of particular soils with the minerals in question. A visitor to the South was told (he believed the claim improbable) that cachexia africana was caused by a slave diet based "too exclusively on Indian corn which is too nourishing and has not a sufficiency in it of inorganic matter" (minerals).[35] In Florida, where visitors saw many blacks in "the most abject state of degeneration imaginable" from dirt eating, a physician believed that the practice originated from a lack of "lime" and other "calcareous matter" in the soils.[36] Thus in that state (as well as Georgia and Mississippi) where the soils were calcium deficient and corn the "principal breadstuff" (also lacking in lime) the physician argued that especially children and pregnant women "were urged by nature to supply that deficiency by going directly to the depleted soils."[37]

Most importantly, several doctors who recommended iron treatment for cachexia africana also claimed cures with this therapy.[38] Significant also is their collective warning that youngsters and pregnant and lactating women were most liable to acquire the habit, precisely those groups with the highest iron and calcium requirements.

Finally then, not only were the nutrients consumed by slaves particularly low in calcium and magnesium, but the efficient absorption of both is enhanced by a sufficient intake of vitamin C, vitamin D, and animal protein. These were seriously wanting in the slave diet. Furthermore, pica usage can be symptomatic of other primary nutritional diseases such as rickets (previously discussed) and beriberi and pellagra (to be taken up shortly).[39]

In conclusion, it should be noted that one school of thought regarding geophagy would have it not the result but rather the cause of mineral deficiency (in this case iron). In other words, ingestion of nonfoods prevents nutrient absorption.[40] But opponents of this position, perhaps frustrated by the chicken–egg nature of the problem, studied cases of pagophagia (ice eating), a practice which could not interfere with iron's absorption. Interestingly, iron therapy was discovered to be almost 100 percent effective in breaking the habit within a week or two.[41] The point here is that mineral deficiencies can produce cravings for substances that do not necessarily contain those minerals, a phenomenon observed as well by antebellum physicians who saw dirt eaters initially nibble specific kinds of clay but graduate to consuming a wide variety of nonfoods. Because iron treatment frequently caused these cravings to disappear, it may be that, in the matter of geophagy at least, the observations of antebellum physicians are particularly germane.

V

It is highly possible that some percentage of the geophagy cases were a form of beriberi, whose symptomatology includes three categories of complaints. The first, neuritis, is characterized by an alternating tingling sensation and numbness in the legs, aching muscles, "knee jerking, an altered gait and shuffling."[42] A second class of symptoms has the victim suffering from "cardiovascular insufficiency" that in addition to palpitations, produces a general sensitivity to cold and a sensation of coldness in the extremities. Finally comes wet beriberi with edema or swelling taking place initially in the legs, then possibly throughout the entire body.

The disease is the result of a deficiency of thiamine (B_1), one of the chief nutrients that seems to be adequately represented in the "hog and hominy" slave fare. In parts of Louisiana, South Carolina, and Georgia, however, rice often replaced corn, and beriberi is most common among rice-eating societies because of a polishing process during milling that strips away the outer cover of the rice grain, a cover rich in thiamine. Because rice mills in the South did polish rice to retard spoilage, a reasonable conjecture is that slaves whose diet centered too closely on this grain could have developed beriberi.

Thus, one student of the South who has looked at the records of rice plantations located along the Savannah River discovered bondsmen who "would suddenly swell in every part of the body, and in five or six days the case would invariably prove fatal." These symptoms are suggestive of virulent beriberi.[43] Again in Louisiana, although here the diet centered on corn, an Italian doctor, Cesare Bressa, who visited the state during the 1820s, described the disease cachexia africana that Piero

Mustacchi has recently diagnosed as wet beriberi with the victim attempting to satisy his body's craving for missing nutrients through dirt eating.[44]

Moreover, Richard Sutch feels that beriberi in the antebellum South need not have been confined to rice-consuming slaves. He argues that the amount of thiamine slaves actually received was deceptively small, because the vitamin is quickly destroyed by heat, alkaline solutions, and prolonged dehydration. Southern practices, such as smoking or pickling pork, substantially reduced the vitamin B_1 yield of the meat, while boiling destroyed even more of the vitamin. Additionally "prolonged dehydration" during storage may well have had a similar pernicious effect on the thiamine in cornmeal, and heat during the cooking process would also have diminished the supply of the vitamin.[45]

We are not completely persuaded by Sutch's argument, for the vitamin B_1 contained in whole cornmeal alone, despite cooking losses, should have been sufficient for most slaves. Yet there may indeed have been subclinical cases of beriberi simply due to a bad diet generally, including a poor intake of the B complex, particularly since it is very important that the B vitamins be in balance in order for each one to be maximally effective. Quite possibly then mild beriberi, which can combine with pellagra and scurvy,[46] was in fact entangled with them, despite an apparent sufficiency of thiamine in cornmeal.

VI

Given the blatant lack of ascorbic acid in the bondsmen diet, scurvy might be expected to have occurred frequently in the slave quarters. Scurvy was a nutritional disease, however, whose etiology was understood, and because very little ascorbic acid can keep the disease at bay planters alert to the meaning of livid spongy gums did as a rule take the precaution of occasionally issuing vegetables.

Not that scurvy was absent from the slave quarters. Rather, antebellum medical literature contains more than a few references to a "scurvy condition among slaves," which physicians linked routinely to a circumscribed diet heavy on salt pork and corn bread and light in vegetables.[47] Moreover subclinical scurvy, which produces anemia, and "other . . . features of vague ill health," was undoubtedly a problem.[48] But because the full-blown disease was so marked in its symptoms and most planters understood its prevention, scurvy was probably confined to the farms of a relatively few mean and/or ignorant masters.

VII

One is mildly surprised at the previously mentioned frequency of skin maladies among the slaves, particularly in light of the tenet that blacks as a group possess an immunity of sorts to these kinds of complaints.[49] The prevalence of pellagra among blacks (of which skin lesions are symptomatic), however, in the South during the early decades of this century and the regimen, centering on corn as the principal cereal, which was discovered to be its cause, refute that idea.[50]

It is, of course, no coincidence that pellagra dogs the heels of heavy consumers of Indian corn. Past medical research has indicted corn as a major etiologic factor by revealing that while insufficient quantities of niacin in the diet may not be the sole cause of pellagra, sufficient quantities will cure the disease and prevent its recurrence. Corn superficially would seem to contain niacin in abundance. The problem is that it contains it too well in a chemically bound form largely unavailable to the body.[51] Moreover, corn has a high leucine (an amino acid) content that interferes with the metabolism of what little niacin corn and other comestibles do yield.[52] Yet a dietary absence of niacin does not automatically condemn one to the ranks of the pellagrins, else the disease historically would have been a much more serious problem.

Sufficient tryptophan (an amino acid and niacin's precursor) in the diet enables the body to manufacture its own niacin and therefore acts as a pellagra preventative. Tryptophan occurs in crude protein. But some proteins are incomplete, and corn as previously noted unhappily falls into this category, yielding as it does only a negligible amount of tryptophan. Furthermore, the leucine content of corn has the same pernicious effect on the ability to metabolize tryptophan as it does on niacin.[53] Thus, those whose diets center on corn have the potential for becoming niacin deficient and pellagra prone. Certainly slaves in the American South who were customarily issued an average of one peck or more of cornmeal weekly fall into this category.

We are not arguing, of course, that all slaves were pellagrins. Indeed, a number of nutritionally mitigating factors undoubtedly acted to spare many slaves the disease. Coffee, for example, is mentioned frequently in connection with the slave regimen, and a single cup of genuine coffee can contribute much of the daily niacin requirement.[54] Sour milk or buttermilk would have provided lactose-intolerant slaves with physically tolerable milk. Beef served regularly is an excellent source of tryptophan, and those slaves who maintained their own gardens and poultry flocks would also have had access to sufficient pellagra preventatives.

Much of the coffee was ersatz, however, the result of roasting corn, bran, okra, or potato peelings.[55] Many plantations made little in the way of dairy products available to slaves, while many more served them exclusively to children. Beef was considered an inferior food by bondsman and master alike, and of course planter whim was the deciding factor in the matter of individual gardens on the plantation.

Hence it is a reasonable assumption that many slaves would not have consumed a sufficient variety of supplements to overcome the low niacin-high leucine yield of the corn–pork core of their diet. This diet, therefore, should have produced pellagra in the antebellum South exactly as it did in the same region after the turn of the twentieth century. Indeed, the peculiar chemical composition of the slave regimen coupled with the blacks' propensity for lactose intolerance suggests strongly that pellagra must have been a serious problem of health in the United States that long went unrecognized because pellagra went unrecognized as a disease.

In diagnosing pellagra, "recognition" is the key factor. It was first observed in eighteenth-century Europe, and as physicians became familiar with the disease, "recognition," rather than the affliction, spread across the continent from Spain, southwestern France and Italy to Austria, Rumania, Hungary, Russia, and finally into Egypt and southern Africa. But recognition of the disease in the United States did not occur until the early twentieth century after which southern physicians admitted to having previously misdiagnosed the disease as everything from eczema to intestinal tuberculosis to malaria to scurvy.[56]

If physicians of the twentieth century equipped with a budding knowledge of parasitic life cycles – helminthic, protozoan, bacterial, and viral – could nonetheless mistake pellagra for diseases with which they were familiar, then certainly their antebellum predecessors, lacking these advantages of scientific research, would have been doubly prone to commit this error.

The problems of diagnosing pellagra are twofold. First, it is extraordinarily protean in its manifestations leading many to believe that it is not one but several diseases, and, second, it rarely develops along classical lines. As the famous pellagrologist Joseph Goldberger noted, although fully developed cases of pellagra form "a picture which, when once seen, can hardly ever fail to be recognized even by one who is not a physician, the diagnosis of the disease is by no means always easy, because the fully developed cases form only a small proportion of the total."[57]

At the onset, the victim has no definite symptoms. He often, however, experiences a feeling of lassitude and perhaps mild digestive disturbances, especially heartburn. He may have a loss of appetite, or he may become a voracious eater. He may develop an insatiable thirst, but he is almost as likely to develop an aversion to water. As the disease progresses in classic cases, the tongue is thickly coated and the mouth sore. Pains develop in the neck and back and muscular weakness occurs, especially in the legs. The victim grows hypersensitive to touch, and the eyes take on a peculiar redness.

In the twentieth-century United States, this so-called first stage of pellagra normally appeared about the first of the year after the beneficial effects of a more varied summer and fall diet (a higher intake of niacin and tryptophan) disappeared. The symptoms might persist for several weeks or months and then vanish only to return the following year. Because those symptoms were scarcely severe, one suspects that antebellum planters, overseers, and slaves alike dismissed them as unimportant indicators of a mild winter complaint or, equally likely, slave laziness or just plain "contrariness."

If the symptoms continued until spring, the disease may well have advanced to a more alarming second stage; here, in addition to retaining (often in intensified form) most of the previous symptoms, the skin that was exposed to sunlight or trauma often became reddened, hence the Spanish appellation *mal de la rosa*. In blacks, however, the color of the skin merely deepened which must also have misled physicians.[58] Later, these areas develop a rough and scaly texture, thus prompting the Italians to call the malady *pelle* (skin) *agra* (rough). Skin lesions as well as an inflammation of the mucous membranes manifested as glossitis, proctitis, vaginitis, stomatitis, and diarrhea might also plague the victim. A high fever is not unusual, and nervous symptoms may develop at the peak of the attack.

With the appearance of this second stage, a doctor was most likely summoned to the plantation. Because antebellum physicians were unacquainted with pellagra, however, they would have regarded the symptoms as indicative of such familiar diseases as typhoid, typhus, putrid sore throat (diphtheria), dropsy, malaria, or scarlet fever, diseases that manifest some symptoms similar to those of pellagra. Generally, these second-stage symptoms last three to four months before disappearing to await the following spring. This characteristic remission of the disease, in fact, must have been still one more source of confusion in that it undoubtedly led many physicians to believe they had "cured" their patient, and this in turn would have obscured the chronic nature of the malady and prevented recognition of this "new" disease.

The third stage of pellagra is characterized by severe cerebrospinal disturbances with the afflicted complaining of itching on the feet and backs of hands, burning sensations in the limbs, shoulders and stomach, a dull headache, and dizziness. Other manifestations include acute melancholia, a conviction of unpardonable sin, delirium, hallucinations, disorientation, and stupor. The fourth and last stage (the wasting stage) sees the onset of increasing weight loss, severe diarrhea, and finally death, often because a weakened condition leaves the victim unable to resist intercurrent diseases. Thus the four Ds of pellagra – diarrhea, dermatitis, dementia, and death – go hand in hand with a myriad of other symptoms.

Because pellagra was not a known and identifiable disease to nineteenth-century physicians combined with the protean manifestations of the illness, any attempt today to discover its presence yesterday is quite complicated. Because the slave diet for many must have been pellagra-producing, however, a few assumptions can be made that may assist in the search.

First, pellagra could easily have gone unrecognized as a disease *sui generis*, while it remained quietly, undramatically endemic during those winter and spring months when the niacin–tryptophan intake was low and the leucine intake proportionately heavy. In other words, so long as pellagra ebbed and flowed with the seasons, and so long as the slaves' margin of dietary safety was sufficient to permit them either to escape the disease entirely or contract it in a mild form to be terminated by seasonal remission, it could easily have escaped detection.

It seems equally reasonable, however (and this brings up the second assumption), that economic vicissitudes on occasion may have forced the exclusion of enough pellagra-preventing "extras" in the slave regimen to have triggered the disease in epidemic form. These epidemics would have compelled antebellum physicians, after searching through their collective corpus of experience, to acknowledge that they were confronted with a new disease.

A search for pellagra during slave days, therefore, must include both a suspicious rummaging through those symptoms that spelled this or that "familiar" disease to antebellum doctors and a ferreting out of an exotic pellagralike malady from the lexicon, as well as the literature, of antebellum medicine. Fortunately, both tasks are facilitated by the peculiar division of that nosologic lexicon into black and white diseases. Interestingly, the black section of that lexicon does include a very likely candidate for the epidemic "new disease" with the pellagralike symptoms. The disease in question became suddenly epidemic in portions of the South during the middle 1840s,[59] poor agricultural years for the region, coming hard on the heels of a few disastrous ones. Because of low cotton prices, a need would have existed for much economy on the plantation. Presumably this led to a cutback of outside food purchases – fertile ground for pellagra.[60]

That this "very extraordinary and fatal epidemic"[61] was "virulent on plantations"[62] and struck at blacks almost exclusively[63] does nothing to lessen its candidacy, while its assigned name – black tongue – positively campaigns for its election, as the term "black tongue" has been employed to denote canine pellagra during this century.[64] Black tongue is a symptomatic appellation that crudely describes that thick brown coating on the tongues of stricken dogs. Antebellum physicians called their new disease "black tongue" because its victims manifested a similar "prominent, though by no means invariable" symptom.[65]

An excellent clinical description of black tongue was given in 1844 by Mississippi physician, W. R. Puckett, who observed the following symptoms: skin – trauma to external skin often caused an inflammation; tongue – "covered with a dirty looking grey coat with red edges";

dermal lesions – included "a serous oozing of an acid character"; glands and mucous membranes – "extensively implicated"; throat – soreness common; limbs, back, and shoulders – pain common; eyes – a "reddish cast."[66] What Dr. Puckett has done is to describe all of the classic prodromal symptoms of pellagra, save perhaps diarrhea, which is an undisturbing omission as diarrhea often does not occur in the early stages of pellagra, and at more advanced stages it would have been purposely induced by purging, a standard medical treatment.

Additionally, the seasonal behavior of black tongue seems as remarkably pellagralike as its symptoms. It first appeared during the *winter* and *spring* months, precisely those months in which pellagra customarily made its appearance during the early decades of this century. Even more significantly, the disease *reappeared* the following winter and spring with even greater virulence, which incidentally had been forecast by the editors of the *New Orleans Medical and Surgical Journal* with more prescience than was customary in the antebellum medical world.[67] This time, too, the disease was not confined to the deep South but was reported in Tennessee and North Carolina as well.[68]

Finally, the protean character of pellagra is suggested by Dr. Puckett's lament that at first "I thought I had several diseases to contend with."[69] As one reads this Mississippi physician, in fact, the impression is that had black tongue not been epidemic throughout the doctor's region, the affliction would have passed as one of those "several diseases." He confessed, for example, to being particularly confused by those symptoms of black tongue that pointed to "typhoid pneumonia."[70] Moreover, he used the term "erysipelatous fever" synonymously with black tongue, and other colleagues too felt that black tongue might simply be a more virulent kind of erysipelas.[71] The latter, also known as St. Anthony's fire, is a disease in its own right – an acute inflammatory affliction of the skin brought on by infection due to various strains of streptococcus – and one more disguise that pellagra could easily have worn.

Again in 1849, a Georgia physician wrote of "black tongue," calling it an "epidemic disease." Its premonitory signs were lethargy, chills, fever and pain. Next came diarrhea, delirium, inflamed skin, and finally the "strength and mind fail."[72] Following this report on black tongue, however, there was little more mention of it in epidemic form throughout the remainder of the antebellum period.[73] Thus, the problem at this point is, simply put, did pellagra (assuming black tongue was pellagra) vanish completely or instead, because of plantation belt tightening, permit a few physicians a glimpse of its cerberus-like countenance in epidemic form and then resume its habit of appearing incognito in a quietly endemic fashion?

A look at a few of the so-called Negro diseases of the period may provide some clues. It has already been noted, for example, that symptoms of "typhoid pneumonia" were manifested by victims of black tongue. Of all the Negro diseases southern medical men agreed that typhoid pneumonia was the most dangerous.[74] But there was little agreement among them as to what exactly constituted this disease. According to Dr. Warren Brickell of New Orleans, it was "comparatively a new disease amongst us" called by many the cold plague, head pleurisy, and bilious pleurisy.[75] Yet despite the manner in which the appellations appear to implicate the lungs, physicians who described this disease often omitted respiratory symptoms entirely.

Rather, most cases of typhoid pneumonia began "in January and February, although it often commences in November and continues through April"[76]; prominent symptoms included a "tongue red at the edges, covered with a dry brown crust" and a dry mouth "parched, with sordes," although often "there are no other symptoms than debility and wandering pains" along with skin lesions.[77] Certainly on the basis of these symptoms, typhoid pneumonia could easily have been pellagra.

Dr. Thompson McGown described epidemics of "typhoid pneumonia" that took place in middle Tennessee and northern Alabama during late 1846 and 1847. The sickness came with late winter and early spring, and was "particularly prevalent and fatal amongst the negroes." Yet young children "seldom, if ever" contracted it.[78] Young children in the twentieth century also were rarely victims of pellagra. Only 1 percent of all pellagra cases involved youngsters, and the disease was *extremely* rare in those under three years of age.[79]

Some believed that typhoid pneumonia was merely an advanced stage of typhoid or typhus, terms which southern physicians employed interchangeably and meant to denote a condition whose symptoms included a black or brown tongue, stupor, and reddened spots on the body. It was generally agreed that blacks were particularly susceptible to the two diseases. Because neither were reputed to have been widespread in the antebellum South, however, one might reasonably suspect pellagra once again on the basis of the pellagralike symptoms and behavior of both diseases.[80]

Epidemics of "typhoid fever" described by Dr. H. G. Davenport of Georgia began in the late fall and winter of 1846 and recurred each winter through the winter of 1850. The symptoms, which mysteriously disappeared in the spring, included skin eruptions, lassitude, "giddiness," back pains, diarrhea, and a coated tongue with a red tip. The doctor was puzzled that poorer whites in the neighborhood did not contract the disease and concluded that poor diet on the part of the slaves, along with their "filthy habits," accounted for it.[81]

More telling still are the remarks that the editors of the *New Orleans Medical and Surgical Journal* appended to Dr. Davenport's article. They felt this article confirmed their earlier warning that an epidemic "characterized by typhoid symptoms, is gradually spreading over the Southwestern portion of the United States."[82] Significantly, they urged that the cure for this form of "typhoid fever" was to *feed your patient* [our italics] . . . The tongue will assume a healthy and natural appearance – the raving delirium will abate, and the secretions will improve, under a well-selected and well-timed system of diet."[83]

Dr. A. V. Faut of Mississippi and Dr. N. H. Morague of South Carolina diagnosed the fever that persisted in their respective regions on the basis of a reddish tongue at the "tip and edges" changing to "black as the disease progresses;" both noted diarrhea and skin lesions in the cases they treated.[84] Dr. E. M. Pendleton of Georgia suggested that "typhoid" in his region actually belonged to "another class of fevers" which occurred during the cold months and was known among the common people as the "*slow fever.*"[85]

Actually, as can be seen by the above, terms such as "typhoid pneumonia," "typhoid," "typhus," and the like had only a hazy meaning, and therefore pellagra's presence may have frequently been disguised by the semantical undergrowth of the antebellum medical world. A whimsical discourse by Dr. Cartwright on "malum egyptiacum" helps make the point. He informed his colleagues that black tongue was synonymous with erysipelas, spotted fever, putrid sore throat, cold plague, typhoid pneumonia, and malignant scarlet fever, and all were in actuality one disease: diphtheria.[86] Fortunately for the reputation of southern medicine, the doctor's place in its history lies elsewhere than the arena of acute clinical diagnosis. He was, however, a self-proclaimed expert on "Negro diseases," and the fact that many southern physicians felt they needed an expert stemmed in large part from the diagnostic problems with which the black patients confronted them.

Darker pigmentation, for example, often served to obscure those external symptoms that physicians had learned to recognize. One Louisiana doctor, who discusses a case encountered during the 1850s, complained that "the dark color of the skin rendered it impossible to recognize the rose-colored eruption, so characteristic of this form of fever," which he called typhoid.[87] That the characteristic rose-colored eruption may have meant pellagra is suggested by another physician who a few years earlier had penned an article which argued that typhoid pneumonia was simply a more virulent manifestation of typhoid fever and that synonyms for the disease included "cold plague," which in turn, according to Cartwright, was black tongue.[88]

Many other "Negro diseases" may also have camouflaged pellagra. An affliction high on the list of slave ailments is dysentery, which of course one usually associates with foul drinking water, spoiled or badly prepared food, and generally unsanitary conditions. Yet dysentery should not have been a malady monopolized by blacks, while a close look at the medical literature reveals that some physicians speaking of "negro dysentery" meant a "peculiar form" of the affliction because it was accompanied by a stage of skin inflammation that progressed to "sloughing" (scabbing) without the usual ulcerative process. One doctor reported that dysentery on certain plantations was a kind of "scarlet fever,"[89] all of which seems remarkably suggestive of the dermatologic ravages of pellagra, and the close connection between the disruptive bowels and eruptive skin that antebellum physicians believed occurred in tandem sharpen the suspicion.[90]

These then are a few of the nineteenth-century black-related diseases which could easily have concealed pellagra in its early stages. A host of other candidates including dengue, dropsy, marasmus, quinsy, and syphilis have not been dealt with, for the point is that pellagralike symptoms, such as a dull headache, dizziness, spasms, weight loss, dermatitis, and diarrhea, would have suggested a myriad of maladies to southern physicians. They, in turn, would have diagnosed on the basis of the most prominent symptoms. Thus, pellagra cases would have been seen as fever, dermatologic, or bowel cases, permitting the disease itself to escape identification for decades with the assistance of recurring spring and summer remissions.

Advanced pellagrins would probably have been few. Even in these cases, however, the pellagrins' well-known susceptibility to pneumonia, tubercular infection, and heart failure suggests that the disease could still in its latter stages have maintained its disguise. In this connection, although admittedly pure speculation, it is interesting to note that advanced pellagrins often display symptoms of mental disorder, ranging from acute melancholia to the conviction that they are being poisoned or possessed by evil spirits, with some revealing a propensity for hurling themselves into bodies of water.[91] Students of the antebellum South are aware of the not infrequent cases of dementia on plantations, including those slaves who insisted they had been poisoned or hexed.[92] They also know of the abnormally large percentage of slave deaths by drowning.[93] African religious and cultural vestiges usually comprise an explanation of the former, while the blacks' addiction to fishing and heavier bone structure has been assumed to at least partially account for the latter. Yet the possibility of an interrelationship between these phenomena and pellagra remains intriguing.

In summary, it is once more stressed that simply because pellagra was not recognized as a disease during the antebellum period does not mean it did not exist. Rather given the chemical composition of the slave diet, it would be amazing if it did not, at least in endemic form. For this reason it seems highly significant that those afflictions most easily mistaken for pellagra were regarded as peculiarly Negro diseases by southern medical men. Furthermore, it is likely that any contraction of the already limited number of supplements in the slaves' diet would have transformed pellagra from an endemic to an epidemic disease. At

a time of economic retrenchment on the part of many planters throughout the South, therefore, it is telling that "black tongue," a new and
strange disease with pronounced pellagralike symptoms, appeared in
epidemic form.

Pellagra most probably did exist as a serious health problem in the
antebellum South. If this is true, and pellagra did pass as many of the
so-called Negro diseases, then the possibility is raised that this one
disease may have constituted a portion of the entire "package."

VIII

Before leaving primary nutritional disease and turning to the problem
of secondary afflictions a few caveats are in order. It has not been
argued (although on occasion it may have seemed that way) that all
slaves were malnourished or that almost all slave morbidity and mortality was a consequence of nutritional deficiencies. Rather, the objec-
tive has been to point out the peculiarly unbalanced nature of the core
of the slaves' regimen, to couple this with some physiologic characteristics possessed by many of West African origin that tended to accentu-
ate the harmful aspects of that diet, and to link the whole with a group
of diseases to which American slaves seemed singularly (and heretofore inexplicably) susceptible.

Unquestionably, the diet of many slaves included foods ranging
from greens to game that successfully offset the deficiencies of the
core; unquestionably, slaves died from legitimate cases of tetanus and
epilepsy and managed to drown themselves on their own without
pellagra prodding them into the water. Certainly, too, the state of
nineteenth-century medicine leaves one uneasy. That physicians and
laymen, believers in "Negro" diseases, diagnosed the diseases of
blacks implies at least some degree of circularity. This means that the
causes of some percentage of the deaths recorded represent little
more than self-fulfilling prophecies.

Finally, there is semantical confusion. Today the term marasmus, for
example, connotes a form of protein–calorie malnutrition. During the
antebellum period it meant simply a "wasting" disease that could have
been protein–calorie malnutrition, or "scrofula" or a manifestation of a
host of ailments. The disease "scrofula" (another black disease), in fact,
underscores the point. Some doctors believed it was a form of consumption (tuberculosis) and called it "Negro consumption."[94] Others
however termed dirt eating "negro consumption," while still others
intended the term "scrofula" to mean skin lesions in a general sort of
way.[95] Thus the word "scrofula" was probably used to describe victims
of diseases as serious as pellagra, kwashiorkor, marasmus, and tuberculosis, as well as afflictions such as pica and worms, and nuisances
such as lice and fleas.

Nonetheless, surely it is more than mere coincidence that the glaring nutritional deficiencies in the diet of many slaves would have produced that set of symptoms which spelled "Negro diseases" to the antebellum physician. "Poor" whites undoubtedly ate the same core, and a reasonable supposition is that they represented the bulk of the whites who succumbed to "Negro" diseases. Yet to reiterate, the slaves would on the whole have suffered more than whites from the same diet because of (1) their lactose intolerance, (2) their difficulty in acquiring sufficient vitamin D, and (3) the tendency of hardworking slaves to average a higher caloric intake than poor whites that would in turn have heightened their requirements for certain chief nutrients.

It seems a reasonable conclusion, therefore, that the slave regimen was accountable for much of the mortality from the so-called Negro diseases, and this in turn suggests the following: As pointed out in Chapter 4, black and white mortality rates have been seen as roughly similar during antebellum days, which has been taken as an important measure of slave well-being. Blacks and whites, however, were not dying of the same diseases at the same rates. Had blacks not possessed relative immunities to yellow fever and malaria (or alternately, had whites not perished in large numbers from these diseases), then it is difficult to escape the suspicion that given their high level of mortality due to "Negro diseases," the collective death rate of blacks might have been far in excess of that of the whites.

Finally, there is the interesting problem of the long-term effects worked on the human personality by a dietary deficiency of the B vitamins. As we have seen, the slave diet was lacking in the B complex, and these vitamins in particular help to determine one's state of mind as well as the manner in which one reacts to outside stimuli. Their relative absence over time can produce lethargy, even apathy and, if severe, acute melancholia – personality disorders which some students of slavery have discovered in abundance on southern plantations.[96] Should it ever be convincingly demonstrated that slaves did indeed possess such personality disorders to an uncommon degree, then, of course, any explanation must include a multitude of factors ranging from the constricting totality of the institution of slavery to chronic illness. But it may be that the slave diet was also at fault and hence responsible for more than physical illnesses.

CHAPTER 9

SELECTION FOR INFECTION

In human experience mortality from infectious diseases appears to
be more closely related to malnutrition than is the incidence of such
diseases.

Ian Taylor and John Knowelden (1964)[1]

A medical gentleman at Savannah told me, that pulmonary complaints are those which prove most fatal to the negroes.

Basil Hall (1829)[2]

I

Antebellum physicians – like old gossips – delighted in passing along
novel observations, and some of their juiciest tidbits dealt with the
peculiar habits of slaves. One custom they tittered about was the "universal practice among them of covering their head and faces, during
sleep, with a blanket, or any kind of covering they can get hold of,"
even when it meant leaving the feet exposed.[3] Another was the slaves'
tendency to bundle up for sleep despite the temperature, while still
another was their tendency to sleep head first close to roaring fires
regardless of the season.[4] Astounded visitors joined physicians in reporting that even "in the hottest days in summer they are never without fires in their huts,"[5] and according to at least one observer, the
bondsmen's fascination with fire had a substantial impact on plantation
architecture. "The kitchens," he remarked "are always at the distance
of several yards from the principal dwelling. This is done as well to
guard against the house negroes through carelessness setting the
house on fire, for they generally sit over it half the night . . . over a
large fire in the summer, when I could scarcely endure the excessive
heat of the night in open air."[6]

It is tempting to view this preoccupation with warmth as a kind of
preventive medicine. True, fires provided them with psychological
comfort and served as a gathering place as well. But at least one observer noted that slaves believed "smoke is wholesome,"[7] while their
custom of sleeping with heads covered in close proximity to a fireplace

134

may have represented a conscious attempt to ward off lung diseases, considered to be "the greatest outlet of life among them."[8]

Antebellum physicians believed that the cause of the extraordinary slave mortality from lung ailments was due to their smaller lungs relative to those of whites. Interestingly, modern science has confirmed at least part of this hypothesis. Black males, and to a lesser extent females, do possess a smaller vital lung capacity than their white counterparts, given similarities in age, weight, and standing height.[9] But whether physicians of yesterday were correct in inferring that this was the cause of an unusual black susceptibility to respiratory disease is another matter that research has not yet resolved. It is true that historically blacks in their West African homeland and throughout the Americas as well have suffered from a higher incidence of fatal respiratory difficulties than Caucasians. Indeed, in North America today, they still suffer a mortality rate from these causes far above that sustained by whites.[10] But how much can be blamed on inheritable susceptibility and how much on nutrition, clothing, housing, and other environmental factors remains to be discovered.

There is, however, another innate characteristic having to do with the relative tolerance for cold on the part of black and white that may bear on the problem. Here again antebellum physicians anticipated modern scientific research with their observation that cold weather punished Negroes far more than Caucasians.[11] Studies conducted in the aftermath of the Korean War demonstrated conclusively that blacks do have a poorer adaptive response to cold exposure than whites. Their metabolic rates are much slower to increase than whites, their cold hemagglutinin titers are higher, and the black's tendency to shiver (a defense to warm the body) occurs later than a white's tendency in the same circumstances.[12] But again, relationships between this relative inability to withstand cold and pulmonary illness have yet to be established.

Nevertheless, on a priori grounds it is justifiable to suspect that a smaller vital capacity coupled with a greater intolerance for cold had something to do with the black's susceptibility to respiratory infection in the slave quarters. Additionally vague suspicions aside, good solid medical reasons exist to explain the susceptibility of some slaves. Victims of sickle cell anemia, for example, suffer more frequently from acute pulmonary infection, while possessors of the sickle trait as well as hemoglobin C disease also are more liable to lung complaints.[13] Moreover, respiratory symptoms are often observed in persons invaded by certain worms which, as we have seen, was an especially acute health problem for slaves.[14] Outdoor work in wet weather, flimsy cabins, and inadequate clothing must all have also played considerable roles in slave susceptibility.

Slave nutrition, however, was very possibly at the root of the high frequency of black mortality from respiratory infection, the catalyst that transformed a genetic or environmental predisposition to illness into death. For as a rule, malnourished peoples suffer a higher rate of mortality from infectious diseases than the well-nourished,[15] in part because antibodies, needed to fight the infection, derive from serum proteins. Thus, malnutrition reduces the level of serum proteins in the body and therefore the antibody level in the blood, retarding the body's ability to intensify other mechanisms with which it combats infection. Finally, poor nutrition can create a kind of vicious malnutrition–infection cycle, whereby infection further taxes already depleted nutritional reserves, leaving the body even more vulnerable when exposed to the next infectious disease.[16]

The slaves' nutritional status then could frequently have made the difference between morbidity statistics and mortality statistics when they were stricken with any of the following diseases of the respiratory system, all of which were statistically far more liable to kill blacks than whites in the South.

II

"An undernourished child contracting whooping cough is more likely to die of this disease than a healthy child similarly infected,"[17] state epidemiologists. Because whooping cough was in a league with worms as a major killer of slave (as opposed to white) youngsters it may be inferred that in the antebellum South the "healthy" children were the whites. Of the 1,820 deaths from this sickness in our sampling of seven states during the year 1849–50, only 28 percent or 512 of the victims were white. The blacks therefore contributed a hefty 72 percent of the fatalities. In terms of live populations, the differential is even more pronounced. Fully 166 of every 100,000 black youngsters aged ten and under succumbed to the disease as opposed to only 47 of every 100,000 white children in the same age cohort.

Mortality data from the city of Charleston provide similar statistics; from 1822 until 1848, 357 deaths from pertussis were registered.[18] Again 72 percent of the victims were black, although the black and white populations were roughly equal throughout the period. Among other things this suggests that the circumstances of plantation living which found children in daily intimate contact did not put them in more jeopardy of contracting whooping cough than urban counterparts. Conversely, the relative isolation of the plantation does not seem to have provided children with any real measure of protection from the disease.

Today pertussis mortality data still reveal an enormous differential by race. During the years 1959–61, the rate of death from whooping cough in the United States was nine times higher in black infants than white, while in 1969 "one and one-half times as many [black infants as white] died from pertussis, even though black infants comprise only 11 percent of the United States infant population."[19] Of course much of today's differential is probably explicable in terms of the greater percentage of white children who are immunized. But some of the difference is probably also attributable to nutritional circumstances. Certainly this was the case on the plantations.

To begin with, pertussis is synergistic with rickets, which means that rachitic children tend to have far more serious cases of pertussis, and rickets was a serious problem on the plantation.[20] Moreover, a vitamin C deficiency not only renders one more susceptible to infection, but enhances considerably the likelihood that the infection in question will become fatal; vitamin C was among the most conspicuous of the chief nutrients denied slaves in adequate amounts.

Additionally, an inadequate supply of protein would have impaired a slave child's chance of recovering from whooping cough for reasons just discussed. It is worth recalling that planters deliberately withheld animal protein from young children especially, because they believed it to be prejudicial to the children's health. Furthermore, the barrier against infective agents also breaks down when vitamins A, D, and the B complex are lacking in the tissue[21]; in the case of A and D it was noted that slaves would have been deficient in these vitamins for at least part of the year, while most were lacking in the B group throughout much of the year.

Finally, pertussis was probably responsible for even more mortality than that reflected in antebellum mortality schedules, because whooping cough deaths are frequently the result of concurrent bacterial infection that enters the lungs causing bronchopneumonia. Because whooping cough involves "catarrh" of the respiratory passages, "catarrh" may well have been given as the cause of some pertussis deaths.

III

While drawing up their lists of black diseases, few southern physicians failed to include pneumonia, often referring to the condition by appellations such as "lung fever" and "winter fever."[22] These synonyms, however, were replaced in the mortality schedules for the 1849–50 census by two categories only: pneumonia and catarrh, the former presumably connoting clear pulmonary symptoms, while the latter signified deadly "colds." Returns from the seven major slave states in 1849–50 reveal that the pair accounted for 6 percent of the white and 8 percent of the black mortality, indicting respiratory difficulties as a major killer of bondsmen. Fully 4,184 deaths in these states were blamed on pneumonia and another 977 on catarrh. By race, pneumonia took 59 percent of its victims from the black population, while catarrh was even more selective. Fully 71 percent of its targets had dark skin. In terms of total live population, the racial preferences of the two diseases were even more pronounced felling 62 of every 100,000 whites yet 125 of every 100,000 blacks. Slaves then were about twice as liable to die from pneumococcal infections as their masters.

When called upon to account for the differential, physicians of the period tended to focus reproachfully on the "weak lungs" of Negroes and in so doing were groping for racially predisposing factors.[23] Some of their modern successors have done the same to explain why blacks in the United States today are afflicted with an incidence of pneumonia about five times greater than whites,[24] and why black pneumonia mortality rates have soared far above the white rate throughout this century.[25]

Quite properly environmental factors have also weighed heavily in their accounting for something of a black monopoly on the disease. In the past, a few thoughtful physicians looked beyond African lungs to the conditions of slave life, castigating planters for exposing bondsmen to the elements, exhorting them to dress slaves warmly in flannel clothing and woolen stockings, and to look to the slave cabins making certain they were dry, adequately ventilated, and well stocked with blankets.[26] These important suggestions surely were beneficial when heeded. But medical men could not know that vitamin D deficiency predisposes an individual to the invasion of viruses and consequently to viral pneumonia.[27]

Undoubtedly, the fact that 25 percent of the pneumonia deaths during the year 1849–50 occurred during the winter and 44 percent took place in the spring signifies more than that these are the coldest months. They are also the months when blacks in particular have grave difficulties in utilizing sunlight to produce an adequate supply of vitamin D. Moreover, the months in question were also those in which fresh vegetables and hence many vitamins were in scarce supply. Rickets, which we have surmised was widespread among black children, frequently leads to pneumonia, and the absence of "garden sass" (a source of calcium) when coupled with vitamin D deficiency would surely have made the winter and spring seasons the worst months for rickets.

Additionally, the pica habit in which many bondsmen indulged diminishes the body's ability to resist infectious disease as does even mild iron deficiency that was both linked to the habit and inherent in slave comestibles.[28] Animals placed on a diet heavy in Indian corn have proven inordinately susceptible to pneumonia, presumably because of the many essential vitamins and minerals that corn fails to provide.[29] Moreover, studies of African tribes have shown that those living only on vegetable diets have a rate of respiratory infection "incomparably greater" than those with animal protein included,[30] and the slave diet, while not devoid of animal protein, was dismally lacking in protein of good quality.

Thus, an unfortunate combination of circumstances ranging from a temperate climate to pica usage created a heightened black susceptibility to pneumonia. Environmental factors such as clothing and housing were also important elements while genetic differences in vital capacity and cold response may have played a role as well. But at bottom, the slave's inability to resist fatal pneumonia may well have stemmed from the absence of those foods that could have helped their bodies to resist the infection.

IV

"Many diseases", wrote a Louisiana physician in 1902, "are more frequent in the Negroes [today] which in the days of their slavery were comparatively rare. By far the most frequent and fatal of these is tuberculosis . . . At the present rate of increase of tuberculosis among the negroes, it is just a question of time when this disease will completely exterminate the race."[31]

This quotation neatly frames another epidemiologic problem, similar to that encountered earlier with pellagra. Tuberculosis *should* have been prevalent among the slaves, but reputedly was a strictly postbellum scourge of blacks. There are two major reasons why the white plague should have been no stranger to slave quarters. First, blacks historically have revealed an inefficient immunologic response to tubercle bacilli, a susceptibility that apparently stems from an abbreviated association with the disease. West Africans knew nothing of tuberculosis until its importation by Europeans and, thus, along with other "virgin soil" peoples such as the American Indians and Eskimos, have proved far more vulnerable to it than individuals of European descent, whose longer familiarity with the disease has endowed them with resistance.[32] Today blacks still develop more malignant cases of the disease and at earlier ages than whites (the black death rate from tuberculosis was 4.7 times that of whites in 1969); and this susceptibility should have been substantially more pronounced yesterday on the plantation.[33]

A second reason for suspecting far more tuberculosis among the slaves than is commonly believed has to do with nutrition, for a high correlation exists between tuberculosis mortality and malnutrition. Lack of vitamins A, C, B_1, B_2, and B_3, along with calcium, iron, and amino acid deficiencies, have all been heavily implicated as factors contributing to the body's inability to fight off the infection. As already seen, vitamin C was chronically absent from the slave diet, vitamin A was for many available only seasonally, while the essential amino acids in many instances were lacking or seriously out of proportion.[34] To illustrate something of the possible relationship between amino acid deficiency and tuberculosis infection, we refer once more to the study of African tribes living exclusively on vegetable diets, as opposed to those whose diets are balanced with animal protein. In the case of tuberculosis, the former tribes sustained a rate six times greater than those who regularly consumed meat.[35]

Immunologically and nutritionally then, slaves should have proven inordinately susceptible to tuberculosis. Yet the judgment of antebellum physicians had "consumption" uncommon in slaves,[36] a judgment accepted by postbellum physicians and modern authorities alike. Indeed postbellum physicians who suddenly found themselves confronted with tubercle bacilli infecting black bodies were emphatic in their near unanimous declaration that the illness was a postwar phenomenon, triggered by the freed slave's inability to care for himself, as opposed, of course, to the slave days when he was supposedly well cared for by his master. Many modern students of the problem, on the other hand, have explained the supposed rarity of the disease in the slave quarters on the basis of the somewhat isolated plantation acting to quarantine the bondsmen from what essentially is an urban disease, requiring more than casual contact for transmission.[37]

Obscured in this effort at explanation, however, is that tuberculosis never was a stranger in the slave huts. A look at differential mortality drawn from the seven southern states during 1849–50 reveals that of the 4,059 deaths from "consumption," blacks, who comprised 44 percent of the population, furnished 37 percent of the consumptives. Thus, although whites had a somewhat greater risk of dying from "consumption," with the disease killing 80 out of every 100,000 whites and 60 out of every 100,000 blacks, it was nonetheless hardly as uncommon to antebellum blacks as the literature would have it.

Still one might argue that because of the immunologic and nutritional factors already discussed blacks should have been far more susceptible than they appear to have been both absolutely and relative to whites. Against this, however, is that the rate of southern mortality from tuberculosis in general was much less than the rate in northern states, as for example in Massachusetts (344 per 100,000 live population in 1849–50), due to the South's predominately rural nature. Because a far larger percentage of blacks than whites were rural dwellers during the antebellum period, therefore, this factor alone may explain why blacks did not suffer more from the disease than whites despite their greater immunologic and nutritional susceptibilities.

What little urban data exist from the period do tend to corroborate this position. In Charleston, the mortality rate of both races was substantially higher than in the South as a whole. During the years 1822–48, "consumption" killed an average of 59 blacks and 47 whites annually for a total of 1,261 white and 1,589 black victims.[38] Based on the city's 1850 population, the annual death rates by race per 100,000 live population would have been 235 for the whites and 257 for the blacks.

Hence blacks and whites similarly exposed to "consumption" in an urban environment died at similar rates, although the black rate was somewhat higher. But the larger problem remains. For the reasons already outlined, when equal numbers of blacks and whites were similarly exposed black fatalities should have substantially outweighed those of whites. Before addressing the problem further, we feel it wise to glance for a moment at the pathology of tuberculosis, a disease that can be acquired in four ways. Bacilli may invade the body through the contaminated milk of tubercular cows or contaminated food; occasionally tubercular mothers pass the disease to unborn children; but most commonly, it travels in air droplets from infected human beings.[39]

Once inside the body the bacilli find their way through the lymph channels to establish infection in the nearest lymph nodes. Bacilli ingested in contaminated milk or food would tend to manifest their presence in the neck and intestinal regions, while those inhaled would concentrate in the lungs. Even as "primary infection" is occurring, however, the invading bacilli are swarmed upon by white cells of the blood and tissues which probably explains why they normally do so little damage at first, and the victim shows few symptoms. The little damaged patches in the organs begin to heal, the lymph glands return to normal size. and the individual with a good state of natural resistance has in effect cured himself.

For those less fortunate the complications that may beset them come under the heading of "postprimary" infection. This can develop from primary infections that fail to heal, but rather lay more or less dormant for months or even years until suddenly still living tubercle bacilli show renewed activity and commence spreading, via the blood, to other organs. Or the host may take in fresh bacilli that produce the same effect, namely a body suddenly sensitized to the toxic effect of tubercular infection that responds much differently to the postprimary than it did to the primary infection. Indeed, the reaction is sometimes quite violent leading to rapid tissue destruction and death.

Yet here again, the body may rally, mount a successful resistance, and heal itself, although the usual form for the disease to assume is the classic lingering one leading ultimately to death, perhaps directly from the infection or indirectly from weakened defenses that lower resistance to other diseases. But the just described behavior of the disease is normal only in populations having generations of intimacy with it. In their case, the widespread distribution of the illness to many organs (miliary tuberculosis) and a rapid degeneration of lung tissue (galloping consumption) were the most terrifying forms of the disease, but not all that common. Usually the tubercle bacillus is eliminated in the primary stage, and even if postprimary infection occurs it spreads quite slowly.

But with inexperienced peoples the disease acts much differently and is far more deadly because of the body's inability to muster defenses against the primary infection. Examples demonstrating the point are legion. One outstanding illustration is the experience of the West African troops and laborers brought to France in large numbers during World War I who suffered a "death rate from tuberculosis . . . enormously higher than amongst white troops and the disease was usually far more rapidly fatal."[40]

It is important to note that this phenomenon occurred among a twentieth-century black population with at least some historical contact with the disease. More demonstrative of the impact of the disease on a virgin people is the dreadful experience of North American Indians, whose sudden exposure to tuberculosis produced death rates some ten times higher than those sustained by Europeans during the worst of their earlier epidemics. Perhaps the most terrible example was the comparatively recent fate of a previously remote Indian tribe in western Canada that was practically decimated after exposure to tuberculosis with an incredible annual mortality rate of 9,000 per 100,000 live population.[41]

Unfortunate as this latter experience was it did have the heuristic effect of yielding precise observations on clinical manifestations of the disease in a "virginal" population. These observations are particularly germane to an understanding of the possible behavior of tuberculosis in many slave bodies. It seems that the first and second generations of Indians infected *revealed few pulmonary cases* ("consumption") but rather "extensive glandular involvement," particularly in school-age children.[42] It was only when the disease passed to the third generation that it revealed a decisive predilection for settling in the lungs, while glandular involvement fell to about 7 percent among schoolchildren. By the time a fourth generation hosted the disease, glandular involvement had fallen to less than 1 percent.[43]

Clearly, tuberculosis followed a much different course in peoples who have had a history of contact with it. The first two Indian generations obviously had difficulty in localizing the infection, so much that "only microscopic analysis allowed doctors to recognize the disease as tuberculosis."[44] Yet with the third and fourth generations, tuberculosis began to assume that form with which western peoples are familiar.

This manifestation of "extraordinary" symptoms in populations inexperienced with a disease (symptoms which later disappear as the populations develop resistance) is a familiar one in the pages of medical history. Generations are required for natural selection to weed out the most susceptible and those who simply cannot adapt; time must pass too while host and pathogen work out a coexistence that permits both to survive. In the case of tuberculosis, it has been hypothesized that "it takes something over a hundred years after its first contact . . . for a race to develop a resistance against the disease equivalent to that of a European population."[45]

In the above quote one suspects that the word "race" was employed very loosely, and what really was meant was a group of people living in close proximity to one another. In the "balkanized" West Africa to which the white plague was introduced from Europe, the disease would have spread slowly; so slowly in fact that despite the presence of tuberculosis in parts of West Africa, most blacks dispatched to the Americas would have had no contact with it. Then, given rural residence and the restrictions on mobility imposed by slavery, contact for many probably would have been delayed for generations.

But to return to the problem, it is not so surprising after all that, although a number of slaves developed recognizable cases of tuberculosis (recognizable because of those pulmonary symptoms with which physicians were familiar), the percentage that did so was somewhat lower than that of white fellow sufferers despite a black nutritional and immunologic liability. Those who did contract "consumption" clearly had made the same adjustments to the disease as Europeans. But the example of the western Canadian Indians suggests that other slaves were less able to come to terms with tuberculosis, and therefore would have displayed those same "extra pulmonary" symptoms that were initially so confusing to physicians attending the Indians, and that would have proved even more baffling to antebellum doctors. In other words, many slaves would have suffered from a form of tuberculosis that would inevitably have been misdiagnosed.

The peculiar antebellum "Negro" disease, scrofula, is interesting in this regard. Today scrofula describes a condition of a tubercular nature derived from infected cows that is especially manifested in a chronic enlargement and cheesy degeneration of the lymphatic glands, particularly in the neck and abdomen.[46] But in times prior to pasteurization, a disease transmitted by milk could hardly have flourished among black people characterized by a high incidence of lactose intolerance and limited access to dairy products while leaving almost untouched white people who had a low incidence of lactose intolerance and a much greater access to milk. Southern medical literature makes at least one clear point on "scrofula": it was preeminently another "Negro" disease.[47]

A Kentucky physician labeled scrofula the "great scourge" of Negroes, a disease he preferred to call "struma Africana," struma being one more synonym for scrofula.[48] Others, however, opted for terms such as "cachexia Africana," Negro consumption, or Negro poison,[49] appellations that also may be suggestive of tubercular conditions. Autopsies performed on black scrofula victims revealed organs "studded with tubercles."[50] Because the lymphatic conditions in the neck and abdomen could not be bovine tuberculosis, the suspicion is that this illness was tuberculosis displaying the same miliary symptoms that it has in other inexperienced populations.

During 1849–50 fully 71 percent (383) of the 537 deaths from scrofula in seven southern states were black suggesting, among other things, that although scrofula deserved its reputation as a "Negro disease" it was not the fearsome killer portrayed by much of the literature. On the other hand, our seven-state sample in this case appears to be yielding somewhat skewed data. Virginia alone contributed almost half (241) of the scrofula deaths, while Louisiana and Alabama combined counted only 70 victims of the disease during the same year. Conversely, Kentucky and Tennessee (states not included in the sample) together buried 284 victims of the disease of whom 67 percent were black. In terms of live black population, the disease killed 42 per 100,000 in the two border states as opposed to only 12 per 100,000 in the two Deep South states. The disease then seems to have entertained geographic as well as racial preferences, with the three upper Southern states of Tennessee, Kentucky, and Virginia supplying the bulk of Dixie's scrofula victims (64 percent of the nine states under scrutiny).

This inclination to pursue prey on more northerly turf was not lost on border state physicians who ascribed to cold "the power of exciting or bringing on scrofulus afflictions," all of which neatly excused the more northerly states their disproportionate share of victims.[51] Yet tuberculosis is a disease of tropical and temperate zones as well as those reputedly "healthy" places in between as Indians in Arizona disastrously discovered.[52] Moreover, one cannot fail to be struck by some of the previously mentioned synonyms for scrofula – "cachexia Africana," "negro poison" or "negro consumption" – which, it will be recalled, were employed in an earlier chapter to connote cases of dirt eating.

Indeed, the fact that cachexia africana meant dirt eating to Louisiana physicians yet scrofula to their Tennessee colleagues becomes doubly intriguing when it is noticed that the lower South states of Louisiana and Alabama accounted for very few black scrofula deaths (less than 14 percent of those counted in the seven states) yet buried 83 percent of the dirt eaters. Tennessee, Kentucky, and Virginia by contrast, as demonstrated, combined to register the bulk of the scrofula deaths in the South but listed only nine fatalities from dirt eating.

As pointed out earlier, dirt eating is rarely fatal, yet antebellum physicians believed it to be deadly. This raises the suspicion that the "tumid" abdomens which lower South physicians thought symptomatic of advanced dirt-eating cases may have been indicative of some other ailment entirely, with miliary tuberculosis a likely candidate. Even if every one of the so-called dirt-eating fatalities was the work of scrofula, however, this would account for very few new black tuberculosis fatalities, which means still more searching.

Julian Lewis (who also suspected that tuberculosis was quite prevalent among blacks in the antebellum South) pointed out in his study, *The Biology of the Negro*, that in early twentieth-century Africa it was observed that "one of the outstanding characteristics of tuberculosis in most natives is the lack of outward signs, even in the presence of massive disease," and therefore "clinical observation alone is insufficient to determine the extent of infection."[53]

During the early decades of the twentieth century, it was noticed that blacks throughout the tropics were more susceptible to tuberculosis than whites, yet as was the case with the Canadian Indians the symptoms were quite different: less extensive lung lesions and "a far greater involvement of lymph nodes all over the body in Africans."[54] Finally, even today, authorities on black-related diseases stress the tendency of tuberculosis to mimic a whole range of other diseases.[55] Thus, the foregoing points lend even more credence to the hypothesis that tuberculosis was widespread among slaves, but because of extrapulmonary symptoms, on the one hand, and the ability of the disease to masquerade as many illnesses, on the other, it was not always diagnosed correctly in slaves; rather, many black tuberculosis deaths must lay concealed under a number of rubrics other than "scrofula," "consumption", and "dirt eating," thereby creating the problem encountered with pellagra.

Two diseases in particular present themselves as likely disguises for miliary tuberculosis. The first is "dropsy," which demonstrated more partiality to blacks than whites; during 1849–50 in the seven-state sample, dropsy killed 74 blacks per 100,000 as opposed to 56 whites per 100,000. Dropsy among whites, however, loosely understood to be an abnormal collection of serous fluid in cellular tissues, was diagnosed on the basis of unusual swellings.[56] But many physicians arrived at the conviction that "dropsy" occurred so often in blacks as to qualify as a "Negro disease" on the basis of "dropsical" tumors in black abdomens and lungs. Because of the absence of specific tuberculosis symptoms that inexperienced peoples manifest, it cannot be unreasonable to suspect that these "dropsical tumors" were in many cases the work of miliary tuberculosis, particularly in view of the apparent urban nature of dropsy. In Charleston, for example, the disease killed 1,040 blacks during 1822–48 but only 375 whites. Not incidentally, it should be recalled that consumption during these years killed 1,589 Charleston blacks as opposed to 1,261 whites, while scrofula accounted for another 57 blacks but only 19 whites.[57]

Another possibility is typhoid (which even today physicians must take care not to confuse with miliary tuberculosis) or better still "typhoid pneumonia." The disease diagnosed as typhoid (or typhus – the symptoms are similar) killed 50 slaves per 100,000 in the 1849–50 seven-state sample and 45 whites per 100,000. The differential is not great. Unfortunately, however, "typhoid pneumonia" is not listed as a cause of death (perhaps subsumed under pneumonia or typhoid), yet antebellum physicians made clear by their writings that this disease was extraordinarily partial to blacks and tended to sweep whole planta-tions, invariably taking the "best" slaves, meaning young men and women.[58] Young adults frequently prove most susceptible to new dis-eases because their immunologic systems in effect react too vigorously. Thus, there are grounds for suspicion that typhoid pneumonia may actually have been miliary tuberculosis.

Doubtless other candidates exist as well, although it seems unneces-sary to ransack antebellum nosology for still more possibilities. For the point is that contrary to belief, slaves suffered from tuberculosis in large numbers and in urban areas at a greater rate than whites when similarly exposed. If, for example, dropsy is added to "consumption" and scrofula deaths in Charleston, then for the twenty-six year period of 1822–48, that city buried 2,686 blacks and 1,655 whites from these combined causes. Assuming that all dropsy deaths were tuberculosis for both black and white (although of course they were not) the respec-tive death rates from this disease (based on the city's 1850 population) would have been 433 per 100,000 for blacks and 306 per 100,000 for whites.

If "consumption" and "scrofula" deaths are lumped together in our seven-state sample, the two in combination killed 81 out of every 100,000 whites and 74 out of every 100,000 blacks. If "dropsy" deaths were also added, the death rates would be virtually the same. Because of the miliary symptoms displayed by many blacks that would have gone unrecognized by physicians, it would appear that even during antebellum days a greater percentage of blacks than whites may well have died of tuberculosis after all. This is a situation to be expected given the blacks' immunologic and nutritional susceptibilities. More-over, the factor of "unrecognizable" symptoms compels a look at the "unknown" death category in the seven-state sample. This reveals that 320 blacks per 100,000 perished from "unknown" causes during 1849–50 as opposed to only 186 per 100,000 whites.

One cannot avoid wondering how much of the differential repre-sented unrecognized tuberculosis? That tuberculosis after all was a seri-ous problem among slaves on the plantation has been demonstrated, despite rural residence, a lack of slave mobility, and the circumstances of the plantation as a quarantining device. The disease was a serious problem during slavery because of a lack of immunities coupled with the state of slave nutrition. After abolition these predisposing factors were accentuated, while the prophylactic circumstances of slavery dis-appeared. Thus, the flashpoint was reached for the disease to explode in epidemic form.

CHAPTER 10

CHOLERA AND RACE

I was so unfortunate as to loose [sic] Anthony with Cholera in August. he was hire in Town at $25.00 a month, it is a great loss to me, he generally made me $1.00 every day that he worked. he died in three days, the leaders of his arms and legs were drawn up in knots as large as hen eggs – his eyes sunk deep in his head – He was large and fleshy when taken but in 3 days his flesh shrunk [sic] away to skin and bones

> Mrs. Walter Raleigh Lenoir, 1852. (Lenoir family papers,
> University of North Carolina)

I

Thus far, the focus has been on diseases to which blacks very definitely manifested special immunities or susceptibilities. This chapter, however, which closes a survey of antebellum "Negro" diseases takes up cholera, a disease to which blacks may well have been no more susceptible than whites, but only appeared to be. Nonetheless, cholera could not be eliminated, because in appearance at least cholera unquestionably preferred black victims and not just in the United States but throughout the hemisphere.

Previously confined to Asia, with India its primordial home, Asiatic cholera, suddenly during the nineteenth century embarked, upon one deadly voyage after another, which ultimately carried the plague to most of the globe. America escaped the first pandemic that began in 1817 and invaded European Russia in 1823. The second, third, and fourth pandemics, however all moved inexorably westward toward the Atlantic and crossed over to the United States during the years 1832, 1848, and 1866.[1]

Historically, inexperienced peoples are dealt with harshly by new diseases against which their bodies have little defense, and Asiatic cholera was definitely a new disease for Americans.[2] In its most severe form, it was not only dramatic in its onset but terrifying in its effects claiming about half of those infected, many within twenty-four hours.[3] Its major symptoms, acute vomiting and diarrhea, are triggered by a

147

toxin released by the *vibrio cholerae* into the small intestine. The normal stool is transformed into a liquid resembling rice water, which rushes through the body in such volume that over the course of four to six days the patient may pass fluid equaling twice his body weight. As dehydration progresses, the victim experiences painful muscular cramps; weakness and lethargy develop, followed by stupor, then finally shock. An assortment of complications, including cardiovascular collapse, signal death.

In none of the foregoing, however – not in a sketch of cholera's history nor in a glance at its symptoms – is there a clue as to why the disease should have treated black and white as differently as it is supposed to have done in the United States and throughout much of the Americas. Cholera vibrios are colorblind and neither Euro- nor Afro-American had descended from peoples who might have developed resistance to them. Yet in the Caribbean, in Brazil, and in the United States, Asiatic cholera became quickly identified by physicians as a peculiarly black affliction.

European colleagues too were struck by the manner in which cholera played racial favorites. The German epidemiologist August Hirsch amassed data from Africa's East Coast, the East and West Indies, Brazil, and the United States that seemed to indicate a greater black susceptibility to the disease, while James Christie's "Notes on the Cholera Epidemics in East Africa" tended to make a case for cholera's black preference in that region.[4] Yet most epidemiologists today feel that there are no racial factors that predispose to the disease, although their contention is admittedly based upon nothing very concrete, because little is known about cholera's immunology and much of what is known remains contradictory and confusing.[5] Perhaps an examination of the black and white differential experience with the disease in the American South, with an eye on the most recent medical knowledge of cholera, will help to illuminate why cholera singled out blacks for special and fatal attention in the United States and thus by implication throughout the hemisphere.

II

It was early in 1832 when cholera symptoms (which have been likened to those of "acute arsenical poisoning")[6] appeared almost simultaneously in Montreal, Philadelphia, and New York. "Cholera morbus" was the initial diagnosis; but this wishful thinking quickly was dashed as it became clear that the plague had crossed the ocean.[7] Cholera vibrios were now loose in American waters, free to spread to human alimentary canals through drinking water, food washed in water, fish and other foods that drew nourishment from water, and, of course, all foods fertilized by contaminated night soil.

By midsummer the severity of the epidemic precipitated publication of *The Cholera Bulletin*, a triweekly newspaper founded by New York physicians to keep the public informed and permit medical men to compare notes on the disease's behavior.[8] From this and a similar enterprise, *The Cholera Gazette* of Philadelphia, southerners learned of the plague, and planters began to worry in earnest, for as cholera advanced on the South, it had begun to demonstrate a preference for black victims.[9]

In Philadelphia, the black cholera rate had been twice that of whites,[10] while a Cincinnati doctor noted "Our black population [is] unquestionably more liable to the disease than the whites."[11] Then from Cuba came word that the disease was decimating that island's slave population. The Spanish governor announced the initial death toll was at least 30,000 souls, and later in 1833 he estimated (wildly) that 55,000 slaves had died during the first fifty-six days of the epidemic.[12]

The approach of cholera galvanized Southerners into prophylactic activity. Cities and plantations alike were subjected to a flurry of scrubbing, polishing, and whitewashing, while low places were drained and filled and lime was spread everywhere.[13] Masters became vigilant about airing slave bedding, cleaning slave clothing, and anxious that all "victuals [were] cooked done," while in case these measures did not keep cholera at bay medicine chests were filled.[14]

Yet more often than not the pestilence ignored these labors. Planters who had "had all filth removed from about their negro quarters," "cabins whitewashed and lime thrown under them", and who had paid "strict attention . . . to the quality of food used" despaired at seeing their plantations harder hit by the plague than those of more careless neighbors.[15]

The worst fears of southern planters were confirmed as the disease did in fact demonstrate a preference for black victims. W. Mazyck Porcher, a prominent South Carolina planter, wrote, "you may suppose that there is a considerable panic here – this is not the case; I never saw people take anything so cool in my life . . . It has killed so few white persons that they are not afraid of it on their account but are distressed about their servants."[16] A colleague of Porcher's puzzled that cholera "is confined to the negroes, as if, like the yaws, it was an African disease,"[17] while the ultimate dread of all slaveholders was succinctly expressed by a planter on the Savannah River. He wrote in 1834 that "the cholera has broken out with great violence."[18] He estimated the death of 250 slaves in his neighborhood alone, and then added somberly, "It is highly probable [that] it [cholera] will ruin me; that is, compel me to sell the plantation and what is left of the negroes to pay for the residue of the purchase."[19]

Not that planters did not fight back and some planters, in fact, took heroic measures. On one stricken plantation where cholera killed three slaves on the first day and ten more within a few more days, two doctors were imported to combat the disease, one of whom was to reside with the slaves around the clock.[20] Yet physicians proved helpless in the face of this plague. "There is something singularly inexplicable," wrote a Louisiana planter, "in the manner the disease makes its appearance. It would really seem that as quick as the doctors and the wise men get a theory up about it, it sets to work to upset the theory."[21]

Baffled, doctors fell back on their old standbys – bleeding leeching, lancing, cupping, and pumping cayenne pepper, calomel, camphor, mustard, laudanum, and turpentine through cholera-ravaged bodies[22] – all of which allied the physicians with the disease against the patient. Today death from cholera has been virtually eliminated by effective therapy which aims at quick replacement of salts and waters lost in the diarrheal stool.[23] Yesterday's treatment with its emphasis on purging and bleeding merely accelerated the process of dehydration. It has aptly been called "benevolent homicide."[24]

One cannot be too harsh with antebellum physicians, however, for cholera has many gradations of severity and affects individuals differently. Because the recovery rate was about 50 percent physicians naturally tended to believe that the recoveries were due to the efficacy of their medications.

On the other hand, the first cholera epidemic had taught many persons to be wary of physicians and their cures, and during the second epidemic doctors complained bitterly of competition from "nostrum vendors," as people chose to treat themselves.[25] Yet if a medical student of the period can be believed, many physicians admitted privately that "one half dies no matter what treatment is employed."[26] Another student wrote to his mother in Virginia that, if cholera "comes through there & I was at home I'd turn doctor. I could cure as many cases as any of the doctors,"[27] which may well have summed up the public's attitude toward the talents of its medical men.

Certainly many slaves were skeptical of medical attention for cholera whether it came at the hands of physicians or slaveholders, and with good reason, considering the draconian nature of the "cures." One planter remedy, for example, included dosing with calomel, castor oil, and soapsuds; bleeding; cupping; blistering; mustard plasters "on the ancles (sic) and the calves of the legs"; and "hot bricks to the feet."[28]

Undoubtedly "remedies" of this kind constituted much of the reason why slaves tried to conceal from their masters the fact that they had contracted the disease. Planters were advised to counter by stationing "competent nurses to watch and examine negro bowel movements."[29] Physicians also fretted about the blacks' fatalism – their "foolish infatuation" which made them "indifferent [to] and unconscious" of the dangers of the plague.[30] Once sick, many simply "lie down and die in a few hours."[31] At least one inspired master defeated the pestilence, however, by ignoring the advice of physicians and breaking every rule as it reached his plantation. All hands were ordered to "quit work" and "permitted . . . to go into a regular frolic; whiskey and fiddle were called in requisition," and the "unrestrained merriment and mirth" lasted for three days.[32] Somehow it worked. There were no new cases.

Obviously the disease defied all understanding. A South Carolina planter was completely bewildered by the fifty cholera cases scattered over his plantation. "The cause," he wrote, "I cannot discover; they live at various settlements, are employed in every kind of work and have . . . the same food."[33] Black susceptibility to the plague was blamed on everything from "rotgut whisky"[34] to diseased oysters.[35] More than a few physicians, struck by similarities between cholera and yellow fever, sought a common cure.[36] Yet the search for cholera's etiology was not totally unsuccessful, particularly in the case of planters who had noticed first in the 1830s and once again in the 1840s that "those places on which cistern water alone was used, were nearly exempt from that dreadful disease," and when cholera did strike on these plantations it was the result of consuming "unwholesome water" elsewhere.[37] Thus masters who learned to be careful about water or those who took their slaves away from the river to inland camps pioneered effective prevention measures for cholera.

Unfortunately, however, despite urgings from physicians at the beginning of both antebellum cholera epidemics that masters move slaves away from rivers to inland camps,[38] slave losses were staggering. During 1833 alone it was calculated that cholera cost Louisiana planters some $4 million in slaves.[39] The epidemic of the late 1840s was only months old when estimations of 10,000 slaves already dead were advanced which meant the loss of at least another $4 million.[40] Thus, although the cost of the two epidemics has yet to be calculated either in terms of lives destroyed or the aggregate worth of chattles lost by planters, these examples alone suggest that both were enormous.

No wonder that in October of 1848 after the disease had crossed the Channel to the British Isles thousands of miles away in Louisiana the price of slaves was significantly affected.[41] Only white nonslaveholders could feel casual about the presence of the disease, such as the New Orleans resident who assured a curious correspondent that "the city is considered healthy, although we have cases of cholera occasionally among the whites *and a great deal among the colored population*" (italics ours).[42]

Thus the two antebellum epidemics convinced planters, citizens, and physicians that in the South at least cholera was peculiarly a black disease, while the latter began classifying it as such. Presumed racial attributes such as sloth, carelessness, and intemperance were thought to be responsible, an explanation that could also account for those whites who perished.[43] Thus "filthy habits" were declared to be the cause of the cholera deaths of two hundred blacks from "St. Martin's to Franklin"[44] Louisiana, but also of those Irishmen bound from New Orleans to Texas who could hardly be thrown overboard "as fast as they died."[45]

III

In 1866 America began its third and last encounter with Asiatic cholera, with some physicians expressing concern for the freedmen.[46] On the whole, however, an absence of concern in the literature of the period suggests that white Southerners were almost nonchalant about the plague, perhaps because there were no slaves to lose. Certainly the impression that cholera was essentially a black man's disease still prevailed, while racists desiring to deport the nation's black population found in the association of filth with black with cholera one more reason for deportation.[47]

But was cholera really a black disease or, to sharpen the question, were blacks innately more susceptible to the disease than whites? Surely impressions gleaned from the antebellum epidemics indicate that blacks suffered more from cholera than whites, but they throw little light on the problem of whether this liability was a function of environmental circumstances or innate susceptibility. Hopefully a look at hard data generated by these and the 1866 epidemic will provide something of an answer.

Certainly environmental circumstances do go far toward explaining the affinity that the Asiatic pestilence seemed to display for blacks. The tendency of cholera to follow water routes meant that in the South, where many plantations were concentrated along rivers, slaves frequently constituted a demographic majority in the path of the disease. Hence blacks should have also contributed the majority of its victims. Figure 1 illustrates vividly the role of the Mississippi River in cholera's march through the state of Mississippi during 1849–50:[48] Of the state's 655 cholera deaths for this period, almost 80 percent occurred in river counties.[49] Because these counties also contained one-quarter of the state's black population, but merely 8 percent of the whites, there seems little mystery as to why blacks were the chief cholera sufferers.

Again in cities, blacks were more likely than whites to reside close to the waterfront and be employed there. Food from the sea, river, and field usually reached the market and kitchen through their hands which naturally increased their risk of infection. Therefore, it is not totally surprising that in Charleston, for example, during 1836 about 80 percent (339 out of 408) of the cholera victims were black even though the white and black populations were roughly equal,[50] or that in the

Figure 1. Deaths from cholera in Mississippi, 1849–50. (Data from "Seventh Census of the United States, Original Returns of the Assistant Marshalls, Third Series, Persons Who Died during the Year Ending June 30, 1850," for the State of Mississippi. Department of Archives and History, Jackson, Miss.)

1852–53 outbreak, 63 percent (55 out of 85) of the dead were blacks.[51] Yet, to an extent during the 1830s, and certainly during the 1850s, blacks shared the poorer sections of Charleston with immigrants (mostly Irish), while cholera deaths were not confined to the waterfront but occurred "in every part of town" according to the chroniclers of the epidemic.[52] Thus, it is questionable whether residence and occupation explain the whole of the differential.

Moreover, a closer inspection of the Mississippi mortality data reveals that after adjusting for the blacks' numerical preponderance in the river counties, they still suffered substantially more than whites, losing 556 per 100,000 of their numbers to the disease as opposed to a white death rate of only 325 per 100,000. Blacks, in other words, had more than a 70 percent greater chance of dying from the disease than whites.

The data, of course, may be skewed. Another student of the problem has pointed out that because cholera was regarded as a lower-class or black disease, many middle- and upper-class white cholera fatalities were probably concealed by thoughtful doctors under rubrics such as diarrhea or dysentery.[53]

On the other hand, cholera struck hard at Federal soldiers stationed in the South during 1866, and it is unlikely that Army doctors conspired to falsify the cause of white deaths. Yet the Army calculated that while white soldiers averaged 193 cholera cases for every 1,000 of mean strength exposed and lost 78 of these cases, black soldiers averaged 259 cases per 1,000 mean strength exposed with 136 failing to recover.[54] Interestingly, the proportion of white to black fatalities (1:1.75) was practically identical to the Mississippi pattern in 1849–50.

Doubtless part of the differential is explicable in terms of black units being disadvantaged in areas such as sanitary facilities and food preparation. Another less explicable phenomenon, however, is gradually becoming apparent. After contracting the disease, blacks had a significantly greater chance of succumbing to it than whites. The Army figures for 1866 reveal that while death claimed ten whites out of every twenty-five cholera cases, it carried off ten black victims for every nineteen cases.

A similar differential was observable during the year 1873 as the plague fired a last salvo at the United States. Table 2 reflects cholera cases and deaths recorded for five southern states. The white fatality rate was ten deaths out of every twenty-four cases, whereas blacks perished at a rate of ten for every sixteen cases. It should be stressed that both rates are remarkably similar to the United States Army data of 1866.

Thus, suspicion increases that southern physicians were correct (and modern epidemiologists wrong) in believing that racial factors were implicated in differential cholera mortality. Those environmental fac-

Table 2. *Cholera cases and deaths by race, recorded*
for five southern states, 1873

	Whites			Blacks		
State	No. of cases	No. of deaths	%	No. of cases	No. of deaths	%
Alabama	151	69	45.6	132	112	84.8
Kentucky	1,051	463	44.0	653	392	60.0
Louisiana	217	147	67.7	188	160	85.1
Mississippi	32	13	40.6	41	20	48.7
Tennessee	1,229	409	33.2	825	431	52.2
Total	2,680	1,101	41.0	1,839	1,115	60.6

Source: John M. Woodward, *Cholera Epidemic of 1873 in the United States* (1875), 35 (table).

tors that may account for a greater incidence of infection among blacks nonetheless do not explain why blacks experienced a more severe form of the disease than whites. Because, as was mentioned previously, medicine was in no way responsible for the patient's survival and no real improvements in cholera treatment were made until the twentieth century, no answers are to be found in differential medical treatment.[55]

Therefore, we are confronted with the following: on the average about 5 to 10 percent of those individuals invaded by cholera vibrios manifested the disease's classic symptoms;[56] and these symptoms meant death for about half of those Americans who displayed them. The remaining 90 percent or so of those infected would have experienced a mild cholera with symptoms difficult to distinguish from other enteric diseases. Their diarrhea would have been self-limiting, they would have had few evacuations, and they would have recovered.

Of those Americans who manifested classic cholera symptoms in 1873, however, by race, six out of ten whites recovered, while six out of ten blacks died. In the U.S. Army during 1866 the situation was roughly the same. For Mississippi during the year 1849–50 there are no figures on deaths per number of persons infected; blacks, however, in the counties hardest hit by the plague had over a 70 percent greater chance of dying from it than whites. Finally impressionistic evidence left in the wake of the pandemics that struck the United States indicates clearly that blacks suffered far more than whites.

Unquestionably then either innate characteristics were at work that made blacks more susceptible to the disease than whites, or there were other less easily distinguishable environmental factors creating the differential. It is in this latter category that modern cholera research may offer some assistance.

First, researchers have demonstrated that gastric acid in the stomach has the ability to destroy many enteric bacteria, cholera vibrios among them.[57] In other words, gastric hypoacidity would predispose to cholera infection, and, although no one has demonstrated that blacks are more prone to this condition than whites, the circumstances of labor in the South may well have frequently produced it. "Large draughts of water," it has been hypothesized, have the effect of temporarily diluting gastric acid sufficiently to permit the passage of vibrios, unharmed, through the stomach into the small intestine.[58] Thus, infected water consumed in large quantities not only carries the infection, but has the ability to deliver vibrios safely to the point where they do maximum harm.

Therefore, field hands before and after abolition who labored long and hard under a hot sun, pausing frequently to gulp water, often from creeks, rivers, ponds, marshes, and other places of potential infection, would have been far more likely to contract cases of severe cholera than those who drank smaller amounts of infected water or consumed contaminated food. In the former case, of course, fewer vibrios would have been ingested, while in the latter gastric acid would have been given much more of an opportunity to do its work. In fact the "large draughts of water" hypothesis probably helps to explain why historically those afflicted first early in a cholera epidemic have been "young hard working adults."[59]

The second reason why blacks may have died at a greater rate than whites is related to a difference in their nutritional statuses. Malnutrition has long been suspected as a predisposing factor to cholera, and all recent summations on the state of cholera research hypothesize a close correlation between severe cholera and a poor nutritional status. Although attempts at specific linkages have thus far proved unsuccessful,[60] the blacks' experience with the malady provides one more reason for continuing the search. We have argued that much of America's nineteenth-century black population was seriously malnourished, both absolutely and relative to whites. Thus their poor cholera survival rate relative to whites may have been still one more price paid for such a condition.

IV

It has been shown statistically that white physicians, planters, and citizens in the South were correct in their impressions of cholera's racial preferences. Yet the black and white cholera mortality figures generated by the cholera epidemics make it clear that whites were not justified in believing the disease struck almost exclusively at blacks, and that they themselves possessed some sort of immunity. It has been seen that much of cholera's discrimination was a result of environmental factors that put blacks at a greater risk of cholera infection than whites in the South. It has been suggested as well that patterns of water consumption dictated by the circumstances of field labor may have induced cases of greater virulence in blacks than would otherwise be expected and that their poor (in relation to whites) nutritional status quite possibly militated against recovery. Whether these subtle environmental factors, in combination with the more blatant, can account for the full magnitude of differential black/white cholera morbidity and mortality remains an open question. Probably they do. The pity is that yesterday these factors were not understood, and consequently the black was unfairly associated with a "filthy" disease in the white mind.

ANTEBELLUM MEDICINE

INTRODUCTION TO PART IV

One must first ask: to what extent did Southern practitioners
achieve a knowledge of such science as was then available, and,
second, to what extent did they apply that knowledge *pro bono
publico*?

Richard H. Shryock (1930)[1]

Thus far the focus has been on black-related disease immunities and
susceptibilities. Minimal attention, however, has been paid to those
individuals (black and white) who dealt daily with problems of slave
health. The following section is intended to remedy this, first by providing a glimpse of the plantation health care system, and second by
examining the attitudes of white physicians toward blacks within the
context of their call for a separate branch of southern medicine devoted
exclusively to the slave.

Postell, Genovese, and Savitt, to name but a few, have all admirably
treated plantation medicine; Fredrickson and Stanton have both done
marvelous work on the burgeoning scientific racism of the antebellum
period, while John Duffy, among others, has demonstrated the role
physicians played in the construction of southern nationalism.

The contribution of this part is in its effort to unite these various
treatments within a causal framework; namely that the physicians' perception of distinctive black health problems led to the South's brand of
scientific racism, which in turn fed the call for slave medicine as part of
a growing southern nationalism.

Unquestionably, the evidence underlying this section is mostly impressionistic, while the presentation is interpretive. Thus some may be
skeptical that the physicians relied upon are truly representative of the
southern medical profession; others may feel that the role of that profession in both the development of scientific racism and southern nationalism is exaggerated.

It would be unfortunate, however, if objections of this nature caused
the major point of this section to be lost. The point is that the phenomenon of southern nationalism has served to obscure the honest

161

conviction of many southern physicians that (based on their own experience) there was a very real need for specialists in black-related diseases. In this sense, they anticipated the present burgeoning appreciation of distinctive black health problems by over a century. The tragedy was that they also anticipated (and fueled) a virulent postbellum scientific racism in the South that is touched upon in the book's final part.

CHAPTER 11

SLAVE MEDICINE

The most profitable kind of practice is that among negroes.

Samuel Cartwright (1853)[1]

Ole Miss, she generally looked after the niggers when they sick
and give them the medicine. And, too, she would get the doctor
iffen she think they real bad off 'cause like I said, Ole Miss, she
mighty stingy, and she never want to los no nigger by them dying.
Howsomever, it was hard to get her to believe you sick when you
tell her that you was, and she would think you just playing off
from work.

Tines Kendrick, Georgia ex-slave[2]

Slave medicine was a strange melange of medical dogma and superstition, pragmatic practice and compulsive conjecturing, insights and ignorance – all of which was aimed at the preservation and perpetuation
of those lives in which planters had invested so heavily.

Nonetheless, all slaveholders did not employ physicians regularly,
and some, particularly masters of marginal units, seldom, if ever, engaged their services either for slaves or for their own families no matter
how grave the illness. Even on these numerous benighted outposts,
however, the antebellum physician made regular bedside appearances if
only by proxy. Sometimes he was present in the form of a cure laboriously jotted down, or vaguely recalled, obtained from a neighbor who
had once consulted a doctor, or perhaps a remedy passed along in the
family – *materia medica* which had become part of the public domain.[3]

He was also frequently represented by one of a multitude of do-it-
yourself home medical guides authored by enterprising physicians
which in themselves are a fascinating mixture of the erudite and the
erroneous. Some of these titles included:[4] Virginia's W. H. Coffin's *The
Art of Medicine Simplified* (1853); Georgia's James Ewell's, *The Planters and
Mariners Medical Companion* (1807); South Carolina's Alfred M. Folger's,
The Family Physician, Being a Domestic Medical Work (1845); Tennessee's A.
G. Goodlett's, *The Family Physician, or Every Man's Companion* (1838); and
Kentucky's John C. Gunn's *Domestic Medicine or Poor Man's Friend* (1838).

All have a great similarity suggesting, as was the case with many travel accounts of the day, that authors consulted their predecessors very carefully before composing their own. But the equating of good health with cleanliness that runs through all of them from Ewell's first edition in 1807 to editions of J. Hume Simon's *The Planter Guide and Family Book of Medicine* appearing on the eve of the War was of such beneficial importance as to compensate for the occasional wrong-headed procedure or prescription. The works contained detailed instructions on how to diagnose everything from asthma to "wind cholic," with "cures" ranging from antimony to zinc. Here one learned to make plasters and poultices, bathe lacerations with lye, fill cuts with saltpeter or turpentine, seal them with wax and oil, and even conquer the bite of a mad dog.

Perhaps ironically these books written by doctors caused the ire of doctors who complained loudly and bitterly that because of them, planters were encouraged to treat cases themselves, calling in professional help only when their own efforts proved unsuccessful.[5] "Take me," recalled one ex-slave, "I was never one for sickness. But the slaves used to git sick. There was jaundice in them bottoms. First off they's give some castor oil, and if that didn't cure, they'd give blue mass. Then if he was still sick they's git a doctor."[6]

Against this procedure stood the physicians, thundering that "above all, we must condemn the almost universal practice, on the part of owners and overseers, of tampering with their sick negroes for one, two or more days before applying for medical aid."[7] Yet plantations large and small strove to be self-sufficient, and small slaveowners in particular did their best to avoid large doctor bills. Thus the mistress of an estate frequently found herself in charge of the medical regimen with preventive medicine her particular forte. Slave children on the first days of sunshine following the winter were lined up for a dose of garlic and tot of rum as their spring tonic.[8] Others were marched to the "big house" semiannually for an infusion of "deadshot" or "vermifuge" (a particularly nauseous compound) in preparation for the impending change of season.[9]

To avoid worms "gittin in dem," the youngsters were given chinaberry[10]; to ward off diphtheria they wore bags of "asafetida" around their necks[11]; to escape the "hooping cough," a simple leather string around the throat sufficed.[12] For the child and adult alike red pepper (particularly in the Cotton South) was an important weapon of prevention, believed to keep at bay "that langor and apathy of the system which renders it so susceptible to chills and fevers."[13]

Every mistress was also armed with two or three general purpose remedies relied upon much the way aspirin is today. Calomel, or castor oil, was in the forefront of almost all medicine chests, "vinegar nail" (concocted by soaking square cut iron nails in vinegar) was also a favorite as were rosin pills (from pine rosin), normally combined with vinegar.[14] Whisky and rum were used as pain killers, while toothaches and earaches were handled by stuffing the offending cavity with tar.[15] Additionally, plantations stocked commercial medicines touted as especially effective for slaves such as "Swaim's panacea," for "negroes who are confined in large numbers on plantations in hot climates."[16]

On larger plantations, the administration of health care frequently fell with myriad other duties on the shoulders of the overseer. That concern for the health of their slaves loomed large in the minds of masters can be found in their many "Plantation Rules" habitually presented to new overseers. A Mississippi planter sternly warned his deputy that "the health of the negroes under your charge is an important matter."[17] "In cases of sickness," commanded another, "the said Ward is to pay the strictest and most unremitting attention to the negroes."[18] A third planter ordered that "all sick persons are to stay in the hospital night and day, from the time they first complain to the time they are able to go to work again."[19] A South Carolina slaveholder could scarcely have been more explicit when he cautioned his overseer that "the Proprietor, in the first place wishes the Overseer *most distinctly* to understand that his first object is to be, under all circumstances, the care and well being of the negroes."[20]

As these instructions suggest, there is much truth in the assertion "that many planters and overseers considered sickness among the Negroes their greatest trouble in the management of plantations."[21] This same impression is given by planters' diaries, correspondence, and journals of the period, as well as their professional organs such as the *Southern Cultivator* and *DeBow's Review* and *American Cotton Planter and Soil of the South* where scarcely an issue appeared without slaveholders trading secrets on "The Management of Negroes," or "The Health of Negroes", which reflect surprisingly good suggestions for improving the physical well-being of their wards.[22]

But no matter how skilled in medical matters a planter or his wife or overseer might have been, the "Rules of Overseers" also clearly recognized the limitations of laymen. "Bloodletting" was usually prohibited and sometimes the prescription of calomel as well "unless by a physician." Slaves who met with serious accident were to be transported forthwith to a hospital, and in the case of any but minor illnesses a physician was to be sent for at once.[23]

Yet as a rule, the regular doctor was only consulted if a patient had proven himself to be definitely ill, a situation one physician likened to that of "a man called in to stay an already rapidly falling wall – a timely prop might have readily stayed the tottering structure, but he who applies his shoulder to it while falling only runs the risk of being buried beneath its ruins."[24] Here, of course, the doctor was bemoaning the risk of arriving at a slave's bedside just in time to receive the blame for losing

him. But despite this professional grousing[25] (which contains more than
a hint of self-interest), physicians were not always stayed from their
desire to be the first to grapple with slave illness. Rather some plantations retained physicians on an annual contract, paying as high as $1200
annually for a doctor's services.[26] This kind of commitment, although
normal in the newer South (the contract was usually for $300 to $400 per
year),[27] was roundly denounced by the medical profession in the eastern
states as smacking of rate cutting, on the one hand, and as a "practice
[which] aims at a species of miserable, petty monopoly . . . in direct
violation of the ethics of the profession" on the other.[28]

More frequently, a physician attended a planter, his family, and his
"people" much as did the now all but extinct family doctor, making
calls when sent for and receiving pay on a piecework basis. A bill
submitted by a Doctor Holcombe to the Butler plantation for his services from 20 May through 22 November, 1843 is illustrative. During
this six-month period, the physician prescribed on occasion "by letter
from office and [the] medicine [was] put up and sent."[29] In this case
the cost was $3.00 per prescription including medicine. Additionally he
paid almost twenty visits to the plantation with daytime calls averaging
$6.00 plus a charge for medicine ranging from $1.00 to $3.00 per visit.
Three times the entry "prof[essional] visit in the *night*" appears, however, and, in these instances, the charge was double or $12.00. The bill
gives little clue as to the nature of the illnesses dealt with, but they
may have been of an epidemic nature, since frequently six to eight
slaves were treated during a visit.

The statement for the six-month period totalled $177.00, which was
marked "paid in full," a particularly happy occurrence for professionals whose chief difficulty seems to have been bill collecting. Typical is
Dr. Richard Arnold's lament, "It runs me almost crazy to think that
with hundreds upon hundreds due me professionally I find the greatest difficulty in raising a simple fifty dollars."[30] Yet Arnold, a Savannah
physician, is more frequently quoted for his observation that the demand for slave medical care was "the true reason why physicians get
into practice more readily at the South than at the North" and that
"here he stands some chance of making his bread while he has teeth to
chew it."[31]

That the bread was sometimes abundant can be seen in the substantial number of plantation owners throughout the South whose names
were preceded by "Dr."; indeed more than one student of southern
physicians has commented on the phenomenon of physician/planters
and that one became the former because it afforded the quickest means
of achieving the latter status.[32] The leavening to hasten this process
was often epidemic disease such as cholera in the Mississippi delta in
1849, which so frightened one planter that he paid a physician $500
weekly to "stay on his place and attend his slaves."[33]

Yet "even without pestilence," wrote another slaveholder in the region, "deaths might bring a planters ruin." He clearly had himself in
mind, bewailing in his journal, "Oh, my losses make me almost
crazy."[34] Thus there was plenty of demand for day-to-day professional
attention on the plantation. Planters acutely aware of their own medical limitations sought a physician's services as a form of insurance
against the loss of their chattels.

For this reason, "the greatest part of the practice of every country
physician is among colored people,"[35] and many physicians, like Dr.
Gibbes of South Carolina, could remark that during the course of their
careers they had attended thousands of Negroes in their respective
regions.[36] Additional testimony to the importance attached to professional medical care comes from plantation records which abound with
numerous entries of medical fees paid, with the cost of slave medical
attention considerably less than that of whites. Thus "ordinary obstet-
ric cases" according to a Georgian fee bill were thirty dollars for whites
but only twenty dollars for slaves. Vaccinations for whites ran three
dollars to six dollars, but slaves were vaccinated for two dollars each or
twelve dollars per dozen. As in many businesses, quantity was rewarded with discounts.[37]

In the normal course of their duties physicians were called upon by
the plantation to perform a range of tasks from extracting teeth to
delivering babies, but mostly their work seems to have been that of
dispensing medicines for routine but chronic complaints. In certain
practical areas such as that of setting broken bones or prescribing
trusses for hernias (which were plentiful on the plantation) or vaccinat-
ing against smallpox,[38] they were at their best; in the face of epidemics
they were mostly ineffectual; against everyday ailments then, as now,
nature cured, and the physicians took the credit.

One solid contribution of the physicians was the good common
sense counsel they provided to planters regarding their bondsmen.
Samuel Cartwright, for example, proved himself to be sympathetic to
both the psychological and the physiologic problems of slaves trans-
ferred from the Old to the New South when he advised a planter that
"In regard to unacclimated negroes, the overseer should watch their
diseases most carefully . . . they should never be pushed [and] they
should have enough of good wholesome food . . . The first thing to be
done when a new set of unacclimated negroes arrives on a plantation is
for the overseer to put on his studying cap & make it a part of his
business to make the whole lot of new negroes as comfortable, as
contented & as happy as possible & to prepare the way for their grad-
ual incorporation with the others."[39]

In like manner the physicians' emphasis on cleanliness must have
greatly benefited the slaves. They interminably urged that plantations
be slicked up, standing water removed, older slave cabins torn down,

and newer ones whitewashed while advising that bondsmens' clothing, like their bedding, should be changed and washed with
regularity.[40]

To help implement these preventative procedures, as well as assist
physicians in the clinical arena, there was the plantation "sick nurse"
or "doctor woman." Often old or even an invalid, she was nonetheless
highly prized for a lifetime of accumulated wisdom on practical medical
matters. On middle-sized plantations she probably doubled as the children's nurse and perhaps as midwife as well; on larger plantations she
could frequently be found overseeing a staff of midwives, nurses, and
the children's cook, a staff which attended the "lying-in women" before, during, and after birth, had charge of the plantation nursery and
maintained its hospital.[41]

Plantation hospitals ran a gamut from a simple one-room cabin to
elaborate six-room affairs such as that on the Allston estate with two
fireplaces and a piazza to a well-equipped Georgia slave hospital complete with "good ventilation, steam heat, an examining study, a
kitchen, a medicine closet, four wards and a bathing room."[42] Hospitals with sufficient space normally contained a confinement ward or a
lying-in room, separate rooms for men and women patients and facilities for segregating contagious individuals. They might also feature a
pharmacy or "medicine room," although normal practice on all but the
largest estates was for the planter or overseer to keep pharmaceuticals
under lock and key in their place of residence.[43]

William Postell, who examined the inventories of some of those
"medicine rooms," turned up an astounding variety of equipment and
medicines. Under the former category, he found one boasting of "mi-
croscopes and slides, nursing bottles, mortar and pestle, pharmaceuti-
cal scales, breast pumps, bleeding cups, feeding cups, liters, alcohol
lamps . . . and vapor-bath aparatus." Another listed "one lot of den-
tists tools, one box of pill molds, and three syringes," along with
forty-three different drugs, representing only a portion of the plantation's total inventory.[44]

For slaves too ill to be cared for on the plantation or slaves whose
masters did not maintain adequate medical facilities there were slave
hospitals in many cities of the South or wards in regular hospitals
specifically for blacks. New Orleans maintained at least two of the
latter, while exclusively slave hospitals could be found in Savannah,
Natchez, Montgomery, and elsewhere.[45]

Thus, despite segregated medical care for slaves, that care was probably as good (or bad) as the age had to offer, a phenomenon that some
have likened to a kind of welfare medicine for the bondsmen.[46] Naturally a few slaves took advantage of the system, and malingering was a
common planter complaint. Referring to a slave hospital one overseer

grumbled that "once a nigger gets in there, he'd like to lie there for the rest of his life."[47] Planters also were forever bemoaning that their hospitals were "crowded . . . with patients who have nothing the matter with them,"[48] while there are many accounts of slaves who appropriated planter's medicine, not for the purpose of curing an ailment, but to make themselves ill to escape work.[49]

Physicians claimed not to be fooled. "The negro is prone to dissemble and feign disease," asserted Dr. Ramsay of Georgia, "probably no race of human beings feign themselves ill so frequently, and are so incapable of concealing their duplicity."[50] Planters had their individual methods for testing the extent of slave illness. One, for example, told his colleagues that "if a negro is sick a pint of corn is deducted from his allowance everyday because if he is really sick the nurse supplies him with good gruel, he therefore does not require corn, and if he is merely shamming, a reduction of rations, like stopping a sailor's grog, will induce him to be more active in the performance of his duties."[51] Physicians and masters alike, however, usually, in cases other than blatant malingering, gave the slave the benefit of the doubt, for a few days confinement was good insurance against losing a case for the doctor and an investment for the planter.

Moreover, it bears noting that planters were moved by other than pecuniary motives in providing medical attention for their wards. At the one extreme in the words of Richard Shryock, "the a priori argument for slave health in terms of a property interest has only a partial validity – men have been known to neglect even their livestock."[52] But at the other extreme, a mixture of peer pressure, planter pride in healthy slaves, and a genuine regard and affection for "his people" prompted many a slaveholder to invest far more in an individual's physical well-being than mere economic self-interest could justify.

For example, a ten-year-old female slave of the North Carolina Pettigrews "seized by rheumatic pains" was sent to a specialist in Norfolk where she remained for eight months. The total cost of treatment was in excess of $220.00, "a substantial portion of her [cash] value."[53] Countless examples exist of planters doing such things as "uneconomically" spending $75 "to furnish a complete upper plate for a negro man," or sending invalids to nursing homes for special care or slaves to Hot Springs Arkansas for four to five weeks to be cured of various illnesses.[54]

In a word then, the influence of the physician at least indirectly on the health of the slave was good. Nonetheless, slaves were often understandably wary of white doctors. Physicians might complain about slaves feigning illness, but others when ill would work harder than ever to avoid the eye of the overseer and thus professional medical attention.[55] Doctors were also annoyed with a fatalistic belief of bondsmen "that every one has his time appointed to die, and if it be 'come,' they expect to die and if not, they will get well without medicine."[56]

Blacks might get along without white medicine, but they also maintained their own medical system. "Oh, de people didn't put much faith to de doctors in dem days," remarked an ex-slave. "Mostly, de would use de herbs in de fields for de medicine."[57] Intimate knowledge of this medicine was normally the property of the "herb doctor," a slave in the neighborhood, very often a plantation nurse, who ambidextrously practiced both black and white man's medicine. Slaves when sick often approached their own herb doctors first for a cure believing that there is "a root for ev'y disease,"[58] and the only trick was to match "root" with disease, which meant of course some experimentation.[59] The most frequently relied on roots and herbs included "lion's tongue" (wintergreen tea), red oak bark, "life everlasting" (rabbit tobacco), garlic, Jerusalem oak, tansy leaves, catnip, sage, snake root, peach tree leaves, elephant tongue, chinaberry tea, comfrey, raspberry leaves, pine needles, dogwood, sea myrtle, orange milkweed, wild cherry bark, polk root, mustard weed, Peter's root, may apple, and sweet william roots.

That "remedies" of this nature or even the more unpalatable such as fried "young mice," "boiled cockroaches," and "sheeps' dung tea"[60] were much less painful than the "mercuralizing," leeching, cupping, and lancing done by white physicians must certainly have been part of their appeal to slaves. This same appeal, incidentally, often drew white people to black practitioners.[61] But mostly the appeal may have been a much better record of patient recoveries, for on a priori grounds alone it can be noted that even if few slave remedies actually cured, they did not kill, which is better than sometimes can be said for heroic white medicine.[62]

But without romanticizing folk practice, many slave cures undoubtedly were effective not only because matches were achieved between "roots" with medicinal properties and diseases that yielded to the medicine, but because African practitioners knew, as good physicians have always known, that a patient's recovery depends as much on psychological factors – whether he believes that a particular treatment will be effective – as on the efficacy of the treatment itself, which at bottom demands a faith in the doctor.

Because many bondsmen seem to have had little faith in white doctors but much in black practitioners, for this reason alone they were likely to be more effective. Then too, much of the faith derived from the comfort given a slave by one of his fellows as opposed to a too often austere aloof white, convinced not only of his own superiority but of black inferiority as well. Much of it also had to do with the ritualistic manner in which herbs and treatments were dispensed: with many flourishes and charms to enlist the supernatural in buttressing the remedy.[63]

Testimony to the efficacy of folk practitioners and their methods comes from whites as well as blacks, for indeed as a rule the plantation herb doctor was not only encouraged by the slaveholder but at times consulted by him, underscoring Eugene Genovese's bland observation that "the medical profession did not enjoy a reputation for infallibility."[64]

"Kitty cured 39 out of 40 cases" of scarlet fever, enthused the mistress of one plantation, "by giving little medicine but snake root tea and saffron tea and rubbing [the] body all over with old bacon skin."[65] "It is seldom" wrote another slaveholder "that I call in a physician. We Doctor upon the old woman slave and have first-rate luck."[66] In fact Negro folk practitioners[67] on occasion were praised even by white competitors such as the eminent Dr. Ramsay who acknowledged that black doctors were often more successful at restoring patients to health than their white counterparts.[68]

In the area of obstetrics, however, black practitioners were less successful. Many cases of the "nine day fits" (tetanus due to an infected umbilicus) discussed in Chapter 7, must have been due to the African practice of applying mud to the umbilical stump. Black midwives also were blamed for a fair amount of the high incidence of uterine disease among slave women, and certainly those who were in the habit of forcing the patient to stand erect right after delivery and shaking her until she delivered the placenta must have contributed to many of the cases of prolapsed uterus endured by black females.[69]

White doctors roared condemnation at the heavy reliance of planters on midwives, and to give the physicians their due planters who employed them [the physicians] in their maternity wards do seem to have enjoyed low levels of infant mortality.[70] Not that physicians actually knew what they were about in preventing tetanus among the newborn, and in fact one of the South's better-known physicians attributed the disease to his observation that black babies lie still except when being fed. The trismus, he claimed, was the result of the occipital bone slipping out of place.[71] But the emphasis of antebellum physicians on cleanliness (and especially their advice to bathe the infants daily) doubtless saved many newborns from the dreaded trismus, while their anatomic knowledge may have spared many females postpartum complications. In this connection too, most physicians prescribed a month's rest for the mother following delivery, although on the better managed plantations this seems to have been a fairly standard practice born of good common sense.

Yet oddly, in spite of the regular physicians' reasonably good showing in matters of maternity, his attendance in these cases was the exception, and midwives remained the rule, whereas he was in great demand when epidemic disease was afoot, yet here his record was usually poor. An explanation for this apparent incongruity is threefold and reflects something of the medical compromise worked out by black patients and practitioners with white planters and doctors.

First, midwifery was an old and venerable institution in most frontier regions, and more importantly it was one cherished by the slaves themselves. Second, most planters avoided interfering in the day-to-day life of the slave community and, like the slaves, viewed birth as a natural occurrence best left in their hands. Third, even if planters were disturbed either financially or morally by the heavy rate of infant mortality in the slave cabins, the very nature of the birth process militated against professional attendance. Then babies did not arrive on demand (as they do too often today at the hands of impatient obstetricians) and to assure the presence of a physician at birth meant something akin to fulltime employment.

In the face of epidemic disease, on the other hand, if planters did not have absolute confidence in white physicians, they had even less faith in the abilities of local black practitioners. The latter might treat common complaints with competence but were not to be trusted in combat with an enemy that could conceivably wipe out the planter. In "serious" matters of health, therefore, the white doctor was normally called.

Perhaps one additional reason why antebellum medical men were not employed for the more routine medical chores, such as child delivery, was their relative scarcity. For, although the roster of physicians swelled considerably throughout the antebellum period, so did the general population, including urban populations that lured many a doctor away from the plantations. Thus, despite the profitability of slave medicine, the field was often one dominated by beginners, aspiring to an urban practice or, better, to a plantation of their own.

The consequence was a high turnover among rural doctors and planter disgruntlement, such as that expressed by Ebenezer Pettigrew who, angered by losing still another doctor, wrote "I do not care much for any of them. I have at last learned that they are but men, and as mean and ignorant as other men and little to be depended upon."[72] Yet in the doctors' defense, the business of slave medicine was a lonely, unrewarding affair; one of incessant travel between plantations, often in the middle of the night, of packing and unpacking saddlebags, of visiting patients who did not always welcome their attentions, and of dealing with planters who recalled their failures far longer than their successes.

Moreover, slave medicine created special frustrations for the physician that he did not experience with white patients. Diagnosis of diseases in the latter was frequently based on skin color, which, if yellowed suggested jaundice, if reddened might indicate scarlet fever and so forth. But the black skin disguised symptoms physicians were trained to look for.[73] Hence they frequently complained "of their inability to make out a satisfactory diagnosis among negro patients, and the little satisfaction they have in treating [those] cases."[74] Indeed it was generally agreed that, although blacks were sick less often than whites, when they did become ill their cases were far more difficult to diagnose and cure.[75] Then, too, physicians were of the belief that a slave could not bear the large doses of medicine prescribed for whites, nor could they stand up so well under bloodletting. Bereft of the standard procedures of massive dosing and venesection, the southern physician viewed the black as an odd and trying patient.

Furthermore, plantation doctors often met with diseases they could neither fathom nor treat because underlying them was the patient's conviction that he had been poisoned or hexed or charmed.[76] Rheumatic or neuralgic pains, for example, were sometimes attributed to witches who descended on sleeping victims, and rode astride their backs making them "caper about on all fours."[77] Much of this illness stemmed from vestiges of West African religious beliefs that lived on in the slave quarters. Some, too, it has been speculated, was symptomatic of a dementia produced by nutritional diseases such as pellagra. But in any event the physician was frequently baffled in dealing with afflictions of this nature.

Another problem with treating slaves was their fatalistic outlook, an acceptance of inevitable death sometimes helped along by their decision that they were going to die and then doing precisely that. Other times, however, slaves, impressed with the physicians' energetic efforts, took a lively interest in their own treatment. Physicians believed that, among other things, sugar-coated pills of a uniform size could be especially effective with slaves due to "the confidence which negroes are apt to place in neatly prepared and tasteless remedies."[78] Thus, plantation journals disclose recipes for such concoctions as Gibson's fever pills, also known as "nigger pills."[79]

Another distinctive part of slave medicine had to do with warranting "soundness" in a slave prior to his sale, a practice which Juriah Harris, professor of physiology at Savannah Medical College, called attention to in his 1858 study of "What constitutes Unsoundness in a Negro." According to Harris, physicians were "daily called upon" for such warranting activity, inspecting for impairments such as rheumatism, hemorrhoids, and hernias that might curtail the usefulness of a slave, while women were especially scrutinized for difficulties that might prevent childbearing.[80] Occasionally this practice offered the opportunity for individual enterprise, whereby the attending physician purchased "unsound" slaves, restored them to health and pocketed a sizable profit.[81]

A final opportunity that was afforded physicians in the unique field of slave medicine was the chance to experiment, which they dared not do with whites. In most cases, experimenting was done on black ca-

davers that were in great demand by medical colleges for dissections –
so great in fact as to support a thriving practice of "body snatching."[82]
But in some cases the experimentation was carried out in surgery. One
notable success was that of Dr. Marion Sims who perfected his technique for operating on vesicovaginal fistulas through a long series of
operations on slave women, achieving success after four years and
thirty operations.[83] The gynecologic breakthrough was of major importance to the medical world. Yet in the words of John Duffy, "It is
highly unlikely that any surgeon, northern or southern, would have
experimented on white women in such a way."[84]

The same was true for advances in the techniques of the cesarean
section. The poor nutritional status of many slave women meant a
plethora of pelvic deformity cases among them, and consequently
many women unable to give normal birth. Led by Francois Marie
Prévost, Louisiana physicians in particular achieved a high degree of
success, performing fifteen such operations between 1822 and 1861
saving eleven mothers and eight children. But again, all the operations
were performed on slave women suggesting "that southern surgeons
and physicians were far more willing to try new procedures upon
slaves than upon other women."[85]

Set against this semiresponsible medical experimentation, which at
least did save lives (although at an awful price in pain in an age that
knew little of anesthesia), was some totally irresponsible tinkering by a
few physicians eager to know not only if blacks did experience less
pain than whites, but how much depletion they could bear.[86] They
were, in other words, anxious for fame in the field of Negro medicine,
a field sown lavishly, as will be seen, with the seeds of political and
professional self-interest with scientific racism the harvest.

CHAPTER 12

PHYSICIANS VERSUS THE SLAVES

When we look at the Southern Negro physically and intellectually, we find him emphatically dissimilar to his bipedal fellow of the white race . . . he is (the negro) palpably antipodal to the white man.

Dr. H. A. Ramsay (1852)[1]

The physician is, par excellence, the slaves' friend.

Dr. S. A. Cartwright (1853)[2]

I

The binomial nomenclature of Linnaeus dominated scientific attitudes on race during most of the eighteenth century. Species were classified neatly by genus and although men might differ, they were more alike than different and certainly all of the same race. Differences were attributed to environmental factors such as a "vertical sun" which had turned the Negro black, temperate zones that colored the Caucasian white, and in-between climates that produced in-between hues.[3]

This "environmentalism" also had the virtue of squaring with the Mosaic account of man's creation. Yet from this flowed a concept of the equality of all men that did not square with the practice of chattel slavery, particularly not in the United States, which was noisily claiming to have constituted a government on that principle.

But uncomfortable as the contradiction was, as the eighteenth century dissolved into the nineteenth, the pain was expected to be of short duration. Provision had been made for closing the slave trade in a few short years, and most states had already ceased slave importations. As for slavery itself, even its defenders described it as a "temporary evil," while few expected the peculiar institution to outlive the demise of the slave trade for any length of time.

Just as the western world was losing its enthusiasm for slavery, however, innovations in technology and transportation breathed new life into the South's peculiar institution, and as short-staple cotton, Whitney's gin, and a transportation revolution joined to perform the

175

economic midwifery that brought about slavery's rebirth, it suddenly became important to justify a practice that only yesterday southerners had come perilously close to agreeing was indefensible. This justifying was first important and then imperative as the Atlantic slave trade to much of the hemisphere and then in many places slavery itself fell victim to unleashed abolitionist pressure, leaving the South in a kind of paranoic isolation with the angry buzz of abolitionists sounding more and more ominous in its collective ear.

The gnawing need to rationalize slavery forced southerners to close ranks and inspect their ideologic defenses. The South's batallions of professionals then went into action. Ministers rolled forth the most venerable of weapons in the southern arsenal – the Scriptures – and Ham's curse from the book of Genesis was fired broadside at slavery's enemies. Meanwhile, to keep up morale on the homefront, reminders were roared from the pulpit that God had ordained slavery. The legal profession was committed to the fray, upholding the rights of slave-holders on constitutional grounds, while politicians scouted terrain favorable to slavery's expansion.[4]

But whether biblical or constitutional, southern thrusts were too easily parried by contrary interpretations. Something more was required, something that might transcend skirmishes over scripture and law and silence critics once and for all. Abolitionists held that it was morally wrong to enslave other men; but what if it could be shown that Negroes were not "men" in the sense that Caucasians were men, but rather something much less, something impossibly inferior?

It was this burden of demonstrating black inferiority on a scientific level that was taken up by some of the more vocal members of the southern medical profession.[5] Armed with the accumulated knowledge of their colleagues on black and white differential disease experiences, they were also able to build on the fact that the concept of the unity of man was no longer the dogma it had been a few decades earlier and indeed was under spirited attack from American science.[6]

Sorties early in the nineteenth century had been carried out by individuals such as Charles Caldwell, who questioned whether climate alone could have wrought the marked physical differences between Europeans and Africans.[7] Yet the first full-scale assault was aimed not at physical but intellectual differences. In 1839, Dr. Samuel George Morton published his *Crania Americana* which, on the basis of skull measurements, divided mankind into twenty-two families, subdivided into five races.[8] In terms of "highest intellectual endowment", the families of the Caucasian race held pride of place, while those of the "Ethiopian" race clustered at the bottom. The work received favorable reviews with much of America's scientific community pleased that at last some hard evidence was at hand to support the theory of man's diversity.[9]

Under Morton's influence, new vistas were quickly opened. Because intellects differed by race but climate had nothing to do with determining intellect, perhaps climate had also been wrongly credited for differences in color, hair texture, and those countless other peculiarities that made one group of men different from another. Indeed many began to suspect that most racial differences might be permanent after all which, if true, suggested that quite possibly man had not originated from a single progenitor. In this case, "species" of man could be conceived of, all at different stages of development, with the implied inevitable inequalities.[10]

The ensuing debate over the question of man's diversity was a vigorous one which saw the coalescence of a group of like-minded thinkers today identified as the "American School of Ethnology." That the "school" was thoroughly dedicated to the notion of innate racial inequality is exemplified by two works both co-authored by member Josiah C. Nott (a student of Morton's) and George Gliddon. Together *Types of Mankind* (1855) and *Indigenous Races of the Earth* (1857) provide a massive compilation of the thought of the "American school" and summarize in detail the attitude of many of America's scientists toward the black on the eve of the Civil War. In short, the black was relegated to a separate class of man – the lowest species – whose intelligence was so far below that of the Caucasian that he was helplessly incapable of governing himself. The logical conclusion, of course, for anyone who cared to reach for it, was that slavery, far from being a necessary evil, was instead a positive good.

Yet southern physicians (and the South generally) dared not reach for it even though Nott was one of their own. For the doctrine of multiple origins upon which the American school was based was anathema to orthodox religion, the most sturdy buttress in the defense of the peculiar institution because of its grass roots foundation. To challenge it with a doctrine certain to offend the clergy, yet one laden with abstruse arguments and abstract theories that could only baffle the layman was unthinkable.

II

The American school was not, as William Stanton has pointed out, "a deliberate construction of Southerners and Southern sympathizers in the North."[11] Its doctrines might have offered much ideological reinforcement to the South's cause, but the cost, also in ideological terms, was far too heavy – particularly when those doctrines could not circulate on the popular level. There did, however, circulate on that less rarified plane an absolute conviction of Negro inferiority which spokesmen for southern physicians could nurture and give conceptual form to, not by recourse to ethnology, but by emphasizing physiology.

The virtue of this approach was that it could produce the desired black inferiority and something of a scientific underpinning for popular persuasion without colliding with the entrenched Mosaic account of creation.[12] Moreover, the materials for constructing a case for black physiologic and intellectual inferiority were readily at hand – those materials the product of different black and white problems of health that physicians observed daily. They knew that blacks possessed disease immunities and susceptibilities peculiar to themselves; they had witnessed their dramatic refractoriness to yellow fever, observed their steadfast resistance to malaria, yet watched them succumb to a score of other diseases from which whites normally recovered.

Interestingly (but not surprisingly), theorizing by nineteenth-century southern physicians to explain disease discrimination by race closely parallels the changing racial thought of the larger scientific community. Early in that century, for example, even though it was customary to think and talk in terms of "Negro diseases," the etiologies of these diseases were conceived of in climatic and environmental terms (as they had been during the eighteenth century) rather than in racial terms. Blacks had more pleurisies and other respiratory sicknesses than whites because their lungs were more accustomed to the "torrid zone" than to North America's temperate climate.[13] Many infant illnesses as well as skin afflictions of adults were attributed to problems of cleanliness, while the black's chronic bowel disorders were blamed on improperly cooked food, bad water, and so forth.[14]

But with the 1830s, these perceived environmental etiologies began to yield to assumptions of racial predisposition to various illnesses. In part, this metamorphosis in southern epidemiologic thought was encouraged by the new racial orientation given to scientific research throughout the western world. Some reinterpretation of the causes of a differing black and white disease experience in the South, however, would probably have come about, regardless of any outside intellectual influence.

A case in point is black susceptibility to respiratory disorders that really could no longer be blamed on lungs unaccustomed to temperate climates; not when those lungs now dwelled in chests of slaves many generations removed from the tropics. Thus, the old explanation was discarded and a new one – that blacks were innately endowed with smaller and weaker lungs – with a decidedly genetic, as opposed to an environmental, emphasis was advanced.[15]

Having settled the matter of the slave's lungs, southern physicians turned their attention to other parts of his body. Not only, it was decided, were the lungs of the Negro smaller than those of Caucasians, but his heart and brain were also diminutive by comparison.[16] On the other hand, his liver, kidneys, and "glands" were both larger and more active than Caucasian counterparts, while his skin dealt with heat more efficiently than that of the white man's.[17] The latter incidentally was believed to make him remarkably suited for hard labor.[18]

Throughout the 1830s and 1840s as these dissimilarities were "discovered" and commented upon, the conviction grew that a direct relationship existed between the Negro's anatomic peculiarities and his disease susceptibilities. Yet the nature of these relationships remained elusive, despite the efforts of some experimentally inclined doctors whose attempts to discover them worked considerable wear and tear on black patients.[19] This was considered excusable, however, because of another medical "discovery." Negroes, it was asserted, did not experience pain to the same degree as whites "because their nervous systems were less well developed."[20] This hypothesis coupled nicely with the Negro's allegedly small brain to explain one more aspect of the black and white differential disease phenomena. Blacks were much less susceptible to brain and nervous disorders than their masters because they engaged in far less intellectual activity.[21]

From a physician's standpoint, the slave's underdeveloped nervous system was believed to pose some tricky problems, among them that large quantities of medicine should not be given to slaves, nor should large quantities of blood be taken from them. In fact to treat a slave as a white patient might kill him, all of which implied a substantially different approach to the black sickbed.[22] By the 1850s then, the dawning medical perception of innate black and white physiologic differences had given rise to the notion that blacks and whites required different medical treatments and that in the South a distinctive practice of medicine (that is, Negro medicine) was called for.[23]

It is at this juncture that many currents converge to muddy the water and obscure the development of racial thought among antebellum physicians. Heretofore the mainstream, as it were, had been the steadily accumulating body of knowledge on black disease immunities and susceptibilities, laboriously compiled by southern medical doctors, and lately attributed to black physiologic differences. But during the early 1850s findings of the American school trickled into a mainstream already clouded by the swirling currents of medical professionalism, white supremacy, Negrophobia, and southern nationalism.

Perhaps the man who knew these waters best, charting and then navigating them with considerable skill was Dr. Samuel Cartwright, a native Virginian, trained in Pennsylvania and Maryland, with practices first in Natchez and then in New Orleans, who became the South's foremost expert on Negro diseases.[24] Cartwright left a large and successful practice in Natchez during the cholera epidemic of 1848 to battle the disease in New Orleans. The following year he found himself still in that city and, by virtue of his observations on black-related diseases, charged by the Louisiana State Medical Convention with preparing a report on these ethnic afflictions. A defense and elaboration of that report submitted in 1850 would occupy most of his remaining life (which ended in 1862), and earn for him the scorn of some colleagues, the admiration of many and the undisputed title of champion of State's Rights medicine.[25]

Indeed, for Cartwright, the major cause of the sectional difficulties between North and South centered on northern ignorance of the medical and physiologic peculiarities of blacks. "The popular error prevalent at the North," declared Cartwright in one of his seminal 1850 polemics on "The Diseases and Physical Peculiarities of the Negro Race," "that the negro is a white man, but, by some accident of climate or locality, painted black, requiring nothing but liberty and equality – social and political – to wash him white, is permitted to go uncorrected by the Northern medical schools."[26] Rather, contended Cartwright, the Negro's blackness was more than just skin deep, and in fact "darkness" pervaded every area of the black's body from the brain to the muscles; tendons, membranes, even the humors were tainted with dark hues.[27]

The implications of this blackness were many. Physiologically, blacks and whites were separated by an enormous gulf, but unfortunately the differences did not end with the physiologic. Rather, black physiologic peculiarities lay at the root of a hopeless mental inferiority due to a Negro "hebetude of intellect." This unhappy condition stemmed from an improper "atmospherization" of Negro blood, in part the fault of small lungs that made impossible the inhalation of sufficient fresh air to accomplish proper "atmospherization" and in part because of an innate black distaste for fresh air.[28]

This antipathy, Cartwright alleged, was common to all infants for whom the "full and free respiration of pure fresh air . . . is hurtful and prejudicial."[29] A baby needed to rebreathe "its own breath, warmed to the same temperature as that of its body, and loaded with carbonic acid and acqueous vapor."[30] Caucasians outgrew this stage, but blacks, being perpetual infants, did not, as demonstrated by the "universal practice among them of covering their head and faces, during sleep, with a blanket, or any kind of covering that they can get hold of."[31] It was this "defective hematosis" the Louisiana physician explained confidently that caused the black to lack courage and mental energy. In tandem with the smaller brain, this bred his "indolence and apathy," and childlike behavior.[32]

Cartwright had a great deal more to say in this vein, much of it ingeniously argued, some of it carefully reasoned, all of it leading to generalizations calculated to further the cause of slavery as well as his own profession. In the latter case, the sum was a plea for the creation of a unique branch of southern medicine (Negro medicine) to treat beings whose physiologic makeup and disease susceptibilities demanded specialized attention. Cartwright was equally dogmatic in advancing the cause of slavery. The unhappy physical and mental state of the blacks made it imperative that a superior race direct and take care of them. Slavery then, under Cartwright's pen became a peculiar institution for peculiar people, a salubrious institution for those "endowed with a will so weak, passions so easily subdued, and dispositions so gentle and affectionate" that they would be lost could they not exercise their "instinctive feeling of obedience to the stronger will of the white man."[33]

Cartwright was obviously an extremist, but it was he, more than anyone else, who has been credited with drawing together the threads of black physiologic peculiarities spun by predecessors and contemporaries and then weaving into them a concept of mental inferiority.

How influential Cartwright was on his profession is difficult to ascertain. Most doctors who wrote for the medical journals of the New South seem to have more or less followed his lead. Physicians in the Old South, however, particularly those of Charleston, balked completely, pronouncing the whole of his arguments "an absurdity."[34] In a scathing 1851 review of one of Cartwright's publications, they challenged him "to distinguish between two specimens of blood taken respectively from the white and black man. We defy him to distinguish between specimens of muscle, tendon, chyle, lymph, bile, brain or nerves."[35] As for the black's love of slavery, the Charleston physicians scoffed, "surely the author does not mean that it was an act of humanity bestowed on the race when we stole them from their native land, and brought them amongst us, to be our hewers of wood and drawers of water."[36]

The following year the same physicians addressed themselves to Cartwright's criticisms of northern medical schools with the declaration that "we were born and bred in the South, but we received our medical eduction in the North. For every dollar paid out there, we take pleasure in saying that we received the fullest value and our only regret is that circumstances would not permit us to remain longer in the capacity of a student in that benighted land."[37]

Yet even such determined opponents as these were quieted as events of the decade prodded North and South toward war. Some moved in Cartwright's direction by observing cautiously that specialists in black medicine were probably needed and a separate branch of the profession called for on diagnostic grounds alone, confessing their own difficulties in spotting disease symptoms when the patients were black. Others, including many of the South's most prolific physician writers, chorused an enthusiastic approval of both Cartwright's reasoning and conclusions and offered their thoughts to bolster the growing discipline.

The sum constituted a medical-cum-political argument for the close study of the black's physiologic distinctiveness or "niggerology" as Nott termed it,[38] with distorting lenses sliding the focus frequently from the physiologic to the psychologic. "Look," commanded a Georgia physician, "at his [the black's] small brain, his deficient intellection, his small lungs and defective atmospherization, his increased liver, his black blood and sluggish circulation, his obtunded nervous sensibility, his enlarged glandular system, all pointing to a physical character, animal in its inclinations and wanting in those attributes of intelligence which elevate the white man and places him far above the brute."[39]

Superstitious, lazy, childlike, sluggish, dull in mind, weak in will: the black became all these things to the South's more vocal physicians who, stimulated by black and white differential experiences with disease, coupled physical traits with moral and mental attributes to forge another link in slavery's defense perimeter. Under their pens the blacks were so inferior that "no education can be of help."[40]

As free men, or left to their own devices, they would invariably succumb to those "unalterable physiological laws" which could only mean a "relapse into barbarism."[41] Slavery then was a positive good, they concluded thereby discharging their obligation to southern nationalism.

Under the circumstances it was the best these doctors could do and still remain clear of questions of multiple origins, so offensive to the religiously orthodox. Moreover, the effort did confront directly the central problem of a South imbued with a faith in democratic government yet dedicated to slavery. For the only resolution of this dilemma was the demonstration of an inherent Negro inferiority.

This demonstration, however, had no chance of uniting whites North and South into ethnocentric ranks, as individuals such as Cartwright may have hoped. They did see their influence penetrate with some vigor north of the Mason-Dixon line, perhaps the most infamous example contained in the pages of New York physician John H. Van Evrie's *Negroes and Negro "Slavery": The First an Inferior Race: the Latter its Normal Condition* (N.Y. 1861). But the nature of the antebellum "science" of the Negro seemed too patently self-serving to have much of an impact outside of a self-interested slaveholding region.

III

Nineteenth-century medical understanding of the black began with "fevers" and a medical appreciation of the black's ability to resist them and was followed by the realization that the black had special disease liabilities. Based upon these twin factors of disease susceptibilities and immunities, antebellum medical men elaborated a theory of physiologic differences between white and black – differences which in time of illness demanded differential medical treatment.

The theory in part reflected nothing more than southern racism. But it was also a product of the accumulated experience of country physicians throughout the South, who had spent much of their careers in tending sick slaves. With the tumult of the 1850s, however, it was appropriated and expressed most vociferously by extremists such as Cartwright who were avid racists, caught in the grip of southern nationalism, but nonetheless spokesmen with a fine eye for opportunity; in this case the opportunity to professionalize the southern medical profession.

Consequently, the call for Negro medicine could be alternately portrayed as a bid for monopoly over the lucrative slave practice and the training of southern practitioners, a popularization of the doctrines of the American school of ethnology, a movement for states' rights medicine, a defense of slavery and an attempt to instruct the North on the difficulties of the white man's burden.

Doubtless it was, in conception and in fact, all of these things. When Dr. Arnold in the shambles of one of Savannah's yellow fever outbreaks declared, "The epidemic has convinced me how utterly impossible it is for the white race to do the outdoor work in this hot climate," he was expressing an age-old defense of slavery on epidemiologic grounds.[42] When during the last years before the War southern medical schools flourished and proliferated as more and more native sons decided that they should study the disease peculiarities of their land and their people at home rather than in the North, those dedicated to the cause of southern medicine must have felt a glow of satisfaction, a glow that burst into the joy of absolute success when just on the eve of hostilities, prospective young members of the antebellum medical establishment (still students in the North) anticipated the future course of their own states by "seceding" en masse from northern medical schools.[43]

And when the *Texas Almanac* three years before the outbreak of the War asserted that "the African is an inferior being, differently organized from the white man, with wool instead of hair on his head – with lungs, feet, joints, lips, nose and cranium so distinct as to indicate a different and inferior grade of being," then neatly dodged the troublesome question of "whether this comes from the curse upon Ham and his descendents forever, or from an original law of God" it succinctly expressed the South's own rendition of the "American School" thought.[44]

Yet what is frequently missed is that the call for a separate branch of Negro medicine was also stimulated by a genuine conviction of unique black health problems that require specialized attention.[45] This conviction was logically arrived at by physicians with much experience in treating the ills of Southerners black and white, with their collective observations antedating by decades the sectional conflict. Thus had there been no debate over slavery, there most probably would still have been a call for Negro medicine, and had there been no Civil War the first textbook on the subject by John Stainback Wilson probably would have appeared.[46] But the War broke out before the book could be published, and following emancipation there was less white interest in black health problems, for then a black "was nobody's nigger but his own," with no one responsible for paying his bills.

In understanding the need for a specialized study of black-related diseases, antebellum medical men anticipated American medical science by over a century. Unhappily in so doing they also, in the words of George Fredrickson, elevated "prejudice to the level of science, thereby giving it respectability,"[47] and their legacy was a "scientific racism" rather than an appreciation of the ethnicity of disease. Sadly then, behind the facade of antebellum medicine, stood strong pillars of racism, and like those buildings of ancient civilizations, the pillars remained long after the facade had crumbled.

PART V

SEQUELAE AND LEGACY

INTRODUCTION TO PART V

Black people in America do not have to be told that they have been the victims of bad medical treatment. They have found this out repeatedly whenever they have presented themselves for care at thousands of hospitals and at innumerable doctors' offices and clinics, where they have often been ridiculed and accused of being the cause of their own medical misfortunes.

Rev. Jesse L. Jackson (1975)[1]

Although antebellum physicians were frustrated in getting a scientific grip on the slippery question of racial origins, their postbellum successors suffered no such disability. Just prior to the opening shots at Fort Sumter the work of Charles Darwin appeared, and scarcely had the guns fallen silent at Appomattox before Josiah Nott synthesized much of the new theory with previous work on race done by the American School.[2] Darwin's theory of evolution might create difficulties for fundamentalists for decades to come, but it proved a godsend to racists willing to interpret the Bible a bit more liberally. For Darwin made it possible to bypass the inherently heretical question of a "recent creation" to account for the black man's lack of development and return to the biblical concept of an original creation. All men had been created as one but following that creation peoples had diverged considerably in their respective evolutionary journeys – whites emerging from that journey forged and tempered – a dynamic, intellectually blessed race, while blacks were still stumbling along a trail that had led to near hopeless retardation as a member of the genus *Homo*, rungs behind on the evolutionary ladder.

The peculiar institution had provided a snug paternal, noncompetitive world for the black in which he thrived. But emancipation had changed all of that. Now the races were thrown together in a competitive situation, and the race least fit was, as Darwin was interpreted, inevitably doomed.

Immediately following emancipation the popular "crude belief" existed that blacks would condemn themselves by refusing to work voluntarily. But when these expectations failed to materialize southern whites decided against gambling on black self-immolation and began constructing those political, economic, and social perimeters that would enclose the black in a second-class world. As it turned out, however, the environmental circumstances of that world coupled with black disease susceptibilities had much to do with resuscitating the concept of racial doom in the minds of southern physicians, suddenly confronted on all sides by what seemed to be a veritable epidemic among blacks of diseases such as scrofula, consumption, and syphilis as well as a frightening frequency of black stillbirths.

Moreover, frequently defective census data also seemed to gloomily toll black extinction. For example, after examining the 1890 data, a physician declared that blacks were dying twice as fast as whites and in some regions four times as fast. "Indeed it is a question," he exclaimed, "whether at this rate there will be ultimately any of the race left."[3]

A few years later Alabama's Dr. Seale Harris, after studying the nation's first census of the twentieth century, found the black death rate to be almost three (2.7) times greater than the white rate, and he too doubted "whether anything we can do will save the negro from racial extermination."[4]

Moreover, adult death rates were only half of the black's demographic problem. Blacks were also failing to reproduce themselves due largely, in the opinion of physicians, to an enormous number of stillbirths as well as heavy infant mortality. A Richmond doctor amassed data for that city during the years 1871–74 which revealed that one black stillbirth occurred for every seven live babies born as opposed to a white ratio of one in eighteen. Another physician presented similar data for Savannah to demonstrate that between 1884–92, 1,040 black stillbirths had occurred in that city as opposed to 252 white stillborns.[5] Frederick Hoffman amassed data on stillbirths from Washington D. C. and Baltimore which showed the rate per 100,000 population for blacks was 20 and 17, respectively as opposed to 6.5 and 7 for the whites,[6] all of which led one physician to the sardonic comment that the "Negro certainly leads in not being born."[7]

Certainly "survival of the fittest" notions as well as racist wishful thinking caused many to exaggerate the extent of the black postbellum health crisis. But it was a crisis nonetheless, which saw black disease susceptibilities exacerbated by diets and housing in many cases far worse than in the slave days.

Tuberculosis and pneumonia were the two major killers. The former had not of course suddenly burst upon blacks. Rather, as has already been discussed, it was only now behaving in a way recognizable to physicians. Crowded, badly ventilated housing abetted its spread as well as that of pneumonia, another disease to which the black has proven historically susceptible.

Moreover, black resistance to these and other diseases must have been low because of their diet, which had gone from bad under slavery to perhaps even worse after emancipation, recent attempts to romanticize "soul food" notwithstanding. Studies indicate that it was seriously lacking in fresh meats, milk, eggs, fruits, and vegetables, while the starchy food which did predominate was either fried in fat or boiled with fat meat.[8] Consequently, the regimen of blacks continued well into this century to be dangerously low in iron, calcium, vitamins, and proteins, precisely those deficiencies that were most glaring in the slave diet, and indeed deficiencies also chronic in the West African diet.

No wonder then that the postbellum list of "Negro diseases" included not only pneumonia and tuberculosis but worms, teething, tetanus, trismus, and smothering, the same diseases that were the biggest killers of slaves. Two "new" (meaning newly recognized) afflictions that joined the list – pellagra and rickets – were both nutritional illnesses and in tandem dramatically highlight the poor quality of the black diet following slavery.

Many southern physicians were sympathetic to black health problems. Most blamed environmental conditions, although a few suspected that another important factor was that Afro-Americans were learning to live with some new ailments. But unfortunately, there were also many physicians who could not resist making racist capital of the black health crisis. Indeed, the medical journals of the period almost bristle with writings of doctors eager to portray the black as a filthy, loathsome, disease-ridden creature who was not only a threat to himself and his own people but an epidemiologic menace to whites as well.

For them the plight of the blacks was the result of "some supreme law . . . doing its work at a terrible rate."[9] That law was the inexorable evolutionary process of weeding out the unfit. "The negro was doomed," declared Dr. Corson in 1893, because "the world has reached a point where the caucasian is supreme and all else must give way before him."[10]

There were some, however, who even urged hurrying the extinction process. In some cases this amounted only to vague talk of entrusting "to the science of medicine . . . the last analysis of the negro problem."[11] Others were far more explicit, arguing for "the sterilization of the entire male negro population by vasectomy," a solution which would "bravely and humanely [solve] the greatest race problem of the ages."[12]

Thus as the twentieth century dawned Afro-Americans were still suffering both from distinctive illnesses and from those who sought to censure them for those illnesses. As the ensuing and final chapter should make clear this phenomenon continues today, just as a widespread ignorance of black health problems is still a fact today. Contagious diseases are no longer the deadly foes we saw them to be, but as the chapter attempts to show, nutritional difficulties continue to plague blacks and, indeed, constitute by far their most serious barrier to collective good health and longevity.

The evidence upon which the chapter rests has been gathered from many sciences and surveys, and for the most part represents the latest findings. An exception is the brief discussion of hypertension that, at this point, cannot be documented as thoroughly as we would like. Most examples of medical ignorance of black physiologic differences and difficulties which close the study do, indeed, seem representative of the medical and nutritional sciences. A few blatant racist statements are hopefully not representative but were included because of the manner in which they echo all the way from the slave days.

CHAPTER 13

EPILOGUE: CRADLE TO GRAVE

Perhaps the greatest need of the Negroes, in the way of reducing sickness and death, is for the dissemination of knowledge on how to take care of the body in both its normal and its pathological state.

Gunnar Myrdal (1944)[1]

All the Negroes I've seen around here are so fat they shine!

Mississippi Governor Paul Johnson in response to a question about hunger among blacks in his state (1967)[2]

President Truman's classic comment on politics, "If you can't stand the heat, stay out of the kitchen," has been stood on its head by officials reacting to heat on the hunger issues. They simply try to destroy the stove or oven responsible for the heat.

John Kramer (1974)[3]

I

The dawn of the twentieth century saw the black death rate standing at 30.2 per 1,000 as opposed to a white rate of 17.3.[4] Seven decades later (1972) the black death rate had been reduced to 9.4 per 1,000 and the white to 9.3 per 1,000.[5] Superficially it would seem that national self-congratulation is in order. Not only has the black death rate been cut by two-thirds, but today it is virtually the same as the white. Tuberculosis, which was killing turn-of-the century blacks at a rate well over 450 per 100,000 (three times the white rate), had by the years 1929–31 declined substantially in virulence removing only 199 for every 100,000 live population (yet still selecting blacks over whites at a 3:1 rate).[6] Today the disease kills a mere 8 blacks per 100,000 population, although parenthetically the racial preference of the disease has increased. As of 1972 the black tuberculosis mortality rate was almost five times that of whites.[7]

In 1900 pneumonia was also winnowing about 350 of every 100,000 blacks in America. By 1929–31, the rate had declined to 254. Today

191

influenza and pneumonia combined shorten life for only 42 blacks per 100,000 live population. But again whereas Afro-Americans throughout most of this century died from the disease at a rate three times that of whites, now that rate is five times greater.[8]

Syphilis, which reached epidemic proportions in the black community prior to World War II with over one-quarter of the black men inducted into the Army suffering from the disease,[9] has now been brought under control with penicillin at least relative to its higher incidence earlier in the century. The disease seems once more to be on the rise, however, with the *reported* cases "significantly higher among Blacks than among Whites."[10]

But returning to the point, despite the fact that the relative disadvantage of blacks in terms of mortality from these diseases has actually increased when compared to whites, these three old enemies are collectively far from the nemesis of the black community they once were. Yet one age-old enemy remains, which the apparent similarity in the death rates of black and white Americans obscures: infant mortality. For the overall death rate calculated without reference to age conceals the tragic truth that blacks are dying at a much younger age than whites with far too many making the journey from cradle to grave in less than a year.[11]

In the slave quarters, slave infants were dying at a rate approaching four times that of their white counterparts. It was noted that the black infant mortality rate in the decades following the Civil War was equally dismaying. But today the level of black infant mortality is still almost twice that of the whites. Thus, as of 1969 the white death rate for those aged less than one year was 18 per 1,000 as opposed to 33 blacks per 1,000 in the same age cohort,[12] and this despite the efforts of the medical and nutritional sciences. These efforts have coupled with an increasing standard of living to cut sharply into those high infant death rates to which the nineteenth century was all too accustomed, and certainly blacks have benefited in absolute terms. But relative to whites their gains have been disappointing in the extreme. In 1960, a black infant had almost a 90 percent greater chance of not reaching his first birthday than a white baby. By the early 1970s, the estimate was 80 percent, yet statistics gathered since 1940 suggest that the "comparative disadvantage of the Black community [in terms of infant mortality] has increased."[13] In other words, today a higher percentage of black as opposed to white babies are dying during their first year than thirty years ago. The implications are doubly disturbing when it is recalled that the period in question has witnessed a multitude of civil rights and affirmative action programs designed as part of a massive attempt to alter the black environment through expanded educational and employment opportunities.

II

Much of the black and white differential seems to stem from the low birth weights of black babies, for it is almost axiomatic that the lower the weight at birth the greater the risk of perinatal death.[14] Of the 50,000 infants born each year in the United States who do not survive a week of life, 75 percent are low birth weight (LBW) babies, meaning they weigh less than 2,500 grams (5½ pounds),[15] while the odds against these babies living out their first year of life are seventeen times greater than those of an infant weighing over 2,500 grams at birth.[16]

Unhappily blacks are heavily represented in this risky LBW category. As just mentioned, in 1960 a black infant born in the United States had a 90 percent greater chance of dying his first year than a white; significantly he also had a 90 percent greater chance of weighing less than 2500 grams at birth.[17] Equally significant the percentage of black LBW babies in proportion to live births has been increasing both absolutely and relative to whites. Between 1950 and 1960, for example, the nonwhite LBW rate in the United States rose from 10 to 13 percent, an increase of 30 percent in a single decade, while the white rate actually declined slightly from 7 to 6.8 percent.[18] In 1974, 13.1 percent of all black birth weights were 2,500 grams or less as opposed to 7 percent of the whites,[19] which in turn dovetails with those statistics that demonstrate that at present a higher percentage of black babies are dying during their first year of life relative to whites than thirty years ago.

Today black infants arrive in the world weighing on the average 200 grams less than whites,[20] reflecting the fact that in percentage terms blacks have twice as many LBW babies in every LBW category than do whites.[21] Some have explained this in racial or genetic terms in effect hypothesizing that blacks have lower "normal" birth weights than whites,[22] and while sketchy there is evidence to indicate that nature has elaborated a different scheme of fetal development as well as perinatal growth for blacks as opposed to Caucasians. Throughout the first and most of the second trimester of pregnancy, for example, the black fetus weighs more on the average than the white; it is only throughout the last trimester that the white fetus becomes heavier.[23] But, although initially smaller at birth, the black infant tends to grow more rapidly than his white counterpart after the first year of life.[24] Moreover if a black infant is born weighing 2,000 grams or less, his chances of survival are two or three times better than a white baby of the same weight, which implies a more mature development at lower weights for blacks than whites.[25] Hence early fetal development and accelerated growth after one year of age do suggest a pattern of development for blacks different than that of whites.

But against the genetic explanation[26] are indications that black birth weights do rise as the parents' level of education and socioeconomic status increase,[27] which leads directly to the most generally accepted determinant of birth weight: maternal nutrition. Many factors, of course, can influence birth weight ranging from the mother's age to cigarette smoking[28]; nonetheless, poor maternal nutrition seems unquestionably to be the most important cause of faulty fetal growth.[29] Thus, maternal deprivation looms large as a major reason for the high percentage of black LBW babies and an equally high infant mortality rate. Moreover, to the extent that genetic factors do account for black LBW, poor nutrition may still be culpable.

For although black birth weights have been shown to rise as parents ascend the socioeconomic ladder, when such variables as per capita income and occupational status are held constant, black birth weights still lag substantially behind those of whites.[30] From this observation the hypothesis has been generated that centuries of black nutritional deprivation have evoked a genetic or biochemical response that selects for small babies, therefore protecting the lives of malnourished mothers whose bodies could not withstand the rigors of giving birth to larger babies.[31]

Historical evidence does exist to suggest that LBW black babies are not simply a phenomenon of the last two or three decades. That the black would have a "smaller infant" seems to have been taken for granted by antebellum and postbellum physicians,[32] while doctors in the 1930s with access to thousands of white and black birth weights found those of the latter to be significantly less.[33] Of course, disregarding the slave days, neither the postbellum period nor the depressed 1930s were years of nutritional plenty for blacks, so evidence of this sort is inconclusive at best. Nevertheless the point is well taken that Afro-Americans have endured centuries of nutritional deprivation, and these centuries most probably have extracted a price.

Finally, the infants of malnourished mothers have a much greater chance of contracting serious illness during their first six months of life.[34] We have seen slave mothers with a poor diet losing an appalling number of their infants. Their badly nourished postbellum daughters and granddaughters had a similar experience, while today their great-granddaughters four and five times removed are caught in the same dilemma. They are still in serious nutritional difficulty and consequently are still losing babies at a much higher rate than white mothers.

III

Whether or not blacks possess a selective mechanism for small babies encouraged by long-run nutritional circumstances, birth weights can be raised even in the short-run if proper attention is given to the nutritional status of the mother. Famous examples can be found in studies

of famine-ridden parts of Europe during and after World War II where
a significant increase in the frequency of LBW babies occurred. As diets
improved following the War, however, so did baby weights.[35] Thus,
clearly the place to attack the problem of black LBW babies is on the
nutritional front.

But it will have to be a massive attack, for much needs to be cor-
rected. The U. S. Department of Health, Education and Welfare's Ten
State[36] Nutrition Survey 1968–1970 (TSNS), the first extensive nutritional survey ever conducted in the United States[37] found that blacks
receive less than half of the calcium and iron that whites do, with their
diet also dangerously low in vitamins A and C,[38] while other recent
studies, including the first Health and Nutrition Examination Survey
(HANES), in addition to confirming these findings, have revealed severely deficient intakes of magnesium, the vitamin B complex and
protein.[39] Because many of these deficiencies occur among black people
regardless of income, and in cases such as calcium deficiency are actually more prevalent among certain segments of the highest income
groups, a lack of dietary information may be as serious a problem as
low incomes in the nutritional plight of many of the nation's blacks.

IV

If the black diet on the whole is nutritionally inadequate, then black
prenatal diets, crucial in building the female's nutritional stores can be
said to border on the disastrous, and today's prospective mother, like
her slave progenitor, frequently faces pregnancy without adequate reserves of vitamin D, calcium, iron, and protein.[40]

It has been pointed out that lactose intolerance means that Afro-
Americans will tend to be calcium deficient unless their diet contains
high calcium-yielding nutriments other than milk (which surveys make
clear they do not). Then it was seen that this problem compounded for
slave mothers, whose dark skin meant that for at least part of the year
her body had difficulty in producing sufficient vitamin D to metabolize
that calcium (and magnesium) she did ingest. This situation can only
be more acute among black city dwellers who spend far less time
out-of-doors than did their slave forebearers and in many cases live in
much colder climates. Moreover, under the added nutritional stress of
pregnancy, the difficulty is once more compounded, because the fetus
will draw hourly up to 7 percent of the mother's serum calcium. Thus,
if the diet does not replace the loss of that mineral, calcium will ultimately have to come from maternal skeletal stores.[41]

Insofar as iron deficiency is concerned, those black hemoglobin abnormalities that may contribute to an anemic situation have already
been discussed. But these aside, in 1960 the diets of only 10 percent of
the South's black women provided them with their recommended daily

allowance (RDA) for iron,[42] while studies in the 1970s reveal that 90 to 95 percent of the black females between ages eighteen to forty-four have iron intakes below the RDA.[43] Then too, anemia frequently accompanies a diet that is too low in protein, and nutritional anemia has an adverse effect on birth weight.[44] That the black diet, which has been chronically low in protein since the slave days, is still severely wanting was determined by the TSNS which, on the basis of blood samples, found that three-quarters of the black expectant mothers surveyed were protein deficient.[45]

Additional confirmation of iron deficiency comes from the custom of geophagy among blacks. Pregnant slave women frequently ate dirt. This practice was often a response to a craving for certain minerals, particularly iron. Geophagy is still widespread among pregnant blacks in both rural and urban areas.[46] Relatives in the South send clay northward to urban dwellers, while starch-eating among pregnant black women is a well-known, if poorly understood, phenomenon.[47]

Vitamin C is also needed to enhance the absorption of iron. But national surveys show that blacks on the average receive only half of the RDA of this vitamin.[48] Then during pregnancy the female's ascorbic acid levels in the blood fall sharply because the fetus draws upon it to the extent that its levels range from two to four times higher than the mother's.[49] Additionally, the B vitamins (particularly riboflavin), also lacking in the black diet,[50] are important for fetal growth, while of course any diet low in all of these essential nutrients will impair the mother's ability to ward off infectious disease.

Finally, that blacks are seriously deficient in vitamin D was indicated by a study which found that 15 percent of American black females examined had significantly deformed pelves as a result of childhood vitamin D deficiency as opposed to only 2 percent of white females. They paid for this with a fetal mortality rate of 10 to 15 percent,[51] and while, of course, D deficiency was not the sole cause of this mortality rate, it was certainly a major contributing factor.

V

Clearly then African genetic characteristics, such as skin color, the decreased activity of the lactase enzyme, and hemoglobin abnormalities, exacerbate the effects of a poor dietary regimen, all of which quite literally makes life difficult for the fetus. Yet its difficulties are scarcely over following birth. During the period of one week to one year of age the biggest destroyer of infants by far is the sudden infant death syndrome (SIDS) discussed in Chapter 7 which strikes much harder at blacks than whites. Today black infants are still plagued by the killer that apparently harvested so many of their slave counterparts.

Large statistical studies in Seattle,[52] Texas,[53] Philadelphia,[54] and

Cleveland[55] have all revealed a black SIDS rate double that of whites. Worse, the absolute SIDS rate is undoubtedly much higher and the black and white differential much greater than even these data suggest. On the one hand, SIDS is a new designation of death (since 1974) and consequently is bound to be underreported by some physicians who habitually employ old "cause of death" rubrics such as "bronchopneumonia."[56]

On the other hand, many physicians, coroners, and law enforcement officers are reluctant to designate the death of an infant as SIDS if the victim is black. If an apparently healthy white child dies unexpectedly a diagnosis of SIDS is common. But if a black youngster dies in an identical manner, criminal child abuse or neglect is more frequently suspected, and incredibly physicians still diagnose the deaths of lower class black babies who sleep with their parents as suffocation or "overlaying" just as was done in slave days.[57]

Previously it was hypothesized that both the magnesium-deprivation growth syndrome and calcium deficiency were to blame for many of the sudden infant deaths on the plantation. Today they may remain very important factors. The HANES revelation that about 20 percent of the nation's black adolescent girls from below poverty level families show signs of serious calcium deficiency suggests that real problems lie ahead for the infants many of them will bear, while lending credence to the hypothesis. Surely the poor maternal diet of many black women, coupled with the demands of the fetus, can only make this nutritional situation more acute. And the maternal characteristics that seem to predispose a black infant to SIDS – relative youth, high parity and short intervals between births – all combine to place tremendous pressure on mineral stores and add even more weight to the hypothesis.[58] So, too, does the fact that LBW babies have a ten times greater chance of falling victim to SIDS than normal weight infants, for LBW babies are much more likely to be mineral deficient.[59]

Certainly this is true for iron, and because those born with low weights will normally undergo a period of accelerated growth following birth, an impossible pressure is put on depleted stores.[60] Iron deficiency, however, can mean anemia, and anemia is another factor known to predispose an infant to SIDS,[61] making it one more black health difficulty, which we first spied at work during the antebellum period. For many blacks the problem is literally life-long beginning at birth. Prematurely born children, LBW babies, and infants born of anemic mothers are frequently anemic.[62] Moreover, infants in all three categories will lose much of their already low hemoglobin mass by four to six months of age, meaning an even more serious depletion of iron stores.[63]

A debate has been waged of late over defining a "normal" hemoglobin concentration for blacks, and the suggestion has been made that perhaps as few as 10 grams per 100 ml for black children under twelve is a "normal" lower limit, whereas 11 grams per 100 ml for whites is considered to be the lower limit.[64] But others have argued that there are no racial differences in hemoglobin concentration and that blacks simply suffer more from anemia.[65] Certainly this is a field where little is known and much is to be done. On the other hand, a debate over a single gram or less per 100 ml may be bordering on quibbling, because anemia is generally defined as below 10 grams per 100 ml for both races.

A 1977 examination of black youngsters aged one through six years in South Carolina disclosed that fully one-half suffered from iron deficiency.[66] In Tennessee, one-quarter of the black children under three years of age in Memphis were found to be anemic.[67] In Washington D. C., one-third of the black preschoolers were classified as anemic, the proportion rising to two-thirds for those in the one to one-and-a-half year age bracket.[68] For the nation as a whole, HANES found that the iron intake of almost all (95 percent) of the black pre-school children was below the RDA, and pronounced one-quarter of them anemic.[69]

Included in this percentage, of course, is a range from moderate to acute anemia, but even mild anemia can be dangerous because it renders the body more susceptible to infection, and once an infection is superimposed on anemia a moderate condition generally becomes acute. Moreover, a victim caught up in this vicious cycle is also left vulnerable to any number of other complications resulting from the original infection.[70] Hence, anemia must undoubtedly play a deadly role in engineering the black death rate from children's diseases (such as measles, meningitis, diphtheria, and scarlet fever) which is fully six times that of whites.[71]

Following his first year of life the black child, although initially smaller, grows at a rate substantially more rapid than that of a white youngster. Teeth make an earlier appearance and the skeletal mass develops more quickly, which means accelerated requirements for calcium, magnesium, phosphorus, and vitamin D, not to mention calories.[72] That black children until recently contracted rickets almost as a rite of passage testifies that many of these requirements were met infrequently. Today, although enriched bread, cereals, and fortified milk manage for the most part to keep rickets at bay, it should not be concluded that the nutrients in question are adequately received by black youngsters. Rather a 1977 national study found vitamin D deficiency signs such as bowed legs, bossed skull, and knock-knees very prevalent among Afro-American preschoolers, implying a good deal of subclinical rickets.[73]

A reason for the school milk programs is to correct some of these deficiencies in nutritionally deprived children. Yet because 40 percent of black elementary school children have already developed symptoms of lactose intolerance, much of the program is wasted on them.[74] As teenagers, the percentage of lactose intolerants jumps to 60 percent, while by the time adulthood is reached 77 to 80 percent of all blacks have difficulty using milk.[75] Thus like anemia, calcium, magnesium, and vitamin D deficiencies plague blacks from the cradle to the grave, and surely these nutritional problems can assist in shortening the journey between the two.

Indeed these deficiencies may even be at the root of the problem of hypertension among Afro-Americans; the disease today is the chief cause of death among black adults, killing fifteen times more males and seventeen times more females than their white counterparts.[76] That one-quarter of America's black population (and nearly 50 percent of those over age forty) are hypertensive has summoned an avalanche of explanations ranging from the genetic, nutritional, and social to the psychological to problems of economic stress.[77]

Naturally diet has been implicated because sodium seems quite definitely to be involved in the problem. Drs. Elijah Saunders and Richard Williams, accompanied by a dietitian, examined soul menus and found the salt content of those menus to be "very high,"[78] while another commentator relying on medical evidence pronounced those menus "literally suicidal."[79] Certainly a drastic reduction of the sodium content of a diet tends to lower the blood pressure of hypertensive patients; conversely, a high sodium intake not only aggravates the problem but frequently produces other cardiovascular complications.[80]

In this connection hypertension must have been a problem yesterday among slaves whose diet centered on salted and pickled pork and bacon, a problem we did not treat because of a dearth of hard or even soft data. In the latter category, however, hypertension is often accompanied by dropsy, and it has already been commented that an inordinate number of slave as opposed to white deaths occurred from this affliction.

Yet, although salt has been implicated in the etiology of hypertension, it is hardly the only factor, and why blacks suffer from the disease far more than whites remains a mystery; therefore, another nutritional common denominator between the slave and his modern descendant, besides a heavy use of salt, should be pointed out. The same calcium, magnesium, and vitamin D deficiencies implicated in so many black health problems may also play a role in the etiology of black hypertension. The pair of minerals and vitamin in question are instrumental in the body's ability to regulate salts. Perhaps even more important, they work against the retention of those salts by facilitating their excretion, a process that may be particularly crucial for blacks, who seem to lose less salt through perspiration than do whites suggesting a dangerous tendency toward excess salt retention.[81]

Additionally, some evidence appears to link magnesium directly with hypertension. Experiments on animals have demonstrated that those deprived of magnesium will in fact become hypertensive.[82] Finally, both calcium and magnesium seem to have important assignments in maintaining a healthy cardiovascular system as well as a soothing effect on the central nervous system.[83] None of these assignments is all that well understood at present, while the nature of the relationship between the heart and nerves and blood pressure is equally obscure. Perhaps, however, investigators ought to consider the possibility of magnesium and vitamin D deficiencies figuring in the etiology of black hypertension.

VI

Before leaving hypertension, we need to glance quickly at the phenomenon of the "toxemia" of pregnancy, responsible for an estimated 30,000 neonatal deaths and stillbirths each year in this country.[84] Toxemia is another of those diseases far more prevalent among blacks than whites.[85] It is characterized by proteinuria (the abnormally high presence of protein in the urine) fluid retention, elevated blood pressure, and the convulsions of eclampsia, which can lead to coma and death for the mother as well as for the fetus. In the past, it was believed that black women suffered more from preeclampsia because of a lack of prenatal care. Recently, however, it has been realized that differential susceptibility is not fully explicable in these terms, and the suspicion has emerged that the same unknown causes of black hypertension are responsible for toxemia as well.[86] Hypertensive mothers also lose their newborn at a high rate and produce an inordinate number of infants who are the victims of fetal retardation.[87] Because of the similarities between chronic hypertension and toxemia as well as their effects on the newborn, we are yielding to the temptation to speculate by flourishing the magnesium, calcium, and vitamin D triad once again.

In Chapter 7, the importance of vitamin D to the proper absorption of minerals was discussed. Difficulties of North American blacks were also noted in manufacturing sufficient vitamin D because of pigment that decreases considerably the transmission of ultraviolet radiation. It is not surprising, therefore, that black mothers have far lower serum levels of 25-hydroxyvitamin D (25-OHD—the product of vitamin D metabolization).[88] Obviously, the fetus cannot metabolize its own vitamin D, hence an increased demand is placed on already low maternal stores creating a situation, it has been hypothesized, in which maternal D deficiency actually triggers premature birth.[89] Toxemia too has been directly linked with prematurity and thus of course to low birth weights.[90]

Premature infants, who have been examined born of mothers low in 25-OHD, revealed levels of their own so low that their antirachitic stores were lost.[91] Infants of mothers deficient in vitamin D also often develop hypocalcemia, which in turn precipitates those same tetanic convulsions today that were so deadly on the plantations of yesterday.[92] The tetany syndrome is most prevalent among those born either prematurely, or with a low birth weight,[93] or of multiparous mothers, and has a definite peak season in late winter when D deficiency is most likely.[94] It was hypothesized that yesterday black children suffered far more from tetany than whites; today they definitely do.

We have returned to the maternity ward to close our look at black health problems because that is where new generations are born to perpetuate those problems, and mothers succumb because of those problems. The rate of black maternal mortality, although almost halved between 1960 and 1970, is still an appalling four times higher than that suffered by white females.[95] Surely much of the explanation must focus on the poor nutritional status of black mothers who pass that status to infants who will continue the vicious cycle.

Depressing as this is, however, still one more difficulty for black people may stem from poor nutrition, a difficulty that must be discussed despite the risk of its misuse by pseudoscientific racists. Just as there is a correlation between maternal nutrition and low birth weights, a correlation also exists between low birth weights and mental retardation.[96]

Thus an investigation of slightly retarded black and white children in Detroit (which excluded those prematurely born) discovered that on the average they had significantly lower birth weights than youngsters with average and above average IQs.[97] When premature children were examined the picture was even bleaker. Mental retardation has been found to be ten times more likely to occur with a premature infant than with a full-term infant.[98]

In this same vein, a classic experiment has demonstrated that vitamin supplements given to socioeconomically deprived mothers during pregnancy can significantly bolster the IQs of their offspring.[99] Finally a recent study found that iron-deficient children had "reduced attentiveness," "reduced motivation" and "reduced resistance to fatigue," all attributes bound to create severe difficulties in the learning process.[100]

There has been enough nonsense about innate black intellectual inferiority. On the other hand, the First National Conference on the Health Status of the Negro that took place at Howard University in 1967 announced that mental retardation was one of the three major health problems facing blacks in this country.[101] Too little attention has been paid to the relationship between nutrition and intellectual decrement. Prematurity, toxemia, and low birth weights are the usual culprits identified. But actually these are only symptoms of the larger problem of widespread malnutrition.

The weight of the brain and the number of its cells depends to a large extent on the weight of the infant at birth. More specifically, the human brain grows fastest in utero and for the first six to twelve months of the infant's life, although rapid growth continues until adult size is reached at age six or so. It is during this period then that the brain is most susceptible to damage from malnutrition.[102] Protein seems to be the most important nutrient in brain development, and protein deficiency before birth and during the first few years of life can cost a child up to 20 percent of his IQ.[103] Thus, during pregnancy an additional thirty grams of protein beyond the recommended daily allowance is required for normal fetal growth.[104] Yet the TSNS discovered that three-quarters of black expectant mothers had low serum albumin levels during the last two trimesters of pregnancy and consequently in many cases too little protein for proper fetal brain development.[105]

Many black infants are also protein-deprived during the crucial first months of life according to a South Carolina study that found two-thirds of those in Greenville County had total protein concentrations below normal, with one-third far below the norm.[106] Again the TSNS found that black children aged six-and-under are five times more likely to be protein deficient than whites.[107]

Iron, magnesium, and B vitamin deficiencies too have been linked with poor intellectual development,[108] while women with deformed pelves are far more likely to produce infants with damaged brains.[109] But the intention here is not to belabor the point, which is very simply that nutritional deprivation adversely affects minds as well as bodies.

Closely connected may be the matter of behavior. Stanley Elkins a few years ago precipitated much controversy by his examination of the personality of the stereotyped slave: the docile, lazy uncaring Sambo.[110] More recently Leslie Owens has hypothesized that nutritional factors may well explain some of these "behavioral manifestations," and he is probably correct.[111] For "Sambo" characteristics are confined neither to those with black skin nor to the antebellum period but rather occur among all peoples who suffer chronic malnutrition, for example, the iron-deficient children – black and white – whose behavior included "reduced attentiveness," "reduced motivation," and "reduced resistance to fatigue."[112]

This brings to a close an unpleasant look at centuries of black-related diseases and nutritional deficiencies. Genetic background and biological factors have been seen to combine with climatic and nutritional circumstances to severely undermine the state of black health and hopefully two points have been made with some clarity. The first is that blacks do have different nutritional requirements than whites.[113] But because this is not appreciated, diseases that killed blacks on the plantations of the South – particularly black infants – are still playing havoc with our Afro-American population during the last third of the "modern" twentieth century. An intensive concerted effort to precisely determine those requirements – the establishment of vitamin and mineral RDAs for black people – and the imparting of this information to blacks should surely be placed high on the nation's list of priorities. The second point is that physicians must be aware of blacks as blacks. Samuel Cartwright of New Orleans, despite his racism, was correct in his insistence that the medical profession should be alert to the unique difficulties of health faced by black people. More than a century elapsed, however, following Cartwright's call for "Negro medicine" before Richard Allen Williams and his associates published the first medical text on the subject. We have relied heavily on their *Textbook of Black-Related Diseases* throughout this study and hope that physicians will take note of it as well, for the medical profession must make itself cognizant of the special health problems of blacks.

Physicians should know that most Afro-Americans who are suffering from hypertension do so without even realizing that they have a problem let alone one that can kill them:[114] America's doctors should realize the potentially disastrous results of not understanding this black-related disease such as the diagnosis of toxemia of pregnancy in 70 percent of the black expectant mothers in a New York hospital, when in fact they were manifesting symptoms of hypertensive vascular disease.[115] The profession must not continue to be oblivious to the phenomenon of lactose intolerance and its high frequency among blacks – an ignorance that among other things has produced instances of black ulcer patients being treated with milk with tragic results.[116] Finally SIDS, although the leading killer of America's very young, especially when their skin is black, is routinely misdiagnosed by most of the nation's doctors, and because until recently nothing on crib death could be found in medical texts or reference books, even many newly "minted" physicians are only vaguely aware that such a syndrome exists.[117]

The medical profession in short must reeducate itself and indeed should be anxious to do so. It is not totally gratuitous to point out that it owes a sizable debt to the black having been so instrumental historically in fostering antiblack attitudes in the first place.

VII

Yet the black health crisis will not be resolved simply by the education (and reeducation) of the American medical profession. Rather its failure in delivering proper medical care to blacks must be viewed within a larger context of public ignorance and policy-making indifference, neither free of racism. A final aim of this study has been to show how racial differences in morbidity and mortality over time have been interpreted and the contribution of those interpretations to an ever burgeoning racism. Today these erroneous interpretations and insidious contributions continue, and blacks still suffer twice: once from their crisis of health and again because those health difficulties are turned against them.

Sickle trait makes a disheartening example. Private as well as public employers have been guilty of discharging employees or simply not hiring them because they possess sickle trait; insurance companies have admitted inflating premiums 25 to 50 percent for the applicant who is a sickle trait carrier; and sickle trait children have been denied participation in school sports.[118] Thus, blacks are punished because of a confusion in the public mind of sickle trait with sickle cell anemia and a terrible ignorance of the effects of sickle trait.

But ignorance is not confined to the public alone. The United States Congress confused sickle trait and sickle cell anemia in Public Law 92-294, 92nd Congress, S2676 May 16, 1962. This "Act to provide for the control of sickle cell anemia" opens with the statement that "the Congress finds and declares (1) that sickle cell anemia is a debilitating, inheritable disease that afflicts approximately *two million American citizens*"[119] (our italics). Congress could scarcely have been further from the truth. It has been estimated that there are about two million sickle trait carriers in the United States, but only 50,000 cases of sickle cell anemia.[120] Even worse, an earlier version of a statute passed in the District of Columbia to bring about mandatory screening for sickle cell anemia declared the disease to be "communicable."[121]

Surely it is with genetic screening for sickle trait that misguided and misinformed legislators have been at their absolute worst. Certainly screening can represent an important step in the elimination of sickle cell anemia, but such a program must be voluntary, else much anxiety will result.[122] A dozen or more states now have sickle cell laws for marriage licenses and public school entrance that have been described as "either outright or ambiguously compulsory."[123] In Virginia, in addition to black marriage license applicants, all black inmates of correctional and mental institutions must submit to sickle cell screening.[124] But perhaps the most insulting law is that of New York State, which requires all marriage license applicants to be tested for the trait "who are not of the Caucasian, Indian or Oriental race."[125]

Clearly such heavy handed efforts to deal with this particular health problem can only increase black wariness of any general policy making aimed at black health problems. Indeed genetic screening has occasioned talk among black leaders of attempted "genocide".[126] This is an apparent paranoia that can be readily understood when the turn-of-the-century enthusiasm among physicians for black eradication is recalled.

Nor do blacks have to reach that far into the past to justify their uneasiness regarding the intentions of physicians in particular and the health services in general. They have only to recall the infamous Tuskegee experiments conducted during this century over a forty-year period (1932–72) by the United States Public Health Service. Incredibly, some 400 black patients who applied for treatment for syphilis in fact went untreated so that the "natural history" of the disease could be observed. One consequence was that many died; a figure over 100 was commonly employed.[127]

Vested interests also present a formidable roadblock to improving the quality of black health. Perhaps it is because babies do not vote, or perhaps it is because SIDS kills a significantly lower percentage of whites than blacks, or maybe it has simply to do with budgetary constraints, but for whatever reason SIDS researchers have encountered great difficulty in prying anything more than token funding out of the United States government.[128] Conversely because sickle cell anemia is a widely publicized black-related disease (even though it affects relatively few blacks) legislators are eager to fund researchers in this area because it gives the appearance of "doing something" for the black community.[129] Thus, in 1972, for example, approximately $40 million was expended on sickle cell anemia research or about $800 per person afflicted with the disease.[130] Only 2¢ per SIDS victim was invested, however, in researching that syndrome.[131]

Today the United States ships millions of dollars worth of dried milk to underdeveloped countries, most of which have populations with a high incidence of lactose intolerance. In Columbia, Indians have employed the milk to whitewash their houses; in Cypress it is fed to lambs; in West Africa natives who developed cramps, bloating, and diarrhea (classic lactose intolerance symptoms) were persuaded that it contained evil spirits and have determinedly buried all subsequent shipments; while in Bali the milk has shrewdly been put to use as a laxative.[132] In the wry words of two British investigators "It could be that aid in this form with the subsequent induction of diarrhea is not the most efficient method of helping a malnourished community."[133]

Yet here at home malnourished, black lactose-intolerant children are daily confronted with free milk in the schools, which they must either drink, refuse, or dispose of. It is known that almost half of the black elementary age schoolchildren are lactose intolerant, and we know further that ingestion of a single glass of milk will produce symptoms for a majority of lactose malabsorbers. Milk, therefore, is positively harmful when its inclusion in the diet contributes to diarrhea and consequently to a worsening of one's nutritional status.[134]

Nonetheless the dairy industry that sells over 100 million dollars worth of half pint milk containers to schools each year has had no difficulty in keeping milk programs both at home and abroad very much alive.[135] Other protein beverages for the lactose intolerant have been recommended by experts,[136] but nutrition advisory groups (financed by and partially composed of members of the dairy industry) have adamantly and successfully opposed these recommendations.[137] Hence a program ostensibly to help needy black children is actually in many cases detrimental to their health.

Another such program is the government-subsidized school lunch program, begun in 1946 with the announced purpose of insuring that all children, particularly those from poor families, received at least one hot nutritious meal every day. Most states have a history of regularly misappropriating the federal funds supplied for this purpose, however, and not paying their share as required by law.[138] The result is poor quality meals as revealed in a 1969 study which discovered that over 40 percent of the lunches consist of fat and that all are low in protein; 75 percent do not supply sufficient calories; 60 to 90 percent are lacking in iron, vitamin C, and magnesium; and 50 percent do not supply even one-third of the vitamins B_1, B_3, and B_6.[139]

Moreover, even these dismal percentages only hold true assuming that a half pint of milk is consumed. The many black children who dare not use milk, therefore, receive even less protein and magnesium, while the absence of iron in the meals can only compound that which has been seen to be a crucial problem of black health.

Pica constitutes another illustration of how blacks pay for their health difficulties twice. Recent studies have shown that over half of those afflicted with iron deficiency anemia manifest serious cravings sometimes for a particular food, but often for nonfoods.[140] Since blacks as a group have a high frequency of iron deficiency anemia they are naturally disproportionately represented among nonfood consumers. Unfortunately, however, the practice is seldom viewed in terms of nutritional deprivation. Rather it is often seen as a manifestation of cultural or mental inferiority, a product of superstition or ignorance or habit.[141] A particularly striking case in point can be found in a recent study that appeared in a respectable nutritional journal depicting nonfood users in Mississippi as individuals who have "psychopathological appetite perversions [which does] not represent anything beyond ignorance, superstition or psychoneurosis."[142]

Lamentably, we could continue this rendition indefinitely, for examples of black-related diseases being turned on blacks are distressingly plentiful. Police who do not understand SIDS compound the grief and self-loathing of parents whose baby was lost to crib death by lumping them with parents caught up in the more highly publicized battered-child syndrome.[143] In this connection, black parents are four times less likely to learn that their child was an SIDS victim than white parents and, consequently, four times more likely to be left with the notion that they are somehow responsible.[144]

Instances have been reported of surgeons who performed surgery on blacks because they did not recognize the symptoms of lactose intolerance and others who refer lactose-intolerant patients to psychiatrists.[145]

At least one case is on record of a black cardiac patient whose medication was discontinued when his physician discovered he had sickle trait, believing that the cardiac symptoms stemmed from sickle cell anemia.[146] In this same vein is the example of the black lad whose appendix ruptured because his doctor was convinced that the abdominal pains were sickle cell anemia symptoms. Again the boy merely possessed sickle trait.[147]

Then there is the nutritionist who argues that *milk* ought to be fortified with iron to correct iron deficiency in blacks,[148] or the nutritionists studying black migrant workers in Florida who, baffled by the phenomenon of blacks refusing to drink milk, recommended the addition of dried skim milk to foods[149] (dried skim milk is even higher in lactose than regular milk).

Blacks are still being labled as "soil polluters," responsible for hookworm's propagation in medical texts,[150] while finally we have the investigator who contends that angina pectoris may rarely be experienced by blacks since " 'more than moronic intelligence' is necessary to perceive the sensation of pain."[151]

The illustrations are endless but the point is clear. Race and disease today as yesterday are thoroughly misunderstood by medicine, by nutritionists, the public, industry, policy makers and lawmakers. Blacks first as slaves and now as citizens have been taxed for this ignorance with their health and lives. Until public policy remedies are forthcoming, the levy will continue.

NOTES

Abbreviations of frequently cited journals

ADC	Archives of Diseases in Childhood
AH	Agricultural History
AHG	Annals of Human Genetics
AIM	Archives of Internal Medicine
AJE	American Journal of Epidemiology
AJCN	American Journal of Clinical Nutrition
AJDC	American Journal of Diseases in Childhood
AJHG	American Journal of Human Genetics
AJMS	American Journal of Medical Science
AJOG	American Journal of Obstetrics and Gynecology
AJPA	American Journal of Physical Anthropology
AJPH	American Journal of Public Health
AJTMH	American Journal of Tropical Medicine and Hygiene
AMCP	American Cotton Planter and Soil of the South
BHM	Bulletin of the History of Medicine
BJN	British Journal of Nutrition
BMJ	British Medical Journal
BMLA	Bulletin of the Medical Library Association
BN	Biology of the Neonate
BNYAM	Bulletin of the New York Academy of Medicine
BTMF	Bulletin of the Tulane Medical Faculty
CMJR	Charleston Medical Journal and Review
DBR	DeBow's Review
EMSJ	Edinburgh Medical and Surgical Journal
GHQ	Georgia Historical Quarterly
HB	Human Biology
JADA	Journal of the American Dietetic Association
JAfH	Journal of African History
JAMA	Journal of the American Medical Association
JFS	Journal of Food Science
JHM	Journal of the History of Medicine
JHMJ	Johns Hopkins Medical Journal
JHR	Journal of Human Relations
JMAG	Journal of the Medical Association of Georgia
JMH	Journal of Mississippi History
JN	Journal of Nutrition
JNE	Journal of Negro Education

JNH	Journal of Negro History
JNMA	Journal of the National Medical Association
JP	Journal of Pediatrics
JSCMA	Journal of the South Carolina Medical Association
JSH	Journal of Southern History
JTMH	Journal of Tropical Medicine and Hygiene
LH	Louisiana History
LHQ	Louisiana Historical Quarterly
MVHR	Mississippi Valley Historical Review
NEJM	New England Journal of Medicine
NOMN	New Orleans Medical News and Hospital Gazette
NOMSJ	New Orleans Medical and Surgical Journal
PCNA	Pediatric Clinics of North America
Ped	Pediatrics
PHR	Public Health Reports
PM	Postgraduate Medicine
PMHS	Publications of the Mississippi Historical Society
PNS	Proceedings of the Nutrition Society
PR	Pediatric Research
RSTMH	Transactions of the Royal Society of Tropical Medicine and Hygiene
SA	Southern Agriculturist
SAMJ	South African Medical Journal
SC	Southern Cultivator
SCMA	Transactions of the South Carolina Medical Association
SJMP	Southern Journal of Medical Pharmacology
SMJ	Southern Medical Journal
SMR	Southern Medical Reports
SMSJ	Southern Medical and Surgical Journal
TJM	Transylvania Journal of Medicine and the Associated Sciences
VMM	Virginia Medical Monthly
VMS	Transactions of the Virginia Medical Society
WAMJ	West African Medical Journal
WHO	Bulletin of the World Health Organization
WHO(MS)	World Health Organization Monograph Series
WMQ	William and Mary Quarterly

Preface

1 Kenneth M. Stampp, *The Peculiar Institution: Slavery in the Ante-Bellum South* (New York, 1956), vii.

2 Richard Allen Williams, "Black Related Disease: An Overview," *Journal of Black Health Perspectives*, 1 (1974), 36.

3 Thomas A. Cockburn, "The Origin of the Treponematoses," *WHO*, 24 (1961), 225.

4 Ian Taylor and John Knowelden, *Principles of Epidemiology* (Boston, 1964), 222.

5 Abnormality of course is a relative term. This is the nomenclature, however, employed by hematologists to indicate the over 100 hemoglobin variants described to date from normal fetal and adult hemoglobins.

6 See for example Ashley Montagu, *Statement on Race*, 3rd ed. (London, 1972), 8–9 and passim.

7 Arno G. Motulsky, "Significance of Genetic Diseases for Population Studies," in *Genetic Polymorphisms and Diseases in Man*, ed. Bracha Ramot et al. (New York, 1974), 286.

8 Roger John Williams, *Biochemical Individuality: The Basis for the Genetotrophic Concept* (New York, 1956).

Introduction to Part I

1 Gerald W. Hartwig and K. David Patterson, eds., *Diseases in African History: An Introductory Survey and Case Studies* (Durham, N.C., 1978), viii.

Chapter 1. The black man's cradle and the white man's grave

1 C. D. Darlington, *The Evolution of Man and Society* (London, 1969), 662.
2 W. H. Frost, "Introduction" in John Snow, *Snow on Cholera, Being a Reprint of Two Papers* (New York, 1965), ix.
3 Philip D. Curtin, *The Atlantic Slave Trade: A Census* (Madison, Wisc., 1969), 268, 269; "Measuring the Atlantic Slave Trade Once Again: A Comment," *JAfH*, 17 (1976), 595–605.
4 K. David Patterson and Gerald W. Hartwig, "The Disease Factor: An Introductory Overview," in *Disease in African History*, eds. Gerald W. Hartwig and K. David Patterson (Durham, N.C., 1978), 6–7.
5 "Richard Eden's Account of John Luk's Voyage to Mina, 1554–55" in *Europeans in West Africa 1450–1560*, Hakluyt Series 2, 87: 339 (London, 1942).
6 G. Ainsworth Harrison, "Pigmentation," in *General Variation in Human Populations*, ed. G. A. Harrison (New York, 1961), 110. For a review of the various hypotheses advanced to account for pigment, see Williams S. Pollitzer et al., "Physical Anthropology of the Negroes of Charleston, S. C.," *HB*, 42 (1970), 274.
7 Mildred Trotter, George E. Broman, and Roy R. Peterson, "Densities of Bones of White and Negro Skeletons," *Journal of Bone and Joint Surgery*, 42–A (1960), 50–8; R. L. Allen and David L. Nickel, "The Negro and Learning to Swim: The Buoyancy Problem Related to Biological Differences," *JNE*, 18 (1969), 405–6; Albert Damon, "Race, Ethnic Group, and Disease," *Social Biology*, 16 (1969), 77; J. M. Tanner, *Foetus into Man: Physical Growth from Conception to Maturity* (Cambridge, Mass., 1978), 139–41; P. T. Baker and J. L. Angel, "Old Age Changes in Bone Density: Sex, and Race Factors in the United States," *HB*, 37 (1965), 118; S. H. Cohn et al., "Comparative Skeletal Mass and Radial Bone Mineral Content in Black and White Women," *Metabolism*, 26 (1977), 171–8.
8 See G. C. Last, "The Geographical Implications of Man and his Future in Africa," in *Man and Africa*, eds. Gordon Wolstenholme and Maeve O'Connor (Boston, 1965), 17.
9 F. MacFarlane Burnet and David O. White, *Natural History of Infectious Disease*, 4th ed. (Cambridge, Engl., 1972), 82.
10 Ibid., 232.
11 Darlington, *Evolution of Man and Society*, 652.
12 Louis H. Miller, "Malaria," in *Infectious Diseases: A Guide to the Understanding and Management of Infectious Processes*, ed. Paul D. Hoeprich (Hagerstown, Md., 1972), 1113.
13 Philip D. Marsden, "African Trypanosomiasis (African Sleeping Sickness)," in *Infectious Diseases: A Guide to the Understanding and Management of Infectious Processes*, ed. Paul D. Hoeprich (Hagerstown, Md., 1972) 1037; J. P. Glasgow, *The Distribution and Abundance of Tsetse* (Oxford and New York, 1963), 1, 3–5.
14 George W. Hunter, William W. Frye, and J. Clyde Swartzwelder, *A Manual of Tropical Medicine*, 4th ed. (Philadelphia, 1966), 396; John Ford, *The Role of the Trypanosomiases in African Ecology: A Study of the Tsetse Fly Problem* (Oxford, 1971), 89.
15 David Lee Chandler, "Health and Slavery: A Study of Health Conditions Among Negro Slaves in the Viceroyalty of New Granada and Its Associated Slave Trade, 1600–1810" (Ph.D. dissertation, Tulane University, 1972), 190; James Thomson, *A Treatise on the Diseases of Negroes As They Occur in the Island of Jamaica* (Jamaica, 1820), 89.

16 See for example John Duncan, *Travels in Western Africa in 1845 and 1846*, 2 vols. (London, 1847; reprint ed., New York, 1967), 2:86; William Freeman Daniell, *Sketches of the Medical Topography and Native Diseases of the Gulf of Guinea, West Africa* (London, 1849), 48.

17 Ralph Linton, *The Tree of Culture* (New York, 1955), 436; Glasgow, *Distribution and Abundance of Tsetse*, 1–3. See Ford, *Trypanosomiases in African Ecology*, 88–9, for the racial immunities of cattle (and man) to the disease. Finally, consult Frederick J. Simoons (*Eat Not This Flesh: Food Avoidances in the Old World*, Madison, Wisc., 1961, 56) who points out that some dwarf breeds of West African cattle were resistant to tsetse-borne sleeping sickness, "but even these were seldom present in large numbers, and where infestation by tsetse flies is particularly bad they are absent altogether."

18 Simoons, *Eat Not This Flesh*, 73–8; Tadeuz Lewicki, *West African Food in the Middle Ages: According to Arabic Sources* (London, 1974), 79, 116–27; Michael Gelfand, *Diet and Tradition in an African Culture* (Edinburgh, 1971), 206; Elizabeth Isichei, *A History of the Igbo People* (New York, 1976), 224.

19 Linton, *Tree of Culture*, 436; William Malcolm Hailey, *An African Survey* (rev. ed., London, 1957), 822; Basil Davidson, *The African Genius: An Introduction to African Cultural and Social History* (Boston, 1969), 33; Oliver Davies, *West Africa Before the Europeans: Archaeology and Prehistory* (London, 1967), 149.

20 Davies, *West Africa Before the Europeans*, 8; Hailey, *African Survey*, 822; Alfred W. Crosby, *The Columbian Exchange: Biological and Cultural Consequences of 1492* (Westport, Conn., 1972), 186–8; C. K. Meek, W. M. Macmillan and E. R. J. Hussey, *Europe and West Africa: Some Problems and Adjustments* (London, 1940), 17; Bruce F. Johnston, *The Staple Food Economies of Western Tropical Africa* (Stanford, 1958), 174–81.

21 H. L. Richardson, "The Use of Fertilizers," in *The Soil Resources of Tropical Africa*, ed. R. P. Moss (London, 1968), 138; Juan Papadakis, *Crop Ecological Survey in West Africa*, 2 vols. (Rome, 1966), I: 31; W. B. Morgan and J. C. Pugh, *West Africa* (London, 1969), 198; R. J. Harrison Church, *West Africa: A Study of the Environment and of Man's Use of It*, 4th ed. (London, 1963), 87–8; Hailey, *African Survey*, 819.

22 Isichei, *Igbo People*, 197–8; Meek, Macmillan, and Hussey, *Europe and West Africa*, 32–33, 42; Gelfand, *Diet and Tradition in an African Culture*, 207; K. V. Bailey, "Malnutrition in the African Region," *WHO Chronicle*, 29 (1975), 354–64; J. C. Carothers, "The African Mind in Health and Disease," *JHR*, 8 (1960), 445.

23 Carothers, "African Mind"; World Health Organization, "Africa's Health," *JHR*, 8 (1960), 440; George H. T. Kimble, *Tropical Africa*, 2 vols. (New York, 1960), 2:41–2; Hailey, *African Survey*, 1070–71; T. R. Batten, *Problems of African Development*, 2 vols. 3rd ed. (London, 1960), II: 13, 15; Jacques M. May, *The Ecology of Malnutrition in the French Speaking Countries of West Africa and Madagascar* (New York, 1968), 10–11; Meek, Macmillan, and Hussey, *Europe and West Africa*, 42; Bo Vahlquist, "Nutrition as a Priority in African Development," *AJCN*, 25 (1972), 346.

24 Johnston, *Staple Food Economies*, 7–9, 21–3, 161–3, 193–203; James L. Newman, "Dietary and Nutritional Conditions," in *Contemporary Africa: Geography and Change*, eds. C. Gregory Knight and James L. Newman (Englewood Cliffs, N.J., 1976), 72–5; May, *Ecology of Malnutrition*, viii, 23, 63–5, 105, 144, 194.

25 May, *Ecology of Malnutrition*, 65, 105, 222–3, 228; "Tackling Nutrition Problems in Africa," *WHO Chronicle*, 30 (1976), 31; R. Cook, "The General Nutritional Problems of Africa," *African Affairs*, 65 (1966), 333; Papadakis, *Ecological Survey*, 1:72. The beef return of West African cattle is only one-third of the European equivalent. Morgan and Pugh, *West Africa*, 136; Batten, *Problems of African Development*, 122.

26 Batten, *Problems of African Development*; Bailey, "Malnutrition in the African Region," 357; Michael Gelfand, *Medicine and Custom in Africa* (Edinburgh, 1964), 97–8; "Tackling Nutrition Problems in Africa," 31; Michael Latham, *Human Nutrition in Tropical*

Africa (Rome, 1965), 191; Isichei, *Igbo People*, 224–5; Cook, "General Nutritional Problems of Africa," 333; Newman, "Dietary and Nutritional Conditions," 74.

27 This is testified to by early European visitors to the region who were startled by the little food consumed by the average individual. See, for example, Gerald Roe Crone, ed. and trans., *The Voyages of Cadamosto and other Documents on Western Africa in the Second Half of the Fifteenth Century* (London, 1937), passim.

28 Robert W. Fogel and Stanley L. Engerman, "Recent Findings in the Study of Slave Demography and Family Structure," *Sociology and Social Research*, 63, (1979), 573; Barry W. Higman, "Growth in Afro-Caribbean Slave Populations," *American Journal of Physical Anthropology*, 50(1979), 373–85.

29 Manuel Moreno Fraginals, "Africa in Cuba; A Quantitative Analysis of the African Populations in the Island of Cuba," in *Comparative Perspectives on Slavery in the New World Plantation Societies*, eds. Vera Rubin and Arthur Tuden, *Annals of the New York Academy of Science*, 292 (1977), 197–8.

30 Peter Dallman, "New Approaches to Screening for Iron Deficiency," *JP*, 90 (1977), 679; Stanley M. Garn et al., "Apportioning Black-White Hemoglobin and Hematocrit Differences in Pregnancy" [letter to editor], *AJCN*, 30 (1977), 461–2; Michael J. Kraemer et al., "Race-related Differences in Peripheral Blood and in Bone Marrow Cell Populations of American Black and White Infants," *JNMA*, 69 (1977), 327–31.

31 Stanley J. Birge et al., "Osteoporosis, Intestinal Lactase Deficiency and Low Dietary Calcium Intake," *NEJM*, 276 (1967), 447; Alexander Walker, "The Human Requirement of Calcium: Should Low Intakes Be Supplemented?" *AJCN*, 25 (1972), 521.

32 For this story, see Crosby's fine study, *Columbian Exchange*, especially 35–58.

33 Alfred W. Crosby, "Virgin Soil Epidemics as a Factor in the Aboriginal Depopulation in America," *WMQ*, 33 (1976), 289–99.

34 Philip D. Curtin, "The 'White Man's Grave': Image and Reality, 1780–1850," *Journal of British Studies*, 1 (1961), 94–110. As a point of interest, the term was originally coined by F. Harrison Rankin, *The White Man's Grave: A Visit to Sierra Leone, in 1834* (London, 1836).

35 See P. M. Ashburn (*The Ranks of Death: A Medical History of the Conquest of America* [New York, 1947], appendix, 213–24) for a glimpse of sixteenth-century medicine.

36 Kenneth G. Davies, "The Living and the Dead: White Mortality in West Africa, 1684–1732," in *Race and Slavery in the Western Hemisphere: Quantitative Studies*, eds. Stanley L. Engerman and Eugene D. Genovese (Princeton, 1975), 97. For some reason, however, the Dutch fared much better in West Africa than the English. See H. M. Feinberg, "New Data on European Mortality in West Africa: The Dutch and the Gold Coast, 1719–1760," *JAfH*, 15 (1974), 357–71.

37 The mean mortality for 598 voyages was 16.9 percent. Curtin, *Atlantic Slave Trade*, 283 (table).

38 Ibid., 285 (table). The estimates are those of the English abolitionist, Thomas Clarkson.

39 This has been ascertained statistically by Curtin, *Atlantic Slave Trade*, 275–86, and Herbert S. Klein, *The Middle Passage: Comparative Studies in the Atlantic Slave Trade* (1978), 197–8 and passim.

40 Philip D. Curtin, "Epidemiology and the Slave Trade," *Political Science Quarterly*, 83 (1968), 202–3.

41 R. Storrs, "The 'White Man's Grave' in the Eighteenth Century," *Journal of the Royal Army Medical Corps*, 53 (1929), 230.

42 William Freeman Daniell, *Sketches of the Medical Topography and Native Diseases of the Gulf of Guinea, Western Africa* (London, 1849), 11–12.

43 Ibid., 11–12.

44 John Adams, *Remarks on the Country Extending from Cape Palmas to the River Congo* (London, 1822; reprint London, 1966), 201–2.

45 Ibid., 200.

46 Curtin, "Epidemiology and the Slave Trade," 203, 204.
47 Philip D. Curtin, *The Image of Africa: British Ideas and Action, 1780–1850* (Madison, Wisc., 1964), 360.
48 Tom W. Shick, "A Quantitative Analysis of Liberian Colonization from 1820 to 1843 with Special Reference to Mortality," *JAfH*, 12 (1971), 45–59.
49 John Peterson, *Province of Freedom: A History of Sierra Leone, 1787–1870* (London, 1969).
50 Michael Gelfand, "Rivers of Death in Africa," *Central African Journal*, Supplement, 11 (1965), 10–13.
51 Ibid., 24–25.
52 Davies, "Living and the Dead," 98.
53 Ibid.
54 Curtin, *Image of Africa*, 181; John H. Parry and P. M. Sherlock, *A Short History of the West Indies*, 3rd ed. (London, 1971), 108.
55 For malaria's pervasiveness around much of the globe see Mark F. Boyd's masterful "Historical Review," in *Malariology: A Comprehensive Survey of all Aspects of this Group of Diseases from a Global Standpoint*, ed. Mark F. Boyd, 2 vols. (Philadelphia, 1949), 1:3–25.
56 A good and relatively nontechnical introduction to malarial types and strains may be found in G. Robert Coatney et al., *The Primate Malarias* (Bethesda, Md., 1971).
57 P. C. C. Garnham, *Malaria Parasites and Other Haemosporidia* (Oxford, 1966), 117–19.
58 Oscar Felsenfeld, *Synopsis of Clinical Tropical Medicine* (St. Louis, 1965), 197. For a more detailed discussion of the characteristics of the various malarial infections, see Martin D. Young, "Malaria," in *Manual of Tropical Medicine*, eds. Hunter, Frye and Swartzwelder, 316–62 (esp. 332–4).
59 Garnham, *Malaria Parasites*, 392; J. W. Field, "Blood Examination and Prognosis in Acute Falciparum Malaria," *RSTMH*, 43 (1949), 33–48; Young, "Malaria," 332.
60 Young, "Malaria," 347, 349–50, 360–2.
61 For an examination of the literature on acquired immunities to *P. falciparum*, see Coatney et al., *Primate Malarias*, 284–5. A thorough discussion of "Immunity to the Malaria Infections," by W. H. Taliaferro can be found in *Malariology*, ed. Boyd, 2:935–65.
62 Garnham, *Malaria Parasites*, 400; I. A. McGregor, "Mechanisms of Acquired Immunity and Epidemiological Patterns of Antibody Responses in Malaria in Man," *WHO*, 50 (1974), 261–2.
63 In hyperendemic areas of malaria, the child is born with antibody protection, which decreases rapidly after birth, and not until the child reaches an age of 5 to 10 years has he experienced sufficient infection to effectively resist the disease. Carol Laderman, "Malaria and Progress: Some Historical and Ecological Considerations," *Social Science and Medicine*, 9 (1975), 588. In the meantime the intitial assaults are fatal to about 5 percent of those children infected. M. J. Colbourne and F. N. Wright, "Malaria in the Gold Coast," *WAMJ*, 4 (1955), 171.
64 Young, "Malaria," 334; Louis H. Miller and Richard Carter, "A Review: Innate Resistance in Malaria," *Experimental Parasitology*, 40 (1976), 133.
65 Arno G. Motulsky, "Hereditary Red Cell Traits and Malaria," *AJTMH*, 13 (1964), 147; George MacDonald, *The Epidemiology and Control of Malaria* (London, 1957), 26.
66 See Graham R. Serjeant for an excellent introduction to *The Clinical Features of Sickle Cell Disease* (New York, 1974).
67 J. B. Herrick, "Peculiar Elongated and Sickle-Shaped Red Blood Corpuscles in a Case of Severe Anemia," *AIM*, 6 (1910), 517–21.
68 Arno G. Motulsky, "Frequency of Sickling Disorders in U. S. Blacks," *NEJM*, 288 (1973), 32; Robert B. Scott, "Health Care Priority and Sickle Cell Anemia," *JAMA*, 214 (1970), 731–4.

69 For an historical summary of the work on the sickle cell, see Joseph Song, *Pathology of Sickle Cell Disease* (Springfield, Ill., 1971).

70 W. H. Taliaferro and J. G. Huck, "The Inheritance of Sickle-Cell Anaemia in Man," *Genetics*, 8 (1923), 594–8.

71 James V. Neel, "The Inheritance of Sickle Cell Anemia," *Science*, 110 (1949), 64–6; Linus Pauling et al., "Sickle Cell Anemia: A Molecular Disease," *Science*, 110 (1949), 543–8.

72 Serjeant, *Sickle Cell Disease*, 28.

73 C. Choremis et al., "Sickle-cell Trait and Blood Groups in Greece," *Lancet*, 2 (1953), 909–11; H. Lehman and Marie Cutbush, "Sickle-cell Trait in Southern India," *BMJ*, 1 (1952), 404–5.

74 E. A. Beet, "Sickle Cell Disease in the Balovate District of Northern Rhodesia," *EAMJ*, 23 (1946), 75–86; P. Brain, "The Sickle Cell Trait: Its Clinical Significance," *SAMJ*, 26 (1952), 925–8.

75 A. C. Allison, "Protection Afforded by Sickle-Cell Trait Against Subtertian Malarial Infection," *BMJ*, 1 (1954), 290–4.

76 Lucio Luzzatto, "Studies of Polymorphic Traits for the Characterization of Populations. African Populations South of the Sahara," in *Genetic Polymorphisms and Diseases in Man*, eds. Bracha Ramot et al. (New York, 1974) 64.

77 Some of the possible reasons are discussed by Motulsky, "Hereditary Red Cell Traits and Malaria," 154–6, and Serjeant, *Sickle Cell Disease*, 32–33.

78 Alan B. Raper, "Malaria and the Sickling Trait," *BMJ*, 2 (1955), 1186–9.

79 Allison, "Protection Afforded by Sickle-cell Trait," 290–4.

80 J. C. Endozien, A. E. Boyo, and D. C. Morley, "The Relationship of Serum Gammaglobulin Concentration to Malaria and Sickling," *Journal of Clinical Pathology*, 13 (1960), 115.

81 M. J. Miller, James V. Neel, and Frank B. Livingstone, "Distribution of Parasites in the Red Cells of Sickle-cell Trait Carriers Infected with *Plasmodium falciparum*," *RSTMH*, 50 (1956), 294–6.

82 Serjeant, *Sickle Cell Disease*, Tables, 28, 34–43.

83 For the turmoil the field of genetics has been plunged into since the middle 1950s along with a glimpse of the increasing complexity of the field, see the humorous introductory remarks of Alexander G. Bearn made at the Sheba International Symposium, 18 to 22 March 1973 (Tel Aviv) in *Genetic Polymorphisms*, eds. Ramot et al., 5–6.

84 Serjeant, *Sickle Cell Disease*, 240–60. For an extensive review of these many hemoglobin abnormalities consult the excellent chapter on "Hematology," by William H. Bullock and Pongrac N. Jilly in *Textbook of Black-Related Diseases*, ed. Richard A. Williams (New York, 1975), 199–316.

85 A. G. Motulsky et al., "Biochemical Genetics of Glucose-6-Phosphate Dehydrogenase Deficiency," *Clinical Research*, 7 (1959), 89–90.

86 See Frank B. Livingstone, "Malaria and Human Polymorphisms," *Annual Review of Genetics*, 5 (1971), 49–51, for a summary of research on malaria and G6PD deficiency.

87 Part of the confusion derives from the fact that the heterozygous female, but not the hemizygous male, appears to be relatively resistant to *P. falciparum*. Ulrich Bienzle et al., "Glucose-6-Phosphate Dehydrogenase and Malaria. Greater Resistance of Females Heterozygous for Enzyme Deficiency and of Males with Non-Deficient Variant," *Lancet*, 1 (1972), 107–10. Moreover, as P. Jilly and F. K. Nkrumah, "A Survey of Anaemia in Children in Korle Bu Hospital, with Special Reference to Malaria," *Ghana Medical Journal*, 3 (1964), 118, have shown, children with the enzyme deficiency are more likely to develop anemia as a result of chronic malaria infection than youngsters with normal activity, which also complicates questions of protection provided.

88 Livingstone, "Malaria and Human Polymorphisms," 49; Arno G. Motulsky, "Theo-
    retical and Clinical Problems of Glucose-6-Phosphate Dehydrogenase Deficiency. Its
    Occurrence in Africans and its Combination with Hemoglobinopathy," in *Abnormal
    Haemoglobins in Africa*, ed. J. H. P. Jonxis (Oxford, 1965), 181; Lucio Luzzatto, Essien
    A. Usanga, and Shunmugam Reddy, "Glucose-6-Phosphate Dehydrogenase Defi-
    cient Red Cells: Resistance to Infection by Malarial Parasites," *Science*, 164 (1969),
    839–42.
89 Livingstone, "Malaria and Human Polylmorphisms," 50–51; Roger A. Lewis, *Sickle
    States: Clinical Features in West Africans* (Accra, Ghana, 1970), 35, 90–1. Paul A.
    Marks, "Glucose-6-Phosphate Dehydrogenase: Its Properties and Role in Mature
    Erythrocytes," in *The Red Blood Cell; A Comprehensive Treatise*, eds. Charles Bishop
    and Douglas M. Sturgenor (New York, 1963), 231–5, discusses possible reasons for
    the different manner in which whites and blacks experience the disease.
90 Arno G. Motulsky and Jean M. Campbell-Kraut, "Population Genetics of Glucose-
    6-Phosphate Dehydrogenase Deficiency of the Red Cell," in *Proceedings of the Confer-
    ence on Genetic Polymorphisms and Geographic Variations in Disease*, ed. Baruch S.
    Blumberg (New York, 1961), 169; Lewis, *Sickle States*, 39, 40.
91 Motulsky, "Frequency of Sickling Disorders in U.S. Blacks," 32; Bullock and Jilly,
    "Hematology," 220 (table), 268.
92 Twenty-five percent may be high because of some overlapping of these defects. In
    this connection there has been considerable interest in the coincidence of the sick-
    ling trait and G6PD deficiency, which some believe occurs more frequently than
    could be expected by chance. The difficulties of identifying both traits in an individ-
    ual are many, and results gathered so far are methodologically suspect. See Ser-
    jeant's discussion in *Sickle Cell Disease*, 74–75.
93 Ibid., 33–34; P. L. Workman, B. S. Blumberg and A. J. Cooper, "Selection, Gene
    Migration and Polymorphic Stability in a U.S. White and Negro Population," *AJHG*,
    15 (1963), 429–37.
94 A. C. Allison reviews the problem in "Malaria in Carriers of the Sickle-cell Trait and
    in Newborn Children," *Experimental Parasitology*, 6 (1957), 418–47. See also Garn-
    ham, *Malaria Parasites*, 94–5. A major difficulty here is that acquired immunity in
    older individuals tends to obscure the benefit, if any, they derive from the sickling
    trait.
95 See for example this assertion by George Metcalf in his discussion of malaria in the
    introduction to the newest edition of Edward Long, *The History of Jamaica*, 2 vols.
    (London, 1774; reprint London, 1970).
96 Livingstone, "Malaria and Human Polymorphisms," 42–3.
97 Martin D. Young et al., "Experimental Testing of the Immunity of Negroes to
    Plasmodium Vivax," *Journal of Parasitology*, 41 (1955), 316.
98 Motulsky and Campbell-Kraut, "Glucose-6-Phosphate Dehydrogenase Deficiency,"
    189.
99 Young, "Malaria," 334; Livingstone, "Malaria and Human Polymorphisms," 42–43.
100 Garnham, *Malaria Parasites*, 401, for example, puts "natural racial resistance" to
    falciparum malaria at the top of his list of factors.
101 Louis H. Miller et al., "The Resistance Factor to *Plasmodium vivax* in Blacks; the
    Duffy-Blood-Group Genotype, FyFy," *NEJM*, 295 (1976), 302.
102 Ibid., 302–4.
103 S. G. Welch, I. A. McGregor and K. Williams, "The Duffy Blood Group and Malaria
    Prevalence in Gambian West Africas," *RSTMH*, 71 (1977), 295–6.
104 Miller et al., "Resistance Factor to *Plasmodium vivax*," 303, 304.
105 Ibid., 304.
106 Coatney et al., *Primate Malarias*, 1–10, contains an excellent chapter on the "Evolu-
    tion of the Primate Malarias."

107 Arthur E. Mourant, *The Distribution of the Human Blood Groups* (Oxford, 1954), 784, advanced a similar argument (without, of course, knowledge of the significance of the Duffy blood group genotype) upon which much of our supposition is based.

108 Motulsky and Campbell-Kraut, "Glucose-6-Phosphate Dehydrogenase Deficiency," 188–9.

109 Luzzatto, "Polymorphic Traits," 58 (table), 59.

110 Lucio Luzzatto, "Genetic Factors in Malaria," *WHO*, 50 (1974), 197, 199, mentions this hypothesis.

111 Curtin, "Epidemiology and the Slave Trade," 192–4, 203–4.

Introduction to Part II

1 Frank D. Ashburn in P. M. Ashburn, *Ranks of Death: A Medical History of the Conquest of America* (New York, 1947).

Chapter 2. Yellow fever in black and white

1 John Parham Dromgoole, *Dr. Dromgoole's Yellow Fever Heros of 1878* (Louisville, Ky., 1879), 58–9.

2 This ability has not gone completely unnoticed by modern epidemiologists, some of whom suspect an innate resistance on the part of blacks. See Telford H. Work, "Virus Diseases in the Tropics," in *A Manual of Tropical Medicine*, eds. George W. Hunter, William W. Frye, and J. Clyde Swartzwelder (Philadelphia, 1966) 31, Richard M. Taylor, "Epidemiology," in *Yellow Fever*, ed. George K. Strode (New York, 1951), 454, and F. MacFarlane Burnet and David O. White, *History of Infectious Disease*, 4th ed. (Cambridge, Engl., 1972), 245.

3 Recent medical histories containing vivid clinical and pathological descriptions of yellow fever are John Duffy, *Sword of Pestilence; The New Orleans Yellow Fever Epidemic of 1853* (Baton Rouge, La., 1966), 10–11, Gordon Willis Jones, "Virginians and 'Calenture'," *VMM*, 88 (1961), 391, and Jo Ann Carrigan, "The Saffron Scourge: A History of Yellow Fever in Louisiana, 1796–1905," (Ph.D. diss., Louisiana State University, 1961), 3, 6–7.

4 Carrigan, "Saffrom Scourge," 6–7.

5 See, for example, Phillip D. Curtin, "Epidemiology and the Slave Trade," *Political Science Quarterly*, 83 (1968), 196–7, and Peter H. Wood, *Black Majority: Negroes in Colonial South Carolina from 1670 through the Stono Rebellion* (New York, 1974), 90–1.

6 There are two epidemiological forms of yellow fever: sylvan or jungle and urban yellow fever. The former is an endemic affliction of monkeys, while the latter is an epidemic disease of man. Sylvan yellow fever is the reservoir from which man becomes infected, although yellow fever does not easily descend from the treetops to humans because monkey and man are assaulted by different vectors. W. H. R. Lumsden, "Probable Insect Vectors of Yellow Fever Virus, From Monkey to Man, in Bwamba County, Uganda," *Bulletin of Entomological Research*, 42 (1951), 317, and passim. Today "endemic" yellow fever is defined as the transmission of the yellow fever virus "from nonhuman primate to mosquito to man," and "epidemic" yellow fever is intended to mean transmission "from man to mosquito to man." "Enzootic" yellow fever, on the other hand, connotes a pattern of transmission "from nonhuman primate to mosquito to nonhuman primate." James W. Mosley, "Yellow Fever," in *Infectious Disease: A Guide to the Understanding and Management of Infectious Processes*, ed. Paul D. Hoeprich (Hagerstown, Md., 1972), 665, has pointed out: "Endemic yellow fever is a misnomer, because the term actually refers to the incidental infection of man in an enzootic area." Nonetheless, the term endemic is convenient and is still regularly employed as it will be in this study to connote (1) a

region in which a reservoir of sylvan yellow fever is maintained and/or (2) a region in which conditions permitted the year-round activity of *A. aëgypti* and hence some fairly frequent yellow fever visitations.

7   Oscar Felsenfeld, *The Epidemiology of Tropical Diseases* (Springfield, Ill., 1966), 379; Ian Taylor and John Knowelden, *Principles of Epidemiology* (Boston, 1964), 162–4; William P. MacArthur, "Historical Notes on Some Epidemic Diseases Associated with Jaundice," *British Medical Bulletin*, 13 (1957), 147.

8   Philip D. Curtin, *Image of Africa: British Ideas and Action, 1780–1850* (Madison, Wisc., 1964), 75–6, was clearly concerned with this possibility, yet he felt that "in West Africa it appears that infection of the African population, and hence its immunity, was maintained at most times," 76.

9   August Hirsch, *Handbook of Geographical and Historical Pathology* (trans. Charles Creighton; 3 vols. [London, 1883–86] 1:318–31), lists every known epidemic in the Caribbean from the mid-seventeenth century onward.

10 For assurances that the "immunity" did seem to be almost absolute, see Francisco Guerra, "The Influence of Disease on Race, Logistics and Colonization in the Antilles," *JTMH*, 69 (1966), 33–4; Alexander von Humboldt, *Political Essay on the Kingdom of New Spain*, trans. John Black, 4 vols. (London, 1811; reprinted, New York, 1966), 4:173; Robert P. Parsons, *History of Haitian Medicine* (New York, 1930), 1; George Pinckard, *Notes on the West Indies, Including Observations Relative to the Creoles and Slaves . . . with Remarks upon the Seasoning or Yellow Fever of Hot Climates*, 2 vols., 2nd ed. (London, 1816), 2:467; Charles Belot, *The Yellow Fever at Havana: Its Nature and its Treatment* (Savannah, Ga., 1878), 39; and William Lempriere, *Practical Observations on the Diseases of the Army in Jamaica, as they Occurred Between the Years 1792 and 1797*, 2 vols. (London, 1799), 1:98 (table), 111 (table).

11 Henry Rose Carter published posthumously the best and most thorough examination of the question of yellow fever's origin and concluded unequivocally that the answer was Africa. *Yellow Fever: An Epidemiological and Historical Study of its Place of Origin*, ed. Laura Armistead Carter and Wade Hampton Frost (Baltimore, 1931).

12 Carlos Juan Finlay ("Yellow Fever, Before and After the Discovery of America," *The Climatologist*, 1882, published in Carlos Juan Finlay, *Obras completas*, 4 vols. [Havana, 1964], 2:111–18) makes a case for an American origin, as do L. J. B. Berenger-Feraud, *Traité théorique et clinique de la fièvre jaune* (Paris, 1890) and George Augustin, *History of Yellow Fever* (New Orleans, 1909).

13 Taylor, "Epidemiology," 530–2. For a first-hand account of Yucatan's 1648 yellow fever epidemic that decimated the Indian population, see R. P. Fray Diego Lopez de Cogolludo, *Historia de Yucatan*, 2 vols.; 3rd ed. (Mérida, Mexico, 1867), 2:561–2.

14 Taylor, "Epidemiology," 592–632, admirably summarized these arguments and reaches this conclusion. See also H. Harold Scott, "The Influence of the Slave Trade in the Spread of Tropical Disease," *RSTMH*, 37 (1943), 172–80. Of course, the final proof awaits "the development of immunological methods reliably applicable to prehistoric human remains." Saul Jarcho, "Some Observations on Disease in Prehistoric North America," *BHM*, 38 (1964), 11.

15 Ashburn, *Ranks of Death*, 129–40, does an excellent job of analysing this and other points in the debate. See also Carter, *Yellow Fever*, 69.

16 Armando Schedl, "Negros prehispánicos en América?" *Revista Geográfica Americana*, 244 (1957), 121–4; L. H. Dudley Buxton, J. C. Trevor, and Alvarez H. Julien, "Skeletal Remains from the Virgin Islands," *MAN*, 38 (1938), 49–51; T. D. Stewart, "Negro Skeletal Remains from Indian Sites in the West Indies," *MAN*, 39 (1939), 49–51; M. D. W. Jeffreys, "Pre-Columbian Maize in Africa," *Nature*, 172 (1953), 965–6. See also Hui-Lin Li, "Mu-lan-p'i: A Case for Pre-Columbia Transatlantic Travel by Arab Ships," *Harvard Journal of Asiatic Studies*, 23 (1960–61), 114–26.

17 Thor Heyerdahl, *The Ra Expeditions*, trans. Patricia Crampton (New York, 1971).

18 Taylor, "Epidemiology," 530.
19 K. H. Uttley, "The Mortality of Yellow Fever in Antigua, West Indies, Since 1857," *West Indian Medical Journal*, 9 (1960), 187.
20 Any number of texts deal with the pathology and pathogenesis of yellow fever. In this case we have employed A. J. Rhodes and C. E. Van Rooyen, *Textbook of Virology*, 5th ed. (Baltimore, 1968), 703–4.
21 The following mosquito lore is based on Loring Whitman, "The Anthropod Vectors of Yellow Fever," in *Yellow Fever*, ed. Strode, 229–98.
22 Felsenfeld, *Tropical Diseases*, 381.
23 L. K. H. Goma, *The Mosquito* (London, 1966), 43.
24 Ibid., 43, Marston Bates, *The Natural History of Mosquitos* (New York, 1949), 107.
25 John Duffy, *Epidemics in Colonial America* (Baton Rouge, La., 1953) 139.
26 John H. Parry and P. M. Sherlock, *A Short History of the West Indies*, 3rd ed. (London, 1971) 106–7.
27 Jones, "Virginians and 'Calenture,' " 391.
28 Felsenfeld, *Tropical Diseases*, 380.
29 Examples are numerous. See Ashburn, *Ranks of Death*, 135–6, for the classic example of Cuba.
30 Parry and Sherlock, *West Indies*, 56.
31 One suggestion is that in prehistoric times (when presumably the continents were close together) winds might even have transmitted infected mosquitoes from one continent to the other. Folke Henschen, *The History and Geography of Diseases*, trans. Joan Tate (New York, 1966), 36.
32 Taylor, "Epidemiology," 532.
33 Carter, *Yellow Fever*, 50–78, mentions many diseases frequently confused with yellow fever.
34 Mark F. Boyd, "Introduction," *Malariology: A Comprehensive Survey of all Aspects of this Group of Diseases from a Global Standpoint*, ed. Mark F. Boyd, 2 vols. (Philadelphia, 1949), I:228.
35 Gordon Willis Jones, "Doctor John Mitchell's Yellow Fever Epidemics," *Virginia Magazine of History and Biography*, 70 (1962), 47–8.
36 But not always. The disease seems to have paid brief seventeenth- and eighteenth-century calls on New York, Boston, Philadelphia and Charleston. See Augustin, *History of Yellow Fever*, 767, and M. Foster Farley, "Stranger's Fever," *South Carolina History Illustrated*, 1 (1970), 54–61, passim.
37 Jones, "Dr. John Mitchell's Yellow Fever Epidemics," 47–8.
38 Events of the period under discussion are covered from different perspectives by Charles R. Boxer, *The Dutch Seaborn Empire, 1600–1800* (New York, 1965); John H. Parry, *The Spanish Seaborne Empire* (New York, 1966); Arthur P. Newton, *The European Nations in the West Indies, 1493–1688* (London, 1933); Richard Pares, *War and Trade in the West Indies, 1739–1763* (Oxford, 1936); and Walter Lewis Dorn, *Competition for Empire, 1740–1763* (New York, 1940).
39 Guerra, "Influence of Disease on Race," 27–28.
40 Lempriere, *Practical Observations on the Diseases of the Army of Jamaica*, I:1.
41 John Hunter, *Observations on the Diseases of the Army in Jamaica*, 3rd ed. (London, 1808), 57, who placed the average annual troop mortality rate at 25 percent.
42 Ibid., 60.
43 Thomas Trotter, *Medicina Nautica: An Essay of the Diseases of Seamen*, 3 vols., 2nd ed. (London, 1804), 1:322.
44 Guerra, "Influence of Disease on Race," 29, 30. William Pym (*Observations upon Bulam, Vomito-Negro, or Yellow Fever* [London, 1848], 269–70) reports that over 10,000 of the British losses (80,000) also occurred in St. Domingue during 1795–6.
45 Robert Collins, *Practical Rules for the Management and Medical Treatment of Negro Slaves in the Sugar Colonies* (London, 1811; reprint, New York, 1971), 200, 259; John Wil-

liamson, *Medical and Miscellaneous Observations Relative to the West India Islands*, 2 vols. (Edinburgh, 1817), I:248; Hunter, *Diseases of the Army in Jamaica*, 269–70; Robert Jackson, *A Sketch of the History and Cure of Febrile Diseases; More Particularly as they Appear in the West Indies Among the Soldiers of the British Army* (London, 1791), 249–50; Humboldt, *Political Essay on the Kingdom of New Spain*, 4:171; Belot, *Yellow Fever at Havana*, 39; Pinckard, *Notes on the West Indies*, 2:475.

46 See Alexandre Moreau de Jonnès, *Essai sur l'hygiène militaire des Antilles* (Paris, 1817), 3, 10, for other statistical examples of the heavy troop mortality sustained by Europe in the West Indies during the eighteenth century.

47 Guerra, "Influence of Disease on Race," 34.

48 See for example Hunter, *Diseases of the Army in Jamaica*, 269–70.

49 Guerra, "Influence of Disease on Race," 35.

50 The French also appreciated the implications of using black troops, but it was too late as the St. Domingue situation was already irreparable. See Alexandre Moreau de Jonnès, "Observations pour servir à l'histoire de la fièvre jaune des Antilles suivies des tables de la mortalité des troupes européenes dans les Indes-Ocidentales," *Bulletin de la Societé Medicale d' Emulation*, 6 (1817), 237–47. Ironically, the Spanish, who had pioneered in their use, did not regularly employ black troops during the nineteenth century. The result, as reported by one visitor to Cuba, was an estimate that Spain lost 25 percent of the soldiers sent to Cuba to yellow fever alone. Richard Henry Dana, *To Cuba and Back: A Vacation Voyage* (reprint ed. Carbondale, Ill., 1966), 128–9.

51 The following data have all been taken from Alexander M. Tulloch, *Statistical Report on the Sickness, Mortality, and Invaliding Among the Troops in the West Indies* (London, 1838), 5–7, 434–7, and passim.

52 Calculated from tables in Philip D. Curtin, *The Atlantic Slave Trade; A Census* (Madison, Wisc., 1969) 25, 119.

53 John L. E. W. Shecut, *An Essay on the Prevailing, or Yellow Fever, of 1817* (Charleston, S. C., 1817), 17; William Hume, "The Yellow Fever of Charleston, Considered in its Relations to the West India Commerce," *CMJR*, 15 (1860), 1–2; Belot, *Yellow Fever at Havana*, 29; Albert W. Diddle, "Medical Events in the History of Key West," *BHM*, 15 (1944), 450; Louisa Breeden to Mrs. Louisa Millard, Port Gibson, 18 September 1824, Miles Taylor and family papers, Louisiana State University; Jacob de la Motta, *An Oration, on the Causes of the Mortality Among Strangers, During the Late Summer and Fall* (Savannah, Ga., 1820), passim. Although representing or writing in different regions of the South, all of the above speak of "stranger's fevers."

54 Editors, "Acclimation; and the Liability of Negroes to the Endemic Fevers of the South," *NOMN*, 5 (1858), 80.

55 Henry P. Russell, comp., *An Official Register of the Deaths Which Occurred Among the White Population in the City of Savannah, During the Extraordinary Season of Sickness and Mortality Which Prevailed in the Summer and Fall Months of the Year 1820 to Which is Annexed . . . the Aggregate Amount of Deaths Among the People of Color* (Savannah, Ga., 1820).

56 J. L. Dawson, "Statistics Relative to the Epidemic Yellow Fever in the City of Charleston," *CMJR*, 10 (1855), 199–200.

57 Unsigned article, "The Yellow Fever of Charleston," *SMR*, 1 (1849), 410.

58 William R. Waring, *Report to the City Council of Savannah, on the Epidemic Disease of 1820* (Savannah, Ga., 1821), 40; Stanford Emerson Chaillé *Life and Death in New Orleans From 1787 to 1869 and More Especially During the Five Years 1856 to 1860* (New Orleans, 1869), 51.

59 [William L. Robinson], *The Diary of a Samaritan by a Member of the Howard Association of New Orleans* (New York, 1860), appendix.

60 Hume, "Yellow Fever of Charleston," 1–2.

61 Daily Morning News Press (Savannah), *Names of the Dead, Being a Record of the Mortality in Savannah During the Epidemic of 1854* (Savannah, Ga., 1854), 5.

62   Thomas Young Simons, *A Report on the History and Causes of the Strangers or Yellow Fever of Charleston* (Charleston, S.C., 1839). For still other examples, consult P. H. Lewis, "Sketch of the Yellow Fever of Mobile, with a Brief Analysis of the Epidemic of 1843," *NOMSJ*, 1 (1845), 417, and Waring, *Report to the City Council of Savannah*, 40, 59.

63   A listing of the yellow fever years for Savannah is provided by Robert L. Usinger, "Yellow Fever from the Viewpoint of Savannah," *GHQ*, 28 (1944), 144–5. For Charleston, see the *Report of the Committee of the City Council of Charleston, Upon the Epidemic Yellow Fever, of 1858* (Charleston, S.C., 1859), 5, 47–65, 67; Simons, *Report on the Strangers Fever of Charleston*, 7–8; and 'E. McC', *A Series of Articles upon the Means of Preventing the Recurrence of Yellow Fever in Charleston Addressed to the Citizens of Charleston* (Charleston, S.C., 1858), 6. For New Orleans, consult the appropriate tables in Frederick Ludwig Hoffman, *Vital Statistics of New Orleans, 1787–1909* (New York, 1913). Many of these outbreaks seem to have been of a relatively mild nature, and while it is true that "there are marked differences in the pathogenic properties of different strains" of yellow fever virus (Kenneth C. Smithburn, "Immunology," in *Yellow Fever*, ed. Strode. 183), some of the so-called epidemics were undoubtedly outbreaks of dengue, which is transmitted by the same vector as yellow fever and therefore has a similar epidemiologic behavior, producing many of the same symptoms but not the widespread mortality. For examples of dengue's frequent confusion with yellow fever, see Richard Dennis Arnold's discussion of *The Identity of Dengue; or Break Bone Fever, and of Yellow Fever* (Savannah, Ga., 1859), W. B. Anderson to S. A. Cartwright, Vicksburg, 30 August 1853, L.S.U., and Diddle, "Medical Events in the History of Key West," 460. See also Joseph Franklin Siler, Milton W. Hall, and A. Parker Hitchins, *Dengue: Its History, Epidemiology* (Manila, 1926), 6–8.

64   United States medical literature from the eighteenth century onward is replete with tracts on yellow fever that never fail to speak of black immunity. Examples range from John Lining's eighteenth-century letter ("A Description of the American Yellow Fever, which Prevailed at Charleston, in the Year 1748" in *Essays and Observations, Physical and Literary, Read Before a Society in Edinburgh* [Edinburgh, 1756], 2:404–32) pronouncing Charleston's blacks immune to yellow fever, to David Ramsay's *The Charleston Medical Register, for the Year 1802* (Charleston, S.C., 1803), 21, which attributed the phenomenon to a better ability of Africans to bear the climate, to P. Tidyman's "A Sketch of the most Remarkable Diseases of the Negroes of the Southern States, with an Account of the Method of Treating them, Accompanied by Physiological Observations," *Philadelphia Journal of the Medical and Physical Sciences*, 12 (1826), 325, which pondered why yellow fever "should be confined to the white population."

65   Computed from materials in J. L. Dawson and H. W. DeSaussure, *Census of the City of Charleston, South Carolina, for the Year 1848* (Charleston, S.C., 1849), 10, and United States Census Office, *Statistics of the United States . . . in 1860 . . .* (Washington, D.C., 1866).

66   Simons, *A Report on the Strangers Fever of Charleston*, 7–8.

67   B[ennet] Dowler, "Yellow Fever of Charleston in 1858," *NOMSJ*, 16 (1859), 596, (table), 597; *Report of the Committee of the City Council of Charleston*, 67 (table).

68   *Report of the Committee of the Physico-Medical Society of New Orleans on the Epidemic of 1820* (New Orleans, 1821), appendix.

69   Hoffman, *Vital Statistics of New Orleans*, 19 (table).

70   Ibid. Moreover, it is probable that the number of white deaths has been understated. Erasmus Darwin Fenner, *History of the Epidemic Yellow Fever, at New Orleans, La., in 1853* (New York, 1854), 71, and Bennet Dowler, *Tableau of the Yellow Fever of 1853, with Topographical, Chronological and Historical Sketches of the Epidemics of New Orleans Since Their Origins in 1796* (New Orleans, 1854), 30, both physicians on the spot, put the total deaths in excess of 8,000.

71   Russell, ed., *An Official Register of the Deaths . . . in the City of Savannah.*

72 Daily Morning News Press (Savannah) *Names of the Dead*, 12.
73 J. D. B. DeBow, ed., *Mortality Statistics of the Seventh Census of the United States, 1850* (Washington, D.C., 1854), 27.
74 The following calculations are based on the populations shown for the cities in question in the 1850 census.
75 Waring, *Report to the City Council of Savannah*, 3–4; Daily Morning News Press (Savannah) *Names of the Dead*, 4–5; Jo Ann Carrigan, "Yellow Fever in New Orleans, 1853: Abstractions and Realities," *JSH*, 25 (1959), 344, writes of joking in New Orleans newspapers about a "Can't Get Away Club." For the white stampede out of Mobile see Howard L. Holley, "A Century and A Half of the History of the Life Sciences in Alabama: Yellow Fever Causes Panic in Mobile," *Alabama Journal of the Medical Sciences*, 14 (1977), 293–4, and for that out of Memphis see Thomas H. Baker, "Yellowjack: The Yellow Fever Epidemic of 1878 in Memphis, Tennessee," *BHM*, 42 (1968), 244–5. S. R. Bruesch, "The Disasters and Epidemics of a River Town: Memphis, Tennessee, 1819–1879," *BMLA*, 40 (1950), 303, points out that even after slavery blacks constituted most of the "can't get aways."
76 Samuel A. Cartwright, "Prevention of Yellow Fever," *NOMSJ*, 10 (1853), 316.
77 Andrew R. Kilpatrick, "An Account of the Yellow Fever which Prevailed in Woodville, Mississippi, in the Year 1844," *NOMSJ*, 2 (1845), 57.
78 Erasmus D. Fenner, "The Epidemic of 1847: A Brief Account of the Yellow Fever that Prevailed at New Orleans, Vicksburg, Rodney, Natchez, Houston, and Covington, Louisiana," *NOMSJ*, 5 (1848–9), 207.
79 Ibid., 207.
80 E. D. Fenner, "The Yellow Fever of 1853," *DBR*, 17 (1854), 42.
81 Dowler, *Tableau of the Yellow Fever of 1853*, 38–9.
82 Donald E. Everett, "The New Orleans Yellow Fever Epidemic of 1853," *LHQ*, 33 (1950), 384.
83 *Report of the Howard Association of Norfolk Va., Summer of 1855*, (Philadelphia, 1857), 49. The epidemic cost Norfolk about 2,000 deaths out of a population of 8,000 to 10,000 which saw it through. See also p. 38. The Howards, named for a prominent nineteenth-century philanthropist, was a voluntary association composed of young men who organized themselves to assist the sick and dying. A unit was normally formed locally wherever the disease appeared.
84 *Report of the Portsmouth Relief Association to the Contributors of the Fund for the Relief of Portsmouth, Virginia During the Prevalence of the Yellow Fever in that Town in 1855* (Richmond, Va., 1856), 142.
85 William S. Forrest, *The Great Pestilence in Virginia* (New York, 1856), 103.
86 For examples of this growing conviction, consult A. P. Merrill, "An Essay on the Distinctive Peculiarities and Diseases of the Negro Race," *DBR*, 20 (1856), 621–2, Fenner, "Epidemic of 1847," 207, and Lewis, "Sketch of the Yellow Fever of Mobile," 416. Statistical evidence to buttress the notion was generated during the Norfolk epidemic where "very few indeed of the pure blacks died," yet "the mulattoes suffered almost as much as the whites." *Report of the Howard Association of Norfolk, Va.*, 38.
87 Josiah C. Nott, "An Examination into the Health and Longevity of the Southern Sea Ports of the United States, with Reference to the Subject of Life Insurance," *Southern Journal of Medicine and Pharmacy*, 2 (1847), 19.
88 Josiah C. Nott and George R. Gliddon, *Indigenous Races of the Earth; or New Chapters of Ethnological Inquiry* (Philadelphia, 1857), 367.
89 Merrill, "Distinctive Peculiarities and Diseases of the Negro Race," 621; René La Roche, *Yellow Fever considered in its Historical, Pathological, Etiological, and Therapeutic Relations. . . .* 2 vols. (Philadelphia, 1855), 2:60–9.
90 Paul Eby Steiner, *Disease in the Civil War: Natural Biological Warfare in 1861–1865* (Springfield, Ill., 1968), 15.

91 Carrigan, "Saffron Scourge," 131.
92 U. S. Surgeon-General's Office, *Report on Epidemic Cholera and Yellow Fever in the Army of the United States, During the Year 1867* (Washington, D.C., 1868), xxvi, 80. See Charles Decéry, *Mémoire sur l'épidemie de fièvre juane qui a régné à la Nouvelle-Orléans et dans les campagnes pendant l'année 1867* (New Orleans, 1868) for a history of the 1867 outbreak.
93 For the dramatic postbellum increase of blacks in New Orleans who came directly from the plantations, see John W. Blassingame, *Black New Orleans, 1860–1880* (Chicago, 1973), 1.
94 Richard Frazer Michel, *Epidemic of Yellow Fever in Montgomery, Ala. During the Summer of 1873* (Montgomery, Ala., 1874), 5.
95 *Savannah Morning News*, 28 November 1876; Julius Caesar Le Hardy, "Yellow Fever: Its Relations to Climate and to Hygienic Measures in the United States," *VMM*, (1894), 9–10; and *Yellow Fever, the Epidemic of 1876 in Savannah* (n.d.), passim.
96 Manning Simons, "A Note on the Epidemic of Yellow Fever at Port Royal in 1877," *Extracts from Transactions, South Carolina Medical Association* (1878), 31–2.
97 Baker, "Yellowjack," 261.
98 Ibid., 252, 261. Bruesch, "The Disasters and Epidemics of a River Town," 304, has calculated an even lower black mortality rate of 7 percent. See also the Memphis and Shelby County Health Department, *Yellow Fever and the Board of Health: Memphis 1878* (Memphis, 1964), 27.
99 Baker, "Yellowjack," 261. Bruesch, "The Disasters and Epidemics of a River Town," 304, has calculated a white mortality rate of 75 percent.
100 New Orleans Howard Association, *Report of the Howard Association . . . in the Epidemic of 1878* (New Orleans, 1878), 18.
101 John Logan Power, *The Epidemic of 1878 in Mississippi; Report of the Yellow Fever Relief Work* (Jackson, Miss., 1879), 162.
102 Ibid., 168–70.
103 Ibid., 162–3.
104 The last outbreak of the disease in the United States occurred in 1905, although the final imported case was registered as late as 1923. Mosley, "Yellow Fever," in *Infectious Diseases*, Hoeprich, ed., 665.
105 Julian Herman Lewis, *Biology of the Negro* (Chicago, 1942) 211.
106 Charles Chassaignac, "Some Lessons Taught by the Epidemic of 1905," in *History of Yellow Fever*, ed. Augustin.
107 This also tends to discount older, sometimes resurrected notions that the "aedes mosquito has a certain repugnancy for the black race." For a discussion, see Siler, Hall and Hitchins, *Dengue*, 13.
108 John Wesley Monette, "An Inaugural Thesis on the Endemial Bilious Fever, as it Generally Occurs in the Vicinity of Natchez" (unpublished thesis, Transylvania University, 1825, 5–6); La Roche, *Yellow Fever*, 2:60–9.
109 Robert William Fogel and Stanley L. Engerman, Vol. 1: *Time on the Cross: The Economics of American Negro Slavery* and Vol. 2: *Time on the Cross: Evidence and Methods – A Supplement* (Boston, 1974); 1:132.
110 Alexander G. Bearn, "Introduction," in Bracha Ramot et al. (eds.) *Genetic Polymorphisms and Diseases in Man* (New York, 1974) 5.
111 Thomas D. Dublin and Baruch S. Blumberg, "An Epidemiologic Approach to Inherited Disease Susceptibility," *PHR*, 76 (1961), 505.
112 See for example Hirsch, *Geographical and Historical Pathology*, 1:344.
113 Rubert Boyce, "Note Upon Yellow Fever in the Black Race and its Bearing Upon the Question of the Endemicity of Yellow Fever in West Africa," *Annals of Tropical Medicine and Parasitology*, 5 (1911), 103.

114 Charles Wilcocks and P. E. C. Manson-Bahr, *Manson's Tropical Diseases*, 17th ed. (Baltimore, 1972), 374: James S. Ward, *Yellow Fever in Latin America: A Geographical Study* (Liverpool, 1972), 7–8.
115 Carter, *Yellow Fever*, 270.

Chapter 3. Bad air in a new world

1 Josiah C. Nott, "Statistics of Southern State Population, with Especial Reference to Life Insurance," *DBR*, 4 (1847), 280.
2 There are some 200 known anopheline species of which sixty have been indicted as vectors of malaria. Martin P. Young, "Malaria," in *Manual of Tropical Medicine*, eds. George W. Hunter, William W. Frye, J. Clyde Swartzwelder (Philadelphia, 1966), 337.
3 G. Canby Robinson, "Malaria in Virginia in the Early Nineteenth Century," *BHM*, 32 (1958), 531.
4 See the comments of Robert L. Usinger, "Yellow Fever from the Viewpoint of Savannah," *GHQ*, 28 (1944), 144, Henry Rose Carter, *Yellow Fever: An Epidemiological and Historical Study of its Place of Origin*, ed. Laura Armistead Carter and Wade Hampton Frost (Baltimore, 1931), 50–78, and Wyndham Bolling Blanton, *Medicine in Virginia in the Eighteenth Century* (Richmond, Va., 1931), 148. An example of the lack of diagnostic precision can be found in the "Monroe McGuire Diary, 1818–50," Mississippi State Archives, Jackson, Miss. and John Wesley Monette, "Observations on the Pathology and Treatment of the Endemic Fevers of the Southeast, Commonly called Congestive Fever," *NOMSJ*, 3 (1844), 131, 4 (1845), 265–6.
5 The current assumption is that Africa was the cradle of all malarial types, that the disease spread up the Nile Valley to the Mediterranean and from there to Europe and the East, and that malaria parasites arrived late in the Americas via Europe and Africa. For an early but masterful "Historical Review," see that by Boyd in his introductory chapter to *Malariology: A Comprehensive Survey of all Aspects of this Group of Diseases from a Global Standpoint*, 2 vols., ed. Mark F. Boyd (Philadelphia, 1949), 1:3–25.
6 Examples of older studies which debated the problem are Wyndham Bolling Blanton, *Medicine in Virginia in the Eighteenth Century* (see also Wyndham Bolling Blanton, *Medicine in Virginia in the Nineteenth Century* [Richmond, 1933], p. 157) and St. Julien Ravenel Childs, *Malaria and Colonization in the Carolina Low Country, 1526–1696* (Baltimore, 1940).
7 For two recent summaries of the question of malaria's New World debut, both of which find it extremely doubtful that malaria preceded Columbus to the New World, see Frederick L. Dunn, "On the Antiquity of Malaria in the Western Hemisphere, *HB*, 37 (1965), 385–93, and Saul Jarcho, "Some Observations on Disease in Prehistoric North America," *BHM*, 38 (1964), 1–19. There are those, however, who, while agreeing that malaria was imported to the Americas, believe it arrived with sea-going peoples prior to 1492. See for example L. J. Bruce-Chwatt, "Paleogenesis and Paleo-Epidemiology of Primate Malaria," *WHO*, 32 (1965), 363–87.
8 Carter, for example (*Yellow Fever*, 69), argues for a European origin.
9 P. M. Ashburn, *The Ranks of Death: A Medical History of the Conquest of America* (New York, 1947), 103–26, presents a lively argument for "malaria's" probable African origin.
10 Blanton, *Medicine in Virginia in the Eighteenth Century*, 54–55; John Duffy, *Epidemics in Colonial America*, (Baton Rouge, La., 1953) 204.
11 Peter H. Wood (*Black Majority: Negroes in Colonial South Carolina from 1670 through the Stono Rebellion* [New York, 1974], chap. 3) presents an excellent analysis of the disease experience of South Carolina's colonists.

12 Ibid., 65.

13 Ibid., chap. 3, and Darrett B. Rutman and Anita H. Rutman, "Of Agues and Fevers: Malaria in the Early Chesapeake," *WMQ*, 33 (1976), 31–60, have advanced arguments similar to our own.

14 Joseph Ioor Waring, *A History of Medicine in South Carolina*, 3 vols. (Columbia S.C., 1964–71), 2: 3.

15 Erwin H[einz] Ackerknecht, *Malaria in the Upper Mississippi Valley 1760–1900* (Baltimore 1945), 4.

16 Wyndham Bolling Blanton, *Medicine in Virginia in the Nineteenth Century* (Richmond, Va., 1933), 157; Guion Griffis Johnson, *A Social History of the Sea Islands* (Chapel Hill, N.C., 1930), 95; August Hirsch, *Handbook of Geographical and Historical Pathology*, trans. Charles Creighton, 3 vols. (London, 1883–86) 1: 243–4; Monroe McGuire, "McGuire Diary 1818–1850." Mississippi Dept. of Archives and History.

17 P. Tidyman, "A sketch of the Most Remarkable Diseases of the Negroes of the Southern States, with an Account of the Method of Treating them, Accompanied by Physiological Observations," *Philadelphia Journal of the Medical and Physical Sciences*, 12 (1826), 315–6.

18 W. G. Ramsay, "The Physiological Differences between the European (or White Man) and the Negro," *SA*, 12 (1839), 413.

19 Lewis, "Sketch of the Yellow Fever of Mobile With a Brief Analysis of the Epidemic of 1843 . . . *NOMSJ*, 1 (1843), 417.

20 George A. Ketchum, "Reports from Alabama," *SMR*, 2 (1850), 307; Josiah C. Nott and George R. Gliddon, eds., *Indigenous Races of the Earth; or New Chapters of Ethnological Inquiry* (Philadephia, 1857), 368–9.

21 *Minutes of the Proceedings of the Medical Society of North Carolina Second Annual Meeting* (Raleigh, N.C., 1851), 7.

22 Stephen N. Harris, "Intermittent and Remittent Fever," *SJMP*, 2 (1847), 615–16.

23 Herbert Anthony Kellar, ed., *Solon Robinson: Pioneer and Agriculturalist*, 2 vols. (Indianapolis, 1936, reprint ed., New York, 1968), 2:354; Duffy, *Epidemics in Colonial America*, 248.

24 Because of the problem of "undifferentiated fevers" lumped together under a general malarial rubric, very few good statistics are available, unlike yellow fever which, because it occurred in epidemic form, yielded more reliable mortality data.

25 *Report of the Committee of the City Council of Charleston upon the Epidemic Yellow Fever of 1858* (Charleston, S.C., 1859), 4–5 (tables), 47–65.

26 W. C. Daniell, *Observations upon the Autumnal Fevers of Savannah* (Savannah, Ga., 1826), 31–2.

27 Frederick Ludwig Hoffman, *Vital Statistics of New Orleans, 1787–1909* (New York, 1913), 18 (table).

28 J. Strobhart, "Some Thoughts on Malaria, and Doubts as to its Existence as a Source of Disease," *CMJR*, 3 (1848), 41.

29 J. D. Rumph, "Thoughts on Malaria, and the Causes Generally of Fever," *CMJR*, 9 (1854), 442.

30 E. M. Pendleton, "Statistics of Diseases of Hancock County," *SMSJ*, n.s.5 (1849), 650.

31 Editors, "Acclimation; and the Liability of Negroes to the Endemic Fevers of the South," *NOMN*, 5 (1858), 84.

32 See, for examples, Franklin L. Riley, ed., "Diary of a Mississippi Planter, January 1, 1840 to April 1863," *PMHS*, 10 (1909), 333 and passim; McGuire Diary (Mississippi Department of Archives and History) and the Records of Good Hope Plantation, 1835–59, (South Carolina Historical Society). See mortality entries for 1833–56 in Wendell Holmes Stephenson, "A Quarter-Century of a Mississippi Plantation: Eli J. Capell of 'Pleasant Hill,' " *MVHR*, 23 (1936), 371, the slave list of M. McCulloch,

1855 (Tulane), and the Hubbard Family Papers (University of Virginia) especially the overseer's letter dated 8 August 1838, Nelson County, Va.
33 Richard H. Shryock, ed., *Letters of Richard D. Arnold, M.D. 1808–1876* (Durham N.C., 1929), 65–67.
34 Lewis, "Sketch of the Yellow Fever of Mobile," 417.
35 Josiah C. Nott, "An Examination into the Health and Longevity of the Southern Sea Ports of the United States, with Reference to the Subject of Life Insurance," *Southern Journal of Medicine and Pharmacy*, 2 (1847), 15–16.
36 Editors, "Acclimation," 81, who discussed the views of a number of physicians.
37 Ibid., 81.
38 Alfred G. Tebault papers, 1853–92 (U. of Va.). See second notebook.
39 Cited by Blanton, *Medicine in Virginia in the Nineteenth Century*, 259.
40 E. M. Pendleton, "General Report on the Topography, Climate and Diseases of Middle Georgia," *SMR*, 1 (1849), 339, and "Diseases of Hancock county," 650–1.
41 It should be stressed, however, that as of this writing there has been no proof that the Duffy-negative trait discourages *P. falciparum*.
42 Anthony Cerami and Elsie Washington, *Sickle Cell Anemia* (New York, 1974), 88.
43 Robert William Fogel and Stanley L. Engerman, *Time on the Cross: The Economics of American Negro Slavery* (Boston, 1974) 1:23 (figure).
44 Ibid., 1:132.
45 H. Rawling Pratt-Thomas, "Plantation Medicine," *JSCMA*, 66 (1970), 154.
46 Thompson McGown, *A Practical Treatise on the Most Common Diseases of the South: Exhibiting Their Peculiar Nature, and the Corresponding Adaptation of Treatment* (Philadelphia, 1849), 27.
47 Rumph, "Thoughts on Malaria," 446.

Chapter 4. Tropical killers, race, and the peculiar institution

1 Philip D. Curtin, *Image of Africa: British Ideas and Actions, 1780–1850* (Madison, Wisc., 1964), 80.
2 By the eighteenth century the miasmatic focus permeated literature on tropical medicine. For examples, see John Huxham, *An Essay on Fevers . . .* ,2nd ed. (London, 1750); William Hillary, *Observations on the Changes of the Air and the Concomitant Epidemical Diseases, in the Island of Barbados* (London, 1759; rev. ed. Philadelphia, 1811); James Lind, *Essay on the Diseases Incidental to Europeans in Hot Climates* (London, 1768); and Lewis Rouppe, *Observations on Diseases Incidental to Seamen* (London, 1772).
3 For the changing state of medical thought and practice from 1660–1820, see Richard Harrison Shryock, *Medicine and Society in America, 1660–1860* (New York, 1960), 44–81.
4 Charles Bisset, *Medical Essays and Observations* (Newcastle-Upon-Tyne, 1766), 12; Huxham, *Essay on Fevers*, 18.
5 Philip D. Curtin, " 'The White Man's Grave': Image and Reality, 1780–1850," *Journal of British Studies*, 1 (1961), 107–9; Wyndham Bolling Blanton, *Medicine in Virginia in the Eighteenth Century* (1931), 67. For the picturesque story of the drug, see Marie Louise Duran-Reynals, *The Fever Bark Tree: The Pageant of Quinine* (Garden City, N.Y., 1946), and for its role in ultimately opening the door to the late nineteenth-century European colonization of Africa, see Dennis G. Carlson, "African Fever, Prophylactic Quinine, and Statistical Analysis: Factors in the European Penetration of a Hostile West African Environment," *BHM*, 51 (1977), 386–96.
6 For the evolution of miasmatic theory, see Owsei Temkin, *The Double Face of Janus and Other Essays in the History of Medicine* (Baltimore, 1977), 456–71.
7 On the subject of heroic medicine, consult Richard Shryock, "Medical Practice in the Old South," *South Atlantic Quarterly*, 29 (1930), 160–78, John Duffy, "Medical Practice in the Ante Bellum South," *JSH*, 25 (1959), 53–72, and Alex Berman, "The Heroic

Approach in 19th-century Therapeutics," in *Sickness and Health in America* . . . , eds. Judith Walzer Leavitt and Ronald L. Numbers (Madison, Wisc., 1978), 77–86.

8 Pinckard, *Notes on the West Indies*, 2 vols. 2nd ed. (London, 1816), 2:467. The notion that yellow fever susceptibility increased with the temperature was still firmly embedded in nineteenth-century epidemiological thought. See *Report of the Board of Health of the State of Georgia for 1876 with Appendix and Mortality Record of the Epidemic in Savannah in 1876* (Savannah, Ga., 1877), xiii–xvi and August Hirsch, *Handbook of Geographical and Historical Pathology*, trans. Charles Creighton, 3 vols. (London, 1883–86) 1:340–1.

9 P. Tidyman, "A Sketch of the Most Remarkable Diseases of the Negroes of the Southern States, with an Account of the Method of Treating them, Accompanied by Physiological Observations," *Philadelphia Journal of the Medical and Physical Sciences*, 12 (1826), 325.

10 John Wesley Monette, "An Inaugural Thesis on the Endemial Bilious Fever, as it Generally Occurs in the Vicinity of Natchez," unpublished thesis, Transylvania University, 1825.

11 René La Roche, *Yellow Fever Considered in its Historical, Pathological, Etiological, and Therapeutic Relations* . . . , 2 vols. (Philadelphia, 1855), 2:66.

12 Editors, "Acclimation; and the Liability of Negroes to the Endemic Fevers of the South," *NOMN*, 5 (1858), 84; W. G. Ramsay, "The Physiological Differences between the European (or White Man) and the Negro," *SA*, 12 (1839), 413; *Minutes of the Proceedings of the Medical Society of North Carolina at its Second Annual Meeting* (Raleigh, N.C., 1851), 6.

13 This notion was already a popular one in the minds of West Indian physicians. Curtin, *Image of Africa*, 85.

14 Henry A. Ramsay, *The Necrological Appearances of Southern Typhoid Fever, in the Negro* (Columbia County, Ga., 1852), 16.

15 Samuel A. Cartwright, "Report on the Diseases and Physical Peculiarities of the Negro Race," *NOMSJ*, 7 (1851), 693.

16 Samuel A. Cartwright, "Philosophy of the Negro Constitution," *NOMSJ*, 9 (1852), 208.

17 Ramsay, *Typhoid Fever*, 16.

18 Ibid., 16. J[osiah] C. Nott, "The Mulatto a Hybrid – Probable Extermination of the Two Races if the Whites and Blacks are Allowed to Intermarry," *AJMS*, 6 (1843), 255; A. P. Merrill, "An Essay on the Distinctive Peculiarities and Diseases of the Negro Race," *DBR* 20 (1856) 621–2; Lunsford P. Yandell, "Remarks on Struma Africana, or the Disease Usually Called Negro Poison, or Negro Consumption," *TJM*, 4 (1831), 91.

19 E. M. Pendleton, "General Report on the Topography, Climate and Diseases of Middle Georgia," *SMR* 1, (1849), 337.

20 Cartwright, "Philosophy of the Negro Constitution," 208; Ramsay, *Typhoid Fever*, 14; Review of Ramsay in *NOMSJ*, 9 (1853), 823; Josiah C. Nott *Instincts of Races* (New Orleans, 1866), 8, 28.

21 Cartwright, "Report on Diseases," 693; Ramsay, *Typhoid Fever*, 19.

22 For other treatments of the subject see John Duffy, "A Note on Antebellum Southern Nationalism and Medical Practice," *JSH*, 34 (1968), 266–76; Weymouth T. Jordan, *Antebellum Alabama Town and Country* (Tallahasse, Fla., 1957), 84–103; James Denny Guillory, "The Pro-Slavery Arguments of Dr. Samuel A. Cartwright," *LH*, 9 (1968), 209–27; Mary Louise Marshall, "Samuel A. Cartwright and States' Rights Medicine," *NOMSJ*, 93 (1940), 74–8; and James O. Breeden, "States-Rights Medicine in the Old South," *BNYAM*, 52 (1976), 348–72.

23 Ramsay, "Physiological Differences," 289; Nott, "The Mulatto a Hybrid," 254; Cartwright, "Report on Diseases," 697 ff.

24 For a look at seventeenth- and eighteenth-century epidemics in North America, see
    John Duffy, *Epidemics in Colonial America,* (Baton Rouge, La., 1953) 138–63. For a
    vivid dramatic portrayal of Philadelphia's epidemic of 1793 see John Harvey Powell,
    Bring out your Dead: The Great Plague of Yellow Fever in Philadelphia in 1793 (Philadel-
    phia, 1949). Peculiarly, some doubt has been expressed as to whether Philadelphia
    did in fact experience a yellow fever epidemic in 1793. P. M. Ashburn (*The Ranks of
    Death; A Medical History of the Conquest of America* [New York, 1947], 233–4) for
    example, argues unconvincingly (for a change) that Rush and others misdiagnosed
    yellow fever as "dengue, malaria, or some mild disease" and that presumably the
    "heroic cures employed dispatched patients rather than the yellow fever."
25 Curtin, *Image of Africa,* 183.
26 Benjamin Rush ("An Account of the Bilious Remitting Yellow Fever, as it Appeared
    in Philadelphia, in the Year 1793," in *Benjamin Rush Medical Inquiries and Observations,*
    4 vols., 4th ed. [New York, 1972, reprint of 1815 ed.], 3 and 4, 98 [table]) put the
    number of deaths at 3,881. However, 5,000 has subsequently become the generally
    accepted figure, largely because of those who died after fleeing the city.
27 William Currie, *A Sketch of the Rise and Progress of Yellow Fever* (Philadelphia, 1800)
    14–15; Powell, *Bring out Your Dead,* 94, 95.
28 Powell, *Bring out Your Dead,* passim, contains numerous accounts of white terror in
    the face of yellow pestilence.
29 Mathew Carey, *An Account of the Malignant Fever, Lately Prevalent in Philadelphia; with
    a List of the Names of all who Died There, of that Disorder, Being, above Four Thousand,* 4th
    ed. (Dublin, 1794), 37.
30 Carey (see note 29) was in the vanguard of the blacks' critics. For the best defense
    see Absalom Jones, *A Narrative of the Proceedings of the Black People during the Late
    Awful Calamity in Philadelphia in the Year 1793, and a Refutation of some Censures Thrown
    upon Them* (Philadelphia, 1794; reprint ed., Philadelphia, 1969).
31 For a glimpse of "Benjamin Rush and the Negro," see the study by Betty L. Plum-
    mer, *American Journal of Psychiatry,* 127 (1970), 793–8.
32 Leonidas H. Berry, "Black Men and Malignant Fevers," *JNMA,* 56 (1964), 45.
33 Powell, *Bring out Your Dead,* 100.
34 The following sketch of the start of an epidemic has been drawn from Gordon Willis
    Jones, "The Year Virginia Mourned: The Sources for a Catastrophe," *BHM,* 35
    (1961), 257–9.
35 W. Monycott to Mrs. Mary E. Waterbury, Portsmouth, Va., 11 Aug. 1855, in William
    Richard Hansford papers (Duke University).
36 M. Foster Farley, "The Mighty Monarch of the South: Yellow Fever in Charleston
    and Savannah," *Georgia Review,* 27 (1973), 68.
37 James Innerarity to John Innerarity, Mobile, 23 Sept. 1834, in John Innerarity papers
    (Louisiana State University).
38 Rosalie Bridget Hart Priour, "Reminiscences" 74–5 (University of Texas).
39 Folke Henschen, *The History and Geography of Diseases,* trans. by Joan Tate (New
    York, 1966) 36,37.
40 Wilson H. Grabill, Clyde V. Kiser, and Pascal K. Whelpton, *The Fertility of American
    Women* (New York, 1958), 19; Reynolds Farley, "The Demographic Rates and Social
    Institutions of the Nineteenth Century Negro Population: A Stable Population
    Analysis," *Demography,* 2 (1965), 389.
41 Frank B. Livingstone, "Sickling and Malaria," *BMJ,* 1 (1957), 763; D. F. Roberts and
    A. E. Boyo, "On the Stability of Haemoglobin Gene Frequencies in West Africa,"
    AHG, 24 (1960), 379; I. Lestor Firschein, "Population Dynamics of the Sickle-cell
    Trait in the Black Caribs of British Honduras, Central America," *AJHG,* 13 (1961), 239; B.
    S. Platt, "Effect of Maternal Sickle-cell Trait on Perinatal Mortality," *BMJ,* 4 (1971),

336; John W. Eaton and Jeffrey I. Mucha, "Increased Fertility in Males with the Sickle Cell Trait?" *Nature*, 231 (1971), 456–7.

42 Darrett Rutman, personal communication.

43 William Hume, "The Yellow Fever of Charleston, Considered in its Relations to the West India Commerce," *CMJR*, 15 (1860) 1–2.

44 Richard S. Dunn, "The Social History of Early New England," *American Quarterly*, 24 (1972), 675.

45 We are indebted to the provocative speculations on malaria in the early Chesapeake of Darrett B. and Anita H. Rutman ("Agues and Fevers: Malaria in the Early Chesapeake," *WMQ*, 33 [1976], 58–9) for inspiring our line of reasoning.

46 David Brion Davis, personal communication.

47 Ramsay, "Physiological Differences," 415–16.

48 Jo Ann Carrigan, "Yellow Fever in New Orleans, 1853: Arbstraction and Realities," *JSH*, 25 (1959) 352.

49 This composite of declarations which appeared in southern journals during the late 1850s was in Kenneth M. Stampp, *The Peculiar Institution: Slavery in the Antebellum South* (New York, 1956), 7.

Introduction to Part III

1 Erwin H. Ackerknecht, *Malaria in the Upper Mississippi Valley, 1760–1900* (Baltimore, 1945), 1.

2 Todd L. Savitt, *Medicine and Slavery: The Diseases and Health Care of Blacks in Antebellum Virginia* (Urbana, Ill., 1978).

3 Examples include Michael Craton, *Searching for the Invisible Man: Slaves and Plantation Life in Jamaica* (Cambridge, Mass., 1978); Orlando Patterson, *The Sociology of Slavery: An Analysis of the Origins, Development and Structure of a Negro Slave Society in Jamaica* (London, 1967); B. W. Higman, *Slave Population and Economy in Jamaica, 1807–1834* (Cambridge, Engl., 1976); and Richard B. Dunn, *Sugar and Slaves: The Rise of the Planter Class in the English West Indies, 1624–1713* (Chapel Hill, N.C., 1972).

Chapter 5. "Negro diseases": an introductory glimpse

1 W. G. Ramsay, "The Physiological Differences between the European (or White Man) and the Negro," *SA*, 12 (1839), 416.

2 William Freeman Daniell, *Sketches of the Medical Topography and Native Diseases of the Gulf of Guinea, Western Africa* (London, 1849), 11–12.

3 Robert Collins, *Practical Rules for the Management and Medical Treatment of Negro Slaves in the Sugar Colonies* (London, 1811; reprint ed., New York, 1971), 354.

4 James Grainger, *An Essay on the More Common West Indian Diseases and the Remedies which that Country itself Produces . . .* , 2nd ed. (London, 1802), 53.

5 Berthold Laufer, "Geophagy," *Field Museum of Natural History: Anthropological Series*, 18 (1930), 156; Bengt Anell and Sture Lagercrantz, *Geophagical Customs* (Uppsala, Sweden, 1958), 65; Donald E. Vermeer, "Geophagy Among the Tiv of Nigeria," *Annals of American Geographers*, 56 (1966), 197–204 and "Geophagy Among the Ewe of Ghana," *Ethnology*, 10 (1971), 56–72; John M. Hunter, "Geophagy in Africa and the United States: A Culture-Nutrition Hypothesis," *Geographical Review*, 63 (1973), 170–95.

6 John Hunter, *Observations on the Diseases of the Army in Jamaica . . .* , 3rd ed. (London, 1808), 248.

7 Ibid., 250; Collins, *Practical Rules*, 293; Bryan Edwards, *The History, Civil and Commercial, of the British Colonies in the West Indies*, 3 vols., 4th ed. (London, 1807), 2:167; John Williamson, *Medical and Miscellaneous Observations Relative to the West India Is-*

lands, 2 vols. (Edinburgh, 1817), 1:110; P. Dons, "Recherches sur la cachexia africaine," *Gazette Medicale de Paris*, 6 (1838), 289–95.

8   David Mason, "On Atrophia a Ventriculo (Mal d'Estomac) or Dirt-eating," *EMSJ*, 39 (1833), 290–4; John Imray, "Observations on the Mal d'Estomac or Cachexia Africana, as it takes Place among the Negroes of Dominica," *EMSJ*, 59 (1843), 306.

9   Hunter, *Diseases of the Army in Jamaica*, 248; Edwards, *History of the West Indies*, 2:167; Collins, *Practical Rules*, 294; and Mason, "Atrophia a Ventriculo," 292.

10 Crosby, *The Columbian Exchange: Biological and Cultural Consequences of 1492* (Westport, Conn., 1972), 209. Interestingly a contemporary physician also linked black tetanus susceptibility to the habit of going barefoot. William Hillary, *Observations on the Changes of the Air and the Concomitant Epidemical Diseases in the Island of Barbados*, (London, 1759), 227.

11 L. A. Dugas, "A Lecture Upon Tetanus," *SMSJ*, n.s., 17 (1861), 435; Williamson, *West India Islands*, 1:66; August Hirsch, *Handbook of Geographical and Historical Pathology*, trans. Charles Creighton, 3 vols. (London, 1883–86), 3:614–5; William Lempriere, *Practical Observations on the Diseases of the Army in Jamaica as they Occurred between the Years of 1792 and 1797*, 2 vols. (London, 1799), vol. 1, 47.

12 Edwards (*History of the West Indies*) quoted by Imray, "Mal d'Estomac," 305; Hirsch, *Geographical and Historical Pathology*, 3:616; Collins, *Practical Rules*, 139.

13 Michael Craton, "Hobbesian or Panglossian? The Two Extremes of Slave Conditions in the British Caribbean 1783 to 1834," *WMQ*, 35 (1978), 343.

14 Lempriere, *Observations on Diseases in Jamaica*, I: 48–9; Collins, *Practical Rules*, 139; Grainger, *West Indian Diseases*, 15; Edwards, *History of the West Indies*, 2:167; Jean Barthelemy, *Observations sur les Maladies des Nègres, leurs causes, leurs traitemens, et les moyens de les prevenir*, 2 vols., 2nd ed. (Paris, 1892), 2:128.

15 Collins, *Practical Rules*, 393–4.

16 Grainger, *West Indian Diseases*, 21. See also M. G. Lewis, *Journal of a West Indian Proprietor, 1815–1817* (London, 1929), 97–8, and Abiel Abbot, *Letters Written in the Interior of Cuba . . .* , (Boston, 1829), 15.

17 Collins, *Practical Rules*, 229.

18 Maturin Murray Ballou, *History of Cuba; or Notes of a Traveller in the Tropics. Being a Political, Historical and Statistical Account of the Island from its first Discovery to the Present Time* (Boston 1854), 276; Hirsch, *Geographical and Historical Pathology*, 3:124, 125, 226–7; Williamson, *West India Islands*, 1:183, 2:1.

19 Collins, *Practical Rules*, 269.

20 Manuel Moreno Fraginals, *El ingenio; el complejo económico social cubano del azúcar* (Havana, 1964), 145. See also the comments of David Turnbull, *Travels in the West. Cuba; with Notices of Porto Rico, and the Slave Trade* (London, 1840), 85, and José García de Arboleya, *Manual de la Isla de Cuba: compendio de su historia, geografía, estadística y administración*, 2nd ed. (Havana, 1859), 51.

21 Luis M. Díaz Soler, *Historia de la esclavitud Negra en Puerto Rico*, 4th ed. (Rio Piedras, 1974), 122–3; José Antonio Saco, *Historia de la esclavitud de la raza africana en el nuevo mundo y en especial en los países Americo-Hispanos*, 4 vols. (Havana, 1938–40), 3:153. See also the estimates of 30,000 slaves lost to the epidemic in "Acting Consul General Kennedy to Lord Palmerston," Havana, 11 April 1850 and 22 February 1851 in *Sessional Papers, Accounts and Papers*, Great Britain, Parliament, House of Commons (London, 1823–64), 56A:183–212, 192–3.

22 Collins, who placed the blame on the black habit of sucking on sugar cane, *Practical Rules*, 313–14; Williamson, *West India Islands*, 1:56, 65, 98.

23 Hillary, *Diseases in Barbados*, 297–304. See also Collins, *Practical Rules*, 287; Grainger, *West Indian Diseases*, 60.

24 Hirsch, *Geographical and Historical Pathology*, 2:576; Henry Harold Scott, *A History of Tropical Medicine*, 2 vols. (London, 1939), 2:913, 917; J. Minteguiaga, "Lettre sur le

Béribéri," *Gazette Médicale de Paris*, 45 (1874), 35; Juan G. Havá, "Comunicacion dirigida á la academia sobre una epidemia de beriberi," *Academia de Ciencias Medical, Fisicas y Naturales de la Habana*, 2 (1865), 158–61. See also Kenneth F. Kiple and Virginia H. Kiple, "Deficiency Diseases in the Caribbean," *Journal of Interdisciplinary History*, 11 (1980), 197–215.

25 Collins, *Practical Rules*, 200.

26 All of the following diseases will be discussed in detail in ensuing chapters.

27 Recent exceptions include Todd L. Savitt, *Medicine and Slavery;The Diseases and Health Care of Blacks in Antebellum Virginia* (Urbana, Ill., 1978); Peter H. Wood, *Black Majority: Negroes in Colonial South Carolina from 1670 through the Stono Rebellion* (New York, 1974); and Leslie H. Owens, *This Species of Property: Slave Life and Culture in the Old South* (New York, 1976).

28 For a multi-faceted look at some of these individuals, see Mary Louise Marshall, "Samuel A. Cartwright and States' Rights Medicine," *NOMSJ*, 93 (1940), 74–8; Saul Jarcho, "Symposium on Josiah Clark Nott, M.D., and 19th Century Medicine in the Southern United States," *BNYAM*, 50 (1974), 496–8; Richard H. Shryock, ed., *Letters of Richard D. Arnold, M.D., 1808–1876* (Durham, N.C., 1929); John S. Haller, "The Negro and the Southern Physician: A Study of Medical and Racial Attitudes 1800–1860," *JMH*, 16 (1972), 238–53; and Walter Fisher, "Physicians and Slavery in the Antebellum Southern Medical Journal," *JHM*, 23 (1968), 36–49.

29 Although we do not seriously argue this, it should be noted that because slaves represented capital, some doctors in fact have insisted that they did receive better care than most whites. See for example John Wesley Monette, "An Inaugural Thesis on the Epidemial Bilious Fever, as it Generally Occurs in the Vicinity of Natchez" unpublished thesis, Transylvania University, 1825, 5–6, and Joseph Ioor Waring, *A History of Medicine in South Carolina,* 3 vols. (Columbia, S.C., 1964–71), 2:5. Chapter II in this volume deals with slave medical care in some detail.

Chapter 6. Nutrients and nutriments

1 James Battle Avirett, *The Old Plantation: How We Lived in Great House and Cabin before the War* (New York, 1901), 139.

2 Robert William Fogel and Stanley L. Engerman, *Time on the Cross: The Economics of American Negro Slavery*, 2 vols (Boston, 1974), 1:115.

3 Kenneth M. Stampp, *The Peculiar Institution: Slavery in the Antebellum South* (New York, 1956), 282.

4 Richard Sutch, "The Treatment Received by American Slaves: A Critical Review of the Evidence Presented in *Time on the Cross*," *Explorations in Economic History*, 12 (1975), 386, 387–94.

5 Benjamin A. Botkin, ed., *Lay My Burden Down: A Folk History of Slavery* (Chicago, 1945), 121. The literature is replete with the testimony of ex-slaves who recalled hunger on the plantation. Abolitionist literature in particular enjoyed portraying hungry thralls. See, for example, Theodore Dwight Weld's *American Slavery as it Is: Testimony of a Thousand Witnesses* (New York, 1839) in one of its many editions since it was first published by the American Anti-slavery Society in 1839.

6 Norman R. Yetman, ed., *Life Under the Peculiar Institution*, (New York, 1970), 36. See also Botkin, ed., *Lay My Burden Down*, 61; Ronald Killion and Charles Waller, eds., *Slavery Time When I Was Chillun Down on Marster's Plantation* (Savannah 1973), 126. During the bleak and hungry depression days of the thirties, when much of the ex-slave testimony was gathered, there was a good deal of nostalgia for the planta-tion days of dietary plentitude. See also George P. Rawick, *From Sundown to Sunup: The Making of the Black Community* (Westport, Conn., 1972), 68–73. The crux of this problem of conflicting accounts was put succinctly enough by one ex-bondsman who

explained, "Now you see, dar was good marsas an' bad marsas. Marsas what was good saw dat slaves lived decen an' got plenty to eat. Marsas what was mean an' skinflinty throw em' scraps like dey feed a dog . . . Warn't no law sayin' dey got to treat slaves decent." Milton Meltzer, ed., *In Their Own Words: A History of the American Negro, 1619–1865*, 3 vols. (New York, 1964), 1:44.

7 Frederick Law Olmsted, *A Journey in the Seaboard Slave States, with Remarks on their Economy*, 2 vols. (New York, 1856), 2:698. Most travelers seem to have given planters the benefit of the doubt, at least in the matter of slave feeding. A chronologic sampling of the literature might include Issac Weld, *Travels through the States of North America . . . 1795, 1796, and 1797*, 3 vols., (London 1799; reprint ed., New York, 1968) 1:148; Basil Hall, *Travels in North America in the Years 1827 and 1828*, 3 vols. (London, 1829, reprint ed., Graz, Austria, 1965), 3:224; and Fredrika Bremer, *Homes of the New World . . .* , 2 vols. trans. by Mary Howitt (New York, 1853), 1:297.

8 Jeremiah Evarts Diary, (Georgia Historical Society).

9 See the following articles by planters on slave feeding in *SC*, 4:8 (1846), 7 (1850), 9:4,6,(1851), 11:8 (1853), 12:7 (1854), 13:6 (1855); *DBR*, 7 (1849), 206–25, 330–89, 13 (1852), 193–4, 25 (1858), 571–2, 28 (1860), 597–9; and *FP*, 1:11 (1851).

10 Killion and Waller, eds., *Slavery Time*, 32.

11 George P. Rawick, ed., *The American Slave: A Composite Autobiography*, 19 vols. 2nd ed. (Westport, Conn., 1973), 2:67.

12 U. B. Phillips, *Life and Labor in the Old South* (Boston, 1929), 197.

13 Stampp, *Peculiar Institution*, 282–3, 289.

14 Eugene D. Genovese, *The Political Economy of Slavery; Studies in the Economy and Society of the Slave South* (New York, 1965), 44–6.

15 Fogel and Engerman, *Time on the Cross*, 2: 97 (table).

16 Sam B. Hilliard, "Pork in the Antebellum South: The Geography of Self-Sufficiency," *Annals of the Association of American Geographers*, 59 (1969), 461–80; Eugene D. Genovese, "Livestock in the Slave Economy of the Old South – a Revised View," *AH*, 36 (1962), 143–9; Orville W. Taylor, *Negro Slavery in Arkansas* (Durham, N.C., 1958), 132.

17 See for example the James Allen Plantation Book, 1860–65 (Mississippi Department of Archives and History); Franklin L. Riley, ed., "Diary of a Mississippi Planter, January 1, 1840 to April, 1863," *Publications of the Mississippi Historical Society*, 10 (1909), 305–41, 427, 452–3; Rudolf Alexander Cleman, *The American Livestock and Meat Industry* (New York, 1923), 34–35, 39; and Sam Bowers Hilliard, *Hog Meat and Hoecake: Food Supply in the Old South, 1840–1860* (Carbondale, Ill., 1972), 98–99, 100.

18 Reminders that plantation pork production was generally insufficient for the needs of the slaves and made outside purchases necessary come from Herbert Anthony Kellar, ed., *Solon Robinson: Pioneer and Agriculturalist*, 2 vols. (Indianapolis, 1936; reprint ed., New York, 1968), 1:456; Charles Sydnor, *A Gentleman of the Old Natchez Region: Benjamin L. C. Wailes* (Durham N.C., 1938), 99–100; Albert Virgil House, ed., *Planter Management and Capitalism in Antebellum Georgia: the Journal of Hugh Fraser Grant, Ricegrower* (New York, 1954), 48; Martin Boyd Coyner, "John Hartwell Cocke of Bremo. Agriculture and Slavery in the Antebellum South," (Ph.D. dissertation, University of Virginia, 1961), 401; Jewell Lynn de Grummond, "A Social History of St. Mary Parish, 1845–1860," *LHQ*, 32 (1949), 48; Hilliard, *Hog Meat and Hoecake*, 106–108; and Genovese, "Livestock in the Slave Economy," 147–8.

19 Kellar, *Solon Robinson*, 2:149.

20 Hilliard, *Hog Meat and Hoecake*, 44.

21 Philip St. George Cocke, "Rules by Mr. St. George Cocke," *DBR*, 14 (1853), 177; a Small Farmer, "Management of Negroes," *DBR*, 11(1851), 372; Guion Griffis Johnson, *A Social History of the Sea Islands . . .* , (Chapel Hill, N.C., 1930) 85–6; Rosser Howard Taylor, *Slaveholding in North Carolina: An Economic View* (New York, 1926;

reprint ed., New York 1969), 90; Ralph Betts Flanders, *Plantation Slavery in Georgia*, (Chapel Hill, N.C., 1933), 156.

22 Richard Osborn Cummings, *The American and his Food: A History of Food Habits in the United States* (Chicago, 1940), 16; Waverly Louis Root and Richard de Rochemont, *Eating in America; A History* (New York, 1976), 122.

23 Agricola (pseudonym), "On the Management of Negroes," *SC*, 13 (1855); J. Hume Simons, *The Planter's Guide and Family Book of Medicine* (Charleston, 1848), 209; Samuel A. Cartwright, "Philosophy of the Negro Constitution," *NOMSJ*, 9(1852) 197; M. W. Philips, "More Meat," *AMCP* 2 (1858), 96–7; John S. Wilson, "The Negro–His Diet, Clothing, etc.," *AMCP*, 3 (1859), 197.

24 Wilson, "The Negro–His Diet, Clothing etc.", 197.

25 Cummings, *American and his Food*, 15.

26 A Rice Planter, "On the Culture of Corn, Sweet Potatoes and Oats, and the Management of Cattle," *SA*, Ser.II, 4 (1831), 175; Lewis Cecil Gray, *History of Agriculture in the Southern United States to 1860*, 2 vols., 2nd ed. (New York, 1941) 2:835.

27 Gray, *History of Agriculture*, 2:833–9; Lewis F. Allen, *American Cattle: Their History, Breeding and Management* (New York, 1868), 23; Riley, ed., "Diary of a Mississippi Planter," 318, 356; Charles T. Leavitt, "Attempts to Improve Cattle Breeds in the United States, 1790–1860," *AG*, 7 (1933), 55; Genovese, "Livestock in the Slave Economy," passim; Cleman, *American Livestock*, 62.

28 Cleman, *American Livestock*, 39; Charles T. Leavitt, "Some Economic Aspects of the Western Meat-Packing Industry, 1830–60," *Journal of Business of the University of Chicago*, 4 (1931), 68; Sam B. Hilliard, "Hog Meat and Cornpone: Food Habits in the Antebellum South," *Proceedings of the American Philosophical Society*, 113 (1969), 5. Cattle of course from the border regions were fattened for northern markets. Frederick Law Olmsted, *The Cotton Kingdom, A Traveller's Observations on Cotton and Slavery in the American Slave States*, ed. Arthur M. Schlesinger (New York, 1953), 398; Cleman, *American Livestock*, 78–9.

29 Root and Rochemont, *Eating in America*, 121.

30 Hilliard, *Hog Meat and Hoecake*, 119–20.

31 H[arry] Toulmin, "A Geographical and Statistical Sketch of the District of Mobile," *American Register*, 6 (1810), 338.

32 Edgar Winfield Martin, *The Standard of Living in 1860: American Consumption Levels on the Eve of the Civil War* (Chicago, 1942), 62.

33 Minnie Clare Boyd, *Alabama in the Fifties, A Social Study* (New York, 1931), 115.

34 Ibid., 115.

35 Olmsted, *Cotton Kingdom*, 281.

36 Root and Rochemont, *Eating in America*, 121; Paul S. Taylor, "Plantation Laborer Before the Civil War," *AH*, 28 (1954), 7; Cummings, *American and his Food*, 20; Ebenezer Starnes, *The Slave-holder Abroad* (Philadelphia, 1860), 507; Gray, *History of Agriculture*, 2: 838.

37 Gray, *History of Agriculture*, 2:838; see also Vernie Alton Moody, "Slavery on Louisiana Sugar Plantations," *LHQ*, 7 (1926), 264.

38 John M. Hunter, "Geography, Genetics, and Culture History: The Case of Lactose Intolerance," *Geographical Review*, 61 (1971), 606; Theodore M. Bayless, et al., "Lactose and Milk Intolerance: Clinical Implications," *NEJM*, 292 (1975), 1157.

39 The exception is those rare babies born with congenital abnormalities that make it impossible for them to digest milk. Today they survive because of soy milk.

40 Bayless et al., "Lactose and Milk Intolerance," 1158.

41 Gebhard Flatz and Hans Werner Rotthauwe, "Lactose Nutrition and Natural Selection," *Lancet*, 2 (1973), 76–7.

42 F. J. Simoons, "The Cultural Geography of Dairying," in *Summary of the Conference on Lactose and Milk Intolerance*, eds. Irving I. Gottesman and Leonard L. Heston (Wash-

ington, D.C., 1972), 21; Norman Kretchmer, "Lactose and Lactase – A Historical Perspective," *Gastroenterology*, 61 (1971), 808–9; Juan Papadakis, *Crop Ecological Survey in West Africa (Liberia, Ivory Coast, Ghana, Togo, Dahomey, Nigeria)*, 2 vols. (Rome, 1966), 1:72; John Ford, *Role of Trypanosomiasis in African Ecology; a Study of the Tsetse Fly Problem* (Oxford, 1971), 88.

43 See Norman Kretchmer, "The Geography and Biology of Lactose Digestion and Malabsorption," *PM*, 53 (1977), 66–7, for a summary of other factors believed to have prevented the development of the lactase enzyme among peoples around the world.

44 Some studies have indicated that the inability to hydrolyze lactose begins with weaning or even earlier. Felicity King, "Intolerance to Lactose in Mother's Milk?" *Lancet*, 2 (1972), 335; G. C. Cook and S. K. Kajubi, "Tribal Incidence of Lactase Deficiency in Uganda," *Lancet*, 1 (1966), 727; G. C. Cook, "Lactase Activity in Newborn and Infant Baganda," *BMJ*, 1 (1967), 529; David M. Paige et al., "Lactose Malabsorption in Preschool Black Children," *AJCN*, 30 (1977), 1019; O. Ransome-Kuti, "Lactose Intolerance – A Review," *PM*, 53 (1977), 77.

45 David M. Paige, Theodore M. Bayless, and George G. Graham, "Milk Programs: Helpful or Harmful to Negro Children?" *AJPH*, 62 (1972), 1487; Keiffer Mitchell et al., "Intolerance of Eight Ounces of Milk in Lactose-Intolerant Teen-Agers," *Ped*, 56 (1975), 720; Theodore M. Bayless, "Milk Intolerance: Clinical, Developmental and Epidemiological Aspects," in *Lactose and Milk Intolerance*, eds. Gottesman and Heston, 14.

46 Hunter, "Geography, Genetics, and Culture History," 606; Bayless et al., "Lactose and Milk Intolerance," 1157.

47 Thomas Affleck, "On the Hygiene of Cotton Plantations and the Management of Negro Slaves," *SMR*, 2 (1850), 435. See also Alabama Planter, "Management of Slaves," *DBR*, 13 (1852) 193, and Cocke, "Rules," 177; and for many ex-slave recollections of having drunk soured milk, see Rawick, ed., *Slave Narratives*, passim. Eugene D. Genovese (*Roll, Jordan, Roll. The World the Slaves Made* [New York, 1974], 508) states that the milk children received was "usually in soured form," and Baird U. Brooks "A Study of Infant Mortality in the Southern States," *SMJ*, 23 (1930), 869 believes that buttermilk feedings "drastically reduced the death rate of colored infants" in the South.

48 Bayless, "Milk Intolerance," 11; David M. Paige et al., "Response of Lactose-Intolerant Children to Different Lactose Levels," *AJCN*, 25 (1972), 468; John D. Johnson, Norman Kretchmer, and Frederick J. Simoons, "Lactose Malabsorption: Its Biology and History," *Advances in Pediatrics*, 21 (1974), 207; George G. Graham and David M. Paige, "Nutritional Implications of Low Intestinal Lactose Activity in Children" in *Intestinal Enzyme Deficiencies and their Nutritional Implications*, eds. Bengt Borgström and Arne Dahlqvist (Stockholm, 1973), 46.

49 Hilliard, *Hog Meat and Hoecake*, 61.

50 Joseph Karl Menn, "The Large Slaveholders of the Deep South, 1860," (Ph.D. dissertation, University of Texas, 1964), 39, n. 5.; James C. Bonner, "Advancing Trends in Southern Agriculture, 1840–1860," *AH*, 22 (1948), 254. Toward the end of the antebellum period, a few planters were beginning to appreciate the plant's ability to renovate the soil as well. Andrew M. Soule, "Vegetables, Fruits and Nursery Products, and Truck Farming in the South," in *The South in the Building of the Nation*, V: *Economic History, 1607–1865*, ed. James Curtis Ballagh (Richmond, Va., 1909), 239.

51 John Hebron Moore, *Agriculture in Antebellum Mississippi* (New York 1958), 124. See also Gray, *History of Agriculture*, 2:836; House, *Planter Management*, 48; and Weymouth T. Jordan, *Hugh Davis and His Alabama Plantation* (Tuscaloosa, Ala., 1948), 124, who stress the importance of cowpeas as food for livestock.

52 See, for example, Agricola [pseudonym], "Management of Slaves," *DBR*, 19 (1855), 359, who was a particularly staunch advocate of the field pea as a slave food. He

cautioned his fellow planters, however, to cook them until "perfectly done," and then season them well with red pepper.

53 Fogel and Engerman, *Time on the Cross*, 2:97 (table), 97.

54 Gray, *History of Agriculture*, 2:827, 844. See also Moore, *Agriculture in Antebellum Mississippi*, 128; Riley, "Diary of a Mississippi Planter," 370.

55 Planters seem to have made the distinction between potatoes grown for hogs and "eating potatoes." Riley, "Diary of a Mississippi Planter," 395.

56 See, for example, Starnes, *Slave-holder Abroad*, 496, for sweet potato consumption "so long as they last." Consult Gray, *History of Agriculture*, 2: 827–8, and Kellar, ed., *Solon Robinson*, 1:482, 2:357–8, for the methods of progressive planters who did store sweet potatoes. Those who did often substituted potatoes for cornmeal rations during the winter. Rupert B. Vance, *Human Geography of the South: A Study in Regional Resources and Human Adequacy* (Chapel Hill, N.C., 1935), 417. A reading of Olmsted (*Cotton Kingdom*, 287), however, suggests that it was a rare planter who could make the claim that "I have sweet potatoes in abundance during six months of the year" (Starnes, *Slave-holder Abroad*, 500).

57 For examples of these practices, consult Simons, *Planter's Guide*, 209; Letitia M. Burwell, *Plantation Reminiscences* (Owensboro, Ky., 1878), 5; Hall, *Travels in North America*, 3:224–5; Robert Q. Mallard, *Plantation Life before Emancipation* (Richmond, Va., 1892), 32; Harvey Wish, ed., *Slavery in the South* (New York, 1964), 198; and Gray, *History of Agriculture*, 2:832.

58 Stampp, *The Peculiar Institution*, 287.

59 Wish, ed., *Slavery in the South* 43. See also Meltzer, ed., *In Their Own Words*, 1:44; Stampp, *The Peculiar Institution*, 287; and Charles L. Perdue, Thomas E. Barden, and Robert K. Phillips, eds., *Weevils in the Wheat: Interviews with Virginia Ex-Slaves* (Charlottesville, Va., 1976), passim.

60 Fogel and Engerman, *Time on the Cross*, 1:113.

61 Computed from data contained in Thomas F. Hunt, "The History of Cereal Farming in the South," in *The South in the Building of the Nation*, ed. Ballagh, V:222; and the appropriate pages of Donald B. Dodd and Wynelle S. Dodd, *Historical Statistics of the South 1790–1970* (Tuscaloosa, Ala., 1973).

62 Fogel and Engerman, *Time on the Cross*, 1:113.

63 Taylor, *Slavery in Arkansas*, 136–7.

64 Menn ("Large Slaveholders," 151), for example, reports that wheat was raised on only 26 percent of the large plantations of the Lower South, and where it was raised it was a *money crop*.

65 Consult, for example, the claims of James M. Towns, "Slave Management," *SC*, 9 (1851), and Agricola [pseudonym], "Management of Negroes," 358, along with the comments of William H. Cook, "Overseers and Plantation Management," *ACP*, n.s., 2 (1858), 112–13. See also the variety provided slaves on the plantation examined by Coyner, "Cocke of Bremo," 129–31; Jordan, *Hugh Davis*, 125–9; and Bennett H. Wall, "Ebenezer Pettigrew, an Economic Study of an Antebellum Planter" (Ph.D. dissertation, University of North Carolina, 1946), 100.

66 Affleck "Cotton Plantations," *SMR*, 2 (1850), 431; H. Perry Pope, "A Dissertation on the Professional Management of Negro Slaves" (Masters Thesis, Medical College of South Carolina, 1837), 3–4; Norman B. Woods, *The White Side of a Black Subject* (Chicago, 1894), 154; William Goodell, *The American Slave Code in Theory and Practice* (New York, 1853), 135. Both Emory Q. Hawk (*Economic History of the South* [New York, 1934], 268) and Vance (*Human Geography*, 412–17), make the point that vegetables were not all that common even in the diet of whites.

67 Wendell Holmes Stephenson, "A Quarter Century of a Mississippi Plantation: Eli C. Capell of Pleasant Hill," *MVHR*, 23 (1936), 371; James Benson Sellers, *Slavery in Alabama*, 2nd ed. (University of Ala., 1964), 92–3; Charles Sackett Sydnor, *Slavery in*

Mississippi (New York, 1933), 35; Ulrich Bonnell Phillips and James David Glunt, eds., *Florida Plantation Records From the Papers of George Nobel Jones* (St. Louis, 1927), 513–4; Theodora Britton Marshall and Gladys Crail Evans, eds., "Plantation Report from the Papers of Levin R. Marshall, of 'Richmond': Natchez, Mississippi," *JMH*, 3 (1941), 52.

68 Affleck, "Cotton Plantations," 435.

69 "Presumably" because molasses for most plantations would have been an "outside" expenditure and therefore recorded along with meat and meal expenditures. Yet the majority of the plantation records we have examined make no mention of molasses purchases. On the other hand, many plantations raised cane for sorghum. It is probable as well that on many of these units bees were kept, and honey was substituted. See Menn, "Large Slaveholders," 160, and Hawk, *Economic History*, 270.

70 Food and Agriculture Organization of the United Nations, *Calorie Requirements* (Washington, D.C., 1950), 13, 24.

71 For the nutritional content of foods discussed in this chapter we are dependent on Catherine F. Adams, *Nutritive Value of American Foods in Common Units*, U.S. Department of Agriculture Handbook No. 456 (Washington, D.C., 1975).

72 But if the intake lacks only one amino acid then the efficiency of all the amino acids falls. A. E. Harper, "Basic Concepts," in *Improvement of Protein Nutriture*, ed. Committee on Amino Acids, Food and Nutrition Board, National Research Council (Washington, D.C., 1974), 7, 12, 15.

73 Martha L. Orr and Bernice K. Watt, *Amino Acid Content of Foods*, U. S. Department of Agriculture, Home Economics Research Report No. 4 (Washington D.C., 1957), 56; R. C. Miller, L. W. Aurand and W. R. Flach, "Amino Acids in High and Low Protein Corn," *Science*, 112 (1950), 57; Ricardo Bressani, "The Importance of Corn for Human Nutrition in Latin America and Other Countries," *Proceedings of the Conference on Nutritional Improvement of Corn* (Guatemala, 1972).

74 Orr and Watt, *Amino Acid Content of Foods*, 54.

75 The RDAs in this chapter come from the Food and Nutrition Board, National Academy of Sciences, National Research Council, *Recommended Dietary Allowances*, 8th rev. ed. (Washington, D.C., 1974).

76 Wilson, "The Negro," 197. The sources are full of references to "fat" pork for slaves. See for example the Allen Plantation Book; J. S. Wilson, "Food, Clothing and General Rules of Health," *DBR*, 28 (1860), 597–8; Cartwright, "Philosophy of the Negro Constitution," 197; Moody, "Louisiana Sugar Plantations," 263; and Vance, *Human Geography*, 424.

77 The RDA of protein has been the subject of some uncertainty of late. Nevin Scrimshaw, a leading nutritionist, for example, believes a RDA of 70 grams is actually too low to maintain long-term health. (Nevin S. Scrimshaw, "Shattuck Lecture – Strengths and Weaknesses of the Committee Approach: An Analysis of Past and Present Recommended Dietary Allowances for Protein in Health and Disease," *NEJM*, 294, 1976, 201–3.) Conversely the latest edition of the National Academy of Sciences RDAs lowered the American RDA from 70 grams to 56 grams as a more realistic figure for today's typically sendentary but healthy American, whose major intake of protein is animal protein of high quality. For slaves, however, 70 grams seems to be the more realistic figure.

78 Hunt, "Cereal Farming," 218; G. S. Fraps, "Variations in Vitamin A and in Chemical Composition of Corn," *Bulletin of the Texas Agricultural Experiment Station*, Bulletin 422 (1931), 34; Gray, *History of Agriculture*, 2:815; Moore, *Agriculture in Antebellum Mississippi*, 121–2; Riley, "Diary of a Mississippi Planter," 390.

79 Boyce D. Ezell and Marguerite S. Wilcox, "Effect of Variety and Storage on Carotene and Total Carotenoid Pigments in Sweet Potatoes," *Food Research*, 13 (1948), 208.

80 Sutch, "Treatment Received by American Slaves," 391.

81 But when vitamin A is no longer ingested it is rapidly eliminated from the liver. Thus the "storage" of vitamin A can only benefit an individual for a period of two to three months. Henrik Dam and Ebbe Sondergaard, "Fat-Soluble Vitamins," in *Nutrition: A Comprehensive Treatise*, eds. George H. Beaton and Earle Willard Mchenry, 3 vols. (New York, 1964), 2:9.

82 Kellar, ed., *Solon Robinson*, 1:476. See also Owens, *This Species of Property*, 63; Killion and Waller, eds., *Slavery Time*, 127; Wilson, "Food and Rules of Health," 597, who regarded fruit as poison and Moore, *Agriculture in Antebellum Mississippi*, 140, who says southern orchards were rare. For the slave's dislike of vegetables in general, see Samuel A. Cartwright, "Ethnology of the Negro of Prognathous Race," *NOMSJ*, 15 (1858), 163, and Kellar, ed., *Solon Robinson*, 1:476.

83 Margaret S. Chaney and Margaret L. Ross, *Nutrition*, 8th ed. (Boston, 1971), 247. See Adams, *Nutritive Value of American Foods*, for the difference in vitamin C content between raw and cooked greens.

84 Ezell and Wilcox, "Effect of Variety and Storage on Carotene in Sweet Potatoes," 118, 206.

85 Leonard William Aurand and A. E. Woods, *Food Chemistry* (Westport, Conn., 1973), 122.

86 Christine E. Parkinson and Isabel Gal, "Vitamin A and Seasonal Variation," *Lancet*, 1 (1974), 937–8; W. M. Politzer and E. H. Clover, "Serum Vitamin-A Concentration in Healthy White and Bantu Adults Living under Normal Conditions on the Witwatersrand," *SAMJ*, 41 (1967), 1014.

87 P. J. Leonard and J. G. Banwell, "The Absorption of Vitamin A as an Index of Malabsorption in African Subjects," *EAMJ*, 41 (1964), 501–4.

88 Cicely D. Williams, "Varieties of Unbalanced Diet and their Effect on Nutrition," in *Hunger and Food*, ed. Josué de Castro (London, 1958), 93; Aurand and Woods, *Food Chemistry*, 210.

89 Chaney and Ross, *Nutrition*, 273.

90 E. Gordon Young, "Dietary Standards," in *Nutrition*, eds. Beaton and McHenry, 2:342.

91 Sylvia Cover and William H. Smith, "Retention of Thiamine and Pantothenic Acid in Pork after Stewing," *Food Research*, 17 (1952), 151.

92 An average of 60 mg (with a variation ranging from 46 to 86 mg) of tryptophan is needed to produce 1 mg of niacin. M. K. Horwitt, "Niacin-Tryptophan Requirements of Man," *JADA*, 34 (1958), 915.

93 Kamala Krishnaswamy and Coluther Gopalan, "Effect of Isoleucine on Skin and Electroencephalogram in Pellagra," *Lancet*, 2 (1971), 1167; Constance Kies and Hazel M. Fox, "Interrelationships of Leucine with Lysine, Tryptophan, and Niacin as They Influence Protein Value of Cereal Grains for Humans," *Cereal Chemistry*, 49 (1972), 223–31; Coluther Gopalan and K. S. Jaya Rao, "Pellagra and Amino Acid Imbalance," *Vitamins and Hormones*, 33 (1975), 516.

94 Chaney and Ross, *Nutrition*, 267; N. Raghuramulu, B. S. Narasinga Rao and C. Gopalan, "Amino Acid Imbalance and Tryptophan-Niacin Metabolism. I. Effect of Excess Leucine on the Urinary Excretion of Tryptophan-Niacin Metabolites in Rats," *JN*, 86 (1965), 105.

95 Chaney and Ross, *Nutrition*, 278; F. A. Robinson, *The Vitamin B Complex* (New York, 1951), 276–7.

96 Robert M. Neer, "The Evolutionary Significance of Vitamin D, Skin Pigment, and Ultraviolet Light," *AJPA*, 54 (1975), 413.

97 W. F. Loomis, "Skin-Pigment Regulation of Vitamin D Biosynthesis in Man," *Science*, 157 (1967), 505.

98 John G. Haddad and Theodore J. Hahn, "Natural and Synthetic Sources of Circulating 25-Hydroxyvitamin D in Man," *Nature*, 244 (1973), 515; Hector F. DeLuca, "Me-

tabolism of Vitamin D: Current Status," *AJCN*, 29 (1976), 1259–62; C. D. Holdsworth, "Calcium Absorption in Man," in *Intestinal Absorption in Man*, eds. Ian McColl and G. E. Sladen (New York, 1975), 230–3.

99 D. M. Hegsted, "Calcium, Phosphorus and Magnesium," in *Modern Nutrition in Health and Disease*, eds. Michael G. Wohl and Robert S. Goodhart, 4th ed. (Philadelphia, 1971), 325–6; Chaney and Ross, *Nutrition*, 125–8; Aurand and Woods, *Food Chemistry*, 253; Holdsworth, "Calcium Absorption," 224, 240–3.

100 Holdsworth, "Calcium Absorption," 224; Aurand and Woods, *Food Chemistry*, 252; Stanley Davidson et al. *Human Nutrition and Dietetics*, 6th ed. (Edinburgh, 1975), 112.

101 Eleanor Noss Whitney and Eva May Nunnelley Hamilton, *Understanding Nutrition* (St. Paul, Minn., 1977), 316, 317.

102 Jane Leichsenring, Loana M. Norris, and Mary L. Halbert, "Effect of Ascorbic Acid and of Orange Juice on Calcium and Phosphorus Metabolism of Women," *JN*, 63 (1957), 428–32.

103 Neer, "Evolutionary Significance of Vitamin D," 412–3; Aurand and Woods, *Food Chemistry*, 253. See also Jennifer Jowsey ("Osteoporosis: Its Nature and the Role of Diet," *PM*, 60 [1976], 76) who emphasizes that even if the intake of calcium is adequate, it cannot be absorbed without vitamin D.

104 Adam Turnbull, "Iron Absorption," in *Iron in Biochemistry and Medicine*, eds. A. Jacobs and M. Worwood (New York, 1974), 371–4; James D. Cook, "Absorption of Food Iron," *Federation Proceedings*, 36 (1977), 2031; B. Brozović, "Absorption of Iron," in *Intestinal Absorption in Man*, eds. McColl and Sladen, 278–80; Miguel Layrisse and Carlos Martinez-Torres, "Food Iron Absorption: Iron Supplementation of Food," *Progress in Hematology*, 7 (1971), 147.

105 Layrisse and Martinez-Torres, "Food Iron Absorption," 140; Virgil F. Fairbanks, John L. Fahey and Ernest Beutler, *Clinical Disorders of Iron Metabolism*, 2nd rev. ed. (New York, 1971), 84; Turnbull, "Iron Absorption," 372.

106 Ezzat K. Amine and D. M. Hegsted, "Effect of Diet on Iron Absorption in Iron-Deficient Rats," *JN*, 101 (1971), 930.

107 Ann Ashworth, P. F. Milner and J. C. Waterlow, "Absorption of Iron from Maize (*Zea mays* L) and Soya Beans (*Glycine hispida* Max) in Jamaican Infants," *BJN*, 29 (1973), 269, 272; Cook, "Absorption of Food Iron," 2029.

108 Arno G. Motulsky and Jean M. Campbell-Kraut, "Population Genetics of Glucose-6-Phosphate Dehydrogenase Deficiency of the Red Cell," in *Proceedings of the Conference on Genetic Polymorphisms and Geographic Variations in Disease*, ed. Baruch S. Blumberg (New York, 1961), 179; John D. Harley and Helen Robin, " 'Late' Neonatal Jaundice in Infants with Glucose-6-Phosphate Dehydrogenase-Deficient Erythrocytes," *Australian Annals of Medicine*, 2 (1962), 153–4; A. Majid Shojana and Samuel Gross, "Hemolytic Anemias and Folic Acid Deficiency in Children," *AJDC*, 108 (1964), 53–61.

109 William Weiss, "The Sickle Cell Trait in Relation to Infection," *Archives of Environmental Health*, 8 (1964), 480–2; N. Nagaratnam, Chitra S. Subawickrama, and Therese Kariyawasam, "Viral Infections in G-6-PD Deficiency," *Tropical and Geographical Medicine*, 22 (1970), 179–82; Elizabeth Barrett-Connor, "Anemia and Infection," *American Journal of Medicine*, 52 (1972), 248; Ernest Beutler, "Glucose-6-Phosphate Dehydrogenase Deficiency," in *Hematology*, eds. William J. Williams et al., 2nd ed. (New York, 1977), 472. For a good summary of the contradictory evidence surrounding sickle cell trait, see David A. Sears, "The Morbidity of Sickle Cell Trait; A Review of the Literature," *American Journal of Medicine*, 64 (1978), 1021–36.

110 Stanley J. Birge et al., "Osteoporosis, Intestinal Lactase Deficiency and Low Dietary Calcium Intake," *NEJM*, 276 (1967), 447; Alexander Walker, "The Human Requirements of Calcium: Should Low Intakes be Supplemented?" *AJCN*, 25 (1972), 521.

111 C. Frank Consolazio et al., "Relationship between Calcium in the Sweat, Calcium Balance, and Calcium Requirements," *JN*, 78 (1962), 82-3; B. Isaksson and B. Sjörgren, "A Critical Evaluation of the Mineral and Nitrogen Balances in Man," *PNS*, 26 (1967), 113.

Chapter 7. The children

1 Andrew Flinn, Plantation Diary: Instructions to the Overseer (1840, University of North Carolina).

2 Nathan Irwin Huggins, *Black Odyssey: The Afro-American Ordeal in Slavery* (New York, 1977), 169.

3 Robert William Fogel and Stanley L. Engerman, *Time on the Cross: The Economics of American Negro Slavery*, 2 vols. (Boston, 1974), 1:123.

4 Reginald C. Tsang and William Oh, "Neonatal Hypocalcemia in Low Birth Weight Infants," *Ped*, 45 (1970), 778; M. Isabel Irwin and Eldon W. Kienholz, "A Conspectus of Research on Calcium Requirements of Man," *JN*, 103 (1973), 1063-8. See note 6 below.

5 Demographers generally agree that black fertility was substantially higher than white during the late antebellum period, with most putting the black fertility at about 250 and endowing slave mothers with an average of at least seven children. Reynolds Farley, "The Demographic Rates and Social Institutions of the Nineteenth Century Negro Population: A Stable Population Analysis," *Demography*, 2 (1965), 389 (table), 395. For the argument that black fertility was even higher during the early decades of the nineteenth century see Melvin Zelnick, "Fertility of the American Negro in 1830 and 1850," *Population Studies*, 20 (1966), 77-83.

6 The belief that the fetus is *totally* parasitic, satisfying all its needs from its mother, is no longer held by nutritionists. The consensus today is that the fetus is parasitic for some nutrients but not for others. Consult for example, Derrick B. Jelliffe, *Infant Nutrition in the Subtropics and Tropics*, 2nd ed. (Geneva, 1968), 113; Myron Winick, *Malnutrition and Brain Development* (New York, 1976), 25, 29. For a convincing argument that when nutrients are in short supply, the mother rather than the fetus is spared, see Pedro Rosso, "Maternal Nutrition, Nutrient Exchange, and Fetal Growth," in *Nutritional Disorders of American Women*, ed. Myron Winick (New York, 1977), 3-25.

7 Oscar Felsenfeld, *The Epidemiology of Tropical Diseases* (Springfield, Ill., 1966), 413, explains that "the value of mother's milk depends on [her] state of nutrition." See also Coluther Gopalan, "Effect of Nutrition on Pregnancy and Lactation," *WHO*, 26 (1963), 203-11; Winick, *Malnutrition and Brain Development*, 25; and Samuel Joseph Foman, *Infant Nutrition*, 2nd ed. (Philadelphia, 1974), 197.

8 Pierre Cantrelle, "Mortality: Levels, Patterns, and Trends," in *Population Growth and Socioeconomic Change in West Africa*, ed. John C. Caldwell (New York, 1975), 108; Felsenfeld, *Tropical Diseases*, 414; John R. K. Robson, *Malnutrition; Its Causation and Control*, 2 vols. (New York, 1972), 1:104.

9 Philip Lanzkowsky, "Iron Deficiency Anemia," in *Pediatric Medicine*, ed. Milton I. Levine (Acton Mass., 1975), 79; Foman, *Infant Nutrition*, 170.

10 See, for example, G. E. Harrison, ed., "Slavery in Virginia: Extract from *Slavery in the United States* by J. K. Paulding," *Virginia Magazine of History and Biography*, 36 (1928), 275-82; Solon Robinson, "Negro Slavery at the South," *DBR*, 7 (1849), 38-82; John B. Cade, "Out of the Mouths of Ex-Slaves," *JNH*, 20 (1935), 300; and George P. Rawick ed., *The American Slave: A Composite Autobiography*, 19 vols. (Westport, Conn., 1973), 2:308.

11 Jules Cartier, "Observations on First Dentition, and the Attentions which Children Require," *NOMN*, 1 (1854), 296.

12 A mitigating factor for some would have been "cush" that was often provided the youngsters, which consisted of leftover "pot liquor" from the master's family dinner with cornbread crumbled in. There are many testimonies to "dat good and greasy liquer" with "a lot of black pepper," all steamed in a skillet. "When she comes off fire and chillun gits a spoon and eat out dis skillet. Honey, dat stuff is good!" (Chas. L. Perdue, Thomas E. Barden, and Robert K. Phillips, eds., *Weevils in the Wheat, Interviews with Virginia Ex-Slaves*. [Charlottesville, Va., 1976], 164). The pot liquor would have contained iron, as well as other important vitamins and minerals, while the iron skillet itself would have imparted some of this mineral.

13 C. C. DeSilva and N. Q. Baptist, *Tropical Nutritional Disorders of Infants and Children* (Springfield, Ill., 1969), 34–5; G. C. Cook, "Lactose Activity in Newborn and Infant Baganda," *BMJ*, 1 (1967), 529.

14 A nursing infant requires 45 mg of calcium per kg daily of which upwards of 50 percent will be absorbed, while the artificaly fed infant needs about 150 mg per kg, for he absorbs much less of the calcium in bovine milk. Abraham Cantarow, "Mineral Metabolism," in *Diseases of Metabolism: Detailed Methods of Diagnosis and Treatment*, ed. Garfield G. Duncan, 3rd ed. (Philadelphia, 1952), 239.

15 Foman, *Infant Nutrition, Table*, 199.

16 David M. Paige and George G. Graham, "Nutritional Implications of Lactose Malabsorption," *PR*, 6 (1972), 329; David M. Paige, "Milk Intolerance: Field Studies and Practical Considerations," in *Summary of the Conference on Lactose and Milk Intolerance*, eds. Irving I. Gottesman and Leonard L. Heston (Washington, D.C., 1972), 34–5; David M. Paige, Theodore M. Bayless, and George G. Graham, "Pregnancy and Lactose Intolerance," *AJCN*, 26 (1973), 239; George G. Graham and David M. Paige, "Nutritional Implications of Low Intestinal Lactase Activity in Children," in *Intestinal Enzyme Deficiencies and Their Nutritional Implications*, eds. Bengt Borgstrom and Arne Dahlqvist (Stockholm, 1973), 49–50; A. Stewart Truswell, "Carbohydrate and Lipid Metabolism in Protein-Calorie Malnutrition," in *Protein-Calorie Malnutrition*, ed. Robert E. Olsen (New York, 1975), 120; Theodore M. Bayless et al., "Lactose and Milk Intolerance: Clinical Implications," *NEJM*, 292 (1975), 1158; David M. Paige et al., "Lactose Intolerance and Lactose Hydrolyzed Milk," in *Physiological Effects of Food Carbohydrates*, eds. Allene Jeanes and John Hodge (Washington, D.C., 1975), 195.

17 John S. Wilson, "The Negro – His Diet, Clothing," *ACP* 3 (1859), 197.

18 Ibid., 197. See also Tattler, "Management of Negroes," *SC*, 8 (1850), 162; Agricola [pseudonym], "On the Management of Negroes," *SC*, 8 (1855); J. Hume Simons, *The Planter's Guide and Family Book of Medicine* (Charleston, S.C., 1848), 209; Samuel A. Cartwright, "Philosophy of the Negro Constitution," *NOMSJ*, 197; and M. W. Philips, "More Meat," *ACP*, 2 (1858) 96–7.

19 Wilson, "The Negro," 197.

20 Rawick, *American Slave*, 2:235.

21 "Seventh Census of the United States. Original Returns of the Assistant Marshalls. Third Series, persons who died during the year ending June 30, 1850" for the states of Mississippi (Dept. of Archives and History, Jackson), South Carolina (Dept. of Archives and History, Columbia), North Carolina (Dept. of Archives and History, Raleigh) and Virginia (Virginia State Library, Richmond).

22 J. D. B. DeBow, ed., *Mortality Statistics of the Seventh Census of the United States, 1850 . . .* (Washington, D.C., 1854). Unless otherwise specified mortality statistics presented were recorded during the year 1849–50 and are for the seven states of Alabama, Georgia, Louisiana, Mississippi, North and South Carolina, and Virginia.

23 The little useful material that does exist outside of manuscript census schedules was published separately as *Statistics of the United States including Mortality, Property, etc. in 1860 . . .* (Washington, D.C., 1866).

24 The compiler of the Seventh Census, J. D. B. Debow (*Mortality Statistics*, 8) comments that "at least one-fourth of the whole number of deaths have not been reported at all." For a study of "J. D. B. Debow and the Seventh Census," see that by Ottis Clark Skipper, *LHQ*, 22 (1939), 479–91.

25 And some will be somewhat misleading because of the method employed to present the mortality data. Deaths in the census were listed by race and by age/sex categories, but unfortunately the two are not combined. Thus, to employ a hypothetical example, one could know that 100 individuals died of "croup" in Alabama of which 80 victims were black and 70 victims were aged 5 and under. He does not, however, know how many of the 80 black victims were aged 5 and under. The reader is therefore cautioned that the rates given in this study in terms of live population for an age cohort are approximations only.

26 Farley ("Demographic Rates," 398) for example finds it "likely" that 30 percent of the slave infants born did not survive their first year of life, while Paul H. Jacobson ("An Estimate of the Expectation of Life in the United States in 1850," *Milbank Memorial Fund Quarterly*, 35 [1957], 198) has placed the white infant mortality rate for males at 160.6 and females at 130.8 per thousand.

27 In the seven states under consideration, there were 14,139 deaths from unknown causes of which blacks accounted for roughly 60 percent. Assuming from this that 60 percent of the 8,273 "unknown" deaths for those aged 9-and-under were Negro, blacks in this age cohort experienced 15,748 "known" deaths and 4,964 "unknown" deaths, while the whites suffered 10,686 deaths with a given cause and another 3,309 for which no cause was given.

28 We do not wish to leave the impression that tetany was unknown during the nineteenth century. Rather John Clarke's *Commentaries on Some of the Most Important Diseases of Children* (London, 1815) contains a chapter "On a Peculiar Species of Convulsion in Infant Children" (Chap. IV) that describes the disease, although the author had no idea of its cause. In 1855 the French clinician Trousseau distinguished tetany from tetanus. For the painfully slow discovery of the etiology of the disease, however, see Arthur L. Bloomfield, "A Bibliography of Internal Medicine: Tetany," *Stanford Medical Bulletin*, 17 (1959), 1–12.

29 Today, as more has been learned about the affliction, mortality from tetany is very low. But as late as the 1950s over one-third of its victims died. F. Cockburn et al., "Neonatal Convulsions Associated with Primary Disturbance of Calcium, Phosphorus, and Magnesium Metabolism," *ACD*, 48 (1973), 106; J. H. Keen, "Significance of Hypocalcaemia in Neonatal Convulsions," *ADC*, 44 (1969), 356.

30 Cantarow, "Mineral Metabolism," 274; Jelliffe, *Infant Nutrition*, 113; Stephen A. Roberts, Mervyn D. Cohen, and John O. Forfar, "Antenatal Factors Associated with Neonatal Hypocalcaemic Convulsions," *Lancet*, 2 (1973), 809, 811; Patsy J. M. Watney et al., "Maternal Factors in Neonatal Hypocalcaemia: A Study in Three Ethnic Groups," *BNJ*, 2 (1971), 435; Allen W. Root and Harold E. Harrison, "Recent Advances in Calcium Metabolism," *JP*, 88 (1976), 179; C. W. G. Turton, "Altered Vitamin-D Metabolism in Pregnancy," *Lancet*, 1(1977), 224.

31 Charles Plowden, and Jennett Weston, "Rules for the Government and Management of _____ Plantation, to be Observed by the Overseer," (n.d., Charleston), 9–10; Wendell Holmes Stephenson, "A Quarter-Century of a Mississippi Plantation: Eli J. Capell of Pleasant Hill" *MVHR*, 23 (1936), 371; William D. Postell, "Birth and Mortality Rates Among Slave Infants on Southern Plantations," *Ped*, 10 (1952), 538. Eugene D. Genovese (*Roll, Jordan, Roll. The World the Slaves Made* [New York, 1974], 497) points out, however, that the "ideal" of a month's confinement (or at least release from field work) prior to giving birth, and another month after, was not always realized.

32 Laura S. Hillman and John G. Haddad, "Perinatal Vitamin D Metabolism, *JP*, 86 (1975), 934; Turton, "Altered Vitamin-D Metabolism in Pregnancy," 224; Martin Moncrieff and T. O. Fadahunsi, "Congenital Rickets due to Maternal Vitamin D Deficiency," *ADC*, 49 (1974), 810–1.

33 Laura Hillman and John G. Haddad, "Human Perinatal Vitamin D Metabolism I: 25-Hydroxyvitamin D in Maternal and Cord Blood," *JP*, 84 (1974), 748.

34 See R. J. Purvis et al., "Enamel Hypoplasia of the Teeth Associated with Neonatal Tetany: A Manifestation of Maternal Vitamin D Deficiency," *Lancet*, 2 (1973), 811; Moncrieff and Fadahunsi, "Congenital Rickets," 811.

35 Alfred F. Hess, *Rickets Including Osteomalacia and Tetany* (Philadelphia, 1929), 368–9; Roberts, Cohen, and Forfar, "Antenatal Factors Associated with Convulsions," 809; Max Friedman, Geoffrey Hatcher, and Lyal Watson, "Primary Hypomagnesaemia with Secondary Hypocalcaemia in an Infant," *Lancet*, 1 (1967), 704; Root and Harrison, "Recent Advances in Calcium Metabolism," 179.

36 J. Cam. Massie, *A Treatise on the Eclectic Southern Practice of Medicine* (Philadelphia, 1854), 455; Samual A. Cartwright, "Report on Diseases and Physical Peculiarities of the Negro Race," *NOMSJ*, 7 (1851), 696; Dr. 'J.,' "On Tetanus," *NOMN*, 7 (1860–61), 526–9; S. L. Grier, "The Negro and his Diseases," *NOMSJ*, 9 (1853), 752–4; W. G. Ramsay, "The Physiological Differences Between the European (or White Man) and the Negro," *SA*, 12 (1839), 412; Daniel Drake, "Diseases of the Negro Population," *SMSJ*, 1 (1845), 584; H. Perry Pope, "A Dissertation on the Professional Management of Negro Slaves," unpublished thesis, Medical College of the State of South Carolina, 1837, 15; L. A. Dugas, "A Lecture Upon Tetanus," *SMSJ*, 17 (1861), 443; W. M. Boling, "Remarks on Remittant Fever Complicated with Symptoms of Tetanus," *NOMSJ*, 3 (1847), 733.

37 Computed from the appropriate pages in J. L. Dawson and H. W. DeSaussure, *Census of the City of Charleston, South Carolina, for the Year 1848* (Charleston, S.C., 1849).

38 Cartier, "Observations on First Dentition," 268; Michael Underwood, *A Treatise on the Diseases of Children . . .* (Philadelphia, 1818), 190; Massie, *Eclectic Southern Practice of Medicine*, 442; Charles S. Tripler, "On the Use of Mustard in the Convulsions of Children," *NOMSJ*, 1 (1845), 75; W. H. Coffin, *The Art of Medicine Simplified . . .* (Wellsburg, Va., 1853), 39; Clarke, *Diseases of Children*, 141.

39 "Teething" is still associated in the popular mind with many infant disorders ranging from the mild to the severe. Yet most medical authorities today hold that teething is not responsible for fevers, convulsions, diarrhea, rashes, respiratory ailments or even sleepless nights (on empirical grounds alone the authors would like to quarrel with this latter assertion). (Ronald Stanley Illingworth, *Common Symptoms of Disease in Children*, 3rd ed., [Oxford, 1971], 186; Editor, "Teething Myths," *BMJ*, 4, 1975, 604; Paul J. Honig, "Teething–Are Today's Pediatricians Using Yesterday's Notions?" *JP*, 87 [1975], 415.) On the other hand, a recent survey of the problem has found that in addition to restless nights, infants do sometimes experience a mild diarrhea, become susceptible to colds, coughs, and manifest a low grade fever. (Harvey Kravitz et al., "Teething in Infancy. A Part of Normal Development," *Illinois Medical Journal*, 151 [1977], 265.) Still, "convulsions" is definitely ruled out as a sign of teething (p. 262).

40 See note 44.

41 Clarke, *Diseases of Children*, 87–88; Underwood, *Diseases of children*, 78, 81, 109; Simons, *Planter's Guide*, 142–3; Samuel Kennedy Jennings, *A Compendium of Medical Science . . .* (Tuscaloosa, Ala., 1847), 576.

42 See for example Boling, "Remarks on Remittant Fever, Complicated with Symptoms, of Tetanus" *NOMSJ* 3 (1847), 737; John Erichsen, "Clinical Lecture on Tetanus,"

NOMN, 6 (1859), 614–5; and Dugas, "Lecture Upon Tetanus," 433, 444. See also William Proctor Gould Diary (Alabama State Archives), 31 March 1853, which laments that "poor little Jerry" died of "supposed tetany" after "much suffering." His body was examined "but no cause discovered."

43 'J,' "On Tetanus," 526, 529.

44 Roberts, Cohen, and Forfar, "Antenatal Factors Associated with Convulsions," 810; Hess, *Rickets*, 367; Paul D. Saville and Norman Kretchmer, "Neonatal Tetany: A Report of 125 Cases and Review of the Literature," *BN*, 2 (1960), 6–8.

45 That one physician boasted of curing tetanus by dosing his patients with milk punch suggests that these individuals at least were suffering from tetany rather than tetanus. (R. H. Goldsmith, "Tetanus – Epidemic or Constitutional Among Negroes?" *Practitioner*, 1, 1880, 23.) Other physicians as well believed that good nutrition would "cure" the difficulty. See, for example, Dugas, "Lecture Upon Tetanus," 442.

46 Cockburn et al., "Neonatal Convulsions," 104; Alvin B. Hayles and Mark D. Cloutier, "The Parathyroid Glands," in *Practice of Pediatrics*, ed. Vincent C. Kelley, 4 vols. (Hagerstown, Md., rev. ed. 1978–79), 1:chap. 51, 6.

47 Dugas, "Lecture Upon Tetanus," 436.

48 Alfred M. Folger, *The Family Physician; Being a Domestic Medical Work* . . . (Spartanburg, S.C., 1845), 138; Dugas, "Lecture Upon Tetanus," 433; A. Hester, "Remarks Upon the Causes, Phenomena and Treatment of Tetanus," *NOMSJ*, 3 (1846), 297–8.

49 See for example 'J.,' "On Tetanus," 529, and S. L. Grier, "The Negro and his Diseases," *NOMSJ*, 9 (1853), 753.

50 Pope, "Management of Negro Slaves," 15.

51 T. J. Grafton, "Oil of Turpentine as a Dressing for the Umbilical Cord," *NOMSJ*, 9 (1853), 15–16; Dugas, "Lecture Upon Tetanus," 435.

52 Underwood, *Diseases of Children*, 182.

53 Dugas, "Lecture Upon Tetanus," 444.

54 We are quite possibly on shaky ground here, for many variables are not yet understood. It may be that some blacks are unusually susceptible to tetanus relative to Caucasians. Arno G. Motulsky, for example, has observed in a survey of "Theoretical and Clinical Problems of Glucose-6-Phosphate Dehydrogenase Deficiency: Its Occurrence in Africans and Its Combination with Hemoglobinopathy" (*Abnormal Haemoglobins in Africa*, ed. J. H. P. Jonxis [Oxford, 1965], 154) that G6PD-deficient infants reveal an unusually high frequency of umbilical sepsis. Perhaps other predisposing factors are awaiting discovery which in tandem with Motulsky's observation will explain why today in the United States the black infant mortality rate from tetanus is fourteen times that of whites. George I. Lythcott, Calvin H. Sinnette and Donald R. Hopkins, "Pediatrics," in *Textbook of Black-Related Diseases*, ed. Richard Allen Williams, (New York, 1975), 163.

55 E. Hughes, "On Trismus Nascentium," *NOMSJ*, 3 (1846), 293. See also Dugas, "Lecture Upon Tetanus," 434, 443–4; Ramsay, "Physiological Differences," 412; Grier, "Negro and his Diseases," 758; 'J,' "On tetanus," passim; Daniel Drake, "Diseases of the Negro Population. . . . ," *SMSJ*, 1 (1845), 342; Boling, "Remittant Fever," 733; D. B. Nailer, "On Trismus Nascentium," *NOMSJ*, 3 (1846), 292. All believed that lockjaw too was a "Negro disease."

56 Illustrative is a recent investigation in Punjab, India, that found 25 percent of the children rachitic although they wore few clothes and were exposed to much sunshine. After an "exhaustive nutritional inquiry" the cause was discovered to be calcium deficiency. Geoffrey Taylor, "Osteomalacia and Calcium Deficiency," *BMJ*, 1 (1976), 960.

57 Moncrieff and Fadahunsi, "Congenital Rickets," 811; Root and Harrison, "Recent Advances in Calcium Metabolism," 179; Lewis A. Barness, "Vitamins in Nutrition," in *Practice of Pediatrics*, ed. Kelley, 1:chap. 28, 25.

58 Barness, "Vitamins in Nutriton," 25–27; L. Paunier, "Rickets and Osteomalacia," *WHO Monograph Series*, 62 (1976), 114–5.

59 Robert M. Neer, "Evolutionary Significance of Vitamin D, Skin Pigment, and Ultraviolet Light," *AJPA*, 43 (1975), 413; Barness, "Vitamins in Nutrition," 25–27.

60 George N. Acker, "Rickets in Negroes," *Archives of Pediatrics*, 11 (1894), 894.

61 Mary Theodora Weick, "A History of Rickets in the United States," *AJCN*, 20 (1967), 1234.

62 Colin George Miller and Winston Chotkan, "Vitamin-D Deficiency Rickets in Jamaican Children," *ADC*, 51 (1976), 215.

63 Advertisements have been drawn from the following antebellum newspapers: *Washington Republic, Alexandria Advertiser, American Beacon, Virginia Gazette, Carolina Centinel, Tennessee Gazette, Raleigh Register, Norfolk Gazette and Public Ledger, Mississippi Republican, The Mississippian, Arkansas State Gazette and Democrat, The Supporter and Scioto Gazette, The Daily Journal, The Memphis Daily Appeal, The Telegraphical Texas Register, The Daily Picayune, The Charleston Courier, Georgia Journal and Messenger, Arkansas State Democrat, Gazette and Democrat.*

64 Hess, *Rickets*, 41, 42; Acker, "Rickets in Negroes," 894. See also Weick, "Rickets in the United States," 1238, and Leslie Howard Owens, *This Species of Property: Slave Life and Culture in the Old South* (New York, 1976), 59–60.

65 F. Thomas Mitchell, "Incidence of Rickets in the South," *SMJ*, 23 (1930) 229–30.

66 J. Wellington Byers, "Diseases of the Southern Negro," *Medical and Surgical Reporter (Phil.)*, 58 (1888), 736. See also Mary Ellison (*The Black Experience: American Blacks Since 1865* [New York, 1974], 90) who says rickets was "rampant" among blacks in the early twentieth century.

67 Alfred F. Hess and Lester J. Unger, "Prophylactic Therapy for Rickets in a Negro Community," *JAMA*, 69 (1917), 1583; Hess, *Rickets*, 89–90.

68 Acker, "Rickets in Negroes," 894; Hess, *Rickets*, 42.

69 See for example the remarks of Fogel and Engerman, *Time on the Cross*, 1:124–6.

70 Paul V. Woolley, "Mechanical Suffocation During Infancy; A Comment on its Relation to the Total Problem of Sudden Death," *JP*, 26 (1945), 572–5.

71 Abraham B. Bergman, "Sudden Infant Death Syndrome," *American Family Physician*, 8 (1973), 96. For statistics outside the United States consult Abraham B. Bergman, J. Bruce Beckwith, and George C. Ray, eds., *Proceedings of the Second International Conference on Causes of Sudden Death in Infants* (Seattle, 1970) and Marie A. Valdes-Dapena, "Sudden And Unexpected Death in Infancy: A Review of the World Literature, 1954–1966," *Ped*, 39 (1967), 123–38, and "Sudden Unexplained Infant Death, 1970 Through 1975: An Evolution in Understanding," *Pathology Annual*, 12 (1977), 117–45.

72 L. A. Chamerovzow, ed., *Slave Life in Georgia: A Narrative of the Life, Sufferings, and Escape of John Brown, a Fugitive Slave, Now In England* (London, 1855), 69.

73 Harry Bloch, "Medical-Social Conditions of Slaves in the South," *JNMA*, 61 (1969), 443.

74 Todd L. Savitt, "Smothering and Overlaying of Virginia Slave Children: A Suggested Explanation," *BHM*, 49 (1975), 402.

75 Bergman, "Sudden Infant Death Syndrome," 96.

76 W. E. Parish et al., "Hypersensitivity to Milk and Sudden Death in Infancy," *Lancet*, 2 (1960), 1106–10.

77 Henry S. Lardy et al., "Defective Phosphosphoenolypyruvate Carboxykinase in Victims of Sudden Infant Death Syndrome," in *Research Perspectives in the Sudden Infant Death Syndrome*, ed. E. G. Hasselmeyer, DHEW Pub. No. (NIH) 76–1976 (Washington, D.C., 1976), 105.

78 Abraham Towbin, "Sudden Infant Death (Cot Death) Related to Spinal Injury," *Lancet*, 2 (1967), 940.

79 K. W. Cross and Sheila R. Lewis, "Upper Respiratory Obstruction and Cot Death," *ADC*, 46 (1971), 211–13.

80 Thaddeus Midura and Stephen S. Arnon, "Infant Botulism, Identification of Clostridium Botulism and its Toxins in Faeces," *Lancet*, 2 (1976), 934–6.

81 Richard L. Naeye, "Hypoxemia and the Sudden Infant Death Syndrome," *Science*, 186 (1974), 837–8.

82 See Richard H. Raring, *Crib Death: Scourge of Infants – Shame of Society* (Hicksville, N.Y., 1975), 92.

83 Preben Geertinger, "Sudden, Unexpected Death in Infancy with Special Reference to the Parathyroids," *Ped*, 39 (1967), 43–8.

84 P. M. Mulvey, "Cot Death Survey: Anaphylaxis and the House Dust Mite," *Medical Journal of Australia*, 2 (1972), 1240–44.

85 Lythcott, Sinnette, and Hopkins, "Pediatrics," 133; Richard L. Naeye, Bertha Ladis, and Joseph S. Drage, "Sudden Infant Death Syndrome: A Prospective Study," *AJDC*, 130 (1976), 1207; S. M. Rabson, "Sudden and Unexpected Natural Death. IV. Sudden and Unexpected Natural Death in Infants and Young Children," *JP*, 34 (1949), 168; Jess F. Kraus and Nemat O. Borhani, "Post-neonatal Sudden Unexpected Death in California: A Cohort Study," *AJE*, 95 (1972), 505; Marie Valdes-Dapena et al., "Sudden Unexpected Death in Infancy: A Statistical Analysis of Certain Socioeconomic Factors," *JP*, 73 (1968), 388; Lester Adelson and Eleanor Roberts Kinney, "Sudden and Unexpected Death in Infancy and Childhood," *Ped*, 17 (1956), 681; Abraham B. Bergman et al., "Studies of the Sudden Infant Death Syndrome in King County, Washington. III Epidemiology," *Ped*, 49 (1972), 863; Jack H. Blok, "The Incidence of Sudden Infant Death Syndrome in North Carolina's Cities and Counties: 1972–1974," *AJPH*, 68 (1978), 370–7

86 Ruth Maxwell, Lewis H. Roht, and Paul Callen, "Incidence of Sudden Death Syndrome in Texas, 1969–1972; Estimation by the Surrogate Method," *Texas Medicine*, 72 (1976), 59; Robert Steele, "Sudden Infant Death Syndrome in Ontario, Canada: Epidemiologic Aspects" in *Second International Conference*, eds. Bergman, Beckwith, and Ray, 65; Naeye, Ladis, and Drage, "Sudden Infant Death Syndrome," 1208.

87 Naeye, Ladis, and Drage, "Sudden Infant Death Syndrome," 1209; R. G. Carpenter and C. W. Shaddick, "Role of Infection, Suffocation, and Bottle Feeding in Cot Death: An Analysis of Some Factors in the Histories of 110 Cases and Their Controls," in *Proceedings of the Conference on Causes of Sudden Death in Infants*, eds. Ralph J. Wedgewood and Earl P. Benditt (Seattle, 1963), 138; T. K. Marshall, "The Northern Ireland Study: Pathological Findings," in *Second International Conference*, eds. Bergman, Beckwith and Ray, 111; Rebecca B. Anderson and Judy F. Rosenblith, "Sudden Unexpected Death Syndrome; Early Indicators," *BN*, 18 (1971), 396–8; Valdes-Dapena, "Sudden Unexplained Infant Death," 122, 126–7.

88 Jean L. Marx, "Crib Death: Some Promising Leads but no Solution Yet," *Science*, 189 (1975), 369; Lewis P. Lipsitt, "Perinatal Indicators and Psychophysiologic Precursors of Crib Death," Paper delivered at a Symposium on Perinatal Factors and Developmental Hazards at the Meetings of the American Association for the Advancement of Science, Denver, Co., February 1977, Table 3.

89 Philip S. Spiers and Lydia Wang, "Short Pregnancy Interval, Low Birthweight, and the Sudden Infant Death Syndrome," *AJE*, 104 (1976), 16; Donald R. Peterson and Nina M. Chinn, "Sudden Infant Death Trends in Six Metropolitan Communities, 1965–1974," *Ped*, 60 (1977), 75–79; R. G. Carpenter and J. L. Emery, "Identification and Follow-up of Infants at Risk of Sudden Death in Infancy," *Nature*, 250 (1974), 729.

90 "Neonatal Calcium, Magnesium, and Phosphorus Homeostasis," *Lancet*, 1 (1974), 155–6.

91 For a discussion and documentation of this point, see note 5.

92 Cross and Lewis, "Upper Respiratory Obstruction and Cot Death," 211–3; Shirley Tonkin, "Sudden Infant Death Syndrome: Hypothesis of Causation," *Ped*, 55 (1975), 650–61; Judy F. Rosenblith and Rebecca B. Anderson-Huntington, "Defensive Reactions to Stimulation of the Nasal and Oral Regions in Newborns: Relations to State," in *Development of Upper Respiratory Anatomy and Function: Implications for Sudden Infant Death Syndrome*, eds., James F. Bosma and June Showacre (Bethesda, Md., 1975) 250–63.

93 Donald R. Peterson et al., "Postnatal Growth and Sudden Infant Death Syndrome," *AJE*, 99 (1974), 389–94; Naeye, Ladis, and Drage, "Sudden Infant Death Syndrome," 1209.

94 Ralph L. Naeye et al., "Sudden Infant Death Syndrome Temperament before Death," *JP*, 88 (1976), 511–5; Lipsitt, "Perinatal Indicators," 97 (table).

95 Alfred Steinschneider, "Prolonged Apnea and the Sudden Infant Death Syndrome: Clinical and Laboratory Observations," *Ped*, 50 (1972), 646–54, and "A Reexamination of 'The Apnea Monitor Business,' " *Ped*, 58 (1976), 1–5; Daniel C. Shannon, Dorothy H. Kelly, and Kathleen O'Connell, "Abnormal Regulation of Ventilation in Infants at Risk for Sudden-Infant-Death Syndrome," *NEJM*, 297 (1977), 747–50; W. W. Dement and T. Anders, "Summary of Research on the Relationship between Sleep Apnea and the Sudden Infant Death Syndrome" in *Research Perspectives*, ed. Hasselmeyer.

96 Juan J. Gershanik, Abner H. Levkoff, and Robert Duncan, "The Association of Hypocalcemia and Recurrent Apnea in Premature Infants," *AJOG*, 113 (1972), 646–52.

97 J. L. Caddell, "Magnesium Deprivation in Sudden Unexpected Infant Death," *Lancet*, 2 (1972) 258–62.

98 Joan L. Caddell, Fulton L. Saier, and Carol A. Thomason, "Parenteral Magnesium Load Tests in Postpartum American Women," *AJCN*, 28 (1975), 1099–104.

99 J. L. Caddell et al., "The Magnesium Load Test III: Correlation of Clinical and Laboratory Data in Infants from One to Six Months of Age," *Clinical Pediatrics*, 14 (1975), 478–84.

100 Caddell, "Magnesium Deprivation in Sudden Unexpected Infant Deaths," 258–62; Joan L. Caddell, "Exploring the Magnesium Deficient Weanling Rat as an Animal Model for the Sudden Infant Death Syndrome: Physical Biochemical, Electrocardiographic, and Gross Pathological Changes," *Pediatric Research*, 12 (1978), 1157–66.

101 Caddell has been criticized by C. A. Lapin et al. ("Hepatic Trace Elements in the Sudden Infant Death Syndrome," *JP*, 89 [1976], 607) who found no differences in magnesium concentrations when they studied the livers of SIDS victims and controls. As Caddell points out in her defense, however, ("Hepatic Trace Elements in the Sudden Infant Death Syndrome [letter]," *JP*, 90 [1977], 1039) their "controls" were aged five days to thirteen years old. Furthermore, a number of studies have indicated that the liver is the least satisfactory tissue for accurately assessing magnesium stores. J. L. Caddell and Rita Scheppner ("The Postmortem Diagnosis of Magnesium Deficiency: Studies in an Animal Model for the Human Infant," *Journal of Forensic Sciences*, 23 [1978], 342–3) have recently determined that bone is the best tissue in which to measure magnesium stores.

102 Felicity King, "Intolerance to Lactose in Mother's Milk?" *Lancet*, 2 (1972), 335; George C. Cook and F. D. Lee, "The Jejunum after Kwashiorkor," *Lancet*, 2 (1966), 1266; Truswell, "Carbohydrate and Lipid Metabolism," 120.

103 Cicely D. Williams, "Nutritional Diseases of Childhood Associated with Maize Diets," *ADC*, 8 (1933), 423.

104 Williams, "Nutritional Disease of Childhood," 423; R. G. Whitehead, "Factors Which May Affect the Biochemical Response to Protein-Calorie Malnutrition," in *Protein-Calorie Malnutrition*, ed. A. von Muralt (Heidelberg, 1969), 39.

105 Michael Latham et al., *Scope Manual of Nutrition* (Kalamazoo, Mich., 1972), 28.
106 Hubert Carey Trowell, *Non-infective Disease in Africans* (London, 1960), 332; Cicely D. Williams, "Kwashiorkor," *JAMA*, 153 (1953), 1282; Aaron A. Altschul, *Proteins: Their Chemistry and Politics* (New York, 1965), 187; G. A. O. Alleyne et al., *Protein-energy Malnutrition* (London, 1977), 2–4.
107 Nevin S. Scrimshaw, Carl E. Taylor, and John E. Gordon, *Interactions of Nutrition and Infection* (Geneva, 1968), 75.
108 Rawick, *American Slave*, 2:235.
109 Ibid., 3:194.
110 Tom Landess, ed., "Potraits of Georgia Slaves," *Georgia Review*, 21 (1967), 126. See also Henry Clay Bruce, *The New Man. Twenty-Nine Years a Slave. Twenty-Nine Years a Free Man* (New York, 1895; reprint ed., New York, 1969), 14; Robinson, "Negro Slavery at the South," 381–2; and Rawick, *American Slave*, 2:316.
111 William Howard Russell, *My Diary North and South*, ed. Fletcher Pratt (New York, 1954), 149.
112 Fredrika Bremer, *Homes of the New World . . .* , transl. by Mary Howitt, 2 vols. (New York, 1853), 1:294. Consult also Eugene D. Genovese (*The Political Economy of Slavery: Studies in the Economy and Society of the Slave South* [New York, 1965], 46), who seems to allude to this phenomenon by remarking that the slave diet guaranteed "the appearance of good health."
113 James Maxwell, "Pathological Inquiry into the Nature of Cachexia Africana, As Generally Connected with Dirt-Eating," *Jamaica Physical Journal*, 2 (1835), 413; Grier, "The Negro and his Diseases," 755; F. W. Craigin, "Observations on Cachexia Africana or Dirt-Eating," *AJMS*, 17 (1836), 356–7.
114 See, for example, Minnie Clare Boyd, *Alabama in the Fifties: A Social Study* (New York, 1931), 190, and Owens, *Species of Property*, 41–2.
115 Simons, *Planter's Guide*, 208.
116 Grier, "The Negro and his Diseases," 754–5. See also Boyd (*Alabama in the Fifties*, 190) who discusses marasmus in slave infants.
117 Maxwell, "Nature of Cachexia Africana," 413; *SMR*, 1 (1849), 194.
118 Cartwright, "Reports on Diseases," 704–7; John R. Hicks, "African Consumption," *Stethoscope*, 4 (1854), 625–9; Grier, "The Negro and his Diseases," 757–63; Drake, "Diseases of the Negro Population," 341; Craigen, "Observations on Cachexia Africana" 358; William Telford, "On the Mal d'Estomac," *London Medical and Physical Journal*, 47 (1822), 450–8; J. Hancock, "Remarks on the Common Cachexia, or Leucophlegmasia, called Mal d'Estomac in the Colonies," *EMSJ*, 25 (1831), 67–73; John Le Conte, "Observations on Geophagy," *SMSJ*, 1 (1845), 430. Dirt-eating was also called "Negro consumption" which led to a bit of semantical confusion among antebellum physicians. See Cartwright, "Philosophy of the Negro Constitution," 697, and Lunsford P. Yandell, "Remarks on Struma Africana or the Disease usually called Negro Poison, or Negro Consumption," *TJM*, 4 (1831) 112.
119 Thompson McGown, *A Practical Treatise on the Most Common Diseases of the South . . .* , (Philadelphia, 1849) 89–91, 93; H. V. Wooten, "On the Diseases of Luwndesboro . . . ," *SMR*, 2 (1850); Maxwell, "Nature of Cachexia Africana," 435; Grier, "The Negro and his Diseases," 758.
120 Joseph Pitt, "Observations on the Country and Diseases near Roanoke River, in the State of North Carolina," *New York Medical Reports*, 2nd Hexade (1808), 340; James B. Duncan, "Report on the Topography, Climate and Diseases of the Parish of St. Mary, La.," *SMR*, I (1849), 195; William Carpenter, "Observations on the Cachexia Africana, or the Habit and Effects of Dirt Eating in the Negro Race," *NOMSJ*, 1 (1844), 158, 166–7; Le Conte, "Observations on Geophagy," 441–4; Craigen, "Observations on Cachexia," 71.
121 Carpenter, "Observations on the Cachexia Africana, or the Habit and Effects of

Dirt-Eating in the Negro Race," *NOMSJ*, 1 (1844), 148, 150–2, 166; Cartwright, "Report on Diseases," 704–6; Maxwell, "Nature of Cachexia Africana," 413, 417; Craigen, "Observations on Cachexia Africana," 358; Thomas Affleck, "On the Hygiene of Cotton Plantations and the Management of Negro Slaves," *SMR*, 2 (1850) 435; Tomlinson Fort, *A Dissertation on the Practice of Medicine* (Milledgeville, Ga., 1849), 596; J. R. Cotting, "Analysis of a Species of Clay Found in Richmond County [Ga.], which is Eagerly Sought After, and Eaten, by many People, Particularly by Children," *SMSJ*, 1 (1836).

122 Affleck, "Cotton Plantations," 435–6; Grier, "The Negro and his Diseases," 756–7; Cartwright, "Report on Diseases," 702; Drake, "Diseases of the Negro Population," 341; P. Tidyman, "A Sketch of the Most Remarkable Diseases of the Negroes of the Southern States . . . ," *Philadelphia Journal of the Medical and Physical Sciences*, 12 (1826), 331.

123 Todd L. Savitt, *Medicine and Slavery, the Diseases and Health Care of Blacks in Antebellum Virginia* (Urbana Ill., 1978), 64ff.

124 Geoffrey M. Jeffery et al., "Study of Intestinal Helminth Infections in a Coastal South Carolina Area," *PHR*, 78 (1963), 49; J. P. Carter et al., "Nutrition and Parasitism Among Rural Pre-School Children in South Carolina," *JNMA*, 62 (1970), 183; Lythcott, Sinnette, and Hopkins, "Pediatrics," 177.

125 Lythcott, Sinnette, and Hopkins, "Pediatrics," 159, 177; Jeffery et al., "Helminth Infections," 49; A. E. Keller, W. S. Leathers, and H. C. Ricks, "An Investigation of the Incidence and Intensity of Infestation of Hookworm in Mississippi," *American Journal of Hygiene*, 19 (1934), 629–56; Gilbert F. Otto, "Hookworm," in *Maxcy-Rosenau Preventative Medicine and Public Health*, ed. Philip E. Sartwell, 10th ed. (New York, 1973), 221; Julian Herman Lewis, *The Biology of the Negro*, (Chicago, 1942), 255–7.

126 Josué de Castro, *The Geography of Hunger* (Boston, 1952), 46.

127 De Silva and Baptist, *Tropical Nutritional Disorders*, 23; Scrimshaw, Taylor, and Gordon, *Nutrition and Infection*, 102, 106; Carter et al., "Nutrition and Parasitism," 183; Asa C. Chandler and Clark P. Read, *Introduction to Parasitology*, 10th ed. (New York, 1961), 429; Robson, *Malnutrition*, I: 113; M. Layrisse and A. Vargas," Nutrition and Intestinal Parasitic Infection," *Progress in Food Nutrition Science*, 1 (1975), 653.

128 Carter et al., "Nutrition and Parasitism," 183; Robson, *Malnutrition*, 1: 113.

129 Savitt, *Medicine and Slavery*, 64, 66; Layrisse and Vargas, "Nutrition and Intestinal Parastic Infection," 655; Carter, "Nutrition and Parasitism," 190.

130 Carter et al. "Nutrition and Parasitism"; De Silva and Baptist, *Tropical Nutritional Disorders*, 23.

131 Layrisse and Vargas, "Nutrition and Intestinal Parasitic Infection," 655–6; Scrimshaw, Taylor, and Gordon, *Nutrition and Infection*, 102; Joe L. Frost and Billy Payne, "Hunger in America: Scope and Consequences," in *Nutrition and Intellectual Growth in Children*, ed. Association for Childhood Education International (Washington, D.C., 1969), 8.

132 Chandler and Read, *Parasitology*, 429.

133 Ibid., 429; Carter et al., "Nutrition and Parasitism," 189; Scrimshaw, Taylor, and Gordon, *Nutrition and Infection*, 47.

134 V. Minnich et al., "Effect of Clay upon Iron Absorption," *AJCN*, 21 (1968), 78–86.

Chapter 8. Aliments and ailments

1 John S. Wilson, "The Negro – His Diet, Clothing, and Ailments," *ACP*, 3 (1859), 197.

2 Ralph Butterfield, "Health of Negroes," *DBR*, 25 (1858), 571.

3 See note 63, chap. 7.

4 Nutritional diseases rather naturally divide themselves into illnesses with a "primary" or direct and those of a "secondary" or complex nutritional origin. Scurvy is an example of the former, where external symptoms are readily apparent, and the cure is normally a matter of correcting the diet whereupon the symptoms disappear. Secondary diseases in which malnutrition is only one of a number of factors are taken up in the following chapters.

5 See in particular, William Dosite Postell, "Surveys on the Chronic Illnesses and Physical Impairments Among the Slave Population in the Antebellum South," *BMLA*, 42 (1954), 161; George F. Cooper, "Vital Statistics of Houston County," *SMSJ*, n.s. 7 (1851), 725.

6 Leslie H. Owens, *This Species of Property: Slave Life and Culture in the Old South* (New York, 1976), 58.

7 See Richard Sutch, "The Treatment Received by American Slaves: A Critical Review of the Evidence Presented in *Time on the Cross*," *Explorations in Economic History*, 12 (1975), 391.

8 P. Tidyman, "A Sketch of the most Remarkable Diseases of the Negroes of the Southern States, with an Account of the Method of Treating them, Accompanied by Physiological Observations," *Philadelphia Journal of the Medical and Physical Sciences*, 12 (1826), 314.

9 E. M. Pendleton, "Statistics of Diseases of Hancock County," *SMSJ*, n.s.5 (1849), 650.

10 William Dosite Postell, *Health of Slaves on Southern Plantations* (Baton Rouge, La., 1951; reprint ed. Gloucester, Mass., 1970), 85.

11 John Duffy, *The Healers: The Rise of the Medical Establishment* (New York, 1976), 140. See also Owens, *Species of Property*, 59–60.

12 Pendleton, "Diseases of Hancock County," 649.

13 Daniel Drake, "Diseases of the Negro Population – in a Letter to Rev. Mr. Pinney," *SMSJ*, n.s. 1 (1845), 342. See also Duffy, *The Healers*, 140–2, and Owens, *Species of Property*, 39–41.

14 Robert N. Neer, The Evolutionary Significance of Vitamin D, Skin Pigment, and Ultraviolet Light" *AJPA* 43 (1975), 411.

15 David Mason, "On Atrophia a Ventriculo (mal d'Estomac), or dirteating," *EMSJ*, 34 (1833), 292.

16 Felice Swados, "Negro Health on the Antebellum Plantations," *BHM*, 10 (1941), 467.

17 William Carpenter, "Observations on the *Cachexia Africana*, or the Habit and Effects of Dirteating in the Negro Race" *NOMSJ*, 1 (1844), 148.

18 See for example Chas. Wardell Stiles, *Soil Pollution as Cause of Ground Itch, Hookworm Disease (Ground-Itch Anemia), and Dirt Eating* (Washington, D.C., 1910), 22; Paul H. Buck, "The Poor Whites of the Antebellum South," *AHR*, 31 (1925), 45; C. C. Bass, "The Symptoms and Diagnosis of Hookworm Disease," *NOMSJ*, 63 (1910), 252.

19 Hilda Hertz, "Notes on Clay and Starch Eating among Negroes in a Southern Urban Community," *Social Forces*, 25 (1947), 343–4; Charles E. Mengel, William A. Carter, and Edward S. Horton, "Geophagia with Iron Deficiency and Hypokalemia: Cachexia Africana," *AIM*, 114 (1964), 470–4; Harry A. Roselle, "Association of Laundry Starch and Clay Ingestion with Anemia in New York City," *AIM*, 125 (1970), 57–61; James A. Halstead, "Geophagia in Man: Its Nature and Nutritional Effects," *AJCN*, 21 (1968), 1384–93; Bengt Anell and Sture Lagercrantz, *Geophagical Customs* (Uppsala, Sweden, 1958) 79–81.

20 J. W. Foster, "Pica," *Kenya and East African Medical Journal* (1927), 68–9, 71; Philip Lanzkowsky, "Investigation into the Aetiology and Treatment of Pica," *ADC*, 34 (1959), 140–8; Pincus Catzel, "Pica and Milk Intake," *Ped*, 31 (1963), 1056; Robert McDonald and Shelia R. Marshall, "The Value of Iron Therapy in Pica," *Ped*, 34 (1964), 558–62; Man Mohan et al., "Iron Therapy in Pica," *Journal of the Indian Medical*

Association, 51 (1968), 16–18; Charles A. Coltman, "Papophagia and Iron Lack," *JAMA*, 207 (1969), 513–16; William H. Crosby, "Pica: A Compulsion Caused by Iron Deficiency," *British Journal of Haematology*, 34 (1976), 341–2.
21 See note 125, Chap. 7.
22 See J. Hancock, "Remarks on the Common Cachexia or Leucophlegmasia; called mal d'Estomac in the Colonies, and its Kindred Affections as Dropsy, etc.," *EMSJ*, 35 (1831), 68, and John Le Conte's discussion ("Observations on Geophagy," *SMSJ*, 1 [1845], 427, 431, 438) as examples of early investigations into the etiology of pica.
23 James Maxwell, "Pathological Inquiry into the Nature of Cachexia Africana as Generally Connected with Dirteating," *Jamaica Physical Journal* 2 (1835) 413; Samuel A. Cartwright, "Report on the Diseases and Physical Peculiarities of the Negro Race," *NOMSJ*, 9 (1851), 705–6.
24 It is also believed by some (e.g., Anell and Lagercrantz, *Geophagical Customs*, 79) that dirt eating was a form of suicide for the purpose of achieving a spiritual return to Africa. This seems, however, an assertion, applicable at best to first-generation slaves. By contrast most black dirt-eaters in the nineteenth-century South would have been generations removed from their native land.
25 Robert W. Twyman, "The Clay Eater: A New Look at an Old Southern Enigma," *JSH*, 37 (1971), 447.
26 Ibid., 444–8.
27 Consult John M. Hunter, "Geophagy in Africa and in the United States: A Culture-Nutrition Hypothesis," *Geographical Review*, 63 (1973), 170–95, who has made efforts to distinguish between the cultural and the nutritional origins of pica. See also Dorothy Dickens and Robert N. Ford, "Geophagy (Dirt Eating) Among Mississippi Negro School Children," *American Sociological Review*, 7 (1942), 60–65; Donald E. Vermeer, "Geophagy Among the Ewe of Ghana," *Ethnology*, 10 (1971), 56–72; Margaret F. Gutelius et al., "Nutritional Studies of Children with Pica," *Ped*, 29 (1962), 1012–23, and Edwin S. Bronstein and Jerry Dollar, "Pica in Pregnancy," *Journal of the Medical Association of Georgia*, 63 (1974), 332–5.
28 Bronstein and Dollar, "Pica in Pregnancy," 333–4; Gutelius et al., "Children with Pica," 1012–23; Sydney Jacobs, ed., "The Starch Eater," *Journal of the Louisiana State Medical Society*, 124 (1972), 79–83; Cecile Hoover Edwards et al., "Clay and Cornstarch-eating Women," *JADA*, 35 (1959), 813–15.
29 O. Carlander, "Aetiology of Pica," *Lancet*, 277 (1959), 569; H. L. Jolly, "Advances in Paediatrics," *Practitioner*, 191 (1963), 417; R. Ber and A. Valero, "Pica and Hypochromic Anaemia," *Harfuah*, 61 (1961), 35; L. Heilmeyer and H. G. Harwerth, "Clinical Manifestations in Iron Deficiency," in *Iron Deficiency Pathogenesis: Clinical Aspects Therapy* (London, 1970), 30; Hunter, "Geophagy in Africa and the United States," 182.
30 Hunter, "Geophagy in Africa and the United States," 178; Cecile Hoover Edwards et al., "Effects of Clay and Cornstarch Intake on Women and their Infants," *JADA*, 44 (1964), 111; Josué de Castro, *Geography of Hunger* (Boston, 1952), 87; Berthold Laufer, "Geophagy," *Field Museum of Natural History: Anthropological Series*, 18 (1930), 177; J. R. Cotting, "Analysis of a Species of Clay Found in Richmond County [Ga.] which is eagerly sought after, and eaten, by many people, particularly by children," *SMSJ*, 1 (1836), 288–92.
31 Mohan et al., "Iron Therapy in Pica," 16–18; Coltman, "Papophagia and Iron Lack," 516; Lanzkowsky, "Etiology and Treatment of Pica," 148; McDonald and Marshall, "Iron Therapy in Pica," 558–62; Bronstein and Dollar, "Pica in Pregnancy," 334.
32 Marcia Cooper, *Pica* (Springfield, Ill., 1957), 87–8.
33 For example, kangaroos in the Baltimore Zoo were able to avoid the nutritional lesions commonly observed in captive animals by ingesting red clay with which they synthesize their own B vitamins. See Cooper, *Pica*, 87–8.
34 Joseph Pitt, "Observations on the Country and Diseases near Roanoke River in the

State of North Carolina" *New York Medical Reports*, 2nd Hexade (1808), 340; James B. Duncan, "Report on the Topography, Climate and Diseases of the Parish of St. Mary, La." *SMR*, 1 (1849), 195; Carpenter, *"Cachexia Africana*," 166–7; Le Conte, "Observations on Geophagy," 441–4; F. W. Craigin, "Observations on Cachexia Africana or Dirt Eating" *AJMS*, 17 (1936), 361–2; William Telford, "On the Mal d'Estomac," *London Medical and Physical Journal*, 47 (1822), 450, 458; Hancock, "Common Cachexia," 71; Daniel H. Whitney, *The Family Physician and Guide to Health* (New York, 1833), 117.

35 Cited by Anell and Lagercrantz, *Geophagical Customs*, 49.
36 Thompson McGown, *A Practical Treatise on the Most Common Diseases of the South: Exhibiting Their Peculiar Nature, and the Corresponding Adaptation of Treatment* (Philadelphia, 1849) 89.
37 Ibid., 91.
38 H. V. Wooten, "On the . . . Diseases of Luwndesboro . . . ," *SMR*, 2 (1850), 333; Maxwell, "Nature of Cachexia Africana," 435; S. L. Grier, "The Negro and his Diseases, *NOMSJ*, 9(1853); 758; Tomlinson Fort, *A Dissertation on the Practice of Medicine. . . . (Milledgeville, Ga., 1849)*, 597–8.
39 Pica was especially prevalent in those regions of Italy where pellagra prevailed. Foster, "Pica," 74.
40 V. Minnich et al., "Effect of Clay Upon Iron Absorption," *AJCN*, 21 (1968), 78–86.
41 Ralph D. Reynolds et al., "Pagophagia and Iron Deficiency Anemia, *AIM*, 69 (1968) 438–9; Coltman, "Pagophagia and Iron Lack," 513–16; Crosby, "Pica," 341–2. See also Kenneth M. Talkington et al., "Effect of Ingestion of Starch and Some Clays on Iron Absorption," *AJOG*, 108 (1970), 262–7.
42 Robert R. Williams, *Toward the Conquest of Beriberi* (Cambridge Mass., 1961), 66.
43 Owens, *Species of Property*, 61.
44 Piero Mustacchi, "Cesare Bressa (1785–1836) on Dirt Eating in Louisiana: A Critical Analysis of his Unpublished Manuscript *De La Dissolution Scorbutique*," *JAMA*, 218 (1971), 229–32.
45 Sutch, "Treatment Received by American Slaves," 430.
46 Williams, *Beriberi*, 61.
47 Duncan, "Diseases of the Parish of St. Mary," 195; Fort, *Practice of Medicine*, 566.
48 Stanley Davidson et al., *Human Nutrition and Dietetics*, 6th ed. (Edinburgh, 1959), 330.
49 Julian Herman Lewis, *Biology of the Negro* (Chicago, 1942), 370.
50 For a history of pellagra in the American South, see Daphne A. Roe, *A Plague of Corn: The Social History of Pellagra* (Ithaca, N.Y., 1973); Elizabeth Williams Etheridge, *The Butterfly Caste: A Social History of Pellagra in the South* (Westport, Conn., 1972); Paul S. Carley, "History of Pellagra in the United States," *Urologic and Cutaneous Review*, 49 (1945), 291, 303; and Virgil P. Sydenstricker, "The History of Pellagra, Its Recognition as a Disorder of Nutrition and Its Conquest," *AJCN*, 6 (1958), 409–14.
51 The discovery of pellagra's cure was largely the work of Dr. Joseph Goldberger. For his story see Joseph Goldberger, *Goldberger on Pellagra*, ed. Milton Jerris (Baton Rouge, 1964). That niacin in corn is bound was discovered by E. Kodichek, "The Effect of Alkaline Hydrolysis of Maize on the Availability of its Nicotinic Acid to the Pig," *BJN*, 10 (1956), 51–67, and "Nicotinic Acid and the Pellagra Problem," *Bibliotheca "Nutritio et Dieta,"* 4 (1962), 109–27.
52 Some nutritionists are convinced that the real pellagra-producing culprit is leucine. Coluther Gopalan, Bhavani Belavady, and D. Krishnamurth, "The Role of Leucine in the Pathogenesis of Canine Black Tongue and Pellagra," *Lancet*, 2 (1969), 956–7; Kamala Krishnaswamy and Coluther Gopalan, "Effect of Isoleucine on Skin and Electroence Phalogram in Pellagra," *Lancet*, 2 (1971), 1167–9; Constance Kies and Hazel M. Fox, "Interrelationships of Leucine with Lysine, Tryptophan and Niacin

as they influenced Protein Value of Cereal Grains for Humans," *Cereal Chemistry*, 49 (1972), 223–31; Coluther Gopalan and K. S. Jaya Rao, "Pellagra and Amino Acids Imbalance," *Vitamins and Hormones*, 33 (1975), 516. See also Jennifer Manson, "The Possible Effect of L-leucine on the Nicotinic Acid Requirement of the Rat," *PNS*, 34 (1975), A120. Additionally, the slave diet was high in threonine which also appears to have an adverse effect on the metabolism of both niacin and tryptophan, yet that same diet was extraordinarly low in riboflavin, crucial in converting tryptophan to niacin. Margaret S. Chaney and Margaret L. Ross, *Nutrition*, 8th ed., (Boston, 1971), 276; N. B. S. Raghuramulu, Narasinga Rao, and C. Gopalan, "Amino Acid Imbalance and Tryptophan-Niacin Metabolism. I. Effect of Excess Leucine on the Urinary Excretion of Tryptophan-Niacin Metabolities in Rats," *JN*, 86 (1965), v. 105.

53   A. S. Truswell, J. D. L. Hansen and Patricia Wannenburg, "Plasma Tryptophan and Other Amino Acids in Pellagra," *AJCN*, 21 (1968), 1319; Coluther Gopalan, "Possible Role for Dietary Leucine in the Pathogenesis of Pellagra,"*Lancet*, 1 (1969), 197–9; Bhavani Belavady, S. G. Srikantia, and Coluther Gopalan, "The Effect of the Oral Administration of Leucine on the Metabolism of Tryptophan," *Biochemical Journal*, 87 (1963), 652–5.

54   Ricardo Bressani and Delia A. Navarrete, "Niacin Content of Coffee in Central America," *Food Research*, 24 (1959), 350; Grace A. Goldsmith et al., "Human Studies of Biological Availabilty of Niacin in Coffee," *Proceedings of the Society for Experimental Biology & Medicine*, 102 (1959), 579–80; Robert L. Squibb et al., "A Comparison of the Effect of Raw Corn and Tortillas (Lime-Treated Corn) with Niacin, Tryptophan or Beans on the Growth and Muscle Niacin of Rats," *JN*, 67 (1959), 359.

55   Eugene D. Genovese, *Roll, Jordan, Roll. The World the Slaves Made* (New York, 1974), 549; John B. Cade, "Out of the Mouths of Ex-Slaves," *JNH*, 20 (1935), 300; George P. Rawick, ed., *The American Slave: A Composite Autobiography*, 19 vols., (Westport Conn., 1973), 4:99, 161; 5:174; 6:68; Ronald Killion and Charles Waller, eds., *Slavery Time When I was Chillun Down on Marsta's Plantation* (Savannah, Ga., 1973), 129–30. See Bressani and Navarrete, "Niacin Content of Coffee," 350, who found that coffee containing large amounts of grains does not yield much niacin.

56   James W. Babcock, "How Long has Pellagra Existed in South Carolina?" *Proceedings of the American Medico-Psychological Association*, 67 (1911), 301–2. See also G. A. Wheeler, "A Note on the History of Pellagra in the United States," *PHR*, 46 (1931), 2228, and William J. Darby, Kristen W. McNutt and E. Neige Todhunter, "Niacin," *Nutrition Reviews*, 33 (1975), 290. Actually, two cases were reported during 1864 in the northeastern section of the country, although in both instances confirmation is lacking. Sydenstricker, "History of Pellagra," 409.

57   Goldberger, *Goldberger on Pellagra*, ed. Terris, 373.

58   Michael Latham, *Human Nutrition in Tropical Africa* (Rome, 1965), 106; Lewis, *Biology of the Negro*, 262, 369–70.

59   The epidemic seems to have begun in 1844 and continued throughout the year 1846. Our description of it is based on accounts by contemporary physicians, among them W. R. Puckett, "Remarks on Erysipelatous Fever, or Black Tongue," *NOMSJ*, 1 (1844), 27–31; P. E. H. Lovelace, "Remarks on the Disease Popularly Known as the 'Black Tongue,' " *NOMSJ*, 3 (1846), 190–5; H. G. Davenport, "Observations on Typhoid Fever," *NOMSJ*, 8 (1852), 580–90; W. H. McKee, "Reports from North Carolina," *SMR*, 2 (1850), 406–20; T. P. Ruse, "A Short Account of an Endemic Fever Which Made its Appearance in Lowndes County, Alabama, in the Spring of 1846," *NOMSJ*, 5 (1848), 366–69; Editors, "Black Tongue," *NOMSJ*, 1 (1844), 116; "Erysipelas," *NOMSJ*, 1 (1844), 61; and Fort, *Practice of Medicine*, 557–8.

60   Herbert H. Aptheker, *American Negro Slave Revolts in the South, 1626–1860*, (New York, 1943), 122. See data on prices and production collected by Lewis C. Gray,

History of Agriculture in the Southern United States to 1860, 2 vols. (New York, 1941) 2:1026–7, 1032–4.

61 Editors, "Black Tongue," 116.

62 Lovelace, "Black Tongue," 190. See also Drake, "Diseases of the Negro Population," 342, and for a description of a black tongue epidemic in Virginia consult Susan D. Smedes, *A Southern Planter: Social Life in the Old South* (New York, 1914), 66.

63 Ruse, "Account of an Endemic Fever," 366.

64 Roe, *Plague of Corn,* 112–13.

65 Editors, "Black Tongue," 116.

66 Puckett, "Erysipelatous Fever," 27–30.

67 Editors, "Black Tongue," 116. See also Puckett, "Erysipelatous Fever," 27; and Lovelace, " 'Black Tongue'," 194.

68 Editors, "Black Tongue," 116; McKee, "Reports from North Carolina," 410.

69 Puckett, "Erysipelatous Fever," 27.

70 Ibid., 27.

71 Thomas Ritter, *A Medical Manual and Medicine Chest Companion . . . ,* 3rd ed. (New York, 1859), 98; 53; "Erysipelas," 61; McKee, "Reports from North Carolina," 410; W. H. Coffin, *The Art of Medicine Simplified . . . .* (Wellsburg, Va., 1853), Fort, *Practice of Medicine,* 557–9. See also Alfred M. Folger, *The Family Physician; Being a Domestic Medical Work* (Spartanburg, S.C., 1845), 121, and Ritter, *Medical Chest Companion,* 537, for a description of St. Anthony's fire.

72 Fort, *Practice of Medicine,* 558–9.

73 Although it does appear as a cause of death in 1850 in the southern states of Mississippi, North Carolina, and Virginia. J. D. B. DeBow, ed., *Mortality Statistics of the Seventh Census of the United States, 1850. . . .* (Washington, D.C., 1854).

74 Grier, "Negro and his Diseases" 759–60; Robert Wilson Gibbes, "On Typhoid Pneumonia, as it Occurs in the Neighbourhood of Columbia, S. C.," *AJMS,* 4 (1852), 289; John Y. Bassett, "On the Climate and Diseases of Huntsville, Ala., and Its Vicinity, for the Year 1850," *SMR,* 2 (1850), 321; McGown, *Diseases of the South,* 28, 310; Warren D. Brickell, "Epidemic Typhoid Pneumonia Amongst Negroes," *NOMN,* 2 (1856), 548.

75 Brickell, "Epidemic Typhoid Pneumonia Amongst Negroes," 352. See also McGown, *Diseases of the South,* 308, and Gibbes, "Typhoid Pneumonia," 209.

76 Gibbes, "Typhoid Pneumonia." See also McGown, *Diseases of the South,* 309, and Ramsay, "Physiological Differences," 414.

77 Gibbes, "Typhoid Pneumonia," 291, 294. Note also the symptoms described by Brickell, "Typhoid Pneumonia," 532–40; Benjamin R. Jones, "On the Treatment of Pneumonia," *NOMSJ,* 7 (1850), 179–84; and Jesse Peebles, "A History of the Diseases of Craven's Creek, and its Vicinity, from 1848, down to the Present Time," *NOMSJ,* 15 (1858), 37–8.

78 McGown, *Diseases of the South,* 310–11.

79 Trowell, *Non-infective Disease in Africa* (London 1960), 358; M. R. Barakat, "Pellagra," *WHO,* 62 (1976), 127.

80 James C. Harris, "An Enquiry into the Nature and Existence of Typhoid Fever in the South," *NOMSJ,* 7 (1851), 679; Edward Montgomery, "A Few Remarks on Typhus Fever, Commonly Called Winter Fever," *NOMSJ,* 2 (1845), 22; *Minutes of the Proceedings of the Medical Society of North Carolina At Its Second Annual Meeting* (Raleigh, N.C., 1851), 11–12; Davenport, "Typhoid Fever," 581; Fort, *Practice of Medicine,* 558. No essential difference was really demonstrated between typhus and typhoid until a Philadelphia doctor (Gerhard) published his study in 1837. See also Edward H. Clarke et al., *A Century of American Medicine. 1776–1876* (Brinklow, Md., 1876), 24; John Duffy, "A Note on Antebellum Southern Nationalism and Medical Practice," *JSH,* 34 (1968), 274.

81 Davenport, "Typhoid Fever," 586–7, 581–3.

82 "Editor's Remarks," *NOMSJ*, 8 (1851), 588.

83 Ibid., 589–90.

84 A. V. Faut, "The History, – Symptoms and Characteristics of Typhoid Fever, as it Presented Itself to the Writer, – with an Outline of the Treatment," *NOMSJ*, 7 (1850), 184–5; N. H. Moragne, "A Brief Sketch of Twenty Cases of Typhoid Fever, Successfully Treated," *SMSJ*, n.s. 8 (1852), 389–92.

85 E. M. Pendleton, "General Report on the Topography, Climate and Diseases of Middle Georgia," *SMR*, 1 (1849), 322.

86 Samuel A. Cartwright, "Malum Egyptiacum, Cold Plague, Diptheria, or Black Tongue," *NOMSJ*, 16 (1859), 378.

87 R. T. Gibbs, "On the Medical Topography and Diseases of the Parish of De Soto, La.," *SMR*, 2 (1850), 194.

88 Gibbes, "Typhoid Pneumonia," 290; Cartwright, "Malum Egyptiacum," 378.

89 Monroe McGuire, "McGuire Diary, 1818–1850," Mississippi Department of Archives and History, 36–7.

90 Grier, "Negro and his Diseases," 760; John C. Gunn, *Domestic Medicine or Poor Man's Friend* (Louisville, 1842), 299–300. Consult also H. V. Wooten, "Dysentery Among Negroes," *NOMSJ*, 11 (1855), 448–56, who describes what appears to be the same puzzling affliction which progressed through many stages. Wooten argued that white plantation overseers contracted it as well.

91 Etheridge, *Butterfly Caste*, 8; Roe, *Plague of Corn*, 3, 5.

92 See, for example, William L. McCaa, "Observations on the Manner of Living and Diseases of the Slaves, on the Wateree River" (Inaugural Essay, University of Pennsylvania, 1822), 9; Cartwright, "Report on Diseases," 705; Postell, *Health of Slaves*, 108–9; and Owens, *Species of Property*, 60–1, who believes large numbers of slaves suffered from the dementia of pellagra.

93 By way of illustration, in Louisiana alone during the year 1849–1850, 164 deaths by drowning were recorded of which 70 percent (115) of the victims were black. DeBow, ed., *Mortality Statistics*, 106–7. In Mississippi of 86 deaths by drowning, 76 percent (66) of the total were Negroes. See also p. 151.

94 Lunsford P. Yandell, "Remarks on Struma Africana or the Disease Usually Called Negro Poison or Negro Consumption," *TJM*, 4 (1831), 93ff.; John R. Hicks, "African Consumption," *The Stethoscope*, 4 (1854), passim.

95 Cartwright, "Report on Diseases," 702. Cartwright, among others, spoke of skin afflictions as "scrofulous affections."

96 For an introduction to the debate over what has been termed "the Sambo personality" see the appropriate portions of *The Debate over Slavery; Stanley Elkins and His Critics*, ed. Ann J. Lane (Urbana, Ill., 1971).

Chapter 9. Selection for infection

1 Ian Taylor and John Knowelden, *Principles of Epidemiology* (Boston, 1964) 227.

2 Basil Hall, *Travels in North America in the Years 1827 and 1828*, 3 vols. (London, 1829), 3:204–5.

3 Samuel A. Cartwright, "Report on the Diseases and Physical Peculiarities of the Negro Race," *NOMSJ*, 7 (1851), 695.

4 Henry A. Ramsay, *The Necrological Appearances of Southern Typhoid Fever in the Negro* (Columbia County, Ga., 1852), 15–16.

5 Issac Weld, *Travels Through the States of North America . . . During the Years 1795, 1796, and 1797*, Johnson reprint ed. (New York, 1968), 245. See also "An Englishman in South Carolina," in *Travels in the Old South Selected from Periodicals of the Time*, ed. Eugene L. Schwaab, 2 vols. (Lexington, Ky., 1973), 2:565.

6   Charles William Janson, *The Stranger in America* . . . (1807), 357.
7   J. Hume Simons, *The Planter's Guide and Family Book of Medicine* (Charleston, S.C., 1848) 207–8.
8   Josiah C. Nott and George R. Gliddon, eds., *Indigenous Races of the Earth; or New Chapters of Ethnological Inquiry* (Philadelphia, 1857) 390.
9   Edward E. Mays, "Pulmonary Diseases," in *Textbook of Black-Related Diseases,* ed. Richard Allen Williams, (New York, 1975), 416.
10 M. Alfred Haynes, "The Gap in Health Status between Black and White Americans," in *Black-Related Diseases,* ed. Williams, 4–5 (tables), 6,7.
11 Ramsay, *Typhoid Fever,* 13; P. Tidyman, "A Sketch of the most Remarkable Diseases of the Negroes of the Southern States, with an Account of the Method of Treating them, Accompanied by Physiological Observations, " *Philadelphia Journal of the Medical and Physical Sciences,* 12 (1826), 317.
12 Thomas Adams and Benjamin G. Covino, "Racial Variations to a Standardized Cold Stress," *Journal of Applied Physiology,* 12 (1958), 9–12; Paul T. Baker, "Racial Differences in Heat Tolerance," *AJPA,* 16 (1958), 287–305, and "American Negro-White Differences in the Thermal Insulative Aspects of Body Fat," *HB,* 31 (1959), 316–24. See also Savitt's discussion of the Negro's "Tolerance of Cold and Heat," (*Medicine and Slavery, The Diseases and Health Care of Blacks in Antebellum Virginia* [Urbana, Ill., 1978], 35–41).
13 Mays, "Pulmonary Diseases," 428–9; John N. Lukens, "Hemoglobin S, the Pneumococcus, and the Spleen," *AJDC,* 123 (1972), 6–7; Ruth Andrea Seeler, William Metzger, and Maurice A. Mufson, "*Diplococcus pneumoniae* Infections in Children with Sickle Cell Anemia," *AJDC,* 123 (1972), 8–10; Elizabeth Barrett-Connor, "Pneumonia and Pulmonary Infarction in Sickle Cell Anemia," *JAMA,* 224 (1973), 997–1000.
14 William H. Tooley, "Respiratory Function and Pulmonary Disease in Older Children" (pp. 1311–12) and Murray Wittner, "Parasitic Disease" (pp. 808–9) in *Pediatrics,* ed. Henry L. Barnett, 15th ed. (New York, 1972); Asa C. Chandler and Clark P. Read, *Introduction to Parasitology with Special Reference to the Parasites of Men* (New York, 1961), 431.
15 But not always. In a few cases nutritional deficiencies actually appear to protect against illness. A paucity of the B-complex, for example, seems to increase resistance to some viral infections such as polio, infectious hepatitis and influenza. Taylor and Knowelden, *Principles of Epidemiology,* 226; R. K. Chandra and P. M. Newberne, *Nutrition, Immunity, and Infection: Mechanisms of Interactions* (New York, 1977), 7–9; M. J. Murray and A. B. Murray, "Starvation Suppression and Refeeding Activation of Infection: An Ecological Necessity?" *Lancet,* 1 (1977), 23–25.
16 Iancu Gontzea, *Nutrition and Anti-Infectious Defence,* 2nd ed. (Basel, 1974), 1–19; Chandra and Newberne, *Nutrition, Immunity, and Infection,* 1–7; Taylor and Knowelden, *Principles of Epidemiology,* 226.
17 Taylor and Knowelden, *Principles of Epidemiology,* 225.
18 Computed from data contained in J. L. Dawson and H. W. DeSaussure, *Census of the City of Charleston, South Carolina, for the Year 1848* (Charleston, S.C., 1849), 249, 252.
19 George I. Lythcott, Calvin H. Sinnette and Donald R. Hopkins, "Pediatrics," in *Black Related Diseases,* 163.
20 Nevin S. Scrimshaw, Carl E. Taylor, and John E. Gordon, *Interactions of Nutrition and Infection,* (Geneva, 1968) 94–5, 99; Gontzea, *Nutrition and Anti-Infectious Defence,* 162, 66.
21 Gontzea, *Nutrition and Anti-Infectious Defence,* 117–18; Scrimshaw, Taylor and Gordon, *Nutrition and Infection,* 102, 109; H. McFarlane and M. R. C. Path, "Malnutrition and Immunity," in *Immunological Aspects of Foods,* ed. Nicholas Catsimpoolas (Westport, Conn., 1977), 379.

22 See, for example, E. M. Pendleton, "Statistics of Diseases of Hancock County," *SMSJ*, n.s. 5 (1849), (table) 648; Cartwright, "Report on Diseases," 699–700; J. Strohart, "Some Thoughts on Malaria and Doubts as to its Existence as a Source of Disease," *CMJR*, 3 (1848), 41; Warren D. Brickell, "Epidemic Typhoid Pneumonia amongst Negroes," *NOMN*, 2 (1856), 548; and S. L. Grier, "The Negro and his Diseases," *NOMSJ*, 9 (1853), 758.

23 Consult Wyndham Bolling Blanton, *Medicine in Virginia in the Nineteenth Century* (Richmond, Va., 1933), 158.

24 Haynes, "Gap in Health Status," 7 (table), 8.

25 Max B. Lurie, *Resistance to Tuberculosis: Experimental Studies in Native and Acquired Defensive Mechanisms* (Cambridge, Mass., 1964), 116.

26 Dr. Robert Wilson Gibbes of Columbia, S. C. to Governor R. F. W. Allston, March 6, 1858, *DBR*, 24 (1858), 323; Cartwright, "Report on Diseases," 699–700.

27 Gontzea, *Nutrition and Anti-Infectious Defence*, 44, 117–18; Scrimshaw, Taylor, and Gordon, *Nutrition and Infection*, 94–95.

28 Scrimshaw, Taylor, and Gordon, *Nutrition and Infection*, 128; Chandra and Newberne, *Nutrition, Immunity, and Infection*, 45, 174–5.

29 Gontzea, *Nutrition and Anti-Infectious Defence*, 44.

30 Ibid., 33.

31 J. M. Barrier, "Tuberculosis among our Negroes in Louisiana," *NOMSJ*, 55 (1902), 226–7.

32 C. St. C. Guild, *Tuberculosis in the Negro* (New York, 1935), 7; Stevenson Lyle Cummins, *Primitive Tuberculosis* (London, 1939), 14–22; Richard Gallagher, *Diseases that Plague Modern Man: A History of Ten Communicable Diseases* (New York, 1969), 8.

33 Mays, "Pulmonary Diseases," 418; Haynes, "Gap in Health Status," 6.

34 Gontzea, *Nutrition and Anti-Infectious Defence*, 34–5, 61, 114–15, 136–7. 138–9; Jan Mayer, "Nutrition and Tuberculosis, Diet and Susceptibility to Tuberculosis," *PM*, 50 (1971), 53–6. See also Thomas McKeown, *The Modern Rise of Population* (New York, 1976), passim, who finds a better diet in England responsible for the decline in tuberculosis mortality during the second half of the nineteenth century. Finally consult E. Palermo ("Nutrition, Tuberculosis and Living Conditions," in *Hunger and Food*, (London, 1958) ed. Josué de Castro, 105–13) who correlates a high incidence of tuberculosis in Argentina with a poor diet.

35 Gontzea, *Nutrition and Anti-Infectious Defence*, 33.

36 See for example, "Cartwright on the Negro Constitution," *Stethoscope and Virginia Medical Gazette* 2 (1852), 697, and Josiah C. Nott, "Statistics of Southern State Population with Special Reference to Life Insurance," *DR*, 4 (1847), 281–2.

37 Thus examples are William Dosite Postell, *The Health of Slaves on Southern Plantations* (Baton Rouge, La., 1951), 80; and Felice Swados, "Negro Health on the Antebellum Plantation," *BHM*, 10 (1941), 471. Savitt, *Medicine and Slavery*, 41–5, on the other hand, reasons much as we do.

38 Computed from data in Dawson and DeSaussure, *Census of the City of Charleston*.

39 The following pathological description of tuberculosis is based upon F. MacFarlane Burnet and David O. White, *Natural History of Infectious Disease*, 4th ed. (Cambridge, Engl., 1972), 213ff; Paul B. Beeson and Walsh McDermott, *Textbook of Medicine*, 2 vols., 13th ed. (Philadelphia, 1971), 1:638–43; and Rene Dubois and Jean Dubos, *The White Plague: Tuberculosis, Man and Society* (Boston, 1952), passim.

40 Burnet and White, *Natural History of Infectious Disease*, 218.

41 Dubos and Dubos, *White Plague*, 191.

42 Rene Dubos, *Man Adapting*, 175.

43 Ibid., 175.

44 William H. McNeill, *Plagues and Peoples* (Garden City, N.Y., 1976), 61.

45 Burnet and White, *Natural History of Infectious Disease*, 219.

46 William W. Stead, "Tuberculosis," in *Harrison's Principles of Internal Medicine*, ed. Maxwell M. Wintrobe et al., 2 vols, 7th ed. (New York, 1974), I:863.
47 Daniel Drake, "Diseases of the Negro Population . . . in a Letter to Rev. Mr. Pinney," *SMSJ* I (1845) 341; Richard H. Shryock, ed., *Letters of Richard D. Arnold, M.D., 1808–1876* (Durham, N.C., 1929), 67; C. H. Jordan, "Thoughts on Cachexia Africana or Negro Consumption," *TJM*, 4 (1832), 18 and passim; H. Perry Pope, "A Dissertation on the Professional Management of Negroes" (unpublished thesis, Medical College of South Carolina, 1837), 9; A. H. Buchanan, "Remarks on Negro Consumption," *Western Journal of Medicine and Surgery*, 2 (1840), 405–18; John Hicks, "African Consumption," *The Stethoscope and Virginia Medical Gazette*, 4 (1854), 625–9; Lunsford P. Yandell, "Remarks on Struma Africana or the Disease usually called Negro Poison, or Negro Consumption," *TJM*, 4 (1831), 83.
48 Yandell, "Struma Africana," 93.
49 Jordan, "Cachexia Africana," 18; Buchanan, "Negro Consumption," 407.
50 Yandell, "Struma Africana," 97, 93.
51 Ibid., 94. See also Jordan, "Cachexia Africana," 20; Buchanan, "Negro Consumption," 413.
52 Dubos and Dubos, *White Plague*, 191.
53 Julian Herman Lewis, *The Biology of the Negro* (Chicago, 1942), 103.
54 E. Cochrane, "Tuberculosis in the Tropics," *Tropical Diseases Bulletin*, 34 (1937), 752.
55 Mays, "Pulmonary Diseases," 419.
56 Simons, *Planter's Guide*, 173–5; Thomas Ewell, *American Family Physician . . .* (Washington, D.C., 1824), 144.
57 Dawson and DeSaussure, *Census of the City of Charleston*.
58 Brickell, "Typhoid Pneumonia," 545, 548. George W. Comstock, "Tuberculosis," in *Preventive Medicine and Public Health*, ed. Philip D. Startwell, *Maxey-Rosenau Preventive Medicine and Public Health*, 10th ed. (New York, 1973), 175, points out that there is more active tuberculosis in blacks than whites under the age of forty-five.

Chapter 10. Cholera and race

1 Roderick E. McGrew, "The Cholera Epidemic and Social History," *BHM*, 34 (1960), 61–73, and *Russia and the Cholera, 1823–1832* (Madison, Wisc., 1965), 4; Charles E. Rosenberg, *The Cholera Years: The United States in 1832, 1849 and 1866* (Chicago, 1962), 1, 13; Charles C. J. Carpenter, "Treatment of Cholera – Tradition and Authority versus Science, Reason, and Humanity," *JHM*, 139 (1976), 154–5.
2 For two fine recent works dealing with the impact of new diseases on inexperienced peoples, see Alfred W. Crosby, *The Columbian Exchange: Biological and Cultural Consequences of 1492* (Westport Conn., 1972) and William H. McNeill, *Plagues and Peoples* (Garden City, N.Y., 1976.)
3 Nathaniel F. Pierce and Arabindo Mondal, "Clinical Features of Cholera," in *Cholera*, eds. Dhiman Barua and William Burrows (Philadelphia 1974), 212–13, Arthur H. Gale, *Epidemic Diseases* (Baltimore, 1959), 66, and Rosenberg, *Cholera Years*, 2–3, all provide descriptions of the clinical course of acute cholera. The former two are highly technical, while the latter is aimed at the layman. For a nineteenth-century description of the disease in classic form, see J. Hume Simons, *The Planter's Guide And Family Book of Medicine* (Charleston, S.C., 1848) 205–07.
4 August Hirsch, *Handbook of Geographical and Historical Pathology*, 3 vols. (London, 1883–86), I, 471–2; James Christie, "Notes on the Cholera Epidemics in East Africa," *Lancet*, 1 (1871), 186–8.
5 Oscar Felsenfeld, *The Epidemiology of Tropical Diseases* (Springfield, Ill., 1966), 116. For an appreciation of the complexity of the problem, see Rolf Freter, "Gut-Associated Immunity to Cholera," in Barua and Burrows, eds., *Cholera*, 315–31.

6 John Duffy, "The Impact of Asiatic Cholera on Pittsburgh, Wheeling, and Charleston," *Western Pennsylvania Historical Magazine*, 47 (1964), 201.
7 Samuel H. Adams, "Our Forefathers Tackle an Epidemy – the Cholera of 1832," *New York Folklore Quarterly*, 3 (1947), 94.
8 *The Cholera Bulletin*, conducted by an Association of Physicians. V.1, nos. 1–24 (1832) reprinted by Arno Press, 1972.
9 Rosenberg, *Cholera Years*, 55.
10 Ibid., 59–60.
11 Daniel Drake, *An Account of the Epidemic Cholera as it Appeared in Cincinnati* (Cincinnati, 1832), 19–20.
12 José García de Arboleya, *Manual de la Isla de Cuba: Compendio de su historia, geografía estadística, y administracion* (Havana, 1852), 51; Captain-General Ricafort to the First Secretary of State, Havana, 27 Aug. 1833 (Estraordinario Reservado), Madrid; Archivo Historico Nacional, Estado, Leg. 6374.
13 S. R. Bruesch, "The Disasters and Epidemics of a River Town: Memphis, Tenessee, 1819–1879," *BLMA*, 40 (1950) 297; William D. Jenkins, "The Cholera in 1849," *PMHS*, 7 (1903), 273.
14 Rachel O'Connor to David Weeks, St. Francisville, La., 26 Aug. 1832, in David Weeks and Family Papers (Louisiana State University).
15 Erasmus D. Fenner, "Special Report on Epidemic Cholera, in the City of New Orleans, During the Year 1850," *SMR*, 2 (1850), 105.
16 W. Mazyck Porcher to Robert Marion Deveaux, 15 Sept. 1836, Samuel Porcher Gaillard Journal (University of South Carolina).
17 James P. Carson, *Life, Letters and Speeches of James Louis Petigru, the Union Man of South Carolina* (Washington, D.C., 1920), 161.
18 Ibid., 161.
19 Ibid., 161.
20 Mary Elizabeth Cheves to Anne Lovell, 20 Sept. 1834 in Anne Lovell Papers (Duke University).
21 Alexander Porter to John King, Oakland Plantation, 8 July 1833 in George M. Lester Collection (Louisiana State University).
22 Samuel A. Cartwright, *Some Additional Observations Relative to the Cholera, and a Prescription for the Treatment of that Disease in all its Stages* (Natchez 1833), 7; C. H. Stone, "Report on Epidemic Cholera, in the Vicinity of Natchez," *SMR*, 1 (1849), 368; Erasmus D. Fenner, "Report on Epidemic Cholera in the City of New Orleans 1848–1849," *SMR*, 1 (1849), 153; Joseph Bieller to Jacob Bieller, 7 June, 1833 in Alonzo Snyder Collection (Louisiana State University); Joseph I. Waring, "Asiatic Cholera in South Carolina," *BHM*, 40 (1966), 461.
23 Norbert Hirschhorn et al., "The Treatment of Cholera" in Barua and Burrows, eds., *Cholera*, 235. For "Cholera Advances in Historical Perspective," see Robert Pollitzer in *Proceedings of the Cholera Research Symposium* (Washington, D.C., 1965), 380–7.
24 Norman Howard-Jones, "Cholera Therapy in the Nineteenth Century," *JHM*, 27 (1972), 373 and passim. See also Frederick Eberson, A Great Purging – Cholera or Calomel?" *Filson Club History Quarterly*, 50 (1976), 28–35.
25 Fenner, "Epidemic Cholera . . . 1848–1849," 143.
26 Robert Partin, "T. H. Roddy: A Nineteenth Century Physician of Old James County, Tennessee," *Tennessee Historical Quarterly*, 11 (1952), 200.
27 Letter dated 19 May 1849, John Monroe Papers (Duke University).
28 Ibid., Rachel O'Connor to Mrs. Mary C. Weeks, St. Francisville, 7 Nov. 1832, in David Weeks and Family Papers (Louisiana State University).
29 Review of C. B. New, "On the Treatment of Cholera on Plantations, *NOMSJ*, 7 (1850), 212; Leland A. Lanridge, "Asiatic Cholera in Louisiana, 1832–1873," (Masters Thesis, Louisiana State University, 1953), 76–7.

30   Fenner, "Special Report on Epidemic Cholera . . . 1850," 105–6.
31   Felice Swados, "Negro Health on the Antebellum Plantations," *Bulletin of the History of Medicine,* 19 (1941), 462–72.
32   Fenner, "Special Report on Epidemic Cholera . . . 1850," 106.
33   Cited in Guion Griffis Johnson, *A Social History of the Sea Islands* . . . . (Chapel Hill, N.C., 1930), 94.
34   "Cholera in Richmond Va.," *CMJR,* 9 (1854), 809–10.
35   P. C. Gaillard and R. A. Kinloch, "Report on the Cholera in Charleston in 1852–53," *Proceedings of the South Carolina Medical Association* (Charleston, S.C., 1854), 27.
36   René La Roche, *Yellow Fever, Considered in its Historical, Pathological, Etiological and Therapeutic Relations,* 2 vols. (Philadelphia, 1855), 1:576; Charles Belot, *The Yellow Fever at Havana; Its Nature and its Treatment,* (Savannah, Ga., 1878) 30.
37   Ralph Butterfield, "Health of Negroes," *DR,* 25 (1858), 571–2.
38   Particularly perceptive and vocal in this regard was Samuel A. Cartwright. See his *Observations Relative to the Cholera,* 7, along with his warnings in the *Concordia Intelligencer,* 21 April 1849 cited in Lanridge, "Asiatic Cholera in Louisiana," 81. Finally see his examination of *The Pathology and Treatment of Cholera* (New Orleans, 1849), 13–14.
39   Richard H. Shryock, *Medicine in America: Historical Essays* (Baltimore, 1966), 65.
40   Rosenberg, *The Cholera Years,* 116.
41   C. G. Forshey to Major St. John R. Liddel, 5 Oct. 1848, in Moses St. John Richardson Liddell and Family Papers (Louisiana State University).
42   A. L. Howard to Annette Koch, 18 June 1854, in Christian D. Koch and Family Papers (Louisiana State University).
43   Rosenberg, *The Cholera Years,* 59–61.
44   Letter dated 20 Jan. 1833, Brashear Family Papers (University of North Carolina).
45   Rosalie Bridget Hart Priour, "Reminiscences," (University of Texas), 28.
46   Physicians, for example, such as Joseph Jones, then City Health officer of Nashville (*Republican Banner,* Nashville, 13 June 1867) predicted outbreaks among the freedmen.
47   Lawrence J. Friedman, "Purifying the White Man's Country: the American Colonization Society Reconsidered 1816–40," *Societas,* 6 (1976), 16.
48   Data for the ensuing discussion of cholera in Mississippi have been drawn from the manuscript Census of 1850 for the state of Mississippi.
49   Ibid. However, James D. B. DeBow (*Statistical View of the United States . . . being a Compendium of the Seventh Census* [Washington, D.C., 1854], 153) shows only 587 deaths for the state. Undoubtedly the discrepancy is due in large part to the careless manner in which federal marshals failed at times to distinguish between "cholera" and cholera morbus as causes of death. One suspects that the manuscript census figure of 655 is probably closer to the truth, because, early in the epidemic, cholera was frequently diagnosed as cholera morbus.
50   Waring, "Asiatic Cholera in South Carolina," 464. Charleston's population numbered about 13,000 whites and 16,700 blacks at the time.
51   Gaillard and Kinloch, "Cholera in Charleston," 32.
52   Ibid., 32–3.
53   Todd L. Savitt, *Medicine and Slavery: The Diseases and Health Care of Blacks in Antebellum Virginia* (Urbana Ill., 1978), 227–8.
54   U.S. Surgeon-General's Office, *Report on Epidemic Cholera in the Army of the United States, During the Year 1866* (Washington, D.C., 1867), xiv–xv.
55   Even as late as 1875, a physician could blast his colleagues for being "unable to distinguish between cholera Asiatica, cholera sporadica, cholera morbus, and some forms of pernicious intermittent and remittent fevers. These gentlemen will tell one *'that they know cholera, for they have treated it all their lives'* and they are seemingly oblivious to the fact that America has known [only] epidemics" of the disease. Ely

McClellan, *A Note of Warning; Lessons to be Learned from the Cholera Facts of the Past Year, and from Recent Cholera Literature* (Louisville, Ky., 1876), 32.
56 Felsenfeld, *Tropical Diseases*, 112.
57 R. B. Hornick et al., "The Broad Street Pump Revisited: Response of Volunteers to Ingested Cholera Vibrios," *BNYAM*, 47 (1971), 1186–90; Eugene J. Gangarosa, "The Epidemiology of Cholera: Past and Present," *BNYAM*, 1147; Jan Holgren and Ann-Mari Svennerholm, "Mechanisms of Disease and Immunity in Cholera: A Review," *Journal of Infectious Diseases*, 136 Supplement (1977), 105.
58 Richard A. Cash, Jamiul Alam, and K. M. Toahu "Gastric Acid Secretion in Cholera Patients," *Lancet*, 2 (1970), 1192.
59 Felsenfeld, *Tropical Diseases*, 116.
60 Eugene J. Gangarosa and Wiley H. Mosley, "Epidemiology and Surveillance of Cholera," in *Cholera*, eds. Barua and Burrows, 385–6; Oscar Felsenfeld, *Synopsis of Clinical Tropical Medicine*, (St. Louis, 1965) 33; I. H. Rosenberg et al., "Nutritional Studies in Cholera; The Influence of Nutritional Status on Susceptibility to Infection," in *Proceedings of the Cholera Research Symposium* (Washington, D.C., 1965), 71–2; Charles C. Carpenter, "Cholera," in *A Manual of Tropical Medicine*, eds. George W. Hunter, William W. Frye, and J. Clyde Swartzwelder, 4th ed. (Philadelphia, 1966), 169.

Introduction to Part IV

1 "Medical Practice in the Old South," *South Atlantic Quarterly*, 29 (1930), 165.

Chapter 11. Slave medicine

1 Samuel A. Cartwright, "Alcohol and the Ethiopian," *NOMSJ*, 10 (1853), 162.
2 Benjamin A. Botkin, ed., *Lay My Burden Down: A Folk History of Slavery* (Chicago, 1945), 71–2.
3 Royce McCrary, ed., "The Use of Home Medical Books in Antebellum Georgia: A Letter by John MacPherson Berrien," *JMAG*, 64 (1973), 137–8.
4 Ibid.
5 Ewell, for example, was severely censured by the profession for publishing *American Family Physician*, (Washington, D.C., 1824). Mary Louise Marshall, "Plantation Medicine," *BTMF* 1 (1942), 57.
6 Botkin, ed., *Lay My Burden Down*, 86.
7 Warren D. Brickell, "Epidemic Typhoid Pneumonia Amongst Negroes" *NOMN* 2 (1856) 546.
8 George P. Rawick, *The American Slave: A Composite Autobiography*, 19 vols. (Westport Conn., 1973), 4:294. Another slave also reported a morning dose of garlic and rum was administered to "Keep us 'wholesome'." Francis N. Boney, ed., *Slave Life in Georgia: A Narrative of the Life, Sufferings, and Escape of John Brown, A Fugitive Slave* (Savannah 1972), 7.
9 David Doar, "Rice and Rice Planting in the South Carolina Low Country," *Charleston Museum*, 8 (1936), 32.
10 Rawick, ed., *American Slave*, 3:175.
11 Ibid., 2:242.
12 Charles S. Johnson, *Shadow of the Plantation* (Chicago, 1934), 196.
13 Robert Collins, "Essay on the Management of Slaves," *SC*, 12 (1854).
14 Rawick, ed., *American Slave*, 4:11; Chas L. Perdue, Thomas E. Barden, and Robert K. Phillips, eds., *Weevils in the Wheat: Interviews with Virginia Ex-slaves* (Charlottesville, Va., 1976), 82–3.
15 Perdue, Barden, and Phillips, eds., *Weevils in the Wheat*, 81–3; James Lindsay Smith, *Autobiography of James L. Smith* (Norwich, Conn., 1881; reprint ed., Miami, Fla., 1969), 10, 21.

16 Weymouth T. Jordan, "Plantation Medicine in the Old South," *Alabama Review*, 3 (1950), 87.

17 Affleck's Cotton Plantation Record and Account Book cited in Marshall, "Plantation Medicine," 52.

18 Judge Sharkey's agreement with Overseer, 1 Jan. 1842. Francis Garvin Davenport, ed., "Judge Sharkey Papers," *MVHR*, 20 (1933), 76.

19 John Spencer Bassett, *The Southern Plantation Overseer as Revealed in His Letters* (Northampton, Mass., 1925), 28. Compare with Andrew Flinn, "Rules for the Overseer," in Andrew Flinn Plantation Diary (University of North Carolina).

20 "Management of a Southern Plantation: Rules Enforced on the Rice Estate of P. C. Weston, Esq. of South Carolina," *DBR*, 22 (1857), 38.

21 Vernie Alton Moody, "Slavery on Louisiana Sugar Plantations," *LHQ*, 7 (1924), 272; Theodora Britton Marshall and Gladys Crail Evans, eds., "Plantation Report from the Papers of Levin R. Marshall of Richmond; Natchez Mississippi," *JMH*, 3 (1941), 45–55.; John Houston to William Allen, 29 Sept. 1861, Springfield, La. in Allen Family Papers (N.C. Dept. of Archives).

22 See for example the series of articles by John S. Wilson such as "The Negro–His Peculiarities as to Disease," *AMCP*, n.s. 3 (1859), 228–9; "Peculiarities and Diseases of Negroes," *DBR*, 28 (1860), 597–9 (1860), 112–5; "Food, Clothing, and General Rules of Health," *DR*, 28 (1860), 597–9, and "The Negro–His Diet, Clothing, etc.," *AMCP*, 3(1859), 197–8.

23 Bassett, *The Southern Plantation Overseer*, 28–9.

24 Brickell, "Typhoid Pneumonia," 546.

25 Complaints of self-treatment were also aimed at whites. See Samuel A. Cartwright, *Statistical Medicine: of Numerical Analysis Applied to the Investigation of Morbid Actions . . .* (Louisville, Ky., 1848) 16.

26 Daniel Drake, "Diseases of the Negro Population," *NOMSJ*, 1 (1845), 584. Also on occasion the literature speaks of physicians resident on the plantation. See Rawick, ed., *American Slave*, 5:31.

27 William D. Postell, "A Review of Slave Care on Southern Plantations," *VMM*, 79 (1952), 103–4.

28 Quoted in Walter Fisher, "Physicians and Slavery in the Antebellum Southern Medical Journal," *JHM*, 23 (1968), 38. Apparently typical in the Savannah region of the 1840s was a physician's annual commitment to a plantation for $1.50 per head. Louis Manigault, "Records of a Rice Plantation in the Georgia Lowlands," Georgia Historical Society, entry 15, April, 1845.

29 This section is based on the Butler journal, summary of medical costs from May 20 to 22 Nov. 1843. Entry for Nov. 22, 1843. In Thomas Butler and Family Papers, Louisiana State University. For other examples of medical costs see Edwin Adams Davis, *Plantation Life in the Florida Parishes of Louisiana, 1836–1846, as reflected in the Diary of Bennet H. Barrow* (New York, 1943), 42, and Alfred H. Conrad and John R. Meyer, "The Economics of Slavery in the Antebellum South," *Journal of Political Economy*, 66 (1958) reprinted in their book, *The Economics of Slavery and other Studies in Econometric History* (Chicago, 1964), 43–92.

30 Richard H. Shryock, ed., *Letters of Richard D. Arnold*, 164, n. 4.

31 Ibid., 34. Consult also Martha Carolyn Mitchell, "Health and the Medical Profession in the Lower South, 1845–1860," *JSH*, 10 (1944), 435.

32 Mitchell, "Health and the Medical Profession," 435; Victor H. Bassett, "Plantation Medicine," *JMAG*, 29 (1940), 120; Marshall and Evans, eds., "Levin R. Marshall," 50.

33 John Q. Anderson, "Dr. James Green Carson, Antebellum Planter of Mississippi and Louisiana," *JMH*, 18 (1956), 253.

34 Quoted in Felice Swados, "Negro Health on the Antebellum Plantations," *BHM*, 19 (1941), 472.

35 Drake, "Diseases of the Negro Population . . . in a Letter to Rev. Mr. Pinney,"
    SMSJ, 1 (1845), 342.
36 Lewright Sikes, "Medical Care for Slaves: A Preview of the Welfare State," *GHQ*, 52
    (1968), 406.
37 Victor H. Bassett, "The Medical Career of John LeConte 1818–1891, who was a
    Physician in Savannah from 1842–1846, with a Discussion of the Status of Medical
    Practice at that Time" *JMAG*, 29 (1940), 155.
38 Most planters vaccinated against smallpox and many plantation books such as that
    of McDonald Furman (Duke University) bear an entry to that effect. Indeed after
    1801 Jenner's vaccine was first used for slaves. Whites followed suit a few years
    later. Bassett, "Plantation Medicine," 117–18.
39 Letter of Dr. S. A. Cartwright, Natchez, 27 June 1844 in John Knight Papers (Duke
    University).
40 J. Hume Simons, *The Planter's Guide and Family Book of Medicine* (Charleston, S.C.,
    1848), 207–10; H. G. Davenport, "Observations on Typhoid Fever," *NOMSJ*, 8
    (1852), 576–87; Robert J. Draughton, "Clothing for Field Hands," *SC*, 7:3 (1850), and
    "Houses of Negroes–Habits, Modes of Living, etc.," *SC*, 8:5 (1850).
41 "Robert Wilson Gibbes to Governor R. F. W. Allston, March 6, 1858," published in
    DR, 24 (1858), 321–2; Doar, "Rice and Rice Planting," 31; Marshall and Evans, eds.,
    "Levin R. Marshall," 54; Ronald Killion and Charles Waller, eds., *Slavery Time When I
    was Chillun Down on Marster's Plantation* (Savannah, 1973), 52; A Mississippi Planter,
    "Management of Negroes upon Southern Estates," *DR*, 10 (1851), 624; Sikes, "Medi-
    cal Care for Slaves," 407.
42 Sikes, "Medical Care for Slaves," 407; William Dosite Postell, *The Health of Slaves on
    Southern Plantations* (Baton Rouge, La., 1951), 129.
43 Plantation records are full of "shopping lists" for medical supplies ranging from
    epsom salts to plaster for wounds. For examples, see Telefair family papers, Thorn
    Island Plantation item 200 (Georgia Historical Society), and Robert Carter papers,
    Letterbook VI (Duke University).
44 Postell, *Health of Slaves*, 132–4.
45 Postell, "Review of Slave Care," 104; "Negro Hospital," *CMJR*, 15 (1860), 850–1;
    Bassett, "Plantation Medicine," 116; Sikes, "Medical Care for Slaves," 408; Ralph
    Betts Flanders, *Plantation Slavery in Georgia* (Chapel Hill, N.C., 1933), 165.
46 Flanders, *Plantation Slavery in Georgia*, 165; Joe Gray Taylor, *Negro Slavery in Louisiana*
    (Baton Rouge, La., 1963), 122; Sikes, "Medical Care for Slaves," 408; Orville W.
    Taylor, *Negro Slavery in Arkansas*, (Durham, N.C., 1958), 163–4; Joseph Ioor Waring,
    A History of Medicine in South Carolina, 3 vols. (Columbia, S.C., 1964–71), 2:5; Samuel
    Cartwright, "The Diseases of Negroes–Pulmonary Congestions, Pneumonia, etc.,"
    DBR, 11 (1851), 209; "Gibbes to Allston," 323; John Wesley Monette, "An Inaugural
    Thesis on the Endemial Bilious Fever, as it occurs in the victinity of Natchez" (un-
    published thesis, Transylvania University, 1825), 5–6.
47 Quoted in Postell, *Health of Slaves*, 141.
48 Marshall, "Plantation Medicine," 55.
49 Consult for example James Silk Buckingham, *The Slave States of America*, 2 vols.
    (London, 1842), 1:402.
50 H. A. Ramsay, *The Necrological Appearances of Southern Typhoid Fever in the Negro*
    (Columbia County, Ga., 1852), 14.
51 Quoted in Jordan, "Plantation Medicine," 89.
52 Shryock, "Medical Practice in the Old South," 175.
53 Bennett H. Wall, "Medical Care of Ebenezer Pettigrew's Slaves," *MVHR*, 37 (1950),
    464.
54 Marshall, "Plantation Medicine," 54; A. J. Leftwich to John Craighead, Hot Springs,
    Ark., 11 July, 1841, in Edward Gay Papers (Louisiana State University).
55 See W. G. Little, "Typhoid Fever," *NOMSJ*, 12 (1855), 146.

56 "Gibbes to Allston," 322.
57 Rawick, ed., *American Slave*, 2:24.
58 Perdue, Barden and Phillips, eds., *Weevils in the Wheat*, 310.
59 Not that the white doctors did not experiment. "They's go around in buggies and on horse. Them that rode had saddle pockets just filled with little bottles and loss of them. He'd try one medicine and if it didn't do no good he' try another until it did do good." Killion and Waller, eds., *Slavery Time*, 31.
60 Victor H. Bassett, "Popular Remedies Used by Southern People," *JMAG*, 29 (1940), 22.
61 James H. Letcher, "The Treatment of Some Diseases by the 'Old Time' Negro," *Railway Surgical Journal*, 17 (1910–11), 173; Bassett, "Plantation Medicine," 121.
62 Many ex-slaves maintained this attitude. "I still believes in them old home-made medicines," reported one, "and I don't believe in so many doctors." Killion and Waller, eds., *Slavery Time*, 32. Doubtless this was due in part to plantation experiences. "Dat calomel what dat doctor would give us would purty nigh kill us," lamented another ex-slave. Rawick, ed., *American Slave*, V:216.
63 Thus "root doctoring" and "conjure doctoring" were not always separable. For the latter see J. E. McTeer and K. Nickerson, *High Sheriff of the Low County* (Beauford, S. C., 1970), 22, 24; A. M. Bacon, "Conjuring and Conjure Doctors," *Southern Workman*, 24 (1895), 193–4, 209–11; Letcher, " 'Old Time' Negro," 17; Leona Herron, "Conjuring and Conjure-Doctors," *Southern Workman*, 24 (1895); D. E. Cadwallader and F. J. Wilson, "Folklore Medicine among Georgia's Piedmont Negroes After the Civil War," *GHQ*, 42 (1965), 217–27; E. A. Barker, "Traditional African Views on Health and Disease," *Central African Journal of Medicine*, 19 (1973), 8–82, and James Haskins, *Witchcraft, Mysticism and Magic in the Black World* (New York, 1974).
64 Eugene D. Genovese, *Roll, Jordan, Roll: The World the Slaves Made* (New York, 1974), 225.
65 Letter to T. Keitt, 20 March 1860 in Thomas Ellison Keitt Papers (Duke University).
66 Quoted in Genovese, *Roll, Jordan, Roll*, 226.
67 Some blacks became public folk practitioners. Following is an oft-quoted advertisement by one written in 1860. "T. Edwards is naturally a doctor . . . My mother was her mother's seventh daughter, and I am her seventh son . . . I am a seven month's child, and walked seven months after I was born, and had shed my teeth seven times." As Shryock ("Medical Practice in the Old South," 172) observed "such professional qualifications must, in certain circles, have proved irresistible." Other blacks were regular practitioners. For a list of these individuals and their accomplishments, see Joel Augustus Rogers, *Africa's Gift to America: The Afro-American in the Making and Saving of the United States* (New York, 1961), 222–5, and for a sketch of *The History of the Negro in Medicine* from the slave days to the present, see Herbert M. Morais (New York, 1967).
68 Ramsay, *Typhoid Fever*, 21.
69 H. Perry Pope, "A Dissertation on the Professional Management of Negro Slaves" (thesis, Medical College of South Carolina, 1837), 14–15.
70 Fisher, "Physicians and Slavery," 43–4. Wall, "Medical Care of Ebenezer Pettigrew's Slaves," 468, for example, points out that Pettigrew, who hired physicians to deliver babies, had a low level of black infant mortality on his plantation. See also Shryock, "Medical Practice in the Old South," 174–5.
71 J. Cam. Massie, *A Treatise on the Eclectic Southern Practice of Medicine* (Philadelphia, 1854) 455–6.
72 Wall, "Medical Care of Ebenezer Pettigrew's Slaves," 461.
73 See Editor, "Dr. Cartwright on the Unity of the Human Race," *Plantation*, 1 (1860), 654–5.

74 "Cartwright on the Negro Constitution," *Stethoscope and Virginia Medical Gazette* 2 (1852) 700.
75 E. M. Pendleton, "General Report on the Topography, Climate, and Diseases of Middle Georgia," *SMR*, 1(1849), 337.
76 Ramsay, *Typhoid Pneumonia*, 15; Todd L. Savitt, *Medicine and Slavery*, (Urbana, Ill., 1978) 176–8; Henry Clay Bruce, *The New Man, Twenty Nine Years a Slave*, (York, Pa., 1895) 57; Newbell Niles Puckett, *Folk Beliefs of the Southern Negro* (Chapel Hill, N.C., 1926), 359.
77 W. S. Forwood, "Serpent Worship among the Negroes," *DBR*, 30 (1861), 98.
78 A. P. Merrill, "Plantation Medicine," *NOMN*, 6 (1859), 226. See also Bassett, "Plantation Medicine," 116.
79 Dr. Walter Wade Papers, 5 June 1851 (Mississippi Dept. of Archives).
80 Juriah Harris "What Constitutes Unsoundness in the Negro?" *Savannah Journal of Medicine*, 1 (1859), 289–95, 2 (1859), 10–16.
81 Marshall, "Plantation Medicine," 48.
82 Fisher, "Physicians and Slavery," 45.
83 Ibid., 48. Consult Duffy, *The Healers: The Rise of the Medical Establishment* (New York, 1976) 136–9, for details of Sim's career.
84 Duffy, *The Healers*, 139.
85 Ibid., 142.
86 Jordan, "Plantation Medicine in the Old South," 85; F. N. Boney, "Doctor Thomas Hamilton: Two Views of a Gentleman of the Old South," *Phylon*, 28 (1967), 288–92; L. A. Chamerovzow, ed., *Slave Life in Georgia, A Narrative of the Life, Sufferings, and Escape of John Brown, a Fugitive Slave, now in England* (London, 1855) 7; Savitt, *Medicine and Slavery*, 176–8.

Chapter 12. Physicians versus the slaves

1 Henry A. Ramsay, *The Necrological Appearances of Southern Typhoid Fever in the Negro* (Columbia County, Ga., 1974) 13.
2 Cartwright, "Alcohol and the Ethiopian," *NOMSJ*, 10 (1853), 150.
3 Excellent studies that treat in detail America's changing perception of the black over time include Winthrop D. Jordan, *White over Black: American Attitudes Toward the Negro, 1550–1812* (Chapel Hill, N.C., 1968), William Stanton, *The Leopard's Spots: Scientific Attitudes Toward Race in America 1815–59* (Chicago, 1960), and George M. Fredrickson, *The Black Image in the White Mind: The Debate on Afro-American Character and Destiny, 1817–1914* (New York, 1971).
4 John Duffy, "A Note on Ante-Bellum Southern Nationalism and Medical Practice," *JSH*, 34 (1968) 267.
5 John S. Haller, "The Negro and the Southern Physician: A Study of Medical and Racial Attitudes 1800–1860," *Journal of Medical History*, 16 (1972), 238; James O. Breeden, "States-Rights Medicine in the Old South," *BNYAM*, 52 (1976), 355.
6 Unless otherwise noted, the following paragraphs dealing with the American school of ethnology are based on the appropriate sections of Jordan, *White Over Black*; Stanton, *The Leopard's Spots*; Fredrickson, *Black Image*; and Donald A. Swan, "The American School of Ethnology," *Mankind Quarterly*, 12 (1971), 78–98. Lest the impression is left that the quest for a scientific sanction for black inferiority was a strictly American or a peculiarly southern affair, let us hasten to add that few Western scientists doubted that whites were intrinsically superior to blacks. The continued existence of slavery in the United States, however, made the question a particularly urgent one for North Americans. Thus the somewhat parochial treatment that follows.

7 [Charles Caldwell], "An Essay on the Causes of the Variety of Complexion and Figure in the Human Species, "*American Review of History and Politics*, 2 (1811), 128–66.

8 Samuel G. Morton, *Crania Americana; or, A Comparative View of the Skulls of Various Aboriginal Nations of North and South America, To which is Prefixed an Essay on the Varieties of the Human Species* (Philadelphia, 1839).

9 For the development, reception, and impact of *Crania Americana*, see Stanton, *Leopard's Spots*, 25–53. And for a revelation of how Morton apparently unconsciously "fudged" his data, see Stephen Jay Gould, "Morton's Ranking of Races by Cranial Capacity," *Science*, 200 (1978), 504, 505.

10 Which, of course, "offered much support to the defense of the peculiar institution." Swan, "American School of Ethnology," 84.

11 Stanton, *Leopard's Spots*, 192. See, however, Fredrickson (*Black Image*, 76–96) who disagrees with this position.

12 Fredrickson, *Black Image*, 86–7; Breeden, "States-Rights Medicine," 349.

13 See for example Victor H. Bassett's ("Plantation Medicine," *JMAG*, 29 [1940], 115) discussion of the comments of Dr. Joshua H. White on Negro lungs early in the nineteenth century.

14 For examples of this environmental emphasis, consult such planter's guides as Thomas Ewell, *American Family Physician* . . . (Washington, D.C., 1824) and J. Hume Simons *The Planter's Gude and Family Book of Medicine* (Charleston, S.C., 1848), 209, as well as studies such as that of H. Perry Pope, "A Dissertation on the Professional Management of Negro Slaves" (unpublished thesis, Medical College of South Carolina, 1837); William L. McCaa, "Observations on the Manner of Living and the Diseases of Slaves on the Wateree River" (Inaugural essay, University of Pennsylvania, 1822), 2, 4, and passim; Franklin, "On the Preservation of the Health of Negroes," *American Farmer*, 2 (1820), 242, and Ralph Butterfield, "Health of Negroes," *DR*, 25 (1858), 571–2.

15 Samuel A. Cartwright, "Philosophy of the Negro Constitution," *NOMSJ*, 9 (1852), 199; Ramsay, *Typhoid Fever*, 16, 19.

16 Ramsay, *Typhoid Fever*, 16, 19; Josiah C. Nott, *Instincts of Races* (New Orleans, 1866), 28; Samuel A. Cartwright, "Report on Diseases, and Physical Peculiarities of the Negro Race," *NOMSJ*, 7 (1851), 692–3.

17 Ramsay, *Typhoid Fever*, 16, 19; Cartwright, "Philosophy of the Negro Constitution, " 208; *Minutes of the Proceedings of the Medical Society of North Carolina At Its Second Annual Meeting* (Raleigh, N.C., 1851), 7.

18 Weymouth T. Jordan, "Plantation Medicine in the Old South," *Alabama Review*, 11 (1850), 96.

19 Ibid., 85; F. N. Boney, "Doctor Thomas Hamilton: Two Views of A Gentleman of the Old South," *Phylon*, 28 (1967), 288–92; Walter Fisher, "Physicians and Slavery in the Antebellum Southern Medical Journal," *JHM*, 23 (1968), 45; John Duffy, *The Healers: The Rise of the Medical Establishment* (New York, 1976) 139–43.

20 Ramsay, *Typhoid Fever*, 16. See also Lunsford P. Yandell, "Remarks on Struma Africana or the Disease Usually Called Negro Poison or Negro Consumption," *TJM*, 4 (1831), 90–1; W. G. Ramsay, "The Physiological Differences between the European (or white man) and the Negro," *SA*, 12 (1839), 412.

21 Ramsay, "Physiological Differences," 294; E. M. Pendleton, "General Report on the Topography, Climate and Diseases of Middle Georgia," *SMR*, 1 (1849), 337; Samuel A. Cartwright, "The Diseases and Physical Peculiarities of the Negro Race," *SMR*, 2 (1850), 425; Josiah C. Nott, "The Mulatto a Hybrid. . ." *AJMS*, 6 (1843), 255.

22 Cartwright, "Report on Diseases," 691–2; S. L. Grier, "The Negro and his Diseases," *NOMSJ*, 9 (1853), 759; *Minutes of the Proceedings of the Medical Society of North Carolina*, 3.

23 Duffy, "Southern Nationalism" 268–9; Breeden, "States-Rights Medicine," 354; Mary Louise Marshall, "Samuel A. Cartwright and States' Rights Medicine," *NOMSJ* 93, (1940), 74–8.
24 See Marshall, "Cartwright and States' Rights Medicine," for the details of Cartwright's career.
25 The "report" in question is the already oft-cited Cartwright, "Report on Diseases," 691–715.
26 Cartwright, "Diseases and Physical Peculiarities," 423.
27 Ibid., 425; and Cartwright, "Report on Diseases," 692.
28 Cartwright, "Report on Diseases," 693–5.
29 Ibid., 695.
30 Ibid.
31 Ibid.
32 Ibid.
33 Ibid., 692–3, 694.
33 Samuel A. Cartwright, "On the Caucasians and the African," *DBR*, 25 (1858), 47–48.
34 Consult D. J. Cain and F. Peyre Porcher's review of "Cartwright on the Diseases, etc., of the Negro Race," *CMJR*, 6 (1851), 829–43 and their review of "Cartwright on the Diseases and Physical Peculiarities of the Negro Race," *CMJR*, 7 (1852), 89–98. See also the highly critical review by James T. Smith, "Review of Dr. Cartwright's Report on the Diseases and Physical Peculiarities of the Negro Race," *NOMSJ*, 8 (1851) 228–37.
35 Cain and Porcher, "Cartwright" (1851).
36 Ibid.
37 Cain and Porcher "Cartwright" (1852).
38 Breeden, "States-Rights Medicine," 352.
39 Ramsay, *Typhoid Fever,* 19.
40 Quoted in "Review of Ramsay," *Necrological Appearances of Typhoid Fever in the Southern Negro, NOMSJ,* 9 (1853), 823.
41 Cartwright, "Report on Diseases," 694.
42 Richard H. Shryock, ed., *Letters of Richard D. Arnold, M.D., 1808–1867* (Durham, N.C., 1929) 70–71.
43 Martha Carolyn Mitchell, "Health and the Medical Profession in the Lower South, 1845–1860," *JSH,* 10 (1944), 442. For the proliferation of medical schools in the South and the growth of the southern medical profession see Breeden, "States-Rights Medicine," 364–8.
44 Quoted in Paul S. Taylor, "Plantation Laborer before the Civil War," *AH,* 28 (1954), 18–19.
45 In addition to the growth of southern medical schools, Negro hospitals also proliferated, which suggests that the call for Negro medicine was more than rhetoric. In announcing the opening of a two-story Negro hospital in 1860, the *CMTR* ("Negro Hospital," 850–1) observed that it will "provide an admirable field for acquainting themselves [students] with those diseases peculiarly incident to a class from which the majority must expect to derive their largest number of patients."
46 Wilson, a Columbus Georgia physician who had practiced previously in southern Alabama, was a regular contributor to the *American Cotton Planter* and had much to say about slave diet and disease. The advertised title of his work was "The Plantation and Family Physician: A Work for Families Generally and for Southern Slaveholders Especially. Embracing the Peculiarities and Disease, the Medical and Hygiene management of Negroes, Together with the Causes, Symptoms, and Treatment of the Principal Diseases Common to Whites and Blacks." Jordan, "Plantation Medicine," 92.
47 Fredrickson, *Black Image,* 89.

Introduction to Part V

1 Rev. Jesse L. Jackson in his "Introduction," to *Textbook of Black-Related Diseases*, ed. Richard Allen Williams (New York, 1974), xxi.
2 Josiah C. Nott, *The Negro Race: Its Ethnology and History*, (Mobile, Ala., 1866).
3 Roy L. Keller, "Syphilis and Tuberculosis in the Negro Race," *Texas State Journal of Medicine*, 19 (1924), 498.
4 L. C. Allen, "Negro Health Problem," *AJPH*, 5 (1915), 194 and passim.
5 Seale Harris, "The Future of the Negro from the Standpoint of the Southern Negro," *Alabama Medical Journal*, 14 (1902), 60–6.
6 Allen, "Negro Health Problems," 194–5, 197. For other examples of this same prediction see E. H. Sholl, "The Negro and his Death Rate," *Alabama Medical and Surgical Age*, 3 (1890–1), 399, and H. L. Sutherland, "Health Conditions of the Negro in the South: with Special Reference to Tuberculosis," *Journal of the Southern Medical Association*, 6 (1909), 402, 405.
7 L. S. Joyens, "Remarks on the Comparative Mortality of the White and Colored Populations of Richmond," *VMM*, 2 (1875), 165–6.
8 Edward Eggleston, *The Ultimate Solution of the American Negro Problem* (Boston, 1913), 258.
9 Paul B. Barringer, "The Negro and the Social Order," in *Race Problems of the South*, ed. Southern Society for the Promotion of the Study of Race Conditions and Problems in the South (Montgomery, Ala., 1900; reprint ed., New York, 1969), 191.
10 Frederick L. Hoffman, *Race Traits and Tendencies of the American Negro* (New York, 1973; reprint of 1896 ed.), 44 (table).
11 Harris, "Future of the Negro," 66.
12 Sholl, "Negro and his Death Rate," 337.

Chapter 13. Epilogue: Cradle to grave

1 Gunnar Myrdal, *An American Dilemma*, 2 vols (New York, 1944), 1:174.
2 Quoted by Nick Kotz, *Let Them Eat Promises: The Politics of Hunger in America* (New York, 1969), 38.
3 John Kramer, "How Not to Feed the Poor: An Overview of Federal Assistance Programs," in *Conference on Public Policy for Urban Minorities and the Poor: The Urban Scene in the Seventies*, eds. James F. Blumstein and Eddie J. Martin (Nashville, Tenn., 1974), 103.
4 Roland B. Scott and Michael R. Winston, "The Health and Welfare of the Black Family in the United States. A Historical and Institutional Analysis," *AJDC* 130 (1976) 706.
5 M. Alfred Haynes, "The Gap in Health Status between Black and White Americans," in *Textbook of Black-Related Diseases*, ed. Richard Allen Williams (New York, 1974), 3.
6 Marion M. Torchia, "The Tuberculosis Movement and the Race Question, 1890–1950," *BHM*, 49 (1975), 152; Myrdal, *American Dilemma*, 1:173).
7 Haynes, "Gap in Health Status," 6 (table).
8 Ibid., 6, 7; Myrdal, *American Dilemma*, 1:173.
9 Joseph A. McFalls, "Impact of VD on the Fertility of the U. S. Black Population, 1880–1950," *Social Biology*, 20 (1973), 6–7; William J. Brown et al., *Syphilis and other Venereal Diseases* (Cambridge, Mass., 1970) 143 (table).
10 George I. Lythcott, Calvin H. Sinnette, and Donald R. Hopkins, "Pediatrics," in *Black-Related Diseases*, ed. Williams, 169. The word *reported* is stressed because today, as in the past, many more white cases than black doubtless go unreported by physicians.
11 Although the overall death rate is the same for black and white, life expectancy tables reveal a considerable differential between blacks and the total population,

with much of that difference accounted for by infant mortality. Thus, based on National Center for Health Statistics data, Haynes ("Gap in Health Status," table, 3) portrayed the "Projected Survival of White and Nonwhite Cohorts Born in 1974" as follows:

Year	White	Nonwhite
1974	1,000	1,000
1975	982	969
1984	977	961
2000	963	936
2039	738	581
2044	639	478

12 Haynes, "Gap in Health Status."
13 Jerry L. Weaver, "The Case of Black Infant Mortality," *Journal of Health Policy*, 1, (1977), 436. Weaver (435) has provided the 1960 figure, while the 1970 estimate has been taken from Lythcott, Sinnette, and Hopkins, ("Pediatrics," 131). Weaver has employed data that produce a lower percentage for the early 1970s but points out that the data are not totally reliable (434). We have therefore chosen to rely on the Lythcott, Sinnette and Hopkins estimate which is closer to the 1969 data showing that a black infant had an 82 percent greater chance of dying during his first year than a white infant.
14 The data for blacks include other races, all under the rubric of nonwhite. Blacks constitute about 90 percent of this group.
15 Frank Falkner, ed., *Key Issues in Infant Mortality, Report of a Conference April 16–18, 1969* (Bethesda, Md., 1969), 18.
16 Helen C. Chase and Mary E. Byrnes, *Trends in Prematurity, United States: 1950–67* (Washington, D.C., 1972), DHEW Pub. No. (HSM), 72–1030, 1.
17 Carl L. Erhardt and Helen C. Chase, "Ethnic Group, Education of Mother, and Birth Weight," *AJPH*, Suppl, 63 (1973), 20.
18 In urban areas the rate was somewhat higher. The average percentage of black LBW babies born in Baltimore during 1961–65 was 15 (Gerald Wiener and Toby Milton, "Demographic Correlates of Low Birth Weight," *AJE*, 91, 1970, 262), while in New York the 1968 percentage was 16 (Erhardt and Chase, "Ethnic Group, Education of Mother and Birth Weight," 20).
19 Chase and Byrnes, *Trends in Prematurity*, 13, and Helen C. Chase, "Time Trends in Low Birth Weight in the United States, 1950–1974," in *The Epidemiology of Prematurity*, eds. Dwayne M. Reed and Fiora L. Stanley (Baltimore, 1977), 20–24, 28.
20 Howard V. Meredith, "North American Negro Infants: Size at Birth and Growth During the First Postnatal Year," *HB*, 24 (1952), 293; Lythcott, Sinnette, and Hopkins, "Pediatrics," 135.
21 Chase, "Time Trends in Low Birth Weights," 28.
22 Stanley M. Garn, Helen A. Shaw, and Kinne D. McCabe, "Effects of Socioeconomic Status and Race on Weight-Defined and Gestational Prematurity in the United States," in *Epidemiology of Prematurity*, eds. Reed and Stanley, 136–7; A. Frederick North and Hugh M. McDonald, "Why are Neonatal Mortality Rates Lower in Small Black Infants than in White Infants of Similar Birth Weight?" *JP*, 90 (1977), 809. Wiener and Milton, "Demographic Correlates of Low Birth Weight," 27.
23 Carl L. Erhardt, "Influence of Weight and Gestation of Perinatal and Neonatal Mortality by Ethnic Group," *AJPH*, 54 (1964), 1849, 1850.
24 Nancy N. Bayley, "Comparisons of Mental and Motor Test Scores for Ages 1–15 Months by Sex, Birth Order, Race, Geographical Location, and Education of Par-

ents," *Child Development*, 36 (1965), 408; Stanley M. Garn and Diane C. Clark, "Problems in the Nutritional Assessment of Black Individuals," *AJPH*, 66 (1976), 263.

25 North and McDonald, "Neonatal Mortality Rates," 809; Joseph Chinnici and Raymond C. Sansing, "Mortality Rates, Optimal and Discriminating Birthweights Between White and Nonwhite Single Births in Virginia (1955–1973)," *HB*, 49 (1977), 343–44; Helen C. Chase, "Infant Mortality and Weight at Birth; 1960 United States Birth Cohort," *AJPH*, 59 (1969), 1622 (table).

26 Another genetic explanation applies only to those mothers with sickle trait whose babies tend on the average to weigh close to 20 percent less than the norm. Michael K. McCormack et al., "A Comparison of the Physical and Intellectual Development of Black Children With and Without Sickle-Cell Trait," *Ped.*, 56 (1975), 1023. One hypothesis to account for this is that the babies of sickle trait mothers may receive an insufficient supply of oxygen. Sanford Brown et al., "Low Birth Weight in Babies Born to Mothers with Sickle Cell Trait," *JAMA*, 221 (1972), 1405.

27 Roland B. Scott, Melvin E. Jenkins, and Robert P. Crawford, "Growth and Development of Negro Infants, I. Analysis of Birthweights of 11,818 Newly Born Infants," *Ped*, 6 (1950), 430; E. Perry Crump et al., "Growth and Development, I. Relation of Birth Weight in Negro Infants to Sex, Maternal Age, Parity, Prenatal Care, and Socioeconomic Status," *JP*, 51 (1957), 692–3; Garn, Shaw, and McCabe, "Effects of Socioeconomic Status and Race," 131–5; Alfred F. Naylor and Ntinos C. Myrianthopoulos, The Relation of Ethnic and Selected Socio-economic Factors to Human Birthweight," *Annals of Human Genetics* 31 (1967) 71.

28 See Janet B. Hardy and E. David Mellits, "Relationship of Low Birth Weight to Maternal Characteristics of Age, Parity, Education, and Body Size," in *Epidemiology of Prematurity*, eds. Reed and Stanley, 105–17, and Lawrence Bergner and Mervyn W. Susser, "Low Birth Weight and Prenatal Nutrition: An Interpretive Review," *Ped*, 46 (1970), 946–66, especially 950–63, for recent reviews of factors influencing birth weight.

29 Richard L. Naeye, William Blanc, and Cheryl Paul, "Effects of Maternal Nutrition on the Human Fetus," *Ped*, 52 (1973), 497, 500; Carol Philipps and Nancy E. Johnson, "The Impact of Quality of Diet and Other Factors on Birth Weight of Infants," *AJCN*, 30 (1977), 216; David Rush, Hillard Davis, and Mervyn Susser, "Antecedents of Low Birthweight in Harlem, New York City," *International Journal of Epidemiology*, 1 (1972), 383; Adebayo S. Ademowore, Norman G. Courey, and James S. Kime, "Relationship of Maternal Nutrition and Weight Gain to Birthweight," *Obstetrics and Gynecology*, 39 (1972), 463–4; Harry Stein and Uda Ellis, "The Low Birthweight African Baby," *ADC*, 49 (1974), 158; C. M. Drillien, "The Small-for-Date Infant: Etiology and Prognosis," *PCNA*, 17 (1970), 9; P. C. Jean, Mary B. Smith and Genevieve Stearns, "Incidence of Prematurity in Relation to Maternal Nutrition," *JADA*, 31 (1955), 576–81.

30 See for example, Garn, Shaw, and McCabe, "Effects of Socioeconomic Status and Race," 135, 137, who demonstrate that black neonates are twice as often below 2500 grams on every income, educational and occupational level, regardless of smoking or parity factors. On the other hand, see Ademowore, Courey and Kime, "Relationships of Maternal Nutrition and Weight Gain to Birthweight," 463–4, whose study showed that black mothers with good nutrition have babies as big or bigger than whites.

31 Weaver, "Case of Black Infant Motality," 439.

32 See, for example, Thomas P. Atkinson, "Report on the Anatomical, Physiological and Pathological Differences Between the White and the Black Races . . ." *VMS*, (1872), 105–14.

33 Lee Bivings, "Racial, Geographic, Annual, and Seasonal Variations in Birth Weights," *AJOG*, 27 (1934), 725–6; H. Bakwin, "Negro Infant," *HB*, 4 (1932); Ethel C. Dunham, R. M. Jenss and A. V. Christie, "Consideration of Race and Sex in Relation to Growth and Development of Infants," *JP*, 14 (1939), 136; A. N. Anderson, E. W. Brown and R.

A. Lyon, "Causes of Prematurity, II. Influence of Race and Sex on Duration of Gesta- tion and Weight at Birth," *AJDC*, 65 (1943), 523.

34 J. H. Ebbs, F. F. Tisdall and W. A. Scott, "The Influence of Prenatal Diet on the Mother and Child," *JN*, 22 (1941), (table), 524; B. J. Van den Ber and J. Yerushalmy, "The Relationship of the Rate of Intrauterine Growth of Infants of Low Birth Weight to Mortality, Morbidity, and Congenital Anomalies," *JP*, 69 (1966), 531–45.

35 A. N. Antonov, "Children Born During the Siege of Leningrad," *JP*, 30 (1947), 250– 9; C. A. Smith, "Effects of Wartime Starvation in Holland on Pregnancy and its Products," *AJOG*, 53 (1947), 599–608; Z. Stein et al., *Famine and Human Development: The Dutch Hunger Winter of 1944–45* (New York, 1975).

36 The states surveyed were California, Kentucky, Louisiana, Massachusetts, Michigan, New York, South Carolina, Texas, Washington and West Virginia.

37 And the most politically explosive because of the policy implications that placed Washington under heavy fire from various ethnic, political, and food lobby groups. Worse, it was embarrassing to a nation posing as a benefactor to the Third World to discover within its own borders nutritional deficiencies common to those of the world's least developed countries. Unhappily, the government reacted by releasing only a portion of the results, and "the final report is likely to become available only when the Administration stops being mesmerized by the fact that it is cheaper in budgetary terms to fight hunger when the public has no firm idea of how extensive hunger really is." Kramer, "How Not to Feed the Poor," 105. At the state level the politics have been no less sensitive. Mississippi, for example, was supposed to be among the states surveyed, but this "was stopped cold by an executive department's fear of one congressman," who in turn presumably feared the political implication of the results of such a survey. Kotz, *Let Them Eat Promises*, 84–85.

38 U. S. Department of Health, Education and Welfare, *Ten-State Nutrition Survey 1968– 1970*, 5 vols., DHEW Pub. No. (HSM) 72-8130-34 (Washington D.C., 1972), here- inafter referred to as TSNS.

39 Jean Mayer, "Food Habits and Nutrition Status of American Negroes," *PM*, 37 (1965), A110–5; Johnnie Prothro, Mary Mickles, and Bernadine Tolbert, "Nutritional Status of a Population Sample in Macon County, Alabama," *AJCN*, 29 (1976), 94–104; George M. Owen et al., "A Study of Nutritional Status of Preschool Children in the United States, 1968–1970," *Ped*, 53, Suppl. (1974), 597–646; Rose E. Jones and Harold E. Schendel, "Nutritional Status of Selected Negro Infants in Greenville County, South Carolina," *AJCN*, 18 (1966), 407–412; J. P. Carter et al., "Nutrition and Parasitism among Rural Pre-school Children in South Carolina," *JNMA*, 62 (1970), 181–91; M. C. Hampton et al., "Caloric and Nutrient Intakes of Teen-Agers," *JADA*, 50 (1967), 385–96; E. Payton, "Growth and Development. VII. Dietary Habits of 571 Pregnant Southern Negro Women," *JADA*, 37 (1960), 129–36; Public Health Services, Health Resources Adminis- tration, *Preliminary Findings of the First Health and Nutrition Examination Survey, United States, 1971–1972: Dietary Intake and Biochemical Findings*, DHEW Pub. No. (HRA) 75-1219-1 (Washington D.C., 1974) (hereinafter referred to as HANES).

40 TSNS 5: (tables), 241–6, Rupert E. Arnell, Daniel W. Goldman, and Frank J. Bertucci, "Protein Deficiencies in Pregnancy," *JAMA*, 127 (1945), 1101–7; Margaret C. Moore et al., "Food Habits of Women During Pregnancy," *JADA*, 23 (1947), 847–53; Mary L. Hinson and J. H. Ferguson, "Food Habits of Pregnant Women in Charity Hospital Clinics," *BTMF*, 10 (1951), 138–42; Icie G. Macy et al., "Physiological Adaptation and Nutritional Status During and After Pregnancy," *JN*, 52 (1954), 1–92; Payton, "Di- etary Habits," 129–36; Graciela Delgado, C. L. Brumback and Mary Brice Deaver, "Eating Patterns among Migrant Families," *PHR*, 76 (1961), 349–55; HANES, (table) 58, 67, 77.

41 Margaret S. Chaney and Margaret L. Ross, *Nutrition*, 8th ed. (Boston, 1971), 339.

42 Payton, "Dietary Habits," 134.

43   Robert O'Neal et al., "The Incidence of Anemia in Residents of Missouri," *AJCN*, 29 (1976), 1159; TSNS (table), 5:245; HANES, 75 (table).

44   K. A. Harrison and P. A. Ibeziako, "Maternal Anaemia and Fetal Birthweight," *Journal of Obstetrics and Gynecology*, 80 (1973), 798–804.

45   TSNS. See also Payton, "Dietary Habits," 133, Arnel, Goldman and Bertucci, "Protein Deficiencies in Pregnancy," 1102, and Mary Hinson and J. H. Ferguson, "Food Habits of Pregnant Women in Charity Hospital Clinics" *BTMF* 10(1951) 138–42 – all of whom found the black prenatal diet to be very deficient in protein.

46   Albert N. Whiting, "Clay, Starch and Soot Eating Among Southern Rural Negroes in North Carolina," *Journal of Negro Education*, 16 (1947), 610–12; James H. Ferguson and Alice Glenn Keaton, "Studies of the Diets of Pregnant Women in Mississippi: I. The Ingestion of Clay and Laundry Starch," *Journal of Louisiana State Medical Society*, 102 (1950), 460–3; Payton, "Dietary Habits," 132; Cecile Hoover Edwards et al., "Effect of Clay and Cornstarch Intake on Women and Their Infants," *JAMA*, 44 (1964), 109; Louis Keith, Eric R. Brown and Cary Rosenberg, "Pica: The Unfinished Story; Background: Correlatives with Anemia and Pregnancy," *Perspectives in Biology & Medicine*, 13 (1970), 626–32; Edwin S. Bronstein and Jerry Dollar, "Pica in Pregnancy," *JMAG*, 63 (1974), 332–5; Harry A. Roselle, "Association of Laundry Starch and Clay Ingestion with Anemia in New York City," *AIM*, 125 (1970), 57.

47   However, a study of the problem looking at 200 pregnant black women in New York City revealed the following: (1) 43 percent of the sample were pica users, (2) pica and iron deficiency were highly correlated, and (3) pica practitioners were anemic and had an incidence of prematurity twice that of the nonpica users. Beverly N. Dunston, "Pica, Hemoglobin and Prematurity and Perinatal Mortality, . . ." (Ph.D. Dissertation, New York University, 1961).

48   Payton, "Dietary Habits," 132, 134; Mayer, "Food Habits and Nutrition Status of American Negroes," A112; Owen et al., "Nutritional Status of Preschool Children," 639; Jones and Schendel, "Nutritional Status of Selected Negro Infants," 410; HANES, 88–95 (tables).

49   Margaret S. Chaney and Margaret L. Ross, *Nutrition*, 8th ed. (Boston, 1971) 343.

50   Mayer, "Food Habits and Nutrition Status of American Negroes," A112; TSNS (tables), 5:249–54.

51   Robert M. Neer, "The Evolutionary Significance of Vitamin D, Skin Pigment, and Ultraviolet Light," *AJPH*, 43 (1975), 411. See also HANES: *Anthropometrical and Clinical Findings*, 21–2, for the prevalence of bowed legs and knock knees "suggestive of past rickets" among blacks. Finally, see H. Ashley Weeks and Benjamin J. Darsky, *"The Urban Aged, Race and Medical Care* (Ann Arbor, 1968), 24–25, who report a higher incidence of black (as compared to white) musculoskeletal illnesses.

52   Abraham B. Bergman et al., "Studies on the Sudden Infant Death Syndrome in King County, Washington. III. Epidemiology," *PCD*, 49 (1972), 863.

53   Ruth Maxwell, Lewis H. Roht, and Paul Callen, "Incidence of Sudden Death Syndrome in Texas 1969–1972; Estimation by The Surrogate Method," *Texas Medicine*, 72 (1976), 65 (table).

54   Maria Valdes-Dapena et al., "Sudden Unexpected Death in Infancy: A Statistical Analysis of Certain Socioeconomic Factors," *JP* 73 (1968) 388.

55   Robert Strimer, Lester Adelson and Robert Oseasohn, "Epidemiologic Features of 1,134 Sudden, Unexpected Deaths: A Study in the Greater Cleveland Area from 1956 to 1965," *JAMA*, 209 (1969), 1496.

56   Maria A. Valdes-Dapena, "Sudden and Unexpected Death in Infancy: A Review of the World Literature: 1954–1966," *Ped*, 39 (1967), 134; J. Bruce Beckwith, "Observations of the Pathological Anatomy of the Sudden Infant Death Syndrome," in *Sudden Infant Death Syndrome: Proceedings of the Second International Conference on Causes of Sudden Death in Infants*, eds. Abraham B. Bergman, J. B. Beckwith, and George C.

Ray (Seattle, 1970) 84; Richard H. Raring, *Crib Death: Scourge of Infants – Shame of Society* (Hicksville, N.Y., 1975), 122–31.

57 Bergman et al., "Sudden Infant Death Syndrome in King County," 861; J. Bruce Beckwith, *The Sudden Infant Death Syndrome*, DHEW Pub No (HSA) 77-5251 (Washington, D.C. 1977), 29.

58 HANES: *Anthropometric and Clinical Findings*, 63 (table); Philip S. Spiers and Lydia Wang, "Short Pregnancy Interval, Low Birthweight, and The Sudden Infant Death Syndrome, *AJE*, 104 (1976), 16; Richard L. Naeye, Bertha Ladis, and Joseph S. Drage, "Sudden Infant Death Syndrome," A Prospective Study," *AJDC*, 130 (1976), 1207; B. G. Carpenter and J. L. Emery, "Identification and Follow-up of Infants at Risk of Sudden Death in Infancy," *Nature*, 250 (1974), 729.

59 Bergman et al., "Sudden Infant Death Syndrome in King County," 865; Elliot D. Weitzman and Leonard Graziani, eds., *Research Planning Workshops on the Sudden Infant Death Syndrome. 4. Neurophysiological Factors*, DHEW Pub. No. (NIH) 74-580 (Washington, D.C., 1972); Maxwell, Roht, and Callen, "Sudden Death Syndrome in Texas," 59; Beckwith, *Sudden Infant Death Syndrome*, 12; Joan L. Caddell, "Magnesium Deprivation in Sudden Unexpected Infant Death," *Lancet*, 11 (1972), 258–9; Murray Davidson, "Feeding the Low-Birth Weight Infant," in *Pediatrics*, ed. Henry L. Barnett, 15th ed. (New York, 1972), 109.

60 Ulla Lundstrom, Martti Siimes, and Peter R. Dallman, "At What Age Does Iron Supplementation Become Necessary in Low-Birth-Weight Infants?" *JP*, 91 (1977), 880, 881–2; Philip Lanzowsky, "Iron Deficiency Anemia," in *Pediatric Medicine*, ed. Milton Levine (Acton, Mass., 1975), 79; George R. Honig and Irving Schulman, "Deficiency of Substances Required for Hemoglobin Synthesis and Erythropoiesis," in *Pediatrics*, ed. Barnett, 1161.

61 Lewis P. Lipsitt, "Perinatal Indicators and Psychophysiological Precursors of Crib Death," Paper presented at a symposium on *Perinatal Factors and Developmental Hazards* at the meetings of the American Association for the Advancement of Science, Feb., 1977, Denver, Colorado (Table 3); Jean L. Marx, "Crib Death: Some Promising Leads But No Solution Yet," *Science* 189 (1975) 369; Naeye, Ladis, and Drage, "Sudden Infant Death Syndrome," 1208.

62 K. A. Harrison and P. A. Ibeziaiko, "Maternal Anaemia and Fetal Birthweight," *Journal of Obstetrics and Gynecology of the British Commonwealth*, 80 (1973), 798, 802; Samuel Joseph Foman, *Infant Nutrition*, 2nd ed. (Philadelphia 1974), 170; Lunzkowsky, "Iron Deficiency Anemia," 79.

63 Lythcott, Sinnette, and Hopkins, "Pediatrics," 148; Honig and Schulman, "Hemoglobin Synthesis and Erythropoiesis," 1160–1.

64 Stanley M. Garn, Nathan J. Smith, and Diane C. Clark, "The Magnitude and the Implications of Apparent Race Differences in Hemoglobin Values," *AJCN*, 28 (1975), 563–5; Peter Dallman, "New Approaches to Screening for Iron Deficiency," *Ped*, 90 (1977), 679; Michael J. Kraemer et al., "Race-related Differences in Peripheral Blood and in Marrow Cell Populations of American Black and American White Infants," *JNMA*, 69 (1977), 331.

65 O'Neal et al., "Incidence of Anemia," 1159; Robert H. Hutcheson, "Iron Deficiency Anemia in Tennessee among Rural Poor Children," *PHR*, 83 (1968), 941; L. J. Filer, "The USA Today – Is it Free of Public Health Nutrition Problems?" *AJPH*, 59 (1969), 333; Kenneth Brown et al., "Prevalence of Anemia among Preadolescent and Young Adolescent Urban Black Americans," *JP*, 81 (1972), 714–8.

66 George Owen, "Nutritional Status of Infants and Young Children: USA," *PCNA*, 24 (1977), 214.

67 Paul Zee, Thomas Walters, and Charles Mitchell, "Nutrition and Poverty in Preschool Children: A Nutritional Survey of Preschool Children from Impoverished Black Families, Memphis," *JAMA*, 213 (1970), 740.

68 Margaret F. Gutelius, "The Problem of Iron Deficiency Anemia in Preschool Negro Children," *AJPH*, 59 (1969), 291. Furthermore Gutelius points out that these were not the highest-risk children, because the test group was composed of subjects brought for baby care, and consequently seldom representative of the poorest families.

69 HANES, 72 (table); O'Neal et al., "Incidence of Anemia," 1162.

70 Hutcheson, "Iron Deficiency Anemia," 939; Gutelius, "Problem of Iron Deficiency Anemia," 294.

71 Thomas F. Pettigrew, *A Profile of the Negro American* (Princeton, N.J., 1964), 82–4. Let us again note, however, that some of this differential is the responsibility of an inefficient health delivery system which has permitted "significant 'pockets' of susceptibles" to go unvaccinated. Lythcott, Sinnette, and Hopkins, "Pediatrics," 162.

72 Stanley M. Garn et al., "Negro-Caucasoid Differences in Permanent Tooth Emergence at a Constant Income Level," *Archives of Oral Biology*, 18 (1973), 609–15; Garn and Clark, "Nutritional Assessment of Black Individuals," 264.

73 Owen, "Nutritional Status of Infants and Young Children: USA," 213. Moreover actual rickets is still seen at least twice as often among black as opposed to white children according to a survey of South Carolina physicians. Julian P. Price and E. Conyers O'Bryan, "Malnutrition in South Carolina as Seen as Practicing Physicians," *JSCMA*, 65 (1969), 112.

74 David M. Paige, Theodore M. Bayless, and George C. Graham, "Milk Programs: Helpful or Harmful to Negro Children," *AJPH*, 62 (1972), 1487.

75 Keiffer Mitchell et al., "Intolerance of Eight Ounces of Milk in Lactose-Intolerant Teen-Agers," *Ped*, 56 (1975), 720; Theodore Bayless et al., "Lactose and Milk Intolerance," *NEJM*, 292 (1975), 1157; John M. Hunter, "Geography, Genetics, and Culture History: The Case of Lactose Intolerance," *Geographical Review*, 61 (1971), 606.

76 Jack Slater, "Hypertension: Biggest Killer of Blacks," *Ebony*, 28 (1973), 76; *Miniconsultation on the Mental and Physical Health Problems of Black Women* (Washington, D.C., 1974), 2. See also J. Stamler et al., "Epidemiologic Studies on Cardio-Vascular-Renal Diseases, I. Analysis of Mortality by Age-Race-Sex-Occupation," *Journal of Chronic Diseases*, 12 (1960), 448; and John H. Phillips and George E. Burch, "A Review of Cardiovascular Diseases in the White and Negro Races,"*Medicine*, 39 (1960), 251–3.

77 *Health Problems of Black Women*, 2; Elijah Saunders and Richard Allen Williams, "Hypertension," in *Black-Related Diseases*, ed. Williams, 334; Joseph A. Wilbur, "Hypertension: An Editorial," *Phylon*, 38 (1978), 353.

78 Saunders and Williams, "Hypertension," 341.

79 Slater, "Hypertension," 80.

80 Lewis K. Dahl, "Salt and Hypertension," *AJCN*, 25 (1972), 231–4; Rene Bine, "Cardiology," in *Nutritional Support of Medical Practice*, eds. Howard A. Schneider, Carl E. Anderson, and David B. Coursin (Hagerstown, Md., 1977), 255–6.

81 Gilbert B. Forbes, "Sodium," in *Mineral Metabolism*, eds. C. L. Comar and Felix Bronner, 4 vols (1969), 2:B, 29.

82 E. E. Hellerstein et al., "Studies on the Relationship Between Dietary Magnesium, Quality and Quantity of Fat, Hypercholesterolemia, and Lipidosis," *JN*, 71 (1960), 339; *Calcium and the Heart*, eds. P. Harris and L. Opie (London and New York, 1971), passim.

83 G. R. Kelman, *Applied Cardiovascular Physiology*, 2nd ed. (London, 1977), 42–3; Warren E. C. Wacker and Bert L. Vallee, "Magnesium," in *Mineral Metabolism*, eds. Comar and Bronner, 1:A, 495–7.

84 Leroy R. Weekes, "Obstetrics and Gynecology," in *Black-Related Diseases*, ed. Williams, 104.

85 Ibid.; Committee on Maternal Nutrition/Food and Nutrition Board National Research Council, *Maternal Nutrition and the Course of Pregnancy* (Washington, D.C., 1970), 163–71.

86 Weekes, "Obstetrics and Gynecology," 104.

87 *Health Problems of Black Women*, 4.

88 Laura Hillman and John G. Haddad, "Human Perinatal Vitamin D Metabolism, I: 25-Hydroxyvitamin D in Maternal and Cord Blood," *JP*, 84 (1974), 748.

89 John Rosen et al., "25-Hydroxyvitamin D: Plasma Levels in Mothers and their Premature Infants with Neonatal Hypocalcemia," *AJDC*, 127 (1974), 222.

90 Ethel C. Dunham, *Premature Infants: A Manual for Physicians*, 2nd ed. (New York, 1955), (table) 32, 34–35; Kenneth R. Niswander, *Obstetrics: Essentials of Clinical Practice*, (Boston, 1976), 205; Ernest W. Page, Claude A. Villee, and Dorothy B. Villee, *Human Reproduction: The Core Content of Obstetrics, Gynecology and Perinatal Medicine*, 2nd ed. (Philadelphia, 1976), 317 (table).

91 Rosen et al., "25-Hydroxyvitamin D," 221–2.

92 Ibid.; Patsy J. M. Watney et al., "Maternal Factors in Neonatal Hypocalcaemia, A Study in Three Ethnic Groups," *BMJ*, 2 (1971), 433–5.

93 Once again it should be noted that calcium/magnesium deficient mothers are far more likely to have LBW babies. Philipps and Johnson, "Impact of Quality of Diet," 216.

94 Reginald C. Tsang and William Oh, "Neonatal Hypocalcaemia in Low Birth Weight Infants," *Ped*, 45 (1970), 778; Paul D. Saville and Norman Kretchmer, "Neonatal Tetany: A Report of 125 Cases and Review of the Literature," *BN*, 2 (1960), 1; J.H. Keen, "Significance of Hypocalcaemia in Neonatal Convulsions," *ADC*, 44 (1969), 357–8; Steven A. Roberts, Mervyn D. Cohen, and John O. Forfar, "Antenatal Factors Associated with Convulsions," *Lancet*, 2 (1973), 809–11. See R.J. Purvis et al., "Enamel Hypoplasia of the Teeth Associated with Neonatal Tetany: A Manifestation of Maternal Vitamin D Deficiency," *Lancet*, 2 (1973), 814; Watney et al., "Maternal Factors in Neonatal Hypocalcaemia," 435, and W. G. Turton, "Altered Vitamin D Metabolism in Pregnancy," *Lancet*, 1 (1977), 224, who believe maternal vitamin D supplements would prevent neonatal tetany.

95 Haynes, "Gap in Health Status," 10. See also Marcus S. Goldstein, "Longevity and Health Status of the Negro American," *Phylon*, 32 (1963), 344, who points out that in 1960 the black maternal mortality rate in Mississippi and Alabama was 14.4 and 14.0, respectively, compared to 3.7 for the total national maternal mortality rate.

96 Benjamin B. Pasamanick and Abraham M. Lilienfeld, "Association of Maternal and Fetal Factors with Development of Mental Deficiency, I. Abnormalities in the Prenatal and Paranatal Periods," *JAMA*, 159 (1955), 158; Drillien, "Small-for-date Infant," 10; Janet B. Hardy, "Perinatal Factors and Intelligence," in *The Bio-Social Basis of Mental Retardation*, eds. Sonia F. Osler and Robert E. Cooke (Baltimore, 1965), 50; George S. Baroff, *Mental Retardation: Nature, Cause, and Management* (New York, 1974), 71; Rick Heber, *Epidemiology of Mental Retardation* (Springfield, Ill., 1970), 91–99; F. H. Wright et al., "A Controlled Follow-up Study of Small Prematures Born from 1952 Through 1956," *AJDC*, 124 (1972), 513, 517–18.

97 John A. Churchill, Joseph W. Neff, and Donald F. Caldwell, "Birth Weight and Intelligence," *Obstetrics and Gynecology*, 28 (1966), 425–9.

98 Rodger L. Hurley, *Poverty and Mental Retardation: A Causal Relationship* (New York, 1969), 55.

99 Ruth F. Harrell, Ella Woodyard, and Arthur I. Gates, *The Effect of Mothers' Diets on the Intelligence of Offspring* (New York, 1955).

100 Jefferson L. Sulzer, Wesley J. Hansche and Frederick Koenig, "Nutrition, and Behavior in Head Start Children: Results from the Tulane Study," in *Nutrition Development and Social Behavior*, ed. David T. Kallen (Washington D.C., 1971), 96–101, 104. See also E. K. Beller and D. A. Howell, *Effects of Iron Deficiency Anemia on Attentiveness in Preschool Children. Final Report Submitted to Office of Economic Opportunity* (Washington D.C., 1971).

101 Paul B. Cornely, "The Health Status of the Negro Today and in the Future," *AJPH*, 58 (1968), 647.

102 J. Dobbing, "The Later Development of the Brain and its Vulnerability," in *Scientific Foundations of Paediatrics*, eds. J. A. Davis and J. Dobbing (Philadelphia, 1974), 573; Peter H. Chase, Cipriano A. Canosa, and Donough O'Brien, "Nutrition and Biochemical Maturation of the Brain," *Modern Problems in Paediatrics*, 14 (1975), 110–18; Roger Lewin, "Starved Brains," *Psychology Today*, 9 (1975), 30–31; Myron Winick, *Malnutrition and Brain Development* (New York, 1976), 64–7, 71–97.

103 Winick, *Malnutrition and Brain Development*, 80–1, 107–10; see B. S. Platt and R. J. C. Stewart for a summary of the work on the "Reversible and Irreversible Effects of Protein-Calorie Deficiency on the Central Nervous System of Animals and Man," *World Review of Nutrition and Dietetics*, 13 (1971), 73; H. P. Chase and L. S. Crnic, "Undernutrition and Human Brain Development," in *Research to Practice in Mental Retardation*. Vol. III: Biomedical Aspects, ed. Peter Mittler (Baltimore, 1977), 338–42.

104 Food and Nutrition Board, National Academy of Sciences, National Research Council, *Recommended Dietary Allowances*, Publ. 1146, 8th Revised Edition (Washington, D.C., 1974), 47. See discussion of protein requirements on pages 41–2.

105 TSNS 4:(Figures), 82; (Tables), 95–7. For earlier studies demonstrating low-protein intakes of the pregnant black female, see Arnell, Goldman, and Bertucci ("Protein Deficiencies in Pregnancy," 1102), who found that one-quarter of the women they studied obtained less than 42 grams of protein daily, and Hinson and Ferguson, "Food Habits of Pregnant Women," 138–42 who also found the *average* protein intake to be 44 grams. Payton, "Dietary Habits of 571 Pregnant Southern Negro Women," 129–36, discovered that only 16 percent met the RDA for protein.

106 Jones and Schendel, "Nutritional Status of Selected Negro Infants," 408–9.

107 TSNS, 4:89 (tables).

108 Winick, *Malnutrition and Brain Development*, 111; Dobbing, "Later Development of the Brain and its Vulnerability," 565–77.

109 Neer, "Evolutionary Significance of Vitamin D," 411.

110 Stanley M. Elkins, *Slavery: A Problem in American Institutional and Intellectual Life* (Chicago, 1959).

111 Leslie Howard Owens, *This Species of Property: Slave Life and Culture in the Old South* (New York, 1976), 69.

112 Sulzer, Hanscha, and Koenig, "Nutrition and Behavior in Head Start Children," 96–101, 104.

113 See Garn and Clark, "Nutritional Assessment of Black Individuals," 264, who argue that due to the black's advanced ossification timing, he will appear "advanced" or "normal" when in fact he is "nutritionally-retarded" if white norms are used.

114 Slater, "Hypertension," 76; Frank A. Finnerty, "Hypertension is Different in Blacks," *JAMA*, 216 (1971), 1634.

115 Frank A. Finnerty, "Does Vascular Damage Follow Toxemia of Pregnancy? An Internist's Appraisal of Three Hundred Three Patients in a Toxemia Clinic," *JAMA*, 154 (1954), 1075–9, and "Toxemia of Pregnancy as Seen by an Internist: An Analysis of 1081 Patients," *Annals of Internal Medicine*, 44 (1956), 358–75.

116 David M. Paige, "Milk Intolerance: Field Studies and Practical Considerations" in *Summary of the Conference on Lactose and Milk Intolerance*, eds. Irving I. Gottesman and Leonard I. Heston (Washington, D.C., 1972), 44.

117 Beckwith, *Sudden Infant Death Syndrome*, 29; Thaddeus J. Bell, Joel S. Saxton and Sandra E. Conradi, "The Status of Sudden Infant Death Syndrome (1975), and SIDS in Charleston County, South Carolina," *JSCMA*, 71 (1975), 312; John J. Lally, "Social Determinants of Differential Allocation of Resources to Disease Research: A Comparative Analysis of Crib Death and Cancer Research," *Journal of Health and Social Behavior*, 18 (1977), 128, 132.

118 James E. Bowman, "Mass Screening for Sickle Hemoglobin: A Sickle Cell Crisis," *JAMA*, 222 (1972), 1650; James M. Gustafson, "Genetic Screening and Human Values" in *Ethical, Social and Legal Dimensions of Screening for Human Genetic Disease*, ed. Daniel Bergsman (Miami, Fla., 1974), 211; Barbara Culliton, "Sickle Cell Anemia: The Route from Obscurity to Prominence," *Science*, 178 (1972), 141–2; Ernest Beutler et al., "Hazards of Indiscriminate Screening for Sickling," *NEMJ*, 285 (1971), 1485–86.

119 Cited by James E. Bowman, "Genetic Screening Programs and Public Policy," *Phylon*, 38 (1977), 123.

120 Anthony Cerami and Elsie Washington, *Sickle Cell Anemia* (New York, 1974), 98.

121 James E. Bowman, "Ethical Issues in Genetic Screening," *NEJM*, 287 (1972), 204.

122 See Barbara J. Culliton, "Sickle Cell Anemia; National Program Raises Problems as Well as Hopes," *Science*, 178 (1972), 283–4; Charles F. Whitten, "Sickle-Cell Programming – An Imperiled Promise," *NEJM*, 288 (1973), 318; Gustafson, "Genetic Screening and Human Values," 209.

123 Tabitha Powledge, "Genetic Screening as a Political and Social Development," in *Screening for Human Genetic Disease*, ed. Bergsman, 38.

124 Bowman, "Ethical Issues in Genetic Screening," 204.

125 N.Y. State Law, Chap. 994, Sec. 13aa, Session Law 1972, found in Powledge, "Genetic Screening," 44.

126 Powledge, "Genetic Screening," 38; Whitten, "Sickle-Cell Programming," 318; Beutler et al., "Hazards of Indiscriminate Screening," 1485–6; Lee A. Calhoun, "The Problem of Human Experimentation from a Black Perspective," in *Social Research and the Black Community: Selected Issues and Priorities*, ed. Lawrence A. Gary (Washington, D.C., 1974), 163.

127 Jesse L. Jackson, "Introduction," in *Black-Related Diseases*, xxi. For the entire story of the experiment, see V. G. Cave, "Proper Uses and Abuses of the Health Care Delivery System for Minorities with Special Reference to the Tuskegee Syphilis Study," *Journal of the National Medical Association*, 67 (1975), 82–84; Thomas G. Benedek, "The 'Tuskegee Study' of Syphilis: Analysis of Moral versus Methodological Aspects," *Journal of Chronic Diseases*, 31 (1978), 35–50; and James H. Jones, *Bad Blood: The Tuskegee Syphilis Experiment* (New York, 1981).

128 See "Politics and Politicians," chapter IX; 122–31, in Raring, *Crib Death*. See also *Examination of the Sudden Infant Death Syndrome. Hearing before the Subcommittee on Children and Youth, United States Senate, 92nd Congress* (Washington, D.C., 1972), passim, and Nicholas Wade, "Crib Death: Foremost Baby Killer Long Ignored by Medical Research," *Science*, 184 (1974), 447–9.

129 Lally, "Differential Allocation of Resources to Disease Research," 132; Culliton, "Sickle Cell Anemia," 283–6; Jerry L. Weaver, *National Health Policy and the Underserved Ethnic Minorities, Women and the Elderly* (St. Louis, 1976), 84–5; Stephen J. Kunitz, "Some Notes on Physiologic Conditions as Social Problems," *Social Science and Medicine*, 8 (1974), 207–9.

130 Calculated from data found in Kunitz, "Some Notes on Physiologic Conditions," 208.

131 Raring, *Crib Death*, 134. See also Lally, "Differential Allocation of Resources to Disease Research," 132, and Wade, "Crib Death," 447–8.

132 Thomas P. Almy, "Evolution, Lactase Levels, and Global Hunger," *NEJM*, 292 (1975), 1184; Robert D. McCracken, "Lactase Deficiency: An Example of Dietary Evolution," *Current Anthropology*, 12 (1971), 497.

133 A. E. Davis and T. Bolin, "Lactose Intolerance in Asians," *Nature*, 216 (1967), 1245.

134 Paige, Bayless, and Graham, "Milk Programs," 1487; Theodore M. Bayless, "Milk Intolerance: Clinical, Developmental and Epidemiological Aspects," in *Conference on Lactose and Milk Intolerance*, eds. Gottesman and Heston, 14; Douglas H. Sandberg,

"Intolerance to Lactose in Negro Children," *Ped*, 46 (1970), 646; Paige, "Milk Intolerance," 35; David M. Paige et al. "Response of Lactose-Intolerant Children to Different Lactose Levels," *ACJN*, 25 (1972), 468; George C. Graham and David M. Paige, "Nutritional Implications of Low Intestinal Lactase Activity in Children," in *Intestinal Enzyme Deficiencies and their Nutritional Implications*, eds. Bengt Borgstrom and Arne Dahlqvist (Stockholm, 1973) 46; John D. Johnson, Norman Kretchmer, and Frederick J. Simoons, "Lactose Malabsorption: Its Biology and History," *Advanced Pediatrics*, 21 (1974), 207.

135   This milk that is distributed "with no regard for whether [it] benefit[s] the needy or the lunch or breakfast programs" is – according the bald admission of the Milk Producers Federation – of more benefit to the milk industry than to the children. Robert Choate, "Special Programs for the Very Poor," in *U.S. Nutrition Policies in the Seventies*, ed. Jean Mayer (1973), 225.

136   Johnson, Kretchmer and Simoons, "Lactose Malabsorption," 228–9; David M. Paige and George G. Graham, "School Milk Programs and Negro Children: A Nutritional Dilemma," *Journal of School Health*, 44 (1974), 10; Mitchell et al., "Intolerance of Eight Ounces of Milk in Lactose-Intolerant Teen-Agers," 721. See also Paige ("Milk Intolerance," 45), Davis and Bolin ("Lactose Intolerance in Asians," 1245), Heli Alzate, Hernando Gonzales, and Javier Guzman ("Lactose Intolerance in South American Indians," *AJCN*, 22 [1969], 123), O. Ransome-Kuti ("Lactose Intolerance – A Review," *PM*, 53 [1977], 86–7), Huang Shi-Shung and Theodore M. Bayless ("Milk and Lactose Intolerance in Healthy Orientals," *Science*, 160 [1968], 84), and G. Cook and S. K. Kajubi ("Tribal Incidence of Lactase Deficiency in Uganda," *Lancet*, 1 [1966], 730) for arguments that our milk programs abroad should be reevaluated in light of the problems connected with lactose intolerance.

137   See the statements by the Protein Advisory Group of the United Nations "Low Lactase Activity and Milk Intake," *Protein Advisory Group Bulletin*, 2, (Washington, D.C., 1972), National Research Council *Background Information on Lactose and Milk Intolerance. A Statement of the Food and Nutrition Board, Division of Biology and Agriculture*, (Washington D.C., 1972), reprinted in *Nutrition Reviews*, 30 (1972), 175–6, and Committee on Nutrition, American Academy of Pediatrics, "Should Milk Drinking by Children be Discouraged? *Ped*, 53, (1974), 576–82.

138   John Perryman, "School Lunch Programs," in *U.S. Nutrition Policies*, ed. Mayer, 216–7; Choate, "Special Programs," 224–5; Hurley, *Poverty and Mental Retardation*, 191–3.

139   Elizabeth W. Murphy, Louise Page, and Bernice K. Watt, "Major Mineral Elements in Type A School Lunches," *JADA*, 57 (1970), 239–45; Mary K. Head, Roma J. Weeks, and Eleanor Gibbs, "Major Nutrients in the Type A Lunch," *JADA*, 63 (1973), 624.

140   William H. Crosby, "Pica: A Compulsion Caused by Iron Deficiency" *British Journal of Haematology*, 34 (1976), 341; Ralph D. Reynolds et al. "Pagophagia and Iron Deficiency Anemia," *AIM*, 69 (1968), 435–40; Dunston, "Pica, Hemoglobin, and Prematurity and Perinatal Mortality," passim.

141   For examples see Perry Craven, "Clay Supply Cherished Secret," *Durham Morning Herald* (Tuesday, May 2, 1967); Ferguson and Keaton, "Diets of Pregnant Women in Mississippi," 462–3; James A. Halstead, "Geophagia in Man: Its Nature and Nutritional Effects," *AJCN*, 21 (1968), 1389; and Donald E. Vermeer and Dennis A. Frate, "Geophagy in a Mississippi County, *Annals of the Association of American Geographers*, 65 (1975), 422–4.

142   Herbert Pollack, "Hunger USA 1968," *AJCN*, 22 (1969), 481.

143   Consult testimonies in the *Examination of the Sudden Infant Death Syndrome*, passim. See also William J. Curran, "An Enigma Wrapped in Swaddling Clothes: Congress

and 'Crib Death,' " *NEJM*, 287 (1972), 235; Wade, "Crib Death," 447, 449; and Luci Horton, "Mystery of Crib Death," *Ebony*, 28 (1973), 60, 61.

144 Abraham Bergman, "Current Classification of Primary Counties in each Standard Metropolitan Statistical Area (SMSA) with Reference to Changes in Management of SIDS Cases in 1972 and 1975," in *Research Perspectives in the Sudden Infant Death Syndrome* (Washington, D.C., 1976).

145 Paige, "Milk Intolerance," 44; Jack D. Welsh, "Lactose Malabsorption: Methodology and Clinical Aspects," in *Lactose and Milk Intolerance*, eds. Gottesman and Heston, 7. See also F. J. Simoons ("The Cultural Geography of Dairying," in *Lactose and Milk Intolerance*, eds. Gottesmann and Heston, 20) who explains that "until recently" lactose intolerance was believed to be psychosomatic in origin.

146 Beutler et al., "Hazards of Indiscriminate Screening," 1486.

147 Ibid.

148 Gutelius, "Problem of Iron Deficiency Anemia," 291.

149 Delagado, Brumback and Deaver, "Eating Patterns among Migrant Families," 354.

150 Ernest Carrol Faust, "History of Human Parasitic Infections," *PHR*, 70 (1955), 959.

151 Cited by Richard Allen Williams, "Cardiology," in *Black-Related Diseases*, ed. Williams, 377.

BIBLIOGRAPHIC ESSAY

The past two or three decades have witnessed an explosion of literature in almost all fields of inquiry including those of history, demography, and the medical and nutritional sciences. The range and diversity of this literature as well as the kinds of primary materials available to the interested researcher should be readily apparent in the footnotes to the text. The following essay is designed for those who are interested in further reading or research in not only the history of the health of blacks but in what promises to be an important field in the decades to come: biologic history.

I

Excellent far-ranging introductions to the impact of disease on man's affairs can be found in William H. McNeill, *Plagues and Peoples* (Garden City, N.Y., 1976); Alfred W. Crosby, *The Columbian Exchange* (Westport, Conn., 1972); and P. M. Ashburn's *Ranks of Death: A Medical History of the Conquest of America* (New York, 1947).

Fine case studies of particular diseases or of particular peoples and their susceptibilities in regions not covered by this work include Hans Zinsser, *Rats, Lice, and History* (New York, 1935); René and Jean Dubos, *The White Plague: Tuberculosis, Man and Society* (Boston, 1952); Roderick E. McGrew, *Russia and the Cholera, 1823–1832* (Madison, 1965); Donald B. Cooper, *Epidemic Disease in Mexico City 1761–1813* (Austin, 1965); and Owsei Temkin, *The Falling Sickness: A History of Epilepsy from the Greeks to the Beginnings of Modern Neurology*, 2nd rev. ed. (Baltimore, 1971).

For black disease immunities, Philip D. Curtin's pioneering epidemiologic studies are crucial. Curtin was the first to employ statistical data to call attention to the fact that blacks did indeed possess immunities to diseases of West Africa that white newcomers did not. See "The White Man's Grave; Image and Reality, 1780–1850," *Journal of British Studies*, 1 (1961), 94–110, *The Image of Africa: British Ideas and Action, 1780–1850* (Madison, 1964), and "Epidemiology and the Slave Trade," *Political Science Quarterly*, 83 (1968), 190–216.

Studies by Kenneth G. Davies, "The Living and the Dead: White Mortality in West Africa, 1684–1732," in *Race and Slavery in the Western Hemisphere*, eds. Stanley L. Engerman and Eugene D. Genovese (Princeton, 1975), 83–98, and H. M. Feinberg, "New Data on European Mortality in West Africa: The Dutch on the Gold Coast, 1719–1760," *Journal of African History*, 15 (1974), 357–71, both represent subsequent elaborations of and reactions to Curtin's work.

Curtin's efforts in demography have been no less seminal. Indeed, far more than any other study, it was his examination of *The Atlantic Slave Trade; a Census* (Madison, 1969) (see also his "Measuring the Slave Trade Once Again: A Comment," *Journal of African History*, 17, 1976, 595–605), which demonstrated how the slave population of the United States must have thrived demographically, while the slave populations of much of the

Caribbean and South America experienced more deaths than births throughout most or all of the slavery period.

On the one hand, this had the effect of throwing cold water on a then heated debate over the "virtues" of South American as opposed to North American slavery. But on the other, it forced scholars to pause and ask themselves why slaves should have enjoyed a greater level of physical well-being in the United States than their brothers elsewhere in the Hemisphere. Much of the answer it seemed must lie within the nebulous purview of the term "health," surrounded by such slippery variables as working conditions, housing, disease environment, nutrition, and the state of the medical art.

To be sure, many studies already existed for the American South that had addressed one or another of these problems. U. B. Phillips in his *American Negro Slavery* (New York, 1918) and again in his look at *Life and Labor in the Old South* (Boston, 1929) had observed that U. S. slaves ate as well, received as much medical attention and lived more or less as long as whites. William D. Postell reached the same conclusions in his study of *The Health of Slaves on Southern Plantations* (Baton Rouge, 1951), while demographic studies such as Charles S. Sydnor, "Life Span of Mississippi Slaves," *American Historical Review*, 35 (1930), 566–74, Robert Evans, "The Economics of American Negro Slavery," in *Aspects of Labor Economics*, Universities–National Bureau for Economic Research (Princeton, 1962), 185–243, and Reynolds Farley, "The Demographic Rates and Social Institutions of the Nineteenth-Century Negro Population: A Stable Population Analysis," *Demography*, 2 (1965), 386–98, confirmed that slave life expectancy (for adults at least) was roughly similar to that of whites.

It was in part by building upon studies such as these that Robert W. Fogel and Stanley L. Engerman constructed their controversial examination of *Time on the Cross; The Economics of American Negro Slavery*, 2 vols. (Boston, 1974). According to Fogel and Engerman the demographic well-being of the United State's slave was indeed a function of a material life as good or better than that enjoyed by most working class whites.

Doubtless the crossfire of debate centering on *Time on the Cross* will continue for some time across the terrain of slavery's historiography. But any ultimate judgment of the study will surely acknowledge that Fogel and Engerman not only forced open many new windows on the subject, but have forced students of slavery, however reluctantly, to peer through those windows.

Thus, because one of these windows concerned nutrition, Richard Sutch found himself grappling with matters of slave diets in his look at "The Treatment Received by American Slaves: A Critical Review of the Evidence Presented in *Time on the Cross*," *Explorations in Economic History*, 12 (1975), 335–448. Again in "Slave Child Mortality: Some Nutritional Answers to a Perennial Puzzle," *Journal of Social History*, 19 (1977), 284–309, Kenneth Kiple and Virginia Kiple were responding in part to questions Fogel and Engerman had already framed, and one suspects that because of the cliometricians, most future studies of slavery in North America and in the Hemisphere will deal in some detail with matters of slave nutrition. They will doubtless also approach their subject with much more methodologic sophistication.

For a pleasant irony of the *Time on the Cross* controversy has been that Fogel and Engerman, while themselves the target of much methodologic criticism, have nonetheless by virtue of a truly multidisciplinary approach worked something of a methodologic revolution in the study of slavery. It is not that economists, demographers, nutritionists, medical researchers, anthropologists, and the like have not had a great deal to say to historians about their subject, but rather that for the most part historians have heretofore been too preoccupied with other facets of their research to recognize the possibilities these disciplines contained. Yet now that the exciting potential of a multidisciplinary approach has been demonstrated so vividly, rapid advances on a broad front seem inevitable.

In the sector of biologic history, investigators will presumably look for inspiration to the methodologic and multidisciplinary experimentation of European scholars appearing in *Annales*. Recent examples of Annalistes articles can be found in Robert Forster and Orest Ranum, eds., *Biology of Man in History: Selections from the Annales: Economies, Sociétés, Civilisations* (Baltimore, 1975) and Elborg and Robert Forster, eds., *European Diet from Pre-Industrial to Modern Times* (New York, 1975). Hopefully too they will acquaint themselves with studies such as those of Thomas McKeowns' pivotal research on the demographic history of Europe. His thesis, presented in several articles and in *The Modern Rise of Population* (New York, 1976), forcefully argues that nutrition (and to a lesser degree sanitation) was far more important in reducing mortality and thus encouraging the growth of nineteenth-century European populations than any of the activities of the medical sciences.

For some examples of a new multidisciplinary orientation among American scholars, see Darrett B. Rutman and Anita H. Rutman, "Of Agues and Fevers: Malaria in the Early Chesapeake," *William and Mary Quarterly* 33 (1976), 31–60, David O. Whitten, "Medical Care of Slaves: Louisiana Sugar Region and South Carolina Rice District," *Southern Studies*, 16 (1977), 153–80, Nicholas Cardell and Mark M. Hopkins, "The Effect of Milk Intolerance on the Consumption of Milk by Slaves in 1860," *Journal of Interdisciplinary History*, 8 (1978), 507–13, Karen O. Kupperman, "Apathy and Death in Early Jamestown" *Journal of American History*, 66 (1979), 24–40, and Phillips Cutright and Edward Shorter "The Effects of Health on the Completed Fertility of Nonwhite and White U. S. Women Born Between 1867 and 1935," *Journal of Social History*, 13 (1979), 191–217.

II

Another stream of historic research that has fed into this study is that of traditional medical history. Numerous studies throughout the past half century have dealt with antebellum medicine and consequently dealt to some extent with the medical treatment of slaves. Examples range from Richard H. Shryock, "Medical Practice in the Old South," *South Atlantic Quarterly*, 29 (1930), 160–78, to Martha Mitchell, "Health and the Medical Profession in the Lower South, 1845–1860," *Journal of Southern History*, 10 (1944), 424–46, to John Duffy, "Medical Practice in the Antebellum South," *Journal of Southern History*, 25 (1959), 53–72.

Other studies have focused almost exclusively on slaves. Illustrative are Felice Swados, "Negro Health on the Ante Bellum Plantations," *Bulletin of the History of Medicine*, 19 (1941), 460–72; Weymouth T. Jordan, "Plantation Medicine in the Old South," *Alabama Review*, 3 (1950), 83–107, Bennett H. Wall, "Medical Care of Ebenezer Pettigrew's Slaves," *Mississippi Valley Historical Review*, 37 (1950), 451–70, Postell's already cited *Health of Slaves*, along with several subsequent articles, Walter Fisher, "Physicians and Slavery in the Antebellum Southern Medical Journal," *Journal of History of Medicine and Allied Sciences* (1968), 36–49, and Lewright Sikes, "Medical Care for Slaves: A Preview of the Welfare State," *Georgia Historical Quarterly*, 52 (1968), 405–13.

One tentative, often halting, theme that runs through much of this literature is that blacks varied somewhat from whites in their disease experience. Yet against this has stood a formidable body of literature including Kenneth Stampp's *The Peculiar Institution: Slavery in the Antebellum South* (New York, 1956) and more recently Winthrop D. Jordan's *White Over Black: American Attitudes Toward the Negro, 1550–1812* (Chapel Hill, 1968), which has denied that blacks and whites had a differential reaction to pathogens, except when those reactions were directly attributed to the inferior environment of the former.

Thus Peter H. Wood (*Black Majority: Negroes in Colonial South Carolina from 1670 through the Stono Rebellion*, New York, 1974) and Philip Curtin must have experienced more than a few qualms while demonstrating that blacks did indeed fare better than whites with malaria and yellow fever. To this literature, Kiple and Kiple added their look at "Black Yellow Fever Immunities, Innate and Acquired, as Revealed in the American South," *Social Science History*, 4 (1977), 419–36.

Todd L. Savitt used his unique combination of medical and historical training to draw together much of this research, combine it with exhaustive archival work, and produce an excellent examination of *Medicine and Slavery: the Health Care of Blacks in Antebellum Virginia* (Urbana, Ill., 1978). This effort was the first major book-length study of slave health since that of Postell and the very first to view the question of black-related diseases within the context of the findings of current medical research.

One nonmedical problem that Savitt had to deal with, one that has vexed the authors of the present work, and one that all who venture into the arena of medicine and slavery will be confronted with is that of the extent to which a black and white differential disease experience fostered racism among whites, a racism that in turn was employed to further exaggerate that disease experience. Clearly it is a problem intermingled with questions of science, physicians' self-interest and sectionalism, as will quickly be discerned by consulting the following literature.

Mary L. Marshall, "Samuel A. Cartwright and States' Rights Medicine," *New Orleans Medical and Surgical Journal*, 92 (1940), 74–8, John G. Greene, "The American Debate on the Negro's Place in Nature, 1780–1815," *Journal of the History of Ideas*, 15 (1954), 384–96, John Duffy, "A Note on Ante-Bellum Southern Nationalism and Medical Practice," *Journal of Southern History*, 34 (1968), 266–76, James D. Guillory, "The Pro-Slavery Arguments of Dr. Samuel A. Cartwright," *Louisiana History*, 9 (1968), 209–77, Donald A. Swan, "The American School of Ethnology," *Mankind Quarterly*, 12 (1971), 78–98, John S. Haller, "The Negro and the Southern Physician; A Study of Medical and Racial Attitudes 1800–1860," *Journal of Medical History*, 16 (1972) 238–53, and James O. Breeden, "States Rights Medicine in the Old South," *Bulletin of the New York Academy of Medicine*, 52 (1976), 348–72, have all dealt with various aspects of the subject in article form. Excellent monographs that treat America's scientific perception of the black are Winthrop D. Jordan, *op. cit;* William Stanton, *The Leopard's Spots: Scientific Attitudes toward Race in America 1815–59* (Chicago, 1960), and George M. Fredrickson, *The Black Image in the White Mind: The Debate on Afro-American Character and Destiny, 1817–1914* (New York, 1971).

III

The area of medical and nutritional research is a formidable one, if for no other reason than the enormous quantity of literature available. Indispensable for locating materials by subject are the *Index Catalogue of the Library of the Surgeon General's Office*, 1st series (Washington, D.C., 1880–95) and its ongoing successor, *Index Medicus*. The *Science Citation Index* is crucial for keeping track of current research. Also important is the National Library of Medicine's annual *Bibliography of the History of Medicine* and the Wellcome Institute of the History of Medicine's *Current Work in the History of Medicine: An International Bibliography*.

Another difficulty with medical research is jargon. Good readable introductions that can ease the reader into the field are Ian Taylor and John Knowelden, *Principles of Epidemiology* (Boston, 1964), F. M. Burnett and D. O. White, *Natural History of Infectious Disease*, 4th ed. (Cambridge, Engl., 1972), and René DuBos, *Man Adapting* (New Haven, Conn., 1965).

The place to begin any consideration of modern black health problems is Richard A. Williams, ed., *Textbook of Black-Related Diseases* (New York, 1975). Also useful is Julian H. Lewis' often overlooked study of *The Biology of the Negro* (Chicago, 1942). Starting points for the study of malaria, yellow fever and cholera as well as other tropical maladies are H. H. Scott, *A History of Tropical Medicine*, 2 vols. (Baltimore, 1939), William W. Frye and Clyde Swartzwelder, *A Manual of Tropical Medicine*, 4th ed. (Philadelphia, 1966), Mark F. Boyd, ed., *Malariology; A Comprehensive Survey of All Aspects of this Group of Diseases from a Global Standpoint*, 4 vols. (Philadelphia, 1949), P. C. C. Garnham, *Malaria Parasites and Other Haemosporidia* (Oxford, 1966), George Strode, ed, *Yellow Fever* (New York, 1951), Dhiman Barua and William Burrows, *Cholera* (Philadelphia, 1974).

Older but nonetheless works invaluable for the data they contain are George Augustine, *History of Yellow Fever* (New Orleans, 1909) and August Hirsch's classic *Handbook of Geographical and Historical Pathology*, 3 vols. (London, 1883–86). Edwin H. Ackerknecht's *History and Geography of the Most Important Diseases* (New York, 1965) represents a modern look at the same illnesses Hirsch covers.

Crosby and McNeill discuss thoroughly the transmission of European pathogens to the Americas but only touch on the transmission of African diseases. Ashburn does more in this regard, while Philip Curtin's "Epidemiology and the Slave Trade" will prove highly useful. In addition, one would do well to consult R. Hoeppli, *Parasitic Diseases in Africa and the Western Hemisphere: Early Documentation and Transmission by the Slave Trade* (Acta Tropica, Suppl. 10, Basel, 1969).

The course of both African and European diseases in early North America is treated by John Duffy, *Epidemics in Colonial America* (Baton Rouge, La., 1953). For malaria one might begin with St. Julian R. Childs, *Malaria and Colonization in the Carolina Low Country, 1526–1696* (Baltimore, 1940) and Erwin H. Ackerknecht, *Malaria in the Upper Mississippi Valley, 1760–1900* (Baltimore, 1945).

A sampling of yellow fever epidemics can be conducted by consulting John H. Powell, *Bring Out Your Dead; The Great Plague in Philadelphia in 1793* (Philadelphia, 1949), Jo Ann Carrigan, "The Saffron Scourge; A History of Yellow Fever in Louisiana, 1796–1905," (Ph.D. dissertation, Louisiana State University, 1961), and John Duffy, *Sword of Pestilence; The New Orleans Yellow Fever Epidemic of 1853* (Baton Rouge, La., 1966). For cholera see Charles E. Rosenberg, *The Cholera Years: The United States in 1832, 1849, and 1866* (Chicago, 1962).

For nutrition, in addition to indexes already mentioned, the *Nutrition Abstracts and Reviews*, published in Aberdeen, Scotland will prove a useful guide. A good text of *Human Nutrition and Dietetics*, 6th ed. (Edinburgh, 1975) has been edited by Stanley Davidson et al. The nutritional status of today's American, black and white, is suggested by the United States Department of Health, Education and Welfare, *Ten State Nutrition Survey 1968–70*, 5 vols. (DHEW Pub. No. (HSM) 72-8130-34, Washington, D. C., 1972) and Public Health Services, Health Resources Administration, *Preliminary Findings of the First Health and Nutrition Examination Survey, United States, 1971–72; Dietary Intake and Biochemical Findings* (DHEW Pub. No. (HRA) 75-1219-1, Washington, D. C., 1974).

The diets of our ancestors are examined by Waverly L. Root and Richard de Rochemont, *Eating in America; A History* (New York, 1976), Andrew M. Soule, "Vegetables, Fruit, and Nursery Products, and Truck Farming in the South," in *The South in the Building of the Nation*, V: *Economic History 1607–1865*, ed. James C. Ballagh (Richmond, 1909), Edgar W. Martin, *The Standard of Living in 1860: American Consumption Level on the Eve of the Civil War* (Chicago, 1942), and Sam B. Hilliard, *Hog Meat and Hoecake: Food Supply in the Old South, 1840–1860* (Carbondale, Ill., 1972).

Of late, numerous scientific studies linking nutrition with disease have appeared. Very useful are Nevin S. Scrimshaw, Carl E. Taylor, and John E. Gordon, *Interactions of Nutrition and Infection* (Geneva, 1968), Donald S. McLaren, *Nutrition and its Disorders*, 2nd ed. (London, 1976), and R. K. Chandra and P. M. Newberne, *Nutrition, Immunity, and Infection: Mechanisms of Interaction* (New York, 1977). For the problems of infants, see Samuel J. Foman, *Infant Nutrition*, 2nd ed. (Philadelphia, 1974) and Derrick B. Jelliffe, *Infant Nutrition in the Subtropics and Tropics*, 2nd ed. (Geneva, 1968).

Good introductions to the problems of lactose intolerance may be found in John M. Hunter, "Geography, Genetics, and Culture History: The Case of Lactose Intolerance," *Geographical Review*, 61 (1971) and Theodore M. Bayless et al., "Lactose and Milk Intolerance: Clinical Implications," *New England Journal of Medicine*, 292 (1975) 1156–9. See Mary T. Weick for "A History of Rickets in the United States," *American Journal of Clinical Nutrition*, 20 (1967), 1234–41, and Marcia Cooper for *Pica: A Survey of the Historical Literature . . . And a Discussion of its Pediatric and Psychological Implications* (Springfield, Ill.,

1957). Pellagra is well treated by Elizabeth W. Etheridge, *The Butterfly Caste: A Social History of Pellagra in the South* (Westport, Conn., 1972) and Daphne A. Roe, *A Plague of Corn; The Social History of Pellagra* (Ithaca, N.Y., 1973).

The vast literature on the Sudden Infant Death Syndrome is examined by M. Maria A. Valdes-Dapena, "Sudden and Unexpected Death in Infancy: A Review of the World Literature, 1954–1966," *Pediatrics*, 39 (1967), 123–38, and "Sudden Unexplained Infant Death, 1970 Through 1975: An Evolution in Understanding," *Pathology Annual*, 12 (1977), 117–45. See Helen C. Chase and Mary E. Byrnes for *Trends in Prematurity, United States: 1950–67* (Washington, D. C., 1972) and Dwayne M. Reed and Fiora L. Stanley, eds., for *The Epidemiology of Prematurity* (Baltimore, 1977).

IV

The body of extant primary material on black-related diseases in the American South is enormous. Perhaps the most valuable and certainly the most voluminous was formed by the contributions of physicians to the medical journals of the period such as the *Charleston Medical Journal and Review* (1846–1860) (known for the years 1846–1848 as the *Southern Journal of Medicine and Pharmacy*), *The New Orleans Medical and Hospital Gazette* (1845–61), the *New Orleans Medical and Surgical Journal* (1844ff), the *Southern Medical Reports* (1849–1850) and the *Southern Medical and Surgical Journal* (1836–67). The medical and nutritional observations of physicians along with planters may also be found in the many agriculture journals of the day. Examples include *DeBow's Review* (1846–64, 1866–70 and 1879–80) and *The American Cotton Planter* known from 1857 on as the *American Cotton Planter and Soil of the South* (1853–61).

Books, on the other hand, dealing with diseases and race are relatively rare. Perhaps most prominent is the study by J. C. Nott and G. R. Gliddon, *Types of Mankind* (Philadelphia, 1854). See also Daniel Drake, *A Systematic Treatise on the Principal Diseases of the Interior Valley of North America* (Cincinnati, 1850), Thompson McGown, *A Practical Treatise on the Most Common Diseases of the South* (Philadelphia, 1849), and J. Cam. Massie, *A Treatise on the Eclectic Southern Practice of Medicine* (Philadelphia, 1854). Examples focusing on specific diseases are Samuel A. Cartwright, *Some Additional Observations Relative to the Cholera* (1833) and Henry A. Ramsay, *The Necrological Appearances of Southern Typhoid Fever, in the Negro* (Columbus County, Ga., 1852).

Slave narratives, the accounts of visitors to the South, and published planter memoirs, letters, and diaries all provide glimpses of slave diets, diseases, and medical treatment, as do the many home medical books such as James Ewell, *The Planters and Mariners Medical Companion* (Philadelphia, 1807 and later editions) or J. Hume Simons, *The Planters Guide and Family Book of Medicine* (Charleston, 1848).

The advertisements for runaway slaves in antebellum newspapers are useful for their physical descriptions, while the newspapers themselves are important sources of information on epidemics. Frequently cities published mortality data in the wake of an epidemic such as *Names of the Dead, Being a Record of the Mortality in Savannah during the Epidemic of 1854* (Savannah, Ga., 1854).

The most important published source of mortality data by race is J. D. B. Debow, *Mortality Statistics, The Seventh Census*, H. R. Ex. Doc. No. 98, 33rd Congress, 2nd session (Washington. D.C., 1855), although local records such as J. L. Dawson and H. W. DeSaussure, *Census of the City of Charleston, South Carolina for the Year 1848* (Charleston, 1849) are also vital.

V

Perhaps the greatest benefit of archival research in the preparation of this book was the discovery of obscure printed pamphlets and rare books, as well as the contemporary newspaper files also housed in the libraries and archives visited. Additionally the following manuscript sources proved valuable.

Alabama

Alabama State Archives, Montgomery
William Proctor Gould diary, 1828–40

Florida

Robert Manning Strozier Library, Florida State University, Tallahassee
Pinehill Plantation papers

Georgia

Georgia Historical Society, Savannah
Jeremiah Evarts diary
Fraser–Couper family papers, 1810–84
Chemonie plantation journal, 1861–4
Louis Manigault, miscellaneous mss. records of "Gowrie" and "East Hermitage" plantations, and "Records of a Rice Plantation in the Georgia Lowlands"
John Orme papers, 1821–45
James Potter papers, 1828–31
Telfair family papers, 1832
Ruth Erwin Welman (Mrs. John Hope) papers, 1841
Caroline Lamar Woodridge papers, 1894

Louisiana

Howard Tilton Library, Tulane University, New Orleans
Evrett family papers "Day Book" (1853–66).
T. J. Grant notebook (n.d.)
M. McCulloch slave list, 1855
Louisiana State Department of Archives and History, Louisiana State University, Baton Rouge
William M. Allen correspondence, 1858–63
Priscilla Bond diary, 1858–66
Audley Britton papers, 1822–94
John C. Burruss papers, 1834
Anna and Sarah Butler correspondence
Richard Butler papers, 1795–1825
Thomas Butler family papers, 1820–1920
Samuel Cartwright family papers, 1851–3
William C. C. Claibourne papers, 1804–5
John Close papers, 1831–5
Nathaniel Evans family papers, 1800–50
G. Mason Graham letters
Edward Gay and family papers
Hazard Company correspondence, 1839–41
Philip Hicky and family papers, 1858
John Innerarity papers
Joseph Jones papers
Christian D. Koch family papers, 1851–9
George M. Lester Collection

Liddell (Moses St. John Richardson and family) papers, 1813–1914
Jeptha McKinney papers, 1846–9
Samuel J. Peters Jr. diary, 1840–62
Alexander Porter letters, 1833
Robert H. Ryland papers, journal, 1849–56
Alonzo Snyder collection, 1800–60
Miles Taylor papers, 1821–90
Benjamin Tureaud papers, 1845–57
David Weeks family papers, 1830–70

Mississippi

Mississippi State Department of Archives and History, Jackson
James Allen plantation book, 1860–5
Aventine plantation diary, 1857–60
William R. Elley plantation record book, 1855–6
Fonsylvania plantation diary, 1863
Robert and James Gorden papers, 1851–76
Monroe McGuire diary, 1818–50
"Seventh Census of the United States, Original Returns of the Assistant Marshalls,
    Third Series, Persons Who Died During the Year Ending June 30, 1850" (Mississippi)
Trask–Ventress family papers, 1791–1854
Dr. Walter Wade papers, 1834–54

North Carolina

William R. Perkins Library, Duke University, Durham, N.C.
Robert Carter papers
Devereaux family papers, 1776–1936
Obediah Fields papers
McDonald Furman papers, plantation book, 1827–73
William Richard Hansford papers
George Noble Jones papers, 1806–72
Thomas Ellison Keitt papers, 1768–1945
John Knight papers, 1788–1891
William Law papers, 1854–6
Anne Lovell papers
Louis Manigault papers, 1776–1886
John Monroe papers
George Poindextor papers
Henry Watson, Jr., papers, 1828–69
North Carolina Department of Archives and History
Allen family papers, 1756–1877
Avery Family papers, 1766–1865
Pettigrew family papers, 1800–65
Mary Jeffreys Rogers collection
"Seventh Census of the United States, Original Returns of the Assistant Marshalls,
    Third Series, Persons Who Died During the Year Ending June 30, 1850" (North
    Carolina)
Southern Historical Collection, University of North Carolina, Chapel Hill
Brashear family papers
Cameron papers, 1739–1921
Andrew Flinn plantation diary
Heyward–Ferguson papers, 1810–40

Jones family papers, 1815–1932
Alexander Robert Lawton papers, 1774–1952
Lenoir family papers, 1763–1929
Macay–McNeely papers, 1791–1856
Minis Collection, physicians account books

South Carolina

Medical College of the State of South Carolina Library, Charleston
  H. Perry Pope, "A Dissertation on the Professional Management of Negro Slaves,"
    presented to the Faculty of the Medical College of South Carolina, 1837.
South Carolina Department of Archives and History, Columbia
  "Seventh Census of the United States, Original Returns of the Assistant Marshalls,
    Third Series, Persons Who Died During the Year Ending June 30, 1850" (South
    Carolina)
South Carolina Historical Society, Charleston
  Clothing and blanket book of John Balls slaves, 1830–41
  Coffin Point record, 1800–21
  Dirleton plantation book, 1859
  Records of Good Hope Plantation, 1835–59
South Caroliniana Library, University of South Carolina, Columbia
  Samuel Porcher Gaillard plantation journal, 1847–9
  James Henry Hammond papers, 1795–1896
  John Stapleton papers, 1800–24
  John O. Wilson journal, 1845–61

Texas

Barker Texas History Center Archives, University of Texas, Austin
  Patrick Churchill Jack letter, 1844
  Rosalie Bridget Hart Priour, mss
  Nathan Thomas papers

Virginia

Alderman Library, University of Virginia, Charlottesville
  Bruce family papers, 1796–1863
  Philip St. George Cocke papers, 1829–71
  Hubbard family papers
  Alfred G. Tebault papers, 1853–92
  Henry Alexander Wise papers, letters, 1846
Virginia Historical Society, Richmond
  James Mina Holladay account book, 1860–3
  Massie family papers
  William Henry Taylor account book, 1839–54
Virginia State Library, Richmond
  "Seventh Census of the United States, Original Returns of Assistant Marshalls, Third
    Series, Persons Who Died During the Year Ending June 30, 1850" (Virginia)
  Slave book of William Massie, 1836–8
Library of Congress
  Robert Carter papers
  Minis, physicians account book, 1824–39

INDEX

Ackerknecht, Erwin H., 71
African trypanosomiasis
  black resistance, 7
  failure in the Americas, 77
  tsetse fly, 6–7, 11, 77
  and West African nutrition, 8, 11
Afro-Americans, *see also* blacks; slaves
  fetal mortality, 188, 196, 200
  health problems misunderstood and ig-
    nored, 203–7
  and hemoglobin abnormalities, *see* ane-
    mia; glucose-6-phosphate dehydroge-
    nase deficiency; sickle trait
  and hypertension, 199–200, 203
  infant mortality, 188, 192, 193, 194, 196,
    197, 200, 266–7 n 11, 267 n 13
  and lactose intolerance, 84, 98, 195,
    198–9, 205–6, 207; *see also* lactose in-
    tolerance
  low-birth-weight babies, *see* low-birth-
    weight babies
  and maternal mortality, 201, 273 n 95
  and medical profession, 203, 204, 205,
    206, 207
  and medical racism, 187–90, 204, 205,
    206, 207
  and mental retardation, 201–2
  mortality rates, 188, 191, 192, 198, 199,
    266–7 n 11
  and nutritional deficiencies, 116, 188–9,
    195, 196, 197, 198, 199, 200, 201, 202,
    205, 206; *see also* particular nutrients
  nutritional requirements, 202–3
  and pica, 196, 206; *see also* pica
  and pneumonia, 188, 191–2
  postbellum diseases, 188–9
  postbellum health crisis, 187–90
  and rickets, 198, 201; *see also* rickets
  and school lunch programs, 206

and sickle trait, 204–5; *see also* sickle
    trait
  and the sudden infant death syndrome,
    196–7, 205, 206; *see also* sudden in-
    fant death syndrome
  and syphilis, 188, 192, 205
  and tetany, 201; *see also* tetany
  and the toxemia of pregnancy, *see* toxe-
    mia of pregnancy
  and tuberculosis, 188, 191
Allen, Richard, 62
Allison, A.C., 17, 18
"American School of Ethnology," 177,
    179, 183
Ancient Mariner, 33
anemia, 9, 10, 93, 97, 108, 115, 195–6,
    197, 198, 199, 204, 206
  see also glucose-6-phosphate dehydroge-
    nase deficiency; sickle trait
Arnold, Dr. Richard D., 54, 166, 183
Ashburn, Frank D., 27

beriberi
  and pellagra, 123
  and pica, 121, 122–3
  and rice consumption, 122
  and scurvy, 123
  symptoms, 122
  and thiamine deficiency, 122–3
  in the West Indies, 77
blacks, *see also* Afro-Americans; slaves
  adjustments to calcium deficiency, 94
  cold susceptibility, 11, 135
  fetal development, 193
  hair texture, 5
  heat tolerance, 10–11
  hemoglobin anomalies, *see* anemia; glu-
    cose-6-phosphate dehydrogenase defi-
    ciency; sickle trait

287

blacks (*cont.*)
lactase enzyme, *see* lactose intolerance
lungs, 5, 135
malaria protection, *see* malaria, innate
immunity
nostrils, 5
physical growth rate, 198
pigment, 5, 10, 92, 94, 196, 200
skeletal structure, 198
susceptible to respiratory problems,
109, 135–6
and vitamin A mobilization, 90
and vitamin D, 91–2, 101; *see also* vitamin D
yellow fever resistance, *see* yellow fever,
black resistance to
bone ailments, 76, 77, 117; *see also* rickets
bowel complaints, 76, 77
Bremer, Fredrika, 112
Bressa, Dr. Cesare, 122
Brickell, Dr. Warren, 129
Brown, John, 107
Butterfield, Dr. Ralph, 117

cachexia africana, *see* pica
Caddell, Dr. Joan L., 110
calcium, 9, 10, 11, 84, 92, 93–4, 96, 98, 99,
101, 102, 106, 108, 110, 115, 117, 118,
120, 121, 139, 189, 195, 197, 198, 199,
200, 201
Caldwell, Charles, 176
Caribbean
European struggle for, 36–8, 58, 60
European troop mortality, 37–8
use of black troops in, 38, 60
Carter, Dr. Henry Rose, 46, 49
Cartwright, Dr. Samuel A., 43, 130, 163,
167, 175, 179–81, 182, 183, 203
Castro, Josué de, 114
catarrh
slave mortality, 137–8
slave susceptibility to, 77, 137–8
census mortality data
discussion of, 99, 188, 240, n 24, n 25, n
26, n 27
cesarean section, 118, 174
chinchona bark, 59
cholera
black susceptibility, 76, 147, 148, 149,
151, 152, 154, 155, 156–7
in Brazil, 148
in Cuba, 76, 149
and gastric hypoacidity, 155–6

hypotheses on etiology, 151
medical treatment, 150, 151, 155
mortality, 149, 151, 152, 154, 155, 156
nineteenth-century pandemics, 147,
258–9 n 55
predisposing factors, environmental,
152, 154, 155, 156–7
preventive measures, 149, 150, 151
in Puerto Rico, 76
and racism, 151–2, 157
symptoms, 147–8
Christie, James, 148
Coffin, Dr. W.H., 163
consumptions, *see* tuberculosis
convulsions, 78, 100, 102; *see also* tetany
Corson, Dr. E.R., 189
crib death, *see* sudden infant death syndrome
Cromwell, Oliver, 14
Curtin, Philip, 23, 39, 58

Darlington, C.D., 4
Darwin, Charles, 187
Davenport, Dr. H.G., 129
Davis, David Brion, 67
dental caries, 76, 77, 117, 118
diphtheria, 76, 77
dirt eating, *see* pica
disease
and demographic history of the South,
64–6
and planter lifestyles, 66–7
resistance as a cause of slavery, 11, 67–8
Duffy, John, 33, 53, 161, 174
Duffy-group antigen determinants, 21–2,
55; *see also* malaria, vivax
Dugas, Dr. L.A., 104

Edwards, Bryan, 75
Elkins, Stanley, 202
Engerman, Stanley L., 79, 80, 81, 88
Europeans
lactose tolerance, 11, 84
mortality in Africa, 12–14, 23
mortality in the West Indies, 36–8
reaction to black disease immunities, 11
susceptibility to African diseases, 7, 11–
14, 22–3; *see also* malaria; yellow
fever, white susceptibility
Ewell, Dr. James, 163
eye ailments, 76, 77, 117–18

Faut, Dr. A.V., 130
Fenner, Dr. Erasmus D., 43

protein-calorie malnutrition, kwashiorkor
in Africa, 9, 11
etiology, 111
and intercurrent disease, 111–12
and lactose intolerance, 111
physical appearance of victims, 98, 111, 112
among slave children, 98, 111–13
symptoms, 111, 112
and worms, 115
protein-calorie malnutrition, marasmus
confused with other diseases, 132
etiology, 112–13
symptoms, 112
Puckett, Dr. W.R., 127, 128
putrid sore throat, see diphtheria

quinine, 59, 66

racism
and black biology, 60–2, 135, 175–84, 187, 263 n 6
and black disease immunities, 23, 52, 60–1, 62, 63–4, 178, 179, 182
and black disease susceptibilities, 23, 106, 151–2, 157, 178, 179, 182, 188–190, 197, 203–7
Ramsay, Dr. W.G., 52, 74, 169, 175
Reed, Dr. Walter, 46
rice cultivation, and malaria, 53, 55
rickets
black susceptibility, 106, 189, 198, 201
described in runaway slave advertisements, 105–6
etiology, 104–5
and the lactase enzyme, 84
mortality, 105
and pelvic deformities, 118–19, 196
and pica, 121
and pneumonia, 138
symptoms, 105
and whooping cough, 137
and tetany, 104–6
Robinson, Solon, 53, 81–2
Rockefeller Foundation, 7
Ross, Sir Ronald, 46
Royal African Company, 12, 14
Rush, Dr. Benjamin, 62
Russell, William, 112
Rutman, Darrett, 66

Saunders, Dr. Elijah, 199
Savitt, Todd L., 71, 107, 161
scabies, 74

scrofula, 78, 132, 143–4, 146, 188; see also tuberculosis
scurvy
symptoms, 123
and vitamin C, 123
in the West Indies, 77
Shryock, Richard H., 161, 169
sickle cell anemia, 17, 55, 205
sickle cell beta-thalassemia, 19
sickle cell hemoglobin C disease, 19, 135
sickle trait
and birth weight, 268 n 26
and fertility, 65
frequencies in Africa, 17, 18
frequencies in the United States, 20, 204, 215 n 92
and genetic screening, 204
in Greece, 17
in India, 17
and malaria protection, 17–19, 55, 65, 215 n 94
and medical misunderstanding, 207
and race discrimination, 204
sickling disorders
and effects on health, 93, 94, 135
SIDS, see sudden infant death syndrome
Sims, Dr. Marion, 174
skin afflictions, 77, 117, 123; see also pellagra
slave nutrition, see also specific vitamins and minerals
adequacy, contemporary observations, 80, 81, 82, 83, 90, 230–1 n 6
adequacy, studies on, 79, 80–1, 89
and beriberi, 122–3
and bone complaints, 117, 118–19
caloric requirements, 88, 133
and dental difficulties, 117, 118
and eye ailments, 117, 118
fishing and hunting, 87
gardens and domesticated animals, 87
infants and children, 96–116, 137
and mortality levels, 133, 136
nursing and weaning, 97, 101–2, 111, 112
and pellagra, 123–33
and personality, 133
physicians on, 82, 112, 123
and pica, 113, 119–22
planters on, 81, 82, 85, 86, 97, 99
pregnant and lactating women, 97, 101, 102, 105, 108, 109, 110, 118, 174